The
Pocket Reader

The
Pocket Reader

David Munger

An imprint of Addison Wesley Longman, Inc.

New York • Reading, Massachusetts • Menlo Park, California • Harlow, England
Don Mills, Ontario • Sydney • Mexico City • Madrid • Amsterdam

Acquisitions Editor: Lynn M. Huddon
Marketing Manager: Carlise Paulson
Cover Design: John Callahan
Cover Photo: PhotoDisc
Interior Design: Dianne Hall, The Davidson Group
Electronic Page Makeup: Dianne Hall, The Davidson Group
Senior Manufacturing Buyer: Dennis J. Para

For permission to use copyrighted material, grateful acknowledgement is made to the copyright holders on pp. 359–361, which are hereby made part of this copyright page.

Library of Congress Cataloging-in-Publication Data

The pocket reader / [compiled by] David Munger.
   p. cm.
"Based on 80 readings"—Pref.
ISBN 0-321-07668-0
   1. College readers. 2. English language—Rhetoric—Problems, exercises, etc.
3. Report writing—Problems, exercises, etc. 1. Munger, David.

PE1417 .P53 1999
808'.0427–dc21

                             99-056569

Please visit our website at http://www.awl.com

ISBN: 0-321-07668-0

12345678910–DOC–03020100

Contents

Example   59

Comparison & Contrast   89

Process Analysis   133

Classification   163

Cause & Effect   191

Analogy   219

Definition   257

Writing Guidelines: Definition   258

Argument   295

Writing Guidelines: Argument   296

Thematic Contents

Customs and Habits

Education

Family

Growing Up/Aging

Nature and the Environment

Poverty/Social Issues

Race and Culture

Science and Society

Self and Society

Women and Men

Writing and Language

Preface

The Pocket Reader provides high-interest, teachable readings organized in the rhetorical arrangement preferred by thousands of instructors. *The Pocket Reader* is based on *80 Readings,* but the selection of readings has been completely updated, it is more concise, and it offers an organization many instructors prefer—one motivated by the writing strategies they teach their students to use in class and expect them to utilize throughout their college career. By focusing each chapter on a particular rhetorical strategy, the text highlights the relationship between reading and writing and allows students to build writing skills in a methodical, step-by-step manner.

However, *The Pocket Reader* does not ignore the context for the readings. Many common threads extend throughout the text: race in America, nature and the environment, gender, medical ethics, as well as many essays on the process of writing itself. While these connections are summarized in the Thematic Contents, they are also embedded in the structure of the book, through strategic juxtaposition of readings.

And, since different instructors place varying degrees of emphasis on readings, and since school terms vary in length, the text is also available in an abridged version: *The Brief Pocket Reader.*

Summary of features

- Two different lengths: *The Pocket Reader* and *The Brief Pocket Reader.*
- Organized according to the most common writing strategies used by college writers.
- Brief and accessible selections for first-year college writers.
- Each chapter begins with writing guidelines for the rhetorical strategy featured in the chapter.

- Each chapter contains a student-written essay.
- Engaging headnotes give students the background they need to appreciate each reading.
- Budget pricing gives instructors the flexibility to assign more than one text.

Acknowledgments

This book could not have been completed without the dedication and attention contributed by many individuals. Lynn Huddon conceived of the project and gave unwavering support as it proceeded to completion. Rich Wohl always encouraged me to think bigger. Deanna Campbell provided valuable research and suggestions both for headnotes and the selection of readings. Lisa Dressler was vigilant in seeking permissions for the works that were selected. Heather Hulett contributed research, words, and work, work, work. Dianne Hall and Mike Shelton did great work in production in the face of ever-changing deadlines. Greta, Jimmy, and Nora Munger contributed inspiration in volumes too great to be measured.

Finally, I offer my gratitude to the teachers and scholars who reviewed the manuscript for this book: Marge Bartelt, Edison Community College; James V. Cervantes, Mesa Community College; Pat Davis, Pima Community College; Norine Ryan, Briar Cliff College; Terry Scambray, Fresno City College; Richard Tomlinson, Richland Community College; Kathryn White, Pima Community College; and Russel Wiebe, Felician College.

—DAVID MUNGER

The
Pocket Reader

1

Narration

Narration

1. **Write for a purpose.** While you may think of narration as simply telling a story, no story is interesting unless it has a point. If your story is about trying to recover lost baggage, your point might be "Airline X's customer service department is unprofessional and rude," or it might be "If you're polite and friendly, people will do amazing things to help you out."

2. **Organize your narrative to make your point.** Most narration is told in chronological order. Usually this strategy is easiest for your readers to understand, and it can often help your purpose by leading directly to your main point. However, sometimes you might want to start in the middle of the story, or even near its end, surprising your reader at key points with details from earlier in the story.

3. **Give plenty of details.** Without details, most stories can be told in just a sentence or two. For example, the airline story could be told as concisely as this: "The airline lost my bags and it took me three days to recover them." The story gains power through its well-chosen details: the empty feeling as you watched the last bag being lifted from the carousel, the cab driver who waited to make sure you found a hotel room, the friendly hotel manager who let you borrow a tie for a business meeting, the shock of watching ice cream dribble down your one clean shirt.

4. **Use a consistent point of view.** If you're telling your story from the first person point of view (I lost my bags, etc.), don't suddenly shift perspectives (Dave went to the baggage counter, etc.). While this advice may seem obvious, it's an easy mistake to make, especially if you're writing your draft over the course of several days. A less obvious and even more common error is to shift tenses. If you're writing in the past tense, keep your entire story in the past. For an excellent example of an essay that maintains a consistent point of view, take a look at Brent Staples' "Black Men and Public Space." Here Staples recounts his story from the perspective of a writer many years later, jumping seamlessly from his descriptions of events which occurred long ago to his current reflections on the subject. Though the strategy is complex, it works because Staples is careful to keep his point of view consistent.

Zora Neale Hurston

I Get Born

Zora Neale Hurston (1901–1961) was born in Eatonville, Florida, the "first incorporated Negro town in America." Zora's early education was sporadic, but she was eventually able to finish high school and go to college. Hurston, like her native town, was uniquely independent. She studied anthropology in college, and was said to be the only woman able to measure the heads of Harlem men with a pair of calipers without getting "bawled out." Hurston's interest in anthropology adds a depth to her fiction, so that when we read we don't just read a story, we explore with her an entire culture. Like her other novels, *Their Eyes Were Watching God* and *Moses, Man of the Mountain*, "I Get Born" from *Dust Tracks on a Road* immediately engages the reader with Hurston's honesty, sense of humor, and gift for storytelling.

THIS IS ALL HEAR-SAY. Maybe some of the details of my birth as told me might   1
be a little inaccurate, but it is pretty well established that I really did get born.

The saying goes like this. My mother's time had come and my father was not   2
there. Being a carpenter, successful enough to have other helpers on some jobs,
he was away often on building business, as well as preaching. It seems that my
father was away from home for months this time. I have never been told why.
But I did hear that he threatened to cut his throat when he got the news. It
seems that one daughter was all that he figured he could stand. My sister, Sarah,
was his favorite child, but that one girl was enough. Plenty more sons, but no
more girl babies to wear out shoes and bring in nothing. I don't think he ever
got over the trick he felt that I played on him by getting born a girl, and while
he was off from home at that. A little of my sugar used to sweeten his coffee
right now. That is a Negro way of saying his patience was short with me. Let me
change a few words with him—and I am of the word changing kind—and he was
ready to change ends. Still and all, I looked more like him than any child in the
house. Of course, by the time I got born, it was too late to make any suggestions,
so the old man had to put up with me. He was nice about it in a way. He didn't
tie me in a sack and drop me in the lake, as he probably felt like doing.

People were digging sweet potatoes, and then it was hog-killing time. Not   3
at our house, but it was going on in general over the country like, being January and a bit cool. Most people were either butchering for themselves, or off
helping other folks do their butchering, which was almost just as good. It is a
gay time. A big pot of hasslits cooking with plenty of seasoning, lean slabs of
fresh-killed pork frying for the helpers to refresh themselves after the work is
done. Over and above being neighborly and giving aid, there is the food, the
drinks and the fun of getting together.

4   So there was no grown folks close around when Mama's water broke. She sent one of the smaller children to fetch Aunt Judy, the mid-wife, but she was gone to Woodbridge, a mile and a half away, to eat at a hog-killing. The child was told to go over there and tell Aunt Judy to come. But nature, being indifferent to human arrangements, was impatient. My mother had to make it alone. She was too weak after I rushed out to do anything for herself, so she just was lying there, sick in the body, and worried in mind, wondering what would become of her, as well as me. She was so weak, she couldn't even reach down to where I was. She had one consolation. She knew I wasn't dead, because I was crying strong.

5   Help came from where she never would have thought to look for it. A white man of many acres and things, who knew the family well, had butchered the day before. Knowing that Papa was not at home, and that consequently there would be no fresh meat in our house, he decided to drive the five miles and bring a half of a shoat, sweet potatoes, and other garden stuff along. He was there a few minutes after I was born. Seeing the front door standing open, he came on in, and hollered, "Hello, there! Call your dogs!" That is the regular way to call in the country because nearly everybody who has anything to watch has biting dogs.

6   Nobody answered, but he claimed later that he heard me spreading my lungs all over Orange County, so he shoved the door open and bolted on into the house.

7   He followed the noise and then he saw how things were, and, being the kind of a man he was, he took out his Barlow Knife and cut the navel cord, then he did the best he could about other things. When the mid-wife, locally known as a granny, arrived about an hour later, there was a fire in the stove and plenty of hot water on. I had been sponged off in some sort of a way, and Mama was holding me in her arms.

8   As soon as the old woman got there, the white man unloaded what he had brought, and drove off cussing about some blankety-blank people never being where you could put your hands on them when they were needed. He got no thanks from Aunt Judy. She grumbled for years about it. She complained that the cord had not been cut just right, and the bellyband had not been put on tight enough. She was mighty scared I was going to have a weak back, and that I would have trouble holding my water until I reached puberty. I did.

9   The next day or so a Mrs. Neale, a friend of Mama's, came in and reminded her that she had promised to let her name the baby in case it was a girl. She had picked up a name somewhere which she thought was very pretty. Perhaps she had read it somewhere, or somebody back in those woods was smoking Turkish cigarettes. So I became Zora Neale Hurston.

10   There is nothing to make you like other human beings so much as doing things for them. Therefore, the man who grannied me was back next day to

see how I was coming along. Maybe it was a pride in his own handiwork, and his resourcefulness in a pinch, that made him want to see it through. He remarked that I was a God-damned fine baby, fat and plenty of lung-power. As time went on, he came infrequently, but somehow kept a pinch of interest in my welfare. It seemed that I was spying noble, growing like a gourd vine, and yelling bass like a gator. He was the kind of man that had no use for puny things, so I was all to the good with him. He thought my mother was justified in keeping me.

But nine months rolled around, and I just would not get on with the walking business. I was strong, crawling well, but showed no inclination to use my feet. I might remark in passing, that I still don't like to walk. Then I was over a year old, but still I would not walk. They made allowances for my weight, but yet, that was no real reason for my not trying. 11

They tell me that an old sow-hog taught me how to walk. That is, she 12 didn't instruct me in detail, but she convinced me that I really ought to try. It was like this. My mother was going to have collard greens for dinner, so she took the dishpan and went down to the spring to wash the greens. She left me sitting on the floor, and gave me a hunk of cornbread to keep me quiet. Everything was going along all right, until the sow with her litter of pigs in convoy came abreast of the door. She must have smelled the cornbread I was messing with and scattering crumbs about the floor. So, she came right on in, and began to nuzzle around.

My mother heard my screams and came running. Her heart must have 13 stood still when she saw the sow in there, because hogs have been known to eat human flesh.

But I was not taking this thing sitting down. I had been placed by a chair, 14 and when my mother got inside the door, I had pulled myself up by that chair and was getting around it right smart.

As for the sow, poor misunderstood lady, she had no interest in me except 15 my bread. I lost that in scrambling to my feet and she was eating it. She had much less intention of eating Mama's baby, than Mama had of eating hers. With no more suggestions from the sow or anybody else, it seems that I just took to walking and kept the thing a-going. The strangest thing about it was that once I found the use of my feet, they took to wandering. I always wanted to go. I would wander off in the woods all alone, following some inside urge to go places. This alarmed my mother a great deal. She used to say that she believed a woman who was an enemy of hers had sprinkled "travel dust" around the doorstep the day I was born. That was the only explanation she could find. I don't know why it never occurred to her to connect my tendency with my father, who didn't have a thing on his mind but this town and the next one. That should have given her a sort of hint. Some children are just bound to take after their fathers in spite of women's prayers.

Annie Dillard

The Chase

Annie Dillard (b. 1945) is probably best known for writing that grapples with her relationship with God and the natural world in such books as *Holy the Firm* and *Pilgrim at Tinker Creek*, which won a Pulitzer Prize in 1975. Although written with the same intense emotion, her book *An American Childhood* takes a different direction from her earlier works, drawing on her memories of growing up in a middle-class neighborhood in Pittsburgh, Pennsylvania. In this selection, Dillard describes one of the adventures of her childhood—writing from a child's perspective, with a little adult wisdom seeping through.

1   SOME BOYS TAUGHT ME TO PLAY FOOTBALL. This was fine sport. You thought up a new strategy for every play and whispered it to the others. You went out for a pass, fooling everyone. Best, you got to throw yourself mightily at someone's running legs. Either you brought him down or you hit the ground flat out on your chin, with your arms empty before you. It was all or nothing. If you hesitated in fear, you would miss and get hurt: you would take a hard fall while the kid got away, or you would get kicked in the face while the kid got away. But if you flung yourself wholeheartedly at the back of his knees—if you gathered and joined body and soul and pointed them diving fearlessly—then you likely wouldn't get hurt, and you'd stop the ball. Your fate, and your team's score, depended on your concentration and courage. Nothing girls did could compare with it. Boys welcomed me at baseball, too, for I had, through enthusiastic practice, what was weirdly known as a boy's arm. In winter, in the snow, there was neither baseball nor football, so the boys and I threw snowballs at passing cars. I got in trouble throwing snowballs, and have seldom been happier since.

2   On one weekday morning after Christmas, six inches of new snow had just fallen. We were standing up to our boot tops in snow on a front yard on trafficked Reynolds Street, waiting for cars. The cars traveled Reynolds Street slowly and evenly; they were targets all but wrapped in red ribbons, cream puffs. We couldn't miss. I was seven; the boys were eight, nine, and ten. The oldest two Fahey boys were there—Mikey and Peter—polite blond boys who lived near me on Lloyd Street, and who already had four brothers and sisters. My parents approved of Mikey and Peter Fahey. Chickie McBride was there, a tough kid, and Billy Paul and Mackie Kean too, from across Reynolds, where the boys grew up dark and furious, grew up skinny, knowing, and skilled. We had all drifted from our houses that morning looking for action, and had found it here on Reynolds Street.

It was cloudy but cold. The cars' tires laid behind them on the snowy   3
street a complex trail of beige chunks like crenellated castle walls. I had
stepped on some earlier; they squeaked. We could have wished for more traffic. When a car came, we all popped it one. In the intervals between cars we
reverted to the natural solitude of children.

I started making an iceball—a perfect iceball, from perfectly white snow,   4
perfectly spherical, and squeezed perfectly translucent so no snow remained
all the way through. (The Fahey boys and I considered it unfair actually to
throw an iceball at somebody, but it had been known to happen.) I had just
embarked on the iceball project when we heard tire chains come clanking
from afar. A black Buick was moving toward us down the street. We all spread
out, banged together some regular snowballs, took aim, and, when the Buick
drew nigh, fired.

A soft snowball hit the driver's windshield right before the driver's face. It   5
made a smashed star with a hump in the middle.

Often, of course, we hit our target, but this time, the only time in all of   6
life, the car pulled over and stopped. Its wide black door opened; a man got
out of it, running. He didn't even close the car door.

He ran after us, and we ran away from him, up the snowy Reynolds side-   7
walk. At the corner, I looked back; incredibly, he was still after us. He was in
city clothes: a suit and tie, street shoes. Any normal adult would have quit,
having sprung us into flight and made his point. This man was gaining on us.
He was a thin man, all action. All of a sudden, we were running for our lives.

Wordless, we split up. We were on our turf; we could lose ourselves in the   8
neighborhood backyards, everyone for himself. I paused and considered.
Everyone had vanished except Mikey Fahey, who was just rounding the corner of a yellow brick house. Poor Mikey, I trailed him. The driver of the Buick
sensibly picked the two of us to follow. The man apparently had all day. He
chased Mikey and me around the yellow house and up a backyard path we
knew by heart: under a low tree, up a bank, through a hedge, down some
snowy steps, and across the grocery store's delivery driveway. We smashed
through a gap in another hedge, entered a scruffy backyard and ran around
its back porch and tight between houses to Edgerton Avenue; we ran across
Edgerton to an alley and up our own sliding woodpile to the Halls' front yard;
he kept coming. We ran up Lloyd Street and wound through mazy backyards
toward the steep hilltop at Willard and Lang.

He chased us silently, block after block. He chased us silently over picket   9
fences, through thorny hedges, between houses, around garbage cans, and
across streets. Every time I glanced back, choking for breath, I expected he
would have quit. He must have been as breathless as we were. His jacket
strained over his body. It was an immense discovery, pounding into my hot
head with every sliding, joyous step, that this ordinary adult evidently knew

what I thought only children who trained at football knew: that you have to fling yourself at what you're doing, you have to point yourself, forget yourself, aim, dive.

10   Mikey and I had nowhere to go, in our own neighborhood or out of it, but away from this man who was chasing us. He impelled us forward; we compelled him to follow our route. The air was cold; every breath tore my throat. We kept running, block after block; we kept improvising, backyard after backyard, running a frantic course and choosing it simultaneously, failing always to find small places or hard places to slow him down, and discovering always, exhilarated, dismayed, that only bare speed could save us—for he would never give up, this man—and we were losing speed. He chased us through the backyard labyrinths of ten blocks before he caught us by our jackets. He caught us and we all stopped.

11   We three stood staggering, half blinded, coughing, in an obscure hilltop backyard: a man in his twenties, a boy, a girl. He had released our jackets, our pursuer, our captor, our hero: he knew we weren't going anywhere. We all played by the rules. Mikey and I unzipped our jackets. I pulled off my sopping mittens. Our tracks multiplied in the backyard's new snow. We had been breaking new snow all morning. We didn't look at each other. I was cherishing my excitement. The man's lower pants legs were wet; his cuffs were full of snow, and there was a prow of snow beneath them on his shoes and socks. Some trees bordered the little flat backyard, some messy winter trees. There was no one around: a clearing in a grove, and we the only players.

12   It was a long time before he could speak. I had some difficulty at first recalling why we were there. My lips felt swollen; I couldn't see out of the sides of my eyes; I kept coughing.

13   "You stupid kids," he began perfunctorily.

14   We listened perfunctorily indeed, if we listened at all, for the chewing out was redundant, a mere formality, and beside the point. The point was that he had chased us passionately without giving up, and so he had caught us. Now he came down to earth. I wanted the glory to last forever.

15   But how could the glory have lasted forever? We could have run through every backyard in North America until we got to Panama. But when he trapped us at the lip of the Panama Canal, what precisely could he have done to prolong the drama of the chase and cap its glory? I brooded about this for the next few years. He could only have fried Mikey Fahey and me in boiling oil, say, or dismembered us piecemeal, or staked us to anthills. None of which I really wanted, and none of which any adult was likely to do, even in the spirit of fun. He could only chew us out there in the Panamanian jungle, after months or years of exalting pursuit. He could only begin, "You stupid kids," and continue in his ordinary Pittsburgh accent with his normal righteous anger and the usual common sense.

If in that snowy backyard the driver of the black Buick had cut off our heads,   16
Mikey's and mine, I would have died happy, for nothing has required so much
of me since as being chased all over Pittsburgh in the middle of winter—running
terrified, exhausted—by this sainted, skinny, furious redheaded man who wished
to have a word with us. I don't know how he found his way back to his car.

Russell Baker

from *Growing Up*

Russell Baker is a journalist whose ideas were shaped as he grew up in a poor family during the Great Depression. He spent his adolescent years in Baltimore, and after college landed a job as a reporter for the *Baltimore Sun*. Eventually he moved to the *New York Times*, where in 1962, he began writing his famous "Observer" column, which he continues to write today. His wry, incisive commentary in "Observer" earned him the Pulitzer Prize in 1979. Shortly thereafter, he began work on his own autobiography, conducting exhaustive interviews with family members in order to create a more accurate picture of depression-era America. The result, in 1983, was the Pulitzer Prize-winning *Growing Up*, which covers Baker's childhood, followed in 1989 by *The Good Times*, which describes the early years of Baker's career in journalism. In this excerpt from *Growing Up*, he recounts the shame of "going on relief" and contrasts it with the joy of Christmas.

[MY] PAPER ROUTE EARNED ME THREE DOLLARS A WEEK, sometimes four, and my   1
mother, in addition to her commissions on magazine sales, also had her
monthly check coming from Uncle Willie, but we'd been in Baltimore a year
before I knew how desperate things were for her. One Saturday morning she
told me she'd need Doris and me to go with her to pick up some food. I had
a small wagon she'd bought me to make it easier to move the Sunday papers,
and she said I'd better bring it along. The three of us set off eastward, passing
the grocery stores we usually shopped at, and kept walking until we came to
Fremont Avenue, a grim street of dilapidation and poverty in the heart of the
West Baltimore black belt.

"This is where we go," she said when we reached the corner of Fremont   2
and Fayette Street. It looked like a grocery, with big plate-glass windows and
people lugging out cardboard cartons and bulging bags, but it wasn't. I knew
very well what it was.

"Are we going on relief?" I asked her.   3

"Don't ask questions about things you don't know anything about," she   4
said. "Bring that wagon inside."

5   I did, and watched with a mixture of shame and greed while men filled it with food. None of it was food I liked. There were huge cans of grapefruit juice, big paper sacks of cornmeal, cellophane bags of rice and prunes. It was hard to believe all this was ours for no money at all, even though none of it was very appetizing. My wonder at this free bounty quickly changed to embarrassment as we headed home with it. Being on relief was a shameful thing. People who accepted the government's handouts were scorned by everyone I knew as idle no-accounts without enough self-respect to pay their own way in the world. I'd often heard my mother say the same thing of families in the neighborhood suspected of being on relief. These, I'd been taught to believe, were people beyond hope. Now we were as low as they were.

6   Pulling the wagon back toward Lombard Street, with Doris following behind to keep the edible proof of our disgrace from falling off, I knew my mother was far worse off than I'd suspected. She'd never have accepted such shame otherwise. I studied her as she walked along beside me, head high as always, not a bit bowed in disgrace, moving at her usual quick, hurry-up pace. If she'd given up on life, she didn't show it, but on the other hand she was unhappy about something. I dared to mention the dreaded words only once on that trip home.

7   "Are we on relief now, Mom?"

8   "Let me worry about that," she said.

9   What worried me most as we neared home was the possibility we'd be seen with the incriminating food by somebody we knew. There was no mistaking government-surplus food. The grapefruit-juice cans, the prunes and rice, the cornmeal—all were ostentatiously unlabeled, thus advertising themselves as "government handouts." Everybody in the neighborhood could read them easily enough, and our humiliation would be gossiped through every parlor by sundown. I had an inspiration.

10   "It's hot pulling this wagon," I said. "I'm going to take my sweater off."

11   It wasn't hot, it was on the cool side, but after removing the sweater I laid it across the groceries in the wagon. It wasn't a very effective cover, but my mother was suddenly affected by the heat too.

12   "It is warm, isn't it, Buddy?" she said. Removing her topcoat, she draped it over the groceries, providing total concealment. "You want to take your coat off, Doris?" asked my mother.

13   "I'm not hot, I'm chilly," Doris said.

14   It didn't matter. My mother's coat was enough to get us home without being exposed as three of life's failures.

15   From then on I assumed we were paupers. . . .

16   [My mother] was a magician at stretching a dollar. That December, with Christmas approaching, she was out at work and Doris was in the kitchen

when I barged into her bedroom one afternoon in search of a safety pin. Since her bedroom opened onto a community hallway, she kept the door locked, but needing the pin, I took the key from its hiding place, unlocked the door, and stepped in. Standing against the wall was a big, black bicycle with balloon tires. I recognized it instantly. It was the same second-hand bike I'd been admiring in a Baltimore Street shop window. I'd even asked about the price. It was horrendous. Something like $15. Somehow my mother had scraped together enough for a down payment and meant to surprise me with the bicycle on Christmas morning.

I was overwhelmed by the discovery that she had squandered such   17
money on me and sickened by the knowledge that, bursting into her room like this, I had robbed her of the pleasure of seeing me astonished and delighted on Christmas day. I hadn't wanted to know her lovely secret; still, stumbling upon it like this made me feel as though I'd struck a blow against her happiness. I backed out, put the key back in its hiding place, and brooded privately.

I resolved that between now and Christmas I must do nothing, absolutely   18
nothing, to reveal the slightest hint of my terrible knowledge. I must avoid the least word, the faintest intonation, the weakest gesture that might reveal my possession of her secret. Nothing must deny her the happiness of seeing me stunned with amazement on Christmas day.

In the privacy of my bedroom I began composing and testing exclamations   19
of delight: "Wow!" "A bike with balloon tires! I don't believe it!" "I'm the luckiest boy alive!" And so on. They all owed a lot to movies in which boys like Mickey Rooney had seen their wildest dreams come true, and I realized that, with my lack of acting talent, all of them were going to sound false at the critical moment when I wanted to cry out my love spontaneously from the heart. Maybe it would be better to say nothing but appear to be shocked into such deep pleasure that speech had escaped me. I wasn't sure, though. I'd seen speechless gratitude in the movies too, and it never really worked until the actors managed to cry a few quiet tears. I doubted I could cry on cue, so I began thinking about other expressions of speechless amazement. In front of a hand-held mirror in my bedroom I tried the whole range of expressions: mouth agape and eyes wide; hands slapped firmly against both cheeks to keep the jaw from falling off; ear-to-ear grin with all teeth fully exposed while hugging the torso with both arms. These and more I practiced for several days without acquiring confidence in any of them. I decided to wait until Christmas morning and see if anything came naturally. . . .

That Christmas morning she roused us early, "to see what Santa Claus   20
brought," she said with just the right tone of irony to indicate we were all old enough to know who Santa Claus was. I came out of my bedroom with my presents for her and Doris, and Doris came with hers. My mother's had been

placed under the tree during the night. There were a few small glittering packages, a big doll for Doris, but no bicycle. I must have looked disappointed.

21   "It looks like Santa Claus didn't do too well by you this year, Buddy," she said, as I opened packages. A shirt. A necktie. I said something halfhearted like, "It's the thought that counts," but what I felt was bitter disappointment. I supposed she'd found the bike intolerably expensive and sent it back.

22   "Wait a minute!" she cried, snapping her fingers. "There's something in my bedroom I forgot all about."

23   She beckoned to Doris, the two of them went out, and a moment later came back wheeling between them the big black two-wheeler with balloon tires. I didn't have to fake my delight, after all. The three of us—Doris, my mother, and I—were people bred to repress the emotional expressions of love, but I did something that startled both my mother and me. I threw my arms around her spontaneously and kissed her.

24   "All right now, don't carry on about it. It's only a bicycle," she said.

25   Still, I knew that she was as happy as I was to see her so happy.

Brent Staples

Black Men and Public Space

The son of a truck driver, Brent Staples grew up in a family of eleven that was constantly on the move due to hard economic times in his hometown of Chester, Pennsylvania. At one point uncertain as to whether he would finish high school, he eventually parlayed a college scholarship into a Ph.D. from the University of Chicago. After an unrewarding career as a lecturer in behavioral science, he found his niche as a writer, first for the *Chicago Sun Times,* then for the *New York Times,* where he continues to work as an editorial writer. While he acknowledges that his race has had a tremendous impact on his life, Staples refuses to let race define him. In this essay, which was originally published in *Harper's* magazine, Staples examines the moment that he discovered that others didn't share his views about his race.

1   MY FIRST VICTIM WAS A WOMAN—WHITE, well-dressed, probably in her early twenties. I came upon her late one evening on a deserted street in Hyde Park, a relatively affluent neighborhood in an otherwise mean, impoverished section of Chicago. As I swung onto the avenue behind her, there seemed to be a discreet, uninflammatory distance between us. Not so. She cast back a worried glance. To her, the youngish black man—a broad six feet two inches with a beard and billowing hair, both hands shoved into the pockets of a bulky mil-

itary jacket—seemed menacingly close. After a few more quick glimpses, she picked up her pace and was soon running in earnest. Within seconds she disappeared into a cross street.

That was more than a decade ago. I was twenty-two years old, a graduate 2 student newly arrived at the University of Chicago. It was in the echo of that terrified woman's footfalls that I first began to know the unwieldy inheritance I'd come into—the ability to alter public space in ugly ways. It was clear that she thought herself the quarry of a mugger, a rapist, or worse. Suffering a bout of insomnia, however, I was stalking sleep, not defenseless wayfarers. As a softy who is scarcely able to take a knife to a raw chicken—let alone hold it to a person's throat—I was surprised, embarrassed, and dismayed all at once. Her flight made me feel like an accomplice in tyranny. It also made it clear that I was indistinguishable from the muggers who occasionally seeped into the area from the surrounding ghetto. That first encounter, and those that followed, signified that a vast, unnerving gulf lay between nighttime pedestrians—particularly women—and me. And I soon gathered that being perceived as dangerous is a hazard in itself. I only needed to turn a corner into a dicey situation, or crowd some frightened, armed person in a foyer somewhere, or make an errant move after being pulled over by a policeman. Where fear and weapons meet—and they often do in urban America—there is always the possibility of death.

In that first year, my first away from my hometown, I was to become thor- 3 oughly familiar with the language of fear. At dark, shadowy intersections in Chicago, I could cross in front of a car stopped at a traffic light and elicit the *thunk, thunk, thunk, thunk* of the driver—black, white, male, or female—hammering down the door locks. On less traveled streets after dark, I grew accustomed to but never comfortable with people who crossed to the other side of the street rather than pass me. Then there were the standard unpleasantries with policemen, doormen, bouncers, cab drivers, and others whose business it is to screen out troublesome individuals *before* there is any nastiness.

I moved to New York nearly two years ago and I have remained an avid 4 night walker. In central Manhattan, the near-constant crowd cover minimizes tense one-on-one street encounters. Elsewhere—visiting friends in SoHo, where sidewalks are narrow and tightly spaced buildings shut out the sky—things can get very taut indeed.

Black men have a firm place in New York mugging literature. Norman 5 Podhoretz in his famed (or infamous) 1963 essay, "My Negro Problem—And Ours," recalls growing up in terror of black males; they "were tougher than we were, more ruthless," he writes—and as an adult on the Upper West Side of Manhattan, he continues, he cannot constrain his nervousness when he meets black men on certain streets. Similarly, a decade later, the essayist and novelist Edward Hoagland extols a New York where once "Negro bitterness bore down mainly on other Negroes." Where some see mere panhandlers, Hoagland sees "a mugger who is clearly screwing up his nerve to do more than just *ask* for money." But Hoagland has "the New Yorker's quick-hunch posture for broken-field maneuvering," and the bad guy swerves away.

6   I often witness that "hunch posture," from women after dark on the warrenlike streets of Brooklyn where I live. They seem to set their faces on neutral and, with their purse straps strung across their chests bandolier style, they forge ahead as though bracing themselves against being tackled. I understand, of course, that the danger they perceive is not a hallucination. Women are particularly vulnerable to street violence, and young black males are drastically overrepresented among the perpetrators of that violence. Yet these truths are no solace against the kind of alienation that comes of being ever the suspect, against being set apart, a fearsome entity with whom pedestrians avoid making eye contact.

7   It is not altogether clear to me how I reached the ripe old age of twenty-two without being conscious of the lethality nighttime pedestrians attributed to me. Perhaps it was because in Chester, Pennsylvania, the small, angry industrial town where I came of age in the 1960s, I was scarcely noticeable against a backdrop of gang warfare, street knifings, and murders. I grew up one of the good boys, had perhaps a half-dozen fistfights. In retrospect, my shyness of combat has clear sources.

8   Many things go into the making of a young thug. One of those things is the consummation of the male romance with the power to intimidate. An infant discovers that random flailings send the baby bottle flying out of the crib and crashing to the floor. Delighted, the joyful babe repeats those motions again and again, seeking to duplicate the feat. Just so, I recall the points at which some of my boyhood friends were finally seduced by the perception of themselves as tough guys. When a mark cowered and surrendered his money without resistance, myth and reality merged—and paid off. It is, after all, only manly to embrace the power to frighten and intimidate. We, as men, are not supposed to give an inch of our lane on the highway; we are to seize the fighter's edge in work and in play and even in love; we are to be valiant in the face of hostile forces.

9   Unfortunately, poor and powerless young men seem to take all this nonsense literally. As a boy, I saw countless tough guys locked away; I have since buried several, too. They were babies, really—a teenage cousin, a brother of 22, a childhood friend in his mid-twenties—all gone down in episodes of bravado played out in the streets. I came to doubt the virtues of intimidation early on. I chose, perhaps even unconsciously, to remain a shadow—timid, but a survivor.

10   The fearsomeness mistakenly attributed to me in public places often has a perilous flavor. The most frightening of these confusions occurred in the late

1970s and early 1980s when I worked as a journalist in Chicago. One day, rushing into the office of a magazine I was writing for with a deadline story in hand, I was mistaken for a burglar. The office manager called security and, with an *ad hoc* posse, pursued me through the labyrinthine halls, nearly to my editor's door. I had no way of proving who I was. I could only move briskly toward the company of someone who knew me.

Another time I was on assignment for a local paper and killing time before an interview. I entered a jewelry store on the city's affluent Near North Side. The proprietor excused herself and returned with an enormous red Doberman pinscher straining at the end of a leash. She stood, the dog extended toward me, silent to my questions, her eyes bulging nearly out of her head. I took a cursory look around, nodded, and bade her good night. Relatively speaking, however, I never fared as badly as another black male journalist. He went to nearby Waukegan, Illinois, a couple of summers ago to work on a story about a murderer who was born there. Mistaking the reporter for the killer, police hauled him from his car at gunpoint and but for his press credentials would probably have tried to book him. Such episodes are not uncommon. Black men trade tales like this all the time. 11

In "My Negro Problem—And Ours," Podhoretz writes that the hatred he feels for blacks makes itself known to him through a variety of avenues—one being his discomfort with that "special brand of paranoid touchiness" to which he says blacks are prone. No doubt he is speaking here of black men. In time, I learned to smother the rage I felt at so often being taken for a criminal. Not to do so would surely have led to madness—via that special "paranoid touchiness" that so annoyed Podhoretz at the time he wrote the essay. 12

I began to take precautions to make myself less threatening. I move about with care, particularly late in the evening. I give a wide berth to nervous people on subway platforms during the wee hours, particularly when I have exchanged business clothes for jeans. If I happen to be entering a building behind some people who appear skittish, I may walk by, letting them clear the lobby before I return, so as not to seem to be following them. I have been calm and extremely congenial on those rare occasions when I've been pulled over by the police. 13

And on late-evening constitutionals along streets less traveled by, I employ what has proved to be an excellent tension-reducing measure. I whistle melodies from Beethoven and Vivaldi and the more popular classical composers. Even steely New Yorkers hunching toward nighttime destinations seem to relax, and occasionally they even join in the tune. Virtually everybody seems to sense that a mugger wouldn't be warbling bright, sunny selections from Vivaldi's *Four Seasons*. It is my equivalent of the cowbell that hikers wear when they know they are in bear country. 14

Amy Tan

Fish Cheeks

Amy Tan is a gifted storyteller whose first novel, *The Joy Luck Club* (1989), met with critical acclaim and huge success. The relationships it details between immigrant Chinese mothers and their Chinese American daughters came from Tan's firsthand experience. She was born in 1952 in Oakland, California, the daughter of immigrants who had fled China's Cultural Revolution in the late 1940s. She majored in English and linguistics at San Jose State University, where she received a B.A. in 1973 and an M.A. in 1974. After two more years of graduate work, Tan became a consultant in language development for disabled children and then started her own company writing reports and speeches for business corporations. Tan began writing fiction to explore her ethnic ambivalence and to find a voice for herself. After *The Joy Luck Club,* she published *The Kitchen God's Wife* (1991), a fictional account of her mother's harrowing life in China, and *The Hundred Secret Senses* (1995), a novel. Tan has also written children's books and contributed essays to *McCall's, Life, Glamour, The Atlantic Monthly,* and other magazines. In this very brief narrative, Tan deftly portrays the ambivalence—the contradictory feelings—of a child with feet in different cultures. "Fish Cheeks" first appeared in *Seventeen* in 1987.

1   I FELL IN LOVE WITH THE MINISTER'S SON the winter I turned fourteen. He was not Chinese, but as white as Mary in the manger. For Christmas I prayed for this blond-haired boy, Robert, and a slim new American nose.

2   When I found out that my parents had invited the minister's family over for Christmas Eve dinner, I cried. What would Robert think of our shabby Chinese Christmas? What would he think of our noisy Chinese relatives who lacked proper American manners? What terrible disappointment would he feel upon seeing not a roasted turkey and sweet potatoes but Chinese food?

3   On Christmas Eve I saw that my mother had outdone herself in creating a strange menu. She was pulling black veins out of the backs of fleshy prawns. The kitchen was littered with appalling mounds of raw food: A slimy rock cod with bulging eyes that pleaded not to be thrown into a pan of hot oil. Tofu, which looked like stacked wedges of rubbery white sponges. A bowl soaking dried fungus back to life. A plate of squid, their backs crisscrossed with knife markings so they resembled bicycle tires.

4   And then they arrived—the minister's family and all my relatives in a clamor of doorbells and rumpled Christmas packages. Robert grunted hello, and I pretended he was not worthy of existence.

5   Dinner threw me deeper into despair. My relatives licked the ends of their chopsticks and reached across the table, dipping them into the dozen

or so plates of food. Robert and his family waited patiently for platters to be passed to them. My relatives murmured with pleasure when my mother brought out the whole steamed fish. Robert grimaced. Then my father poked his chopsticks just below the fish eye and plucked out the soft meat. "Amy, your favorite," he said, offering me the tender fish cheek. I wanted to disappear.

At the end of the meal my father leaned back and belched loudly, thanking my mother for her fine cooking. "It's a polite Chinese custom to show you are satisfied," explained my father to our astonished guests. Robert was looking down at his plate with a reddened face. The minister managed to muster up a quiet burp. I was stunned into silence for the rest of the night.   6

After everyone had gone, my mother said to me, "You want to be the same as American girls on the outside." She handed me an early gift. It was a miniskirt in beige tweed. "But inside you must always be Chinese. You must be proud you are different. Your only shame is to have shame."   7

And even though I didn't agree with her then, I knew that she understood how much I had suffered during the evening's dinner. It wasn't until many years later—long after I had gotten over my crush on Robert—that I was able to fully appreciate her lesson and the true purpose behind our particular menu. For Christmas Eve that year, she had chosen all my favorite foods.   8

Edith Wharton

The Valley of Childish Things

Edith Wharton (1862–1937) began her life as the daughter of wealthy New York socialites, who expected her to become one herself. She performed as required for a time, but became bored with social obligations. Around the turn of the century, she disappointed her family by becoming a writer. Her first novel, *The House of Mirth* (1905), established her as one of America's finest writers. She went on to write a succession of novels, essays, and short stories. Several of her novels, including *Ethan Frome* and *The Age of Innocence,* have been made into successful films.

ONCE UPON A TIME A NUMBER OF CHILDREN LIVED TOGETHER in the Valley of Childish Things, playing all manner of delightful games, and studying the same lesson books. But one day a little girl, one of their number, decided that   1 it was time to see something of the world about which the lesson books had taught her; and as none of the other children cared to leave their games, she set out alone to climb the pass which led out of the valley.

2   It was a hard climb, but at length she reached a cold, bleak tableland beyond the mountains. Here she saw cities and men, and learned many useful arts, and in so doing grew to be a woman. But the tableland was bleak and cold, and when she had served her apprenticeship she decided to return to her old companions in the Valley of Childish Things, and work with them instead of with strangers.

3   It was a weary way back, and her feet were bruised by the stones, and her face was beaten by the weather; but halfway down the pass she met a man, who kindly helped her over the roughest places. Like herself, he was lame and weather-beaten; but as soon as he spoke she recognized him as one of her old playmates. He too had been out in the world, and was going back to the valley; and on the way they talked together of the work they meant to do there. He had been a dull boy, and she had never taken much notice of him; but as she listened to his plans for building bridges and draining swamps and cutting roads through the jungle, she thought to herself, "Since he has grown into such a fine fellow, what splendid men and women my other playmates must have become!"

4   But what was her surprise to find, on reaching the valley, that her former companions, instead of growing into men and women, had all remained little children. Most of them were playing the same old games, and the few who affected to be working were engaged in such strenuous occupations as building mudpies and sailing paper boats in basins. As for the lad who had been the favorite companion of her studies, he was playing marbles with all the youngest boys in the valley.

5   At first the children seemed glad to have her back, but soon she saw that her presence interfered with their games; and when she tried to tell them of the great things that were being done on the tableland beyond the mountains, they picked up their toys and went farther down the valley to play.

6   Then she turned to her fellow traveler, who was the only grown man in the valley; but he was on his knees before a dear little girl with blue eyes and a coral necklace, for whom he was making a garden out of cockleshells and bits of glass and broken flowers stuck in sand.

7   The little girl was clapping her hands and crowing (she was too young to speak articulately); and when she who had grown to be a woman laid her hand on the man's shoulder, and asked him if he did not want to set to work with her building bridges, draining swamps, and cutting roads through the jungle, he replied that at that particular moment he was too busy.

8   And as she turned away, he added in the kindest possible way, "Really, my dear, you ought to have taken better care of your complexion."

Student Essay

Katherine Crane

Handling Room 15

Katherine wrote this essay in response to an assignment asking her to write a personal essay about an illness that she or someone she knew had experienced. It offers a very realistic glimpse into the world of mentally retarded children.

"ARE YOU SURE YOU ARE INTERESTED IN THIS, KATIE?" Mr. Becker asked. "Not   1
everyone can handle what you are going to witness this afternoon." My math
teacher's tone matched his expression: precise, pointed, cold and pensive.
Years of right triangles and permutations made him a calculating man, confident in his assessment of students and their potential. When he wasn't solving equations or summing up students, Mr. Becker took volunteers to the Hattie Larlham Foundation, a home for severely retarded children, a place especially significant to him. I didn't understand why he cared about HLF until I
heard his daughter spent the short five years of her life there, fluttering between life and death, stricken with a rare brain-deteriorating condition. Seeing my name on the volunteer list obviously surprised him. He knew I wasn't
a mathematician or a "visually minded student," and I knew I only took his
class to pass it, so we were not especially close.

I grimaced. I took offense at his doubts about my ability to "handle" the   2
children at the Hattie Larlham Foundation. My impeccable self-confidence as
a "spring senior" prohibited me from envisioning myself as weak and vulnerable to a bunch of kids, no matter what their condition. I effectively "handled" the school newspaper, AP European History, a boyfriend, the college application process, my worried mother, fickle friends, and the Moore Street
Mens' Shelter, so the prospect of baby-sitting a retarded child did not seem
like a daunting task, much less one I would be incapable of handling.

I did not see any patients, or "special children," as they called them, when   3
I entered the warm lobby, which smelled of the tangible "Band-Aid" stench of
health care. Four of us stood there, I the only female, chatting idly until a
male nurse, dressed in street clothes, welcomed us to the Foundation. He
thanked us in advance for volunteering to work with a "special child" two days
a week. He explained that the rest of our experience would come naturally,
that there was not anything he could really instruct us to do. "Love them," he
politely asked, or maybe he instructed, and he pointed at me to follow. I do

not know now what I expected then to see behind the door to Room 15, but I was fairly confident that my job would be to rock a small, sickly infant until he fell asleep.

4   "His name is Daniel," the nurse explained before we entered, "we don't make it practice to reveal any information about our children, but I will tell you that Daniel is an exception at HLF. He's been here the longest of anyone, including staff. He's exceeded our age limitation by two years and we're not sure if Medicare will cover him next after he turns twenty-one. He likes girls, hates his diaper, so if he tries to take it off, hold his hands. I'm going to let you go in alone."

5   I opened the door slowly, wishing there was an observation window like the ones in asylums so I could prepare myself for Daniel. A glance from a window would allow me to see without detection, experience without contact. I entered. His massive body had curled itself into fetal position on a large blue mat in the center of the room, between his crib, stuffed animals and television which played a "Barney" video. His face tucked itself away from me, so I gingerly circled his body to view him face to face, half out of curiosity, half out of respect. A foul odor emanated from him, a putrid combination of teenage body odor, feces, and the palpable, decrepit smell of my great-grandmother. A puddle of mucus and phlegm had gathered under his mouth and heaving, stuffy nose, and my disgust caused me to take a jerking step backwards into a neatly sorted pile of Curious George books. The sudden movement woke the man, and his crusted brown eyes stared at my disbelieving face, yet his head did not move from the blue mat. His features were grossly distorted, his brown hair matted and tangled, his mouth gaping and groping for words he had never spoken.

6   "I'm Katie," I said stupidly, "what's your name?"

7   Daniel let out a sickening grunt.

8   Not knowing whether to run or stay, speak or remain silent, I did nothing. I tried to suppress feelings of sympathy in order to shield myself from despair, sensing, yet not knowing for sure whether pity would help or harm the situation. I crouched down to the floor, held his chaffed, cold hand which reflexively held mine and started to tell him about my day; how I lost my keys that morning; how Mr. Becker's class bored me more than usual; how Jessie kissed another boy, making him the third of the week. He smiled, showing his tremendously stained, yellow, crooked teeth. Certain topics seemed funny to him, especially those which made my voice inflect and those which were appropriate to teenagers. He laughed and snorted while I spoke, still clutching my hand until I broke away during the end of the session. As I tried to disengage my hand from his, he held on tighter, and I had to use my other hand to pry his grip apart. Freed, I started to stand up when he let out a horrifying

bellow and tears began streaming down his face. I ran towards the door expecting him to lash out at me physically, but all his body did was futilely attempt to swivel around to see me as I closed the door to Room 15.

Later the nurse would tell me the scientific name for Daniel's reaction, 9
how he established some sort of bond with me they had never witnessed before in him. The nurse said he might have fallen in love on some basic, incomprehensible level, and he encouraged me to come back and see him if I wished. He congratulated me for handling the situation well, for making the effort to communicate with Daniel and effectively doing so.

"Please come back," he said, and I politely smiled, nodded my head, put 10
on my coat, and left. Mr. Becker picked us up and asked how our experiences were; everyone told him about the sick babies they rocked to sleep. I said nothing. The next Thursday I "missed the bus." Tuesday I had "homework." The next week, the roads were "too icy." And the next week I just stayed home. Sometimes I wonder if he remembers me or if he's moved from the blue mat. And I worry.

2

Description

Description

1. **Tell your readers what to see.** The most effective descriptions frame themselves around a dominant impression. Do you want your readers to see a dark room, or the glistening Olympic medal in the corner? Do you want them to feel saddened by the gloom, or inspired by momentary achievement that may have occurred decades ago? Depending on how you frame your description, you can tell the story of a dedicated athlete now devoting herself to public service, or a wasted talent rotting away in a tenement.

2. **Give concrete details.** In grade school, we all learn that adjectives describe. While this may be true from a technical standpoint, the best descriptions don't tell, they show, using precise nouns and active verbs. Instead of "a shiny silver medal was in the corner," it's more effective to say "a trickle of light illuminated a silver medallion, which had been carefully propped in the corner of the room."

3. **Choose words that express your purpose.** The English language contains a tremendous variety of words that each convey subtle (or not-so-subtle) connotations. As you compose and revise, select words that not only convey the meaning you intend, but also the subjective feeling or emotions you want your readers to experience. Was the medal *casually tossed* in the corner or *carefully propped* there? Was the woman *reclining* or *sprawled* on the sofa?

4. **Use a consistent method to organize details.** When describing a physical object or space, don't jerk the reader from side to side or back to front—select a method and stick to it. You might go from left to right, top to bottom, or outside to inside, but whatever method you choose, make sure you give your reader enough clues to create an image of the space in their mind. Martin Gansberg uses both a chronological and physical arrangement of details to achieve a chilling effect in "38 Who Saw Murder Didn't Call the Police." By tracing the path Kitty Genovese took as she was brutally attacked and murdered, Gansberg makes the objective details of the story come to life. Organization is equally important when describing abstract concepts such as *time* or *love*. If you don't proceed through your description in a methodical manner, your readers will get lost.

Martin Gansberg

38 Who Saw Murder Didn't Call the Police

After starting as a reporter for the *New York Times* in 1942, Martin Gansberg worked his way up through many editorial positions, rising to the level of editor of the *Times'* international edition. This column, based on a 1964 incident that shocked even the most jaded New Yorkers, merited Gansberg several journalism awards for the "vivid picture" it created. Reprinted to the sobered readers of newspapers across the country, it remains one of the most elegantly crafted pieces of journalistic writing in American history. Note how Gansberg makes his dramatic point simply by describing the events that happened that morning.

FOR MORE THAN HALF AN HOUR 38 RESPECTABLE, law-abiding citizens in   1
Queens watched a killer stalk and stab a woman in three separate attacks in
Kew Gardens.

Twice their chatter and the sudden glow of their bedroom lights inter-   2
rupted him and frightened him off. Each time he returned, sought her out,
and stabbed her again. Not one person telephoned the police during the assault; one witness called after the woman was dead.

That was two weeks ago today.   3

Still shocked is Assistant Chief Inspector Frederick M. Lussen, in charge   4
of the borough's detectives and a veteran of 25 years of homicide investigations. He can give a matter-of-fact recitation on many murders. But the Kew
Gardens slaying baffles him—not because it is a murder, but because the "good
people" failed to call the police.

"As we have reconstructed the crime," he said, "the assailant had three   5
chances to kill this woman during a 35-minute period. He returned twice to
complete the job. If we had been called when he first attacked, the woman
might not be dead now."

This is what the police say happened beginning at 3:20 A.M. in the staid,   6
middle-class, tree-lined Austin Street area:

Twenty-eight-year-old Catherine Genovese, who was called Kitty by al-   7
most everyone in the neighborhood, was returning home from her job as
manager of a bar in Hollis. She parked her red Fiat in a lot adjacent to the
Kew Gardens Long Island Rail Road Station, facing Mowbray Place. Like
many residents of the neighborhood, she had parked there day after day since
her arrival from Connecticut a year ago, although the railroad frowns on the
practice.

She turned off the lights of her car, locked the door, and started to walk   8
the 100 feet to the entrance of her apartment at 82-70 Austin Street, which is

in a Tudor building, with stores in the first floor and apartments on the second.

9   The entrance to the apartment is in the rear of the building because the front is rented to retail stores. At night the quiet neighborhood is shrouded in the slumbering darkness that marks most residential areas.

10   Miss Genovese noticed a man at the far end of the lot, near a seven-story apartment house at 82-40 Austin Street. She halted. Then, nervously, she headed up Austin Street toward Lefferts Boulevard, where there is a call box to the 102nd Police Precinct in nearby Richmond Hill.

11   She got as far as a street light in front of a bookstore before the man grabbed her. She screamed. Lights went on in the 10-story apartment house at 82-67 Austin Street, which faces the bookstore. Windows slid open and voices punctuated the early-morning stillness.

12   Miss Genovese screamed: "Oh, my God, he stabbed me! Please help me! Please help me!"

13   From one of the upper windows in the apartment house, a man called down: "Let that girl alone!"

14   The assailant looked up at him, shrugged and walked down Austin Street toward a white sedan parked a short distance away. Miss Genovese struggled to her feet.

15   Lights went out. The killer returned to Miss Genovese, now trying to make her way around the side of the building by the parking lot to get to her apartment. The assailant stabbed her again.

16   "I'm dying!" she shrieked, "I'm dying!"

17   Windows were opened again, and lights went on in many apartments. The assailant got into his car and drove away. Miss Genovese staggered to her feet. A city bus, Q-10, the Lefferts Boulevard line to Kennedy International Airport, passed. It was 3:35 A.M.

18   The assailant returned. By then, Miss Genovese had crawled to the back of the building, where the freshly painted brown doors to the apartment house held out hope for safety. The killer tried the first door; she wasn't there. At the second door, 82-62 Austin Street, he saw her slumped on the floor at the foot of the stairs. He stabbed her a third time—fatally.

19   It was 3:50 by the time the police received their first call, from a man who was a neighbor of Miss Genovese. In two minutes they were at the scene. The neighbor, a 70-year-old woman, and another woman were the only persons on the street. Nobody else came forward.

20   The man explained that he had called the police after much deliberation. He had phoned a friend in Nassau County for advice and then he had crossed

the roof of the building to the apartment of the elderly woman to get her to make the call.

"I didn't want to get involved," he sheepishly told the police.   21

Six days later, the police arrested Winston Moseley, a 29-year-old business-   22
machine operator, and charged him with homicide. Moseley had no previous record. He is married, has two children and owns a home at 133-19 Sutter Avenue, South Ozone Park, Queens. On Wednesday, a court committed him to Kings County Hospital for psychiatric observation.

When questioned by the police, Moseley also said that he had slain Mrs.   23
Annie May Johnson, 24, of 146-12 133rd Avenue, Jamaica, on Feb. 29 and Barbara Kralik, 15, of 174-17 140th Avenue, Springfield Gardens, last July. In the Kralik case, the police are holding Alvin L. Mitchell, who is said to have confessed to that slaying.

The police stressed how simple it would have been to have gotten in touch   24
with them. "A phone call," said one of the detectives, "would have done it." The police may be reached by dialing "O" for operator or SPring 7-3100.

Today witnesses from the neighborhood, which is made up of one-family   25
homes in the $35,000 to $60,000 range with the exception of the two apartment houses near the railroad station, find it difficult to explain why they didn't call the police.

A housewife, knowingly if quite casually, said, "We thought it was a lover's   26
quarrel." A husband and wife both said, "Frankly, we were afraid." They seemed aware of the fact that events might have been different. A distraught woman, wiping her hands on her apron, said, "I didn't want my husband to get involved."

One couple, now willing to talk about that night, said they heard the first   27
screams. The husband looked thoughtfully at the bookstore where the killer first grabbed Miss Genovese.

"We went to the window to see what was happening," he said, 'but the   28
light from our bedroom made it difficult to see the street." The wife, still apprehensive, added: "I put out the light and we were able to see better."

Asked why they hadn't called the police, she shrugged and replied: "I don't   29
know."

A man peeked out from the slight opening in the doorway to his apart-   30
ment and rattled off an account of the killer's second attack. Why hadn't he called the police at the time? "I was tired," he said without emotion. "I went back to bed."

It was 4:25 A.M. when the ambulance arrived to take the body of Miss   31
Genovese. It drove off. "Then," a solemn police detective said, "the people came out."

George Simpson

The War Room at Bellevue

George Simpson, who runs a public relations firm specializing in Internet and online communications, has been public affairs director for *Newsweek* and vice president of corporate communications for Simon & Schuster. He writes stories for newspapers and magazines such as the *New York Times*, *Glamour*, and *Sport* in his spare time. Simpson wrote "The War Room at Bellevue" for *New York* magazine while he was still working for *Newsweek*.

1 BELLEVUE. THE NAME CONJURES UP IMAGES of an indoor war zone: the wounded and bleeding lining the halls, screaming for help while harried doctors in blood-stained smocks rush from stretcher to stretcher, fighting a losing battle against exhaustion and the crushing number of injured. "What's worse," says a longtime Bellevue nurse, "is that we have this image of being a hospital only for. . ." She pauses, then lowers her voice, "for crazy people."

2 Though neither battlefield nor Bedlam is a valid image, there is something extraordinary about the monstrous complex that spreads for five blocks along First Avenue in Manhattan. It is said best by the head nurse in Adult Emergency Service: "If you have any chance for survival, you have it here." Survival—that is why they come. Why do injured cops drive by a half-dozen other hospitals to be treated at Bellevue? They've seen the Bellevue emergency team in action.

3 9:00 P.M. It is a Friday night in the Bellevue emergency room. The after-work crush is over (those who've suffered through the day, only to come for help after the five-o'clock whistle has blown) and it is nearly silent except for the mutter of voices at the admitting desk, where administrative personnel discuss who will go for coffee. Across the spotless white-walled lobby, ten people sit quietly, passively, in pastel plastic chairs, waiting for word of relatives or to see doctors. In the past 24 hours, 300 people have come to the Bellevue Adult Emergency Service. Fewer than 10 percent were true emergencies. One man sleeps fitfully in the emergency ward while his heartbeat, respiration, and blood pressure are monitored by control consoles mounted over his bed. Each heartbeat trips a tiny bleep in the monitor, which attending nurses can hear across the ward. A half hour ago, doctors in the trauma room withdrew a six-inch stiletto blade from his back. When he is stabilized, the patient will be moved upstairs to the twelve-bed Surgical Intensive Care Unit.

9:05 P.M. An ambulance backs into the receiving bay, its red and yellow ⁴ lights flashing in and out of the lobby. A split second later, the glass doors burst open as a nurse and an attendant roll a mobile stretcher into the lobby. When the nurse screams, "Emergency!" the lobby explodes with activity as the way is cleared to the trauma room. Doctors appear from nowhere and transfer the bloodied body of a black man to the treatment table. Within seconds his clothes are stripped away, revealing a tiny stab wound in his left side. Three doctors and three nurses rush around the victim, each performing a task necessary to begin treatment. Intravenous needles are inserted into his arms and groin. A doctor draws blood for the lab, in case surgery is necessary. A nurse begins inserting a catheter into the victim's penis and continues to feed in tubing until the catheter reaches the bladder. Urine flows through the tube into a plastic bag. Doctors are glad not to see blood in the urine. Another nurse records pulse and blood pressure.

The victim is in good shape. He shivers slightly, although the trauma room ⁵ is exceedingly warm. His face is bloodied, but shows no major lacerations. A third nurse, her elbow propped on the treatment table, asks the man a series of questions, trying to quickly outline his medical history. He answers abruptly. He is drunk. His left side is swabbed with yellow disinfectant and a doctor injects a local anesthetic. After a few seconds another doctor inserts his finger into the wound. It sinks in all the way to the knuckle. He begins to rotate his finger like a child trying to get a marble out of a milk bottle. The patient screams bloody murder and tries to struggle free.

Meanwhile in the lobby, a security guard is ejecting a derelict who has ⁶ begun to drink from a bottle hidden in his coat pocket. "He's a regular, was in here just two days ago," says a nurse. "We checked him pretty good then, so he's probably okay now. Can you believe those were clean clothes we gave him?" The old man, blackened by filth, leaves quietly.

9:15 P.M. A young Hispanic man interrupts, saying his pregnant girl ⁷ friend, sitting outside in her car, is bleeding heavily from her vagina. She is rushed into an examination room, treated behind closed doors, and rolled into the observation ward, where, much later in the night, a gynecologist will treat her in a special room—the same one used to examine rape victims. Nearby, behind curtains, the neurologist examines an old white woman to determine if her headaches are due to head injury. They are not.

9:45 P.M. The trauma room has been cleared and cleaned mercilessly. The ⁸ examination rooms are three-quarters full—another overdose, two asthmatics, a young woman with abdominal pains. In the hallway, a derelict who has been sleeping it off urinates all over the stretcher. He sleeps on while attendants change his clothes. An ambulance—one of four that patrol Manhattan for Bellevue from 42nd Street to Houston, river to river—delivers a middle-aged white woman and two cops, the three of them soaking wet. The woman has escaped from the psychiatric floor of a nearby hospital and tried to drown herself in the East River. The cops fished her out. She lies on a stretcher shivering beneath white blankets. Her eyes stare at the ceiling. She speaks clearly when an administrative worker begins routine questioning. The cops are given hospital gowns and wait to receive tetanus shots and gamma globulin—a hedge against infection from the befouled river water. They will hang around the E.R. for another two hours, telling their story to as many as six other policemen who show up to hear it. The woman is rolled into an examination room, where a male nurse speaks gently: "They tell me you fell into the river." "No," says the woman, "I jumped. I have to commit suicide." "Why?" asks the nurse. "Because I'm insane and I can't help [it]. I have to die." The nurse gradually discovers the woman has a history of psychological problems. She is given dry bedclothes and placed under guard in the hallway. She lies on her side, staring at the wall.

9 The pace continues of increase. Several more overdose victims arrive by ambulance. One, a young black woman, had done a striptease on the street just before passing out. A second black woman is semiconscious and spends the better part of her time at Bellevue alternately cursing at and pleading with the doctors. Attendants find a plastic bottle coated with methadone in the pocket of a Hispanic O.D. The treatment is routinely the same, and sooner or later involves vomiting. Just after doctors begin to treat the O.D., he vomits great quantities of wine and methadone in all directions. "Lovely business, huh?" laments one of the doctors. A young nurse confides that if there were other true emergencies, the overdose victims would be given lower priority. "You can't help thinking they did it to themselves," she says, "while the others are accident victims."

10 10:30 P.M. A policeman who twisted his knee struggling with an "alleged perpetrator" is examined and released. By 10:30, the lobby is jammed with friends and relatives of patients in various stages of treatment and recovery. The attendant who also functions as a translator for Hispanic patients adds chairs to accommodate the overflow. The medical walk-in rate stays steady—between eight and ten patients waiting. A pair of derelicts, each with battered eyes, appear at the admitting desk. One has a dramatically swollen face laced with black stitches.

11 11:30 P.M. The husband of the attempted suicide arrives. He thanks the police for saving his wife's life, then talks at length with doctors about her condition. She continues to stare into the void and does not react when her husband approaches her stretcher.

12 Meanwhile, patients arrive in the lobby at a steady pace. A young G.I. on leave has lower-back pains; a Hispanic man complains of pains in his side; occasionally parents hurry through the adult E.R. carrying children to the pediatric E.R. A white woman of about 50 marches into the lobby from the walk-

in entrance. Dried blood covers her right eyebrow and upper lip. She begins to perform. "I was assaulted on 28th and Lexington, I was," she says grandly, "and I don't have to take it *anymore*. I was a bride 21 years ago and, God, I was beautiful then." She has captured the attention of all present. "I was there when the boys came home—on Memorial Day—and I don't have to take this kind of treatment."

As midnight approaches, the nurses prepare for the shift change. They must brief the incoming staff and make sure all reports are up-to-date. One young brunet says, "Christ, I'm gonna go home and take a shower—I smell like vomit." 13

11:50 P.M. The triage nurse is questioning an old black man about chest pains, and a Hispanic woman is having an asthma attack, when an ambulance, its sirens screaming full tilt, roars into the receiving bay. There is a split-second pause as everyone drops what he or she is doing and looks up. Then all hell breaks loose. Doctors and nurses are suddenly sprinting full-out toward the trauma room. The glass doors burst open and the occupied stretcher is literally run past me. Cops follow. It is as if a comet has whooshed by. In the trauma room it all becomes clear. A half-dozen doctors and nurses surround the lifeless form of a Hispanic man with a shotgun hole in his neck the size of your fist. Blood pours from a second gaping wound in his chest. A respirator is slammed over his face, making his chest rise and fall as if he were breathing. "No pulse," reports one doctor. A nurse jumps on a stool and, leaning over the man, begins to pump his chest with her palms. "No blood pressure," screams another nurse. The ambulance driver appears shaken, "I never thought I'd get here in time," he stutters. More doctors from the trauma team upstairs arrive. Wrappings from syringes and gauze pads fly through the air. The victim's eyes are open yet devoid of life. His body takes on a yellow tinge. A male nurse winces at the gunshot wound. "This guy really pissed off somebody," he says. This is no ordinary shooting. It is an execution. IV's are jammed into the body in the groin and arms. One doctor has been plugging in an electrocardiograph and asks everyone to stop for a second so he can get a reading. "Forget it," shouts the doctor in charge. "No time." "Take it easy, Jimmy," someone yells at the head physician. It is apparent by now that the man is dead, but the doctors keep trying injections and finally they slit open the chest and reach inside almost up to their elbows. They feel the extent of the damage and suddenly it is all over. "I told 'em he was dead," says one nurse, withdrawing. "They didn't listen." The room is very still. The doctors are momentarily disgusted, then go on about their business. The room clears quickly. Finally there is only a male nurse and the still-warm body, now waxy-yellow, with huge ribs exposed on both sides of the chest and giant holes in both sides of the neck. The nurse speculates that this is yet an- 14 other murder in a Hispanic political struggle that has brought many such victims to Bellevue. He marvels at the extent of the wounds and repeats, "This guy was really blown away."

15   MIDNIGHT. A hysterical woman is hustled through the lobby into an examination room. It is the dead man's wife, and she is nearly delirious. "I know he's dead, I know he's dead," she screams over and over. Within moments the lobby is filled with anxious relatives of the victim, waiting for word on his condition. The police are everywhere asking questions, but most people say they saw nothing. One young woman says she heard six shots, two louder than the other four. At some point, word is passed that the man is, in fact, dead. Another woman breaks down in hysterics; everywhere young Hispanics are crying and comforting each other. Plainclothes detectives make a quick examination of the body, check on the time of pronouncement of death, and begin to ask questions, but the bereaved are too stunned to talk. The rest of the uninvolved people in the lobby stare dumbly, their injuries suddenly paling in light of a death.

16   12:30 A.M. A black man appears at the admissions desk and says he drank poison by mistake. He is told to have a seat. The ambulance brings in a young white woman, her head wrapped in white gauze. She is wailing terribly. A girl friend stands over her, crying, and a boyfriend clutches the injured woman's hands, saying, "I'm here, don't worry, I'm here." The victim has fallen downstairs at a friend's house. Attendants park her stretcher against the wall to wait for an examination room to clear. There are eight examination rooms and only three doctors. Unless you are truly an emergency, you will wait. One doctor is stitching up the eyebrow of a drunk who's been punched out. The friends of the woman who fell down the stairs glance up at the doctors anxiously, wondering why their friend isn't being treated faster.

17   1:10 A.M. A car pulls into the bay and a young Hispanic asks if a shooting victim has been brought here. The security guard blurts out, "He's dead." The young man is stunned. He peels his tires leaving the bay.

18   1:20 A.M. The young woman of the stairs is getting stitches in a small gash over her left eye when the same ambulance driver who brought in the gunshot victim delivers a man who has been stabbed in the back on East 3rd Street. Once again the trauma room goes from 0 to 60 in five seconds. The patient is drunk, which helps him endure the pain of having the catheter inserted through his penis into his bladder. Still he yells, "That hurts like a bastard," then adds sheepishly, "Excuse me, ladies." But he is not prepared for what comes next. An X-ray reveals a collapsed right lung. After just a shot of local anesthetic, the doctor slices open his side and inserts a long plastic tube. Internal bleeding had kept the lung pressed down and prevented it from reinflating. The tube releases the pressure. The am-

bulance driver says the cops grabbed the guy who ran the eight-inch blade into the victim's back. "That's not the one," says the man. "They got the wrong guy." A nurse reports that there is not much of the victim's type blood available at the hospital. One of the doctors says that's okay, he won't need surgery. Meanwhile blood pours from the man's knife wound and the tube in his side. As the nurses work, they chat about personal matters, yet they respond immediately to orders from either doctor. "How ya doin'?" the doctor asks the patient. "Okay," he says. His blood spatters on the floor.

So it goes into the morning hours. A Valium overdose, a woman who   19
fainted, a man who went through the windshield of his car. More overdoses. More drunks with split eyebrows and chins. The doctors and nurses work without complaint. "This is nothing, about normal, I'd say," concludes the head nurse. "No big deal."

Student Essay

Adam Burrell

Time Torture

In this essay, Adam describes what truly must be every student's object of hatred—the clock radio. Notice how he uses the device of personification to make his loathing of his clock seem more . . . well, personal. Adam uses hyperbole—like the "millions" of dials—to excellent comic effect. You must be brave to use comedy well: there are many situations where it may be seen as inappropriate.

DON'T GET ME WRONG—I'M REALLY NOT PARANOID. I mean, my alarm clock   1
looks like a typical generic style clock radio. Nothing appears outwardly abnormal at all. In fact, it doesn't have any truly distinguishing features at all, and I'm tempted to say that it's an average, run-of-the-mill, nondescript clock radio. But, since it's a cop-out to describe something as "nondescript" (if not outright contradictory), I'll give a quick rundown of it. I've owned this clock radio, a Realistic Chronomatic 213, for a month now, and it's still difficult to remember exactly what it looks like. There it is, a rectangular box sitting on my desk in the corner, six feet from my bed, with a bright red digital readout saying 9:39. The colon between the 9 and the 39—no, now 40—flashes on and off once per second, 24 hours a day.

To the right of the time display is the radio tuning dial, set near 97 FM, probably KBCO Boulder. Also on the rectangular front face, just below the clock display and the radio tuning dial, is a row of four small round switches, used to set the time and the alarm. The top and the sides of the radio are an artificial wood-grain finish, trimmed with black and separated from the front panel by a chrome strip. Centered on its top is a small square speaker grill.

2   Yeah, this alarm clock would seem like a normal, well-adjusted appliance to most people, but that's because they don't have to live with it. Just by looking at it, a person wouldn't sense that this clock radio carried a grudge and had general anti-social tendencies. Even I didn't notice anything strange until recently. First, small irritating things became apparent. For instance, the way it stares at night, annoyingly blinking its stupid red colon. After a half-hour of watching the clock gaze back, it's obvious that the stare isn't a benign one; it has the qualities of an unpleasant sneer, that certain executioner's look of someone in ultimate control. Then, I noticed how time always seemed to speed up at night while I slept. I could almost hear that damn blood-red colon flashing faster and faster, but as soon as I would open my eyes it would skid back down to once per second, once per second. The unnerving part, though, is that the clock speeds up in direct proportion to the amount of sleep that I need—so even if I go to bed early the night before a big exam, I still wake up with severe jetlag.

3   This clock's attitude problem doesn't become blatantly apparent until early morning, however. The hours of darkness slowly convert it into a remorseless predatory creature, primed to terrorize. Yes, terrorize. Remaining utterly silent and motionless so as not to stir its unsuspecting comatose victim, the clock waits. Mercilessly it savors its position of power as the final seconds slip by. And then it strikes. Noise and chaos, resembling the detonation of a medium-sized nuclear device in the corner of my room, slam out of its tiny speaker. At five in the morning. Actually, at five in the morning, the sound has more of a physical quality, roughly equivalent to a chainsaw being started in the left ear while a rake crashes into the jaw. Instinctively, my body, instantly brought from suspended animation to adrenaline overload, lunges in the general direction of the demonic box on the desk. My hand swats at every small knob—there are now millions of them—until it slaps the right switch in the right direction, snuffing out the noise and the pain.

4   Every morning, as I lie limply on the floor, I can see the clock display staring straight ahead, blinking its damned red colon in the morning sun, once per second, once per second, and I know it's trying not to snicker. I'm not paranoid—the clock really does hate me.

Melvin Konner

Kick Off Your Heels

Melvin Konner, an M.D. and professor of anthropology at Emory University, is an expert on health-care reform who has testified before the U.S. Congress on the issue. He has written several books for the popular press including *The Tangled Wing: Biological Constraints On the Human Spirit*, *Becoming a Doctor*, and *The Paleolithic Prescription*. In this essay, he examines the allure and the dangers of high-heeled shoes.

A FRIEND OF MINE, A SEDATE HISTORIAN, ALLOWS HOW HE USED TO sit in the library as a graduate student at Princeton trying to bury his thoughts in some thick tome. In those bad old days, when Princeton was all-male, the appearance of a female visitor would sometimes be signaled by a sound outside the window in the summer evening: the unmistakable click, click of high heels on the garden walk. Like the bell that made Pavlov's dog salivate, the mere sound of the walk triggered a physiological cascade. Such is the drift of the male brain that it can be drawn off course, for at least minutes, by the sound of a symbol of sexuality.

Yet consider what those heels do with the female form. The legs are slimmed and lengthened; this makes them what students of animal behavior call a supernormal stimulus—recalling, yet exaggerating the lengthening that occurs at puberty. (Pin-up drawings always exaggerate length.) At the same time, the feet are shortened—daintier? For some reason, both men and women seem to prefer smaller feet. Heels tighten the calves and make them prominent. The buttocks are thrown up and out (a distant echo, perhaps, of the sexual "presenting" of female mammals) and the bosom thrust forward, producing the S-curve for which women bustled and corseted brutally in time past. That certain something—not a ponytail—that sways when she walks (because women's hips are wider and not poised over the knees) sways more than usual. And she is hobbled. She is charmingly (to him) off-balance on her pedestal, and unable to flee. (A convicted mugger has said, "We would wait under a stairwell in the subway station and, when we heard the click of the wobbly spiked heel, we knew we had one.")

The message is not unambiguous helplessness. The heels just about abolish the average male advantage in height. The points of the heels and the toes are suitable weapons. But regardless of ambiguity, they convey a message: Look at me; get close if you can—or, if you haven't the courage, try to go back to your book.

4   Courting creatures signal sex in myriad ways. Often the males do the strutting. The peacock spreads his magnificent eyed feathers, and antelope like the Uganda kob prance and clang great antlers against each other. Other species leave some posing to the female. In the 10-spined stickleback, a little freshwater fish of the British Isles, the female flashes a bit of swollen silver belly and triggers the male's courtship dance. The female zebra finch, an Australian perching bird, sits on a branch and stretches in a horizontal posture. While the male watches nearby, she bends her legs, sleeks her gray feathers and flutters her black-and-white tail. The female great crested grebe, ordinarily a graceful diving waterbird, assumes an even more awkward posture, sitting on the water with her wings spread and shoulders pointing down.

5   Humans are no slouches when it comes to sexual signaling. On the contrary, we take the signals nature has given us—an arched brow, a descending eyelid, a smile—and embellish them with every conceivable cultural brush stroke. Draping or painting or piercing or molding the body has gone on for millenniums. New Guinea men paint themselves dramatically for dancing, and marriageable Papuan maidens bear elegant tattoos. Extensive, patterned scars variously signified femininity and manliness in many African cultures. Lip plugs, head molding, circumcision, ear stretching, tooth filing—the list goes on.

6   Fewer than a hundred years ago, Western women tied themselves in corsets that damaged abdominal organs and made them respiratory wrecks. At the same time, the Chinese were still practicing the extraordinary 1,000-year-old tradition of foot-binding. The resulting foot was shortened, with all toes but the first curled under and the arch drastically raised—essentially, high heels made of bone. This distortion was a matter of pride, a sign of nobility and allure.

7   How close do our own artificial high heels come to that old Chinese ideal? Not very, but there are similarities. Both signify sex and class, and achieve femininity. And both, to different degrees, result in impairment.

8   Orthopedists and chiropractors see the consequences in backache and knee problems. One orthopedics textbook describes the gait in such shoes as "ungainly" and "mincing," and notes that the normal cushioning is lost. Authorities agree that the toes and balls of the feet in high heels must bear too much weight in striking the ground, and that they transmit the shock upward. After prolonged wearing of high heels, the calf muscles and the Achilles' tendon may permanently contract. Robert Donatelli, a physical therapist, says shortened calf muscles may cause the knees to be slightly flexed; this in turn may cause chronic flexion of hips. The ultimate result may produce a shape of buttocks suggestive to the male, but at the cost of increased lumbar lordosis, harmful pressure on the lumbar discs that can cause low-back pain.

Richard Benjamin, a podiatrist at the Greater Southeastern Hospital in Washington, says, too, that throwing the weight on the ball of the foot diminishes the normal roles of both heel and big toe. Incorrect turning of the foot throws the knee out, affecting the hip and back. Like the S-shaped stance, the exaggerated pelvic sway provides allure at a cost in physical damage.

Podiatrists do see several times more women than men, primarily because   9
of high-heeled shoes with pointed toes. Pain in foot bones is almost inevitable, but this is only the beginning. Abrasions, calluses, bunions (hallux valgus), tendinitis, ingrown toenails and serious bone deformities such as hammer toes and "pump bump"—a bony enlargement of the heel where the shoe rim bites into it—are frequent. Bunions can be serious; they can force the joint between the big toe and the adjacent metatarsal bone to become so bent for so long that calcium buildup renders it permanently and painfully deviated. The ratio of women to men who have this disorder is estimated to be 40-to-1. High heels also cause abnormal thickening of skin and bone at the ball of the foot, and this can force the small toes under the foot, crushing them, in some rare cases. Sheldon Flaxman, a foot surgeon, concludes: "These shoes should be worn for special occasions only." Even then, he says, they should not be pointed and the heels should be as low as possible.

High heels are, after all, relatively new in Western tradition. In the 16th   10
century, the elegant—men and women alike—began to like upward-tilting footwear. Before the Elizabethan period in England, flatness in shoes was consistent with both elegance and sex. One will search in vain in earlier paintings and sculpture for evidence of shoes that lever people off the ground. By the mid-18th century, men's shoes had returned to normalcy, but women were stuck on their awkward platforms, and there they have remained. The most extreme form—the stiletto of the 1950s—was often banned, to prevent damage to floors. No laws, written or unwritten, prevent damage to feet—or to women's sense of freedom.

Why do we have such an attachment to this hurtful fashion? The Freudi-   11
ans have had a field day with it, likening it to a mild version of the condition in which a fetishist (always a man) can be aroused only by a shoe. They even invoke sadomasochism as well, and in this explanation the pain and harm are no longer incidental. As I get older, the pain is what I most often see. But I have to admit that a woman will sometimes take me by surprise—dressed to the nines, high-heeled shoes and all.

I'm fighting it though, the part of it that comes from bad shoes. I expect   12
to win. I think of adjectives that apply to women in flat shoes: lithe, graceful, earthy, athletic, sensible, fleet, dancing, practical, fresh, nimble, strong—and sexy, definitely sexy. (Don't look for logic here, we're talking about hormones.) I think of the women depicted by Greek and Roman art—they didn't need to be hobbled to interest men. I think of the polka and the hora instead of the

waltz and the tango—and as for whatever it is we do to rock music, that works just as well in flats.

13   Still, it's hard to visualize a great formal party without stylish women kicking up their high heels. Like some of the other indulgences of that and like occasions, they're probably O.K. in moderation. But for everyday wear they make as little sense as a three-martini lunch. They're a relatively recent innovation. They've wormed their way into our sexual imagery. But it's hard to see why they have to stay there.

Lani Kwon Meilgaard

An "Other" American

On Being Multiracial-American

Lani Kwon Meilgaard grew up on the islands of Oahu and Maui, where being multi-ethnic was not unusual. She graduated with honors from the University of Hawaii at Manoa with a degree in English. She received her M.A. in Creative Writing from the University of Colorado at Boulder, where she wrote this essay, which originally appeared in the e-zine _Interracial Voice_. Meilgaard lives in California where she is a professor of English writing. She has just completed her first novel, _A Place Without Regret_.

San Bernardino, California
December 1967

1   "But Sharon," said my grandmother, sitting across from Mom at the dinner table, buttering a piece of white bread, "won't your children be. . . ." She paused, searching for the right words, ". . . confused?"

2   It was incredibly hot in the kitchen, and Mom could feel rivulets of sweat running down her sides under her pullover and in the waistband of pink pedal pushers. Heat continued to radiate from the gas oven. Mom's mind was only half on the conversation. She was thinking of the most recent letter she had received. She was thinking of Dad, who was no longer a music major at Redlands University and had narrowly escaped being drafted into the Army. They had both realized that he could have been mistaken for Vietnamese and shot in "friendly fire" if he was fighting on the ground. Enlisted in the Navy instead, he was at boot camp in San Diego, soon to be 2nd class petty officer/machinist mate on the U.S.S. Hancock, stationed off the northern coast of Vietnam.

3   "Don't you think it will be difficult for your children?" Grandma held the

slice of bread out as if it were a crystal ball or flattened palm in which Mom would certainly see her future.

"What do you mean, Mom?"   4

"Getting married to this . . . this . . . Japanese person." Grandma's thin   5
lips shriveled as if she had tasted something bitter.

"Mom," she sighed long-sufferingly, "Michael's an American, not Japa . . ."   6

"He's dark, Sharon." Grandma hissed what she had up until that point   7
kept to herself.

"So?" Mom said, only realizing she had spoken aloud when she saw her   8
mother's pursed lips.

Grandma sighed, "Don't you see?"   9

"We've already set the date. January 26th."   10

"Sharon, I'm trying to help you . . ."   11

Mom stabbed at the dry roast chicken breast on her plate. She didn't look   12
up as she said,

"The best way to help is to give me your blessing."   13

"Your children will hate you."   14

Grandma spat out the words.   15

Mom sat there stunned. She heard the screen door slam behind her and   16
exhaled, not realizing that she had been holding her breath. She turned to her
father.

It had been a rough day for him, working construction in Riverside   17
County. He carefully wiped his face, bald head and neck with an old red ban-
danna—an indication of his reluctance to get involved—before saying, "It's your
choice."

It was my parents' choice. California was the first state, in 1948, to decide   18
that interracial marriages were *not* unconstitutional. It took almost twenty
years, until 1967, for anti-miscegenation laws to be struck down nationwide in
the aptly named Supreme Court decision, *Loving vs. Virginia.*

Grandma did not "forgive" Mom for marrying my father until after I was   19
born, until after she got to know my father and his family. It wasn't easy for
her. I think she genuinely believed she had been trying to help, offering my
mother "good" advice. I became the living symbol of what my grandmother
had feared most—World War II propaganda come to life—"the enemy" marrying into the family, changing the blood, changing the future.

I am not sure if I have forgiven *her* yet.   20

I look into the mirror and try to see myself as a stranger might: dark brown   21
eyes and hair, full lips and light skin. I can see in the slight curving of my eyes
my paternal grandparents' Asian faces, my mother's Native American features.
Under bright, artificial light, I can see the slight yellow cast of my skin, my
irises so dark that I can only see the pupil if I look close.

In Hawaii, I grew up *hapa haole*, of *mixed race*. But in England and in Col-   22 orado, the identity *hapa* was taken from me; I was labeled *white*, rather than being categorized as *other*, like many of my darker-skinned friends. In California, I am once again *hapa* and difficult to conveniently categorize, although here, often other Asian-Americans (unless they are originally from Hawaii) do not recognize me as another Asian. Never before was my race and ethnicity an issue to me, and I have tried to discover why. How has my racial identity shifted? It wasn't a change from the inside, but rather from the outside. It is based upon other people's assumptions, differing in each of the places I have lived.

23   For many years, the cultural model of assimilation, "the melting pot," was touted as the only way to be an American. Yet the standard for this model was based on the politically and economically more powerful European settlers' values and cultural norms. In the 1960s and '70s, a more inclusive ideology was suggested—"a stew" or "mixed salad"—whereby immigrants to America might maintain their distinct cultures, languages and traditions, their *ethnicity* or *ancestry*, while at the same time recognizing their "Americanness."

24   Today, rising numbers of Americans are, like myself, of mixed ethnicity. Many of us are proud of this heritage and interested in our multiple ancestries. We do not fit the limiting, artificial categories of race—White, Black or Negro, American Indian or Alaskan Native, and Asian or Pacific Islander—outlined in Statistical Directive 15, which was adopted in 1978 by the Office of Management and Budget and used in the 1990 U.S. Census of the Population. We are "Multiracial-Americans."

25   Nationality is a complex and often shifting set of political, historical and socio-economic circumstances. A group of people recognize themselves as a country. They identify themselves by their country of origin. At the birth of our relatively young nation, perhaps people wanted to be known *only* by their new national identity—American.

26   Yet saying I am simply "American" not only fails to address the complexity of my being: It nullifies the elements that make me whole. It disregards my ethnicity and ancestry and the many cultural values attached. When I am labeled *white*, I am not seen in relation to the other parts of myself I value. For in addition to being of several European ethnicities—Scottish, Irish, Dutch, German, English, French, and Spanish—I am also Japanese, Korean, Chinese, and Native American (Iroquois and Delaware).

27   When your veins flow with the blood of twelve nations, you belong to none, yet are encompassed by all.

Brunswick, Georgia
March 30, 1969

28 When Mom filled out the application for my birth certificate, she was faced with the following question:

Race of child: 29
__White __Black.   30

"But my baby's half-Asian."   31
   The nurse, a Caucasian matriarch dressed in starched white, many shades   32
lighter than her skin, replied, "Honey, that baby ain't Black, so she's White."
And so I am, according to Georgia Department of Public Health records.
   My father, too, was classified *"White"* on my birth certificate, but he gained   33
none of the privileges whites at this time took for granted—something as simple
as the right to walk by or to go into a store without being stared at by others.
   Lea, the middle sister, was born in Jacksonville, Florida and was classified   34
"Malaysian," even though she has no Malay blood. This practice was appar-
ently discontinued in 1971, when my youngest sister, Laura, was born in
Lamar, California. According to my mother, she is not classified by race.
   Have these slips of paper changed who we are?   35
   A paper that says you're white means nothing when your dark-skinned,   36
Asian father moves back to Hawaii—where many Asian-Americans live—taking
his family with him just to feel he belongs.

Makakilo, Hawaii 1978
Defining the "Other," Hawaiian Style

   Haole n. White person, American, Englishman, Caucasian; formerly,   37
   any foreigner.
         v. ["To be haole"] To act like a white person, to ape the white peo-   38
   ple, or assume airs of superiority, often said disparagingly, especially of
   half-whites. (Pukui 58)

   At my elementary school, the last day of school was called "Kill Haole   39
Day." It was when kids of the non-white races, who were in the majority,
would pick on white kids—call them names, throw rotten eggs at them, beat
them up.
   I don't remember anything ever actually happening on this day; most of   40
the white kids stayed at home, and most of the kids talking about participating were part-white themselves. All I remember was trying to fit in, being a
tomboy, acting as if I were tough. I did not know that there were decades of
suppressed rage behind what we were doing.
   We were unaware of the implications behind racial jokes—which in Hawaii   41
were common but not taken seriously or intended to offend. Everybody made
fun of everybody, knew all the local stereotypes—that Chinese were *pake*, interested only in money; that Japanese were xenophobic and ambitious; that
whites were greedy and loud; while Hawaiians were labeled lazy. In some ways,

these racial jokes provided a safety valve for the unnamed feelings many of us did not acknowledge.

42   Our persecution of white children re-enacted on a smaller scale the resentment of some of our parents, grandparents and great-grandparents, the collective anger against generations of oppression by white *lunas*, overseers on the plantations, and white missionaries. We were emulating a dangerous precedent about which we knew nothing, and yet we somehow remained ignorant that this was racism—in our own school, our own neighborhood.

43   Would I have held down little Aaron—the boy whose breath was tinged with the sour odor of milk and fear—while Kaui beat his white skin red and purple? These were the colors of our anger, of misunderstanding and revenge. For what? The fact that Aaron did better in class than we? Or that his clothes were newer and more expensive? Or was it his Southern accent that we disliked, his way of ignoring the taunts and jeers every day as he got off the bus?

44   Aaron does not exist. He is all the children who did not fit in, some white, some black, but more often defined as *from the Mainland*, a place that was too far away and alien for many of us to understand.

45   "Racism" was something that happened on the Mainland: Whites against Blacks. We did not think that racism could happen in Hawaii. We did not think.

Pearl City, Hawaii
Christmas 1982

46   Christmas festivities in my family consisted of a mixture of American tradition and several local customs unique to the region: eating *kim chee* and sushi with our Christmas turkey or ham, making a gingerbread house garnished with imported Japanese candy bought at Shirokiya, and sometimes having a picnic of hamburgers and *lomi lomi* salmon at the beach.

47   On this occasion, my sisters and I had decorated our living room with the usual Christmas finery. In one corner a Douglas Fir (one of the trees shipped in by the thousands from the mainland U.S. in refrigerated Matson shipping containers, the oddity of which we took for granted) wilted in its solution of sugar water. We made a construction paper fireplace where we hung our stockings. Antique hand-blown glass ornaments and handicrafts we had made in school (like the blue sequin-covered eggshell ornament which held my front-toothless 5th grade portrait) were in positions of prestige on the tree.

48   On Christmas morning we woke our parents up at 5 a.m. and began digging into our loot. The room smelled of Christmas pine and excitement. There are several gifts I remember from that year: a pink Barbie sportscar, silly

putty and, from our paternal grandparents on Maui, dolls in costumes from around the world.

The card was inscribed, "To the girls. Value your ancestors. Love, Grandma and Grandpa Kwon." 49

Each doll stood about six inches tall and, as promised, was dressed in a "traditional" costume. Miss Japan wore a kimono adorned with a cherry blossom pattern and a golden *obi*, and she had an elaborate hairstyle. Was she from Tokyo or Osaka? The box did not specify. Miss America wore leather buckskin and beaded moccasins. She was an amalgam of popular images of Native Americans, like the Disneyfied Pocahontas would be years later. Miss Spain had a long flamenco-style dress, and in her hair there was a veil held by a miniature carved wooden comb. She was not from Galicia, the Northwestern region of Spain (once a part of Portugal) from whence our great-grandmother came. Yet we thought of her as being Spanish. 50

Each doll had some item of clothing that made her representative of her nation, and each doll had the appropriately colored skin and eyes to match the perceived norm of her country of origin. But each doll failed to fully represent the ethnic and cultural diversity within each country. 51

What I discovered later is something difficult to explain. My sisters and I are Japanese, Native American, Spanish, etc. . . , but who we are as people, as "individuals," differs greatly from each of the nations represented by the dolls. 52

We have an identity, but it is not determined by country of origin. It is based on what our family has done together or what we have done individually—like driving to Hanauma Bay to snorkel, or taking a Kentucky Fried Chicken picnic up to the mountains of Aiea, or helping Grandma Kwon prepare *bul go gi*, Korean bar-be-cue beef—that makes us who we are. 53

Growing up was a mish-mash of cultural traditions. We'd watch Disney movies like *The Jungle Book* and *Cinderella* on one day and dance hula the next. Hawaii's multiethnic "culture" offered us these choices, choices we could make according to individual taste and inclination. The cultural activities I enjoyed, like the Japanese *Obon* festivals in the summer at the local Hongwanji to honor our dead relatives, were sometimes different than those my sisters chose to attend. 54

My sisters and I are *individuals*. Doesn't the intrinsic meaning of that word allow for difference? 55

Oxford, England
1992

Justin, my husband, had been working in England for about two years. He was responsible for arranging housing, excursions and social events for an Ameri- 56 can agency which brought American students to Oxford to study. Justin's father is Danish, his mother English, Irish and Huguenot French. He is a British citizen by birth but grew up in Monterrey, Mexico and Detroit, Michigan. He, like myself, has always felt "different." But for him this feeling has come from inside—the feeling of being an observer, antsider—a person who has adapted to living in many different countries. It is an altogether different experience when this feeling of being an outsider is imposed on you from the outside.

57   On a typically gray evening, Justin and I were invited to a dinner party by an estate agent ("real estate agent" in American-English) with whom Justin often consulted. The night air smelled of ivy and dampness. The estate agent and his mother had offered to pick us up.

58   "So, how're you adjusting to our weather?"

59   At first I did not realize that the estate agent was speaking to me. He glanced at me in the rearview mirror, his horn-rimmed glasses and balding pate glowing slightly red from a traffic light. He and Justin had been talking business, while I was looking out the window at the rapidly passing landscape, lights whizzing by. "Oh, yes . . . I am. Thank you," I replied, uncertain as to why I had become unaccountably shy and withdrawn since I had come to England—a 180 degree turn from my usual personality.

60   The estate agent continued talking with Justin. His mother—a woman roughly in her sixties, wearing an old-fashioned overcoat, wool dress and stockings, whom I (knowing it was a stereotype) imagined knitted, owned a cat and never turned up the heat in her house—offered a word or two occasionally. I tuned in and out on what they were saying: "Yes, housing starts these days . . . outrageous. . . . New apartments available? . . . Oxford's growing too fast. . . . students. . . . would be a suburb of London if not for the zoning laws. . . ."

61   We spun around one of the freeway medians, which in England are circular and called "roundabouts." Suddenly, I heard the words, ". . . Japanese . . . yes, my wife is part Asian." Justin said this proudly, holding my hand. I noticed the mother's shoulders stiffen. Her son said nothing until we arrived at the house.

62   For the rest of the evening the estate agent's mother refused to speak with me, avoided my gaze. Her son eyed me strangely from under his bushy eyebrows.

63   At the time I racked my brain to discover what I might have said or done to offend them. Later, I realized it was nothing I had done, but simply who I was.

64   USA 1990 Census of Population Form: When it comes to the question of race, here's what you see:

RACE
Fill ONE circle for the race that the person considers himself/herself to be.

O White   O Black or Negro   O Indian (Amer.)
     If Indian (Amer.), print the name of the enrolled or principal tribe
O Eskimo   O Chinese   O Japanese
O Asian Indian If Other Asian or Pacific Islander (API),
O Aleut Asian or Pacific Islander (API)
O Other API (Print below) Cambodian, and so on.
O Samoan print one group, for example: Hmong, Guamanian Fijian, Laotian, Thai, Tongan, Pakistani
O Filipino   O Hawaiian   O Korean
O Vietnamese O Other race (Print below)

Census records are kept as statistical data for a variety of Federal and State   65
Government uses—educational funding, city and state grants, to enforce the
Voting Rights Act and equal employment regulations, just to name a few. People are asked to "Fill ONE circle for the race each person considers himself/herself to be" (Census E-2). But the race categorizations seem so arbitrary when you read:

> White—Includes persons who indicated their race as "White" or re-   66
> ported entries such as Canadian, German, Italian, Lebanese, Near
> Easterner, Arab, or Polish.

> Black—Includes persons who indicated their race as "Black or Negro"   67
> or reported entries such as African American, Afro-American, Black
> Puerto Rican, Jamaican, Nigerian, West Indian, or Haitian (B-29).

If you consider yourself of European or even Middle Eastern descent, you are   68
categorized by the government as "White." If you consider yourself African or
Caribbean (which historically has also had interracial children born to parents
of African, Indian and/or European races), you are categorized "Black."
    An article entitled "The 'Other' Americans" in the June 1994 issue of   69
American Demographics, illustrates how outdated this thinking is:

> The 1990 census questionnaire asked respondents to put themselves   70
> into a racial category and to indicate their ethnicity and ancestry else-
> where. Respondents who felt that they didn't fit into one of the four
> categories checked a box marked "other race." The number of people
> who checked that box increased 45 percent between the 1980 and
> 1990 censuses, to 9.8 million. That's about 1 in 25 Americans (37).

71   Part of this increase is due to the fact that if you write in a "race" which is categorized by the government as an "ethnicity," your responses are categorized "other race." According to *American Demographics,* Statistical Directive 15 "defines Hispanic origin as an ethnic category separate from race" (37). People of Hispanic ethnicity are often categorized as either "white" or "black."

72   But if you are of multiracial heritage, like myself, you cannot list more than one "race" in the box marked "other." The box and classificatory system are too narrow.

73   You cannot, for example, check each and every box that applies to you. If you do so, according to the U.S. Census and Department of Commerce, either "the race of the mother [is] used" or "the first race reported by the person [is] used" (B-28) to define your race. You may fill in "multiethnic" or "multiracial," but you are categorized anonymously as "other." If you choose to rebel and fill in nothing, "race [is] assigned based upon the reported entries of race by other household members" (B-30). In most cases "White" is used. It just happens to be the first category provided on the census form.

Denver, Colorado
October 29, 1994

74 It was chilly, though still unseasonably warm that fall; the steam vents in the Denver streets released masses of white cloud. I was standing outside Currigan Exhibition Hall, site of the 2nd Annual Rocky Mountain Book Festival, with several friends—to see Linda Hogan, a professor of ours at the University of Colorado, and other writers we admired.

75   Linda arrived, wearing a black velvet tunic, long flowing pants and silver hoop earrings, which brushed against her shoulders. She smiled as she recognized our group.

76   There was a communal shout. "Linda!" "It's good to see you!" "How are you?"

77   "Linda, you're the only woman I'd get up at six to see," I said laughing as I gave her a hug.

78   "Me, too," she said, and we all laughed.

79   Linda was swept aside by one of the organizers of the festival toward the author's entrance, as we dashed up the stairs and into the "Agatha Christie" room for her reading.

80   Our room was full of rows of black, uncomfortable-looking chairs. The ceiling was high, and there was a raised stage before which stood an inauspicious wooden podium. We took seats in the second and third rows, amazed that we were so close to the front, having expected mobs for this first reading of the day.

I looked around the room, noticing a few others who had come to hear   81
Linda read: a couple of older men—white hair, denim; a group of women in
broomstick skirts and fancy embroidered blouses; a newspaper reporter from
the *Rocky Mountain News* who had interviewed Linda a couple of weeks earlier about her Colorado Book Award and Lannan Literary Prize; and Sher-
man Alexie, the next reader in the room, another writer whom I had come
to meet.

The room was too large, yet I felt as if I was in class. Linda was only about   82
five feet away, and her soothing voice reassured me. She read from *Dwellings*,
a book of essays about nature she had just completed, then several poems
from *The Book of Medicines*. She read well, slowly, yet with a rhythmic cadence.
I blinked with surprise when it was over.

The question and answer session that followed was fairly straightforward: 83
How long have you been writing? Who have been your influences? What procedure do you follow when you write? Do you write on a computer or long-
hand? What inspires your writing? etc. . . . etc. . . .

Then, suddenly, one of the men in denim, a throwback, an anachro-   84
nistic cowboy, asked "the question." His tone of voice was skeptical, as if
he thought he was exposing a fraud: a woman who identifies herself as a
Native American writer, but who is really white. He asked, "What kind of
Indian are you, if you are an Indian . . . and do you pray . . . How do you
pray?"

Linda took a deep breath, and I saw the anger flash briefly across her eyes.   85
This all occurred in less than a second.

I have felt the same twisting in my gut, the blood burning in my veins, at   86
being labeled a fake by those who have read my writing and thought my work
"exploitive" and "presumptuous," that I am cashing in on the popularity of
minority literature.

I have often felt an odd sort of guilt, as well. For by being labeled white by   87
others when I know myself to be part Asian, I have been granted privileges my
friends have not. I have felt like an impostor or a spy.

Linda's answer was one I wish I could emulate at times like these, full of   88
grace and dignity. She did not get into a lengthy argument. She described herself in terms of the culture with which she most closely identifies. She responded in an even tone of voice, "I am Chickasaw, and my poems are my
prayers."

Palo Alto, California
April 13, 1996

Filling out applications in order to teach English Composition in local com-   89
munity colleges, I find the following at the end of each questionnaire:

90   The information that you provide will be used for statistical record keeping and reporting only. You will not be identified by name when these statistics are reported, and this information will not be forwarded as part of your application materials.

What is your Racial/Ethnic Group? (Check one)

○ Caucasian   ○ Black   ○ Native American
○ Hispanic/Latino   ○ Asian/Pacific Islander

91   I could check Asian/Pacific Islander and Caucasian. I am both, but the instructions clearly say, "Check one." And what does it mean to be Asian/Pacific Islander anyway? The cultures in this region, the "Pacific Rim," are as different and unique from one another as Canada, the United States and Mexico are from each other. Within these countries there are many distinct linguistic and cultural differences.

92   According to U.S. Census Statistics, published in a February 13, 1995 article in *Newsweek*, there were 310,000 interracial married couples in 1970. In 1993 that number grew to 1,195,000 (72). It is estimated by the National Center for Health Statistics that the total number of interracial births from 1970 to 1990 has increased from 39,012 to 124,468 (Sandor 39). "If current trends continue, minorities will be approaching half of the total U.S. population as early as 2050" (Sandor 37).

93   Race is an artificial category, imposed by governments or political interest groups—easily altered and incapable of fully classifying everyone. Should this be an argument to abolish race or race-based issues in America? While race is an artificial categorization of a group of people by another group of people, it is still an inescapable issue in a country that wants to ignore what it is not willing to confront or understand.

94   I add the following to some of the applications:

95   __Multiracial or __Multiethnic.

96   On others, if there is room, I list my entire ethnic heritage. I check these twelve boxes in dark ink and press the pen down firmly.

Works Cited

"The Loving Generation." *Newsweek*. February 13, 1995. 72.
Pukui, Mary Kawena and Samuel H. Elbert. *Hawaiian Dictionary: Hawaiian-English, English-Hawaiian*. Revised and Enlarged Edition. Honolulu: University of Hawaii Press, 1986.

Sandor, Gabrielle. "The 'Other' Americans." *American Demographics.* June 1994. 36–42.

United States Department of Commerce. *1990 Census of Population: Social and Economic Characteristics.* Washington: Government Printing Office, November 1993.

Gordon Parks

Flavio's Home

Gordon Parks emerged from the poverty and racial isolation of a large Midwestern family to become one of the most influential photographers in American history. The youngest of 15 children, Parks departed home at the age of 16 after his mother died. He supported himself through odd jobs until the early 1930s, when he became inspired by the work of the social documentary photographers of the Great Depression. He bought an inexpensive camera and obtained a position taking photographs for the federal government. Working his way up through jobs at *Vogue* and *Life* magazines, he gradually built a reputation for himself. By the time he wrote "Flavio's Home" in 1961, he was already one of the most admired photographers in the nation. On its publication with its accompanying photographs, "Flavio's Home" elicited a groundswell of public support that eventually allowed Flavio to be brought to the U.S. for treatment and to buy a new home for his family.

I'VE NEVER LOST MY FIERCE GRUDGE AGAINST POVERTY. It is the most savage of   1
all human afflictions, claiming victims who can't mobilize their efforts against
it, who often lack strength to digest what little food they scrounge up to survive. It keeps growing, multiplying, spreading like a cancer. In my wanderings
I attack it wherever I can—in barrios, slums and favelas.

Catacumba was the name of the favela where I found Flavio da Silva. It   2
was wickedly hot. The noon sun baked the mud-rot of the wet mountainside.
Garbage and human excrement clogged the open sewers snaking down the
slopes. José Gallo, a *Life* reporter, and I rested in the shade of a jacaranda tree
halfway up Rio de Janeiro's most infamous deathtrap. Below and above us
were a maze of shacks, but in the distance alongside the beach stood the
gleaming white homes of the rich.

Breathing hard, balancing a tin of water on his head, a small boy climbed   3
toward us. He was miserably thin, naked but for filthy denim shorts. His legs
resembled sticks covered with skin and screwed into his feet. Death was all
over him, in his sunken eyes, cheeks and jaundiced coloring. He stopped for
breath, coughing, his chest heaving as water slopped over his bony shoulders.

Then jerking sideways like a mechanical toy, he smiled a smile I will never forget. Turning, he went on up the mountainside.

4   The detailed *Life* assignment in my back pocket was to find an impoverished father with a family, to examine his earnings, political leanings, religion, friends, dreams and frustrations. I had been sent to do an essay on poverty. This frail boy bent under his load said more to me about poverty than a dozen poor fathers. I touched Gallo, and we got up and followed the boy to where he entered a shack near the top of the mountainside. It was a leaning crumpled place of old plankings with a rusted tin roof. From inside we heard the babblings of several children. José knocked. The door opened and the boy stood smiling with a bawling naked baby in his arms.

5   Still smiling, he whacked the baby's rump, invited us in and offered us a box to sit on. The only other recognizable furniture was a sagging bed and a broken baby's crib. Flavio was twelve, and with Gallo acting as interpreter, he introduced his younger brothers and sisters: "Mario, the bad one; Baptista, the good one; Albia, Isabel and the baby Zacarias." Two other girls burst into the shack, screaming and pounding on one another. Flavio jumped in and parted them. "Shut up, you two." He pointed at the older girl. "That's Maria, the nasty one." She spit in his face. He smacked her and pointed to the smaller sister. "That's Luzia. She thinks she's pretty."

6   Having finished the introductions, he went to build a fire under the stove—a rusted, bent top of an old gas range resting on several bricks. Beneath it was a piece of tin that caught the hot coals. The shack was about six by ten feet. Its grimy walls were a patchwork of misshapen boards with large gaps between them, revealing other shacks below stilted against the slopes. The floor, rotting under layers of grease and dirt, caught shafts of light slanting down through spaces in the roof. A large hole in the far corner served as a toilet. Beneath that hole was the sloping mountainside. Pockets of poverty in New York's Harlem, on Chicago's south side, in Puerto Rico's infamous El Fungito seemed pale by comparison. None of them had prepared me for this one in the favela of Catacumba.

7   Flavio washed rice in a large dishpan, then washed Zacarias's feet in the same water. But even that dirty water wasn't to be wasted. He tossed in a chunk of lye soap and ordered each child to wash up. When they were finished he splashed the water over the dirty floor, and, dropping to his knees, he scrubbed the planks until the black suds sank in. Just before sundown he put beans on the stove to warm, then left, saying he would be back shortly. "Don't let them burn," he cautioned Maria. "If they do and Poppa beats me, you'll get it later." Maria, happy to get at the licking spoon, switched over and began to stir the beans. Then slyly she dipped out a spoonful and swallowed them. Luzia eyed her. "I see you. I'm going to tell on you for stealing our supper."

Maria's eyes flashed anger. "You do and I'll beat you, you little bitch."   8
Luzia threw a stick at Maria and fled out the door. Zacarias dropped off to
sleep. Mario, the bad one, slouched in a corner and sucked his thumb. Isabel
and Albia sat on the floor clinging to each other with a strange tenderness. Isabel held onto Albia's hair and Albia clutched at Isabel's neck. They appeared
frozen in an act of quiet violence.

Flavio returned with wood, dumped it beside the stove and sat down to   9
rest for a few minutes, then went down the mountain for more water. It was
dark when he finally came back, his body sagging from exhaustion. No longer
smiling, he suddenly had the look of an old man and by now we could see
that he kept the family going. In the closed torment of that pitiful shack, he
was waging a hopeless battle against starvation. The da Silva children were living in a coffin.

When at last the parents came in, Gallo and I seemed to be part of the   10
family. Flavio had already told them we were there. "Gordunn Americano!"
Luzia said, pointing at me. José, the father, viewed us with skepticism. Nair,
his pregnant wife, seemed tired beyond speaking. Hardly acknowledging our
presence, she picked up Zacarias, placed him on her shoulder and gently pat-
ted his behind. Flavio scurried about like a frightened rat, his silence plainly
expressing the fear he held of his father. Impatiently, José da Silva waited for
Flavio to serve dinner. He sat in the center of the bed with his legs crossed beneath him, frowning, waiting. There were only three tin plates. Flavio filled
them with black beans and rice, then placed them before his father. José da
Silva tasted them, chewed for several moments, then nodded his approval for
the others to start. Only he and Nair had spoons; the children ate with their
fingers. Flavio ate off the top of a coffee can. Afraid to offer us food, he edged
his rice and beans toward us, gesturing for us to take some. We refused. He
smiled, knowing we understood.

Later, when we got down to the difficult business of obtaining permission   11
from José da Silva to photograph his family, he hemmed and hawed, wallow-
ing in the pleasant authority of the decision maker. He finally gave in, but his
manner told us that he expected something in return. As we were saying good
night Flavio began to cough violently. For a few moments his lungs seemed to
be tearing apart. I wanted to get away as quickly as possible. It was cowardly of
me, but the bluish cast of his skin beneath the sweat, the choking and spitting
were suddenly unbearable.

Gallo and I moved cautiously down through the darkness trying not to ap-   12
pear as strangers. The Catacumba was no place for strangers after sundown.
Desperate criminals hid out there. To hunt them out, the police came in
packs, but only in daylight. Gallo cautioned me. "If you get caught up here
after dark it's best to stay at the da Silvas' until morning." As we drove toward
the city the large white buildings of the rich loomed up. The world behind us

seemed like a bad dream. I had already decided to get the boy Flavio to a doctor, and as quickly as possible.

13   The plush lobby of my hotel on the Copacabana waterfront was crammed with people in formal attire. With the stink of the favela in my clothes, I hurried to the elevator hoping no passengers would be aboard. But as the door was closing a beautiful girl in a white lace gown stepped in. I moved as far away as possible. Her escort entered behind her, swept her into his arms and they indulged in a kiss that lasted until they exited on the next floor. Neither of them seemed to realize that I was there. The room I returned to seemed to be oversized; the da Silva shack would have fitted into one corner of it. The steak dinner I had would have fed the da Silvas for three days.

14   Billowing clouds blanketed Mount Corcovado as we approached the favela the following morning. Suddenly the sun burst through, silhouetting Cristo Redentor, the towering sculpture of Christ with arms extended, its back turned against the slopes of Catacumba. The square at the entrance to the favela bustled with hundreds of favelados. Long lines waited at the sole water spigot. Others waited at the only toilet on the entire mountainside. Women, unable to pay for soap, beat dirt from their wash at laundry tubs. Men, burdened with lumber, picks and shovels and tools important to their existence threaded their way through the noisy throngs. Dogs snarled, barked and fought. Woodsmoke mixed with the stench of rotting things. In the mist curling over the higher paths, columns of favelados climbed like ants with wood and water cans on their heads.

15   We came upon Nair bent over her tub of wash. She wiped away sweat with her apron and managed a smile. We asked for her husband and she pointed to a tiny shack off to her right. This was José's store, where he sold kerosene and bleach. He was sitting on a box, dozing. Sensing our presence, he awoke and commenced complaining about his back. "It kills me. The doctors don't help because I have no money. Always talk and a little pink pill that does no good. Ah, what is to become of me?" A woman came to buy bleach. He filled her bottle. She dropped a few coins and as she walked away his eyes stayed on her backside until she was out of sight. Then he was complaining about his back again.

16   "How much do you earn a day?" Gallo asked.

17   "Seventy-five cents. On a good day maybe a dollar."

18   "Why aren't the kids in school?"

19   "I don't have money for the clothes they need to go to school."

20   "Has Flavio seen a doctor?"

21   He pointed to a one-story wooden building. "That's the clinic right there. They're mad because I built my store in front of their place. I won't tear it down so they won't help my kids. Talk, talk, talk and pink pills." We bid him good-

bye and started climbing, following mud trails, jutting rock, slime-filled holes and shack after shack propped against the slopes on shaky pilings. We side-stepped a dead cat covered with maggots. I held my breath for an instant, only to inhale the stench of human excrement and garbage. Bare feet and legs with open sores climbed above us—evils of the terrible soil they trod every day, and there were seven hundred thousand or more afflicted people in favelas around Rio alone. Touching me, Gallo pointed to Flavio climbing ahead of us carrying firewood. He stopped to glance at a man descending with a small coffin on his shoulder. A woman and a small child followed him. When I lifted my camera, grumbling erupted from a group of men sharing beer beneath a tree.

"They're threatening," Gallo said. "Keep moving. They fear cameras. 22 Think they're evil eyes bringing bad luck." Turning to watch the funeral procession, Flavio caught sight of us and waited. When we took the wood from him he protested, saying he was used to carrying it. He gave in when I hung my camera around his neck. Then, beaming, he climbed on ahead of us.

The fog had lifted and in the crisp morning light the shack looked more 23 squalid. Inside the kids seemed even noisier. Flavio smiled and spoke above their racket. "Someday I want to live in a real house on a real street with good pots and pans and a bed with sheets." He lit the fire to warm leftovers from the night before. Stale rice and beans—for breakfast and supper. No lunch; midday eating was out of the question. Smoke rose and curled up through the ceiling's cracks. An air current forced it back, filling the place and Flavio's lungs with fumes. A coughing spasm doubled him up, turned his skin blue under viscous sweat. I handed him a cup of water, but he waved it away. His stomach tightened as he dropped to his knees. His veins throbbed as if they would burst. Frustrated, we could only watch; there was nothing we could do to help. Strangely, none of his brothers or sisters appeared to notice. None of them stopped doing whatever they were doing. Perhaps they had seen it too often. After five interminable minutes it was over, and he got to his feet, smiling as though it had all been a joke. "Maria, it's time for Zacarias to be washed!"

"But there's rice in the pan!" 24

"Dump it in another pan—and don't spill water!" 25

Maria picked up Zacarias, who screamed, not wanting to be washed. Irri- 26 tated, Maria gave him a solid smack on his bare bottom. Flavio stepped over and gave her the same, then a free-for-all started with Flavio, Maria and Mario slinging fists at one another. Mario got one in the eye and fled the shack calling Flavio a dirty son-of-a-bitch. Zacarias wound up on the floor sucking his thumb and escaping his washing. The black bean and rice breakfast helped to get things back to normal. Now it was time to get Flavio to the doctor.

The clinic was crowded with patients—mothers and children covered with 27 open sores, a paralytic teenager, a man with an ear in a state of decay, an aged blind couple holding hands in doubled darkness. Throughout the place came wailings of hunger and hurt. Flavio sat nervously between Gallo and me. "What will the doctor do to me?" he kept asking.

28   "We'll see. We'll wait and see."

29   In all, there were over fifty people. Finally, after two hours, it was Flavio's turn and he broke out in a sweat, though he smiled at the nurse as he passed through the door to the doctor's office. The nurse ignored it; in this place of misery, smiles were unexpected.

30   The doctor, a large, beady-eyed man with a crew cut, had an air of impatience. Hardly acknowledging our presence, he began to examine the frightened Flavio. "Open your mouth. Say 'Ah.' Jump up and down. Breathe out. Take off those pants. Bend over. Stand up. Cough. Cough louder. Louder." He did it all with such cold efficiency. Then he spoke to us in English so Flavio wouldn't understand. "This little chap has just about had it." My heart sank. Flavio was smiling, happy to be over with the examination. He was handed a bottle of cough medicine and a small box of pink pills, then asked to step outside and wait.

31   "This the da Silva kid?" Yes.

32   "What's your interest in him?"

33   "We want to help in some way."

34   "I'm afraid you're too late. He's wasted with bronchial asthma, malnutrition and, I suspect, tuberculosis. His heart, lungs and teeth are all bad." He paused and wearily rubbed his forehead. "All that at the ripe old age of twelve. And these hills are packed with other kids just as bad off. Last year ten thousand died from dysentery alone. But what can we do? You saw what's waiting outside. It's like this every day. There's hardly enough money to buy aspirin. A few wealthy people who care help keep us going." He was quiet for a moment. "Maybe the right climate, the right diet, and constant medical care might. . . ." He stopped and shook his head. "Naw. That poor lad's finished. He might last another year—maybe not." We thanked him and left.

35   "What did he say?" Flavio asked as we scaled the hill.

36   "Everything's going to be all right, Flav. There's nothing to worry about."

37   It had clouded over again by the time we reached the top. The rain swept in, clearing the mountain of Corcovado. The huge Christ figure loomed up again with clouds swirling around it. And to it I said a quick prayer for the boy walking beside us. He smiled as if he had read my thoughts. "Papa says 'El Cristo' has turned his back on the favela."

38   "You're going to be all right, Flavio."

39   "I'm not scared of death. It's my brothers and sisters I worry about. What would they do?"

40   "You'll be all right, Flavio."

Jerry Colonna

The Big Schmooze
How to Give Good Cell Phone

A member of the "new boys network" of New York's Silicon Alley, Jerry Colonna is a past editor of *Infoweek* who helped to establish it as an influential publication for information professionals. He is currently a founding partner of Flatiron Partners in New York City and Chairman of Heaven Inc., a non-profit organization that provides media opportunities for inner-city youth. He lives in Port Washington, New York with his wife Barbara Chang, his three children, and their pet Gecko, Lil' Tom.

A FEW MONTHS AGO, three of my fellow venture capitalists and I rushed out of   1
a board meeting for one of the companies in our portfolio and hopped in a
cab. As usual—and because each of us reveled in our self-importance—we all
slipped Nokia 6160 cell phones out of our pockets.

I remember looking around the cab, noting the absurdity of four people   2
traveling together, each one of us talking to someone hundreds of miles away.
Then I glanced at the driver. I think he had a StarTAC. Need I say more?

At about the same time, New York City decided to honor arguably the best   3
baseball team ever, the '98 Yankees. It was thrilling to watch future Hall of
Famers such as Derek Jeter make their way up Broadway amid a blizzard of toilet paper and shredded documents.

Among the luminaries in the parade were two politicians: state comptrol-   4
ler Carl McCall and public advocate Mark Green. As my pin-striped heroes
reveled in the cheers of millions, the TV camera zoomed in on the two pols.
Yup. Both were talking on their cell phones. Is nothing sacred?

How did this cell-phone-yapping, pants-pocket-vibrating, wireless mania   5
come to dominate our lives?

My cell phone tales are legion. I remember one conference call in partic-   6
ular. I was working on a deal and we needed to talk with all of the principals
and their attorneys. My phone, a landline, rang at 7:30 a.m. Everyone was
there. About two hours later, one of the attorneys had to, um, leave. He had
been on his cell phone, lying on a gurney, awaiting an MRI.

The worst victimizer—and victim—of the wireless gestalt is Brad Feld.   7
Known by some as the high priest of Colorado venture capital, Brad is the
gadget deity to whom I pray. Ever logical, he moved to Colorado not only to
live amid the natural splendor of Eldorado Canyon but also because he could
just as easily fly to the West Coast as the East. Brad was the first person I know

to have multiple cell phones (a Sony D-Wave Zuma and a Qualcomm Q), taking advantage of his 617 phone when traveling east and his 415 phone when out west. I'm not even sure Brad has a landline.

8   But this need to remain connected has drawbacks. Brad once accidentally called me from a restaurant. I was home, busy programming my latest cell phone, when the landline rang. "Hello," I said. No answer. "Hello?" I repeated, and I heard the clink of utensils on china. "Hello?!" Nothing. And then a voice: "So, after MIT, Feld Technologies was off and running and I began to meet with GE Capital." Hey, it's Brad Feld! "Brad!" I shouted. "Brad, can you hear me?" No reply.

9   I hung up the phone. Then I picked it up: "And the best strategy for a roll-up is—" I hung up the phone. I picked it back up, "Of course, valuations, will have to come down."

10   Brad's a pretty unique case, but my favorite victims are those who've combined their addictions. You know, the pager goes off when there's a voicemail message on the cell phone. Or the Pilot has a paging card. The cell phone gets pages, but they pack a pager anyway—"just in case." All right, I'm one of these universal messagers. I have a cell phone that can receive pages (even emailed pages), and I carry a pager and a laptop.

11   I suppose the thing to do would be to get one of those automated services, Wildfire or General Magic's Portico. But my first real encounter with Wildfire was disconcerting.

12   It was December 1996, cold and snowy. I tromped through the streets of Manhattan to the offices of General Internet to meet Scott Kurnit and hear his vision for "taking back the Net." He was about to launch The Mining Co., an interesting idea that my firm ultimately passed on.

13   Anyway, as Scott paced excitedly around a cramped office, his phone—a StarTAC—began ringing incessantly. Without breaking stride, he slipped the phone off his belt, flipped it open, flipped it shut, and slipped it back on his belt. The phone rang again. He unholstered and reholstered a second time. It rang and he repeated the dance. After five or six times, I stopped him and pointed at his phone. "Oh, this?" he said. "It's Wildfire trying to reach me."

14   Wildfire aside, at the very least Scott deserves credit for owning a Star-TAC, which was the first status symbol in the battle for cell superiority. Indeed, with its palm-sized shape and a flip cover out of *Star Trek*, the StarTAC was a must-have. Of course, within six months it was passé, surpassed by other tiny phones with better services. And now Motorola is back with its new minuscule V Series phones.

15   I remember the first time I took my Nokia 6160 out of my pocket and placed it on the table at the start of a meeting. Everyone at the table turned and stared.

16   "Um . . . is that a PCS phone?" asked a nervous entrepreneur.

Mind you, this guy was two weeks away from running out of cash, and the   17
meeting was his last chance to save his company. But he couldn't ignore that
most basic modern emotion: gadget envy.

Cell phone jealousy borders on the absurd. And nothing, nothing, is   18
worse than taking out your new toy, expecting "oohhh"s and "ahhh"s, only to
be bested by the person who whips out an even smaller, lighter, sleeker, cooler
piece. Your only recourse, as you sink into your chair, is to surreptitiously send
a two-way page to your assistant to run out and buy you the latest and greatest cell phone.

But when it comes down to it, jealousy is the nicer cousin of a baser con-   19
dition: total dependency.

I'm as hooked as anyone. I got this writing assignment because my partner   20
Fred Wilson and I happened to argue over a cell phone battery (we have the
same phones) in front of a *Wired* editor. There we were, in the pressroom at
Internet World, almost coming to blows over a little more airtime. It made for
an amusing spectacle—though Fred might not have thought so if he'd known
about the extra, fully charged battery stashed in my briefcase.

3

Example

Example

1. **Use examples to support a major point.** Without examples, it would be nearly impossible to write a persuasive essay. Readers aren't convinced by "artists these days create too many works that are vulgar and profane." The point becomes much more persuasive when supported by an example: "One 'artist' dumped elephant dung on a portrait of the Virgin Mary—an act considered blasphemous by millions of Catholics worldwide." The same logic holds true in reverse—examples are worthless if you don't use them to make a point.

2. **Think of a variety of examples.** Your work is most effective when you use a variety of examples to support your point. Use brainstorming techniques such as freewriting, listing, and clustering to come up with as many examples as you can. At this stage, just write down every idea you come up with—you'll winnow down your list later.

3. **Select the most relevant examples for your purpose.** While well-selected examples persuade and engage your readers, too many examples will put them to sleep. In her essay on pickup lines, Stephanie Crockett offers just enough examples to tempt the reader. Rather than continuing on and on, she simply stops, and leaves the rest to imagination.

4. **Arrange the examples effectively.** Unlike narration and description, examples can be presented in almost any order without disorienting your reader. But while you have many choices for organizing your examples, some strategies work better than others. One tried and true method is to finish with your most effective example to drive your point home. If you're worried that readers won't be engaged in your topic, you might want to lead off with your best example. Finally, you can use almost any strategy in this book (narration, comparison and contrast, analogy, etc.) to arrange examples.

Charles Sykes

The "Values" Wasteland

A journalist by trade, Charles Sykes has built a reputation as a strong-voiced critic of America's educational system. In 1989, inspired by his father's work as a journalism professor, he published *ProfScam*, a blistering attack on higher education and the tenure system. Sykes' characterization of professors as petty liars who build reputations by publishing in obscure journals at the expense of students won him many fans in conservative circles. In *Dumbing Down Our Kids*, from which this selection is excerpted, he brings the same hard-hitting approach to K–12 education. Sykes sees the American education system as a failure because it teaches children a watered-down set of morals instead of (in his view) the higher principles still taught in other countries.

ERIC RICHARDSON WAS A SEVENTEEN-YEAR-OLD MEMBER of the Spur Posse, a   1
group of boys accused of raping girls as young as ten years old. After their ar-
rests, the posse members reportedly returned to school as heroes, applauded
for their exploits by their fellow students. In talk show appearances and media
interviews, the boys were unrepentant. "They pass out condoms, teach sex education and pregnancy this and pregnancy that," Eric said after polishing off
a Nacho Supreme and necking with his girlfriend in a booth at the Taco Bell.
"But they don't teach us any rules." His response was too glib and too convenient; it wasn't our fault, he was saying, you taught us to be like this. No
school, however misguided, can ever be blamed for a piece of work like Eric
Richardson. Even so, the evidence suggests that his ethical compass is not an
isolated aberration.

A 1988 study of more than 2,000 Rhode Island students in grades six   2
through nine found that two-thirds of the boys and half of the girls thought
that "it was acceptable for a man to force sex on a woman" if they had been
dating six months or more. A write-in survey of 126,000 teenagers found that
25 to 40 percent of teens see nothing wrong with cheating on exams, stealing
from employers, or keeping money that wasn't theirs. A seventeen-year-old
high school senior explained: "A lot of it is a gray area. It's everybody doing
their own thing."

A 1992 survey by the Josephson Institute for Ethics of nearly 7,000 high   3
school and college students, most of them from middle- and upper middle-
class backgrounds, found the equivalent of a "hole in the moral ozone"
among American youth.

- A third of high school students and 16 percent of college students said   4
  they have shoplifted in the last year. Nearly the same number (33 percent

of high school students and 11 percent of college students) said they have stolen from their parents or relatives at least once.

5 • One in eight college students admitted to committing an act of fraud, including borrowing money they did not intend to repay, and lying on financial aid or insurance forms.

6 • A third of high school and college students said they would lie to get a job. One in six said they have already done so at least once.

7 • More than 60 percent of high school students said they had cheated at least once on an exam.

8 • Forty percent of the high school students who participated in this survey admitted that they "were not completely honest" on at least one or two questions—meaning that they may have lied on a survey about lying.

9   "I think it's very easy to get through high school and college these days and hardly ever hear, 'That's wrong,'" commented Patrick McCarthy of Pasadena's Jefferson Center for Character Education. Michael Josephson, the president of the Josephson Institute of Ethics, describes a large and growing population as the "I-Deserve-Its," or IDIs. "Their IDI-ology is exceptionally and dangerously self-centered, preoccupied with personal needs, wants, don't-wants and rights." In pursuit of success, or comfort, or self-gratification, the IDIs are blithely willing to jettison traditional ethical restraints, and as a result "IDIs are more likely to lie, cheat and engage in irresponsible behavior when it suits their purposes. IDIs act as if they need whatever they want and deserve whatever they need. . . ." American youth's culture of entitlement cannot, of course, be laid solely at the feet of the schools. If there has been an ethical meltdown among young Americans we need to look first to their parents, communities, the media, and even the churches for explanations. Society's shift from a culture of self-control to one of self-gratification, self-actualization, and self-realization, and its changing norms regarding personal responsibility and character, was not restricted to the arena of public education. Even so, the ethical state of America's young people may, at least in part, have something to do with the way our schools teach them about right and wrong.

10   At one time, American students used to study historical role models like Benjamin Franklin, Florence Nightingale, Thomas Edison, Madame Curie, Abraham Lincoln, and George Washington—whose stories were used to provide object lessons in inventiveness, character, compassion, curiosity, and truthfulness. Following Aristotle, ethicists recognized that humanity does not become virtuous simply by precept, but by "nature, habit, rational principle." "We become just by the practice of just actions," Aristotle observed, "self-controlled by exercising self-control." This process was most effectively begun by placing examples of such virtues in front of young people for them to emulate. But while Asian children continue to read about stories of perseverance,

hard work, loyalty, duty, prudence, heroism, and honesty, [educational researcher] Harold Stevenson finds that "For the most part, such cultural models have been displaced in the United States today." In its place, we provide children a jumbled smorgasbord of moral choices.

How Do You *Feel* About Cheating?

The course is officially about "citizenship," but the subject is values. Specially 11 prepared for students in the fourth to sixth grades, the class is designed to help students clarify and discover their own values on issues like lying and cheating. As a group or by secret ballot, the fourth, fifth, and sixth graders are asked: "How many of you. . ."

> Think children should have to work for their allowances?
> Think most rules are dumb?
> Think that there are times when cheating is ok?
> Wish you didn't have grades in school?
> Think prizes should be awarded for everything?

The section on cheating asks students: "What are your attitudes toward cheat- 12 ing?" They are asked to complete the following statements:

> Tests are _____
> Grades are _____
> The bad thing about cheating is _____
> The good thing about cheating is _____
> If there were no such things as grades, would your attitude toward cheating change?
> Is school the only place cheating takes place? Where else does cheating take place?
> Is it ever OK to cheat? When?

It is not clear whether there are ever any right and wrong answers to these 13 questions. The class takes a similar approach to lying. Students are asked, "Lying, What's Your View?" . . . Children in the class are . . . presented with a series of ethical problems. They are not asked to define right and wrong or moral or immoral. Instead, they are asked to say which actions are "acceptable . . . and . . . which are . . . unacceptable. Do any of the situations involve lying?"

> A factory worker oversleeps and is late for work. He tells his supervi- 14 sor that he was involved in a minor traffic accident.

15   Janine just can't face a big history exam for which she hasn't studied. She convinces her mother that she has a terrible sore throat and must stay home.

16   Bill runs into a friend he hasn't seen in months. The friend asks how he is. Bill smiles and answers "great!" even though his dog just died, he's flunking English, and he just broke up with his girl-friend. . . .

17   Such nonjudgmentalism is a feature of the approach known as "values clarification," in which, as [journalist] William Kirk Kilpatrick writes, class-room discussions are turned into "'bull sessions' where opinions go back and forth but conclusions are never reached." . . . Many of these classes seem to be based on the rather fantastic notion that since none of the civilizations any-where in the world throughout the entire sweep of human history has been able to work out a moral code of conduct worthy of being passed on, we should therefore leave it to fourth graders to work out questions of right and wrong on their own.

The Values Clarifiers

18   The developers of Values Clarification and other nonjudgmental approaches to moral decision making often claimed to be value-free, but their agenda was quite specific. Their bête noir was "moralizing" in any form. "Moralizing," the authors of *Values Clarification: A Handbook of Practical Strategies for Teachers and Students* wrote in 1978, "is the direct, although sometimes subtle inculcation of the adults' values upon the young." For the authors of the new curriculum, this was not merely authoritarian and stifling, but also dangerous to the ethi-cal health of children. By passing on a set of moral values, they argued, par-ents were hampering the ability of children to come up with their own values. "Young people brought up by moralizing adults are not prepared to make their own responsible choices," they warned. In any case, moralizing was no longer practical. Children were bombarded with so many different sets of val-ues and parents were only some of the many voices they heard. In the end, they argue, every child had to make his own choices. That, of course, is true—making choices is the essence of free will. But where values clarification de-parted from older moral philosophies was in its contention that children do not need to be grounded in value systems or provided with moral road maps before they are asked to make such choices. Values clarifiers also did not care what values the child chose to follow. Specifically, values clarification did not concern itself with inculcating values such as self-control, honesty, responsi-bility, loyalty, prudence, duty, or justice. In its purest form, values clarification did not even argue that these virtues were superior or preferable to their op-

posites and had little to say about concepts of right and wrong. The goal of values clarification was not to create a virtuous young person, or young adult with character or probity; its goal was empowering youngsters to make their own decisions, *whatever those decisions were.* . . .

The assumption behind such programs was that children had the capacity   19 to develop character on their own; that students as young as third grade had the knowledge, insight, and cognitive abilities to wrestle through difficult dilemmas and thorny moral paradoxes without the benefit of a moral compass, either from parents or teachers. . . .

At the heart of the values clarification program was the effort to have stu-   20 dents develop an individual identity. One exercise was "Are You Someone Who . . ." followed by a long list of options, including: "is likely to marry someone of another religion?"; "is likely to grow a beard?"; "would consider joining the John Birch Society?"; "is apt to go out of your way to have a black (white) neighbor?"; "will subscribe to *Playboy* magazine?"; will change your religion?"; "will be likely to win a Nobel Peace Prize?"; "is apt to experiment with pot?"; "would get therapy on your own initiative?"; "will make a faithless husband? wife?"

The authors explain that such questions will cause students "to consider   21 more thoughtfully what they value, what they want out of life and what type of persons they want to become." But the questions send another message as well by treating the various options simply as different choices of apparently equal weight, like choices on a personality buffet line: Will you win the Nobel Prize or experiment with pot? Subscribe to *Playboy* or change your religion? There is no suggestion that growing a beard or cheating on your wife might be decisions that carry rather different moral weights.

Ultimately, the values clarification approach reduces moral choice to a   22 matter of personal taste with no more basis in objective reality than a preference for a red car rather than a blue one. There is no right or wrong answer and no real ground to regard your own choice either as better or more valid than any other.

But is this really a process of working out moral values or is it simply a   23 process of rationalization? Humans rationalize because it is convenient and it suits our interests. If we choose, we can shape morality to meet out inclinations and impulses, rather than try to shape our inclinations to accord with moral law. Moral reasoning, in contrast, involves asking whether an act is good, whether it is made with right intent, and examining the act's circumstances. To make such judgments requires an understanding of what the moral law might be, not simply how we feel about the act. But to take the subjective state of mind and make it the sole test of morality is to rationalize and call it moral reasoning. Checking one's inclinations is not the same as examining one's conscience, precisely because the conscience needs to be educated.

24   One would never get that idea from watching a values clarification "simulation" of a moral choice. In one popular exercise, students have to imagine that their class has been trapped in a cave-in. In the exercise, students are asked to imagine that they have to form a single line to work their way out of the cave. At any moment, another rock slide may close the way out. Those at the head of the line are therefore the most likely to survive. In the class exercise, each member of the class must give the reason he or she should be at the head of the line. The teacher tells them: "Your reasons can be of two kinds. You can tell us what you want to live for or what you have yet to get out of life that is important to you. Or you can talk about what you have to contribute to others in the world that would justify your being near the front of the line." After hearing all of the pleas, the class then decides the order in which they will file out of the cave.

25   Like other values clarification chestnuts, youngsters are asked to make life-and-death decisions. But what are the practical implications? Do students emerge from the class more empathetic? More willing to sacrifice for others? Are they likely to treat their peers with more respect? Show more self-restraint in the presence of their parents? Or are they likely to have a keener sense of their own egos? . . .

26   Other exercises ask students to choose who should be allowed to stay in a fallout shelter (and who should be left to die) during a nuclear attack; to decide whether it is morally permissible for a poor man to steal a drug that his desperately ill wife needs; to work through the dilemma of trapped settlers who must decide whether to turn to cannibalism or starve to death; to put themselves in the place of a mother who must choose which of her two children she will save; and consider the ethical dilemma of a doctor who must decide to operate on an injured child despite the religious objections of the parents. "Like a roller-coaster ride," William Kilpatrick writes, "the dilemma approach can leave its passengers a bit breathless. That is one of its attractions. But like a roller-coaster ride, it may also leave them a bit disoriented—or more than a bit." As entertaining as such problems may be, they are hardly a guide for developing a moral code; morality is more than solving a complex and perhaps even unsolvable puzzle. Take the case of the man whose wife is dying of an incurable illness and who needs a rare and expensive drug. Kilpatrick wonders whether youngsters who spend a diverting and lively class period debating whether stealing is right or wrong in this case would be less likely to steal themselves? Or lie? Or cheat? Or will they come to the conclusion that moral questions are inevitably so complicated, so fraught with doubt, that no one answer is necessarily ever any better than any other and that all moral questions come down in the end simply to a matter of opinion? Or will they get the idea that it is less important whether one steals or not than that one has developed a system of "valuing" with which one is comfortable?

One of the striking things about spending time with high school students is the near universality of this notion that values are something they work out on their own. One frequent speaker on ethical issues recounts his experience with high school students in which he presents them with a typical values clarification dilemma. They must imagine that they are on a lifeboat with another person and their family dog; the students can save only one, so they must choose either the human being, who is a complete stranger, or the beloved and cherished family dog. Typically, some of the students choose to save the dog and allow the man to die; most students choose to save the human being. But then the speaker asks them what they thought of their classmates who had opted for the dog over the man. Almost never, says the speaker, do students say that those choices were "wrong" or morally objectionable. Even for those who made the correct moral choice, it was merely a matter of personal opinion, and they refuse to be judgmental toward those who put the dog's life ahead of the human being's. The concept that there might be universal and objective moral principles at stake is completely alien to these youngsters. 27

Barbara Ehrenreich

In Defense of Talk Shows

Best known for her wry and witty essays in *Time* magazine, Barbara Ehrenreich has been a social critic since the early 1970s, when she burst onto the scene with *Complaints and Disorders: The Sexual Politics of Sickness,* a bitter critique of America's health care system coauthored with Dierdre English. A self-described "socialist and feminist," much of Ehrenreich's work is framed by her politics. In *The Hearts of Men* she suggests that men have simply abandoned their familial obligations, freed from guilt by publications like *Playboy.* Her essays often touch on issues of feminist politics, but in this essay, which originally appeared in *Time*, she tackles a wider issue of society's voyeuristic tendencies, with typical wit.

UP UNTIL NOW, the targets of Bill (*The Book of Virtues*) Bennett's crusades have at least been plausible sources of evil. But the latest victim of his wrath—TV talk shows of the *Sally Jessy Raphael* variety—are in a whole different category from drugs and gangsta rap. As anyone who actually watches them knows, the talk shows are one of the most excruciatingly moralistic forums the culture has to offer. Disturbing and sometimes disgusting, yes, but their very business is to preach the middle-class virtues of responsibility, reason and self-control. 1

Take the case of Susan, recently featured on *Montel Williams* as an exam- 2 ple of a woman being stalked by her ex-boyfriend. Turns out Susan is also stalking the boyfriend and—here's the sexual frisson—has slept with him only days ago. In fact Susan is neck deep in trouble without any help from the boyfriend: She's serving a year-long stretch of home incarceration for assaulting another woman, and home is the tiny trailer she shares with her nine-year-old daughter.

3   But no one is applauding this life spun out of control. Montel scolds Susan roundly for neglecting her daughter and failing to confront her role in the mutual stalking. A therapist lectures her about this unhealthy "obsessive kind of love." The studio audience jeers at her every evasion. By the end Susan has lost her cocky charm and dissolved into tears of shame.

4   The plot is always the same. People with problems—"husband says she looks like a cow," "pressured to lose her virginity or else," "mate wants more sex than I do"—are introduced to rational methods of problem solving. People with moral failings—"boy crazy," "dresses like a tramp," "a hundred sex partners"—are introduced to external standards of morality. The preaching—delivered alternately by the studio audience, the host and the ever present guest therapist—is relentless. "This is wrong to do this," Sally Jessy tells a cheating husband. "Feel bad?" Geraldo asks the girl who stole her best friend's boyfriend. "Any sense of remorse?" The expectation is that the sinner, so hectored, will see her way to reform. And indeed, a Sally Jessy update found "boy crazy," who'd been a guest only weeks ago, now dressed in schoolgirlish plaid and claiming her "attitude [had] changed"—thanks to the rough-and-ready therapy dispensed on the show.

5   All right, the subjects are often lurid and even bizarre. But there's no part of the entertainment spectacle, from *Hard Copy* to *Jade*, that doesn't trade in the lurid and bizarre. At least in the talk shows, the moral is always loud and clear: Respect yourself, listen to others, stop beating on your wife. In fact it's hard to see how *The Bill Bennett Show*, if there were to be such a thing, could deliver a more pointed sermon. Or would he prefer to see the reckless Susan, for example, tarred and feathered by the studio audience instead of being merely booed and shamed?

6   There *is* something morally repulsive about the talks, but it's not anything Bennett or his co-crusader Senator Joseph Lieberman has seen fit to mention. Watch for a few hours, and you get the claustrophobic sense of lives that have never seen the light of some external judgment, of people who have never before been listened to, and certainly never been taken seriously if they were. "What kind of people would let themselves be humiliated like this?" is often asked, sniffily, by the shows' detractors. And the answer, for the most part, is people who are so needy—of social support, of education, of material resources and self-esteem—that they mistake being the center of attention for being actually loved and respected.

7   What the talks are about, in large part, is poverty and the distortions it vis-

its on the human spirit. You'll never find investment bankers bickering on *Rolonda*, or the host of *Gabrielle* recommending therapy to sobbing professors. With few exceptions the guests are drawn from trailer parks and tenements, from bleak streets and narrow, crowded rooms. Listen long enough, and you hear references to unpaid bills, to welfare, to twelve-hour workdays and double shifts. And this is the real shame of the talks: that they take lives bent out of shape by poverty and hold them up as entertaining exhibits. An announcement appearing between segments of *Montel* says it all: The show is looking for "pregnant women who sell their bodies to make ends meet."

This is class exploitation, pure and simple. What next—"homeless people   8 so hungry they eat their own scabs"? Or would the next step be to pay people outright to submit to public humiliation? For $50 would you confess to adultery in your wife's presence? For $500 would you reveal your thirteen-year-old's girlish secrets on *Ricki Lake*? If you were poor enough, you might.

It is easy enough for those who can afford spacious homes and private   9 therapy to sneer at their financial inferiors and label their pathetic moments of stardom vulgar. But if I had a talk show, it would feature a whole different cast of characters and category of crimes than you'll ever find on the talks: "CEOs who rake in millions while their employees get downsized" would be an obvious theme, along with "Senators who voted for welfare and Medicaid cuts"—and, if he'll agree to appear, "well-fed Republicans who dithered about talk shows while trailer-park residents slipped into madness and despair."

Gish Jen

Challenging the Asian Illusion

A novelist and short story writer, Gish Jen's work has been called "stunning," "startling," "funny," and "heartrending." Her fiction work has received tremendous acclaim. Her first book, *Typical American*, was a finalist for the National Book Critics' Circle award. More recently, she was awarded the prestigious Lannan Award for Literary Fiction. Her work has appeared in *The Atlantic Monthly*, the *New York Times*, the *New Yorker*, and *Best American Short Stories of the Century*. The following selection originally appeared in the *New York Times*.

FOR A VERY LONG TIME, when people talked about race, they talked about   1 black America and white America. Where did that put Asian-Americans?

Spike Lee touches on the Asian-American dilemma in *Do the Right Thing*   2 when the Korean grocer, afraid of having his business attacked by rioting blacks, yells: "I not white! I black! Like you! Same!"

3   Unlike the grocer, though, my family and I identified mostly with white America, which, looking back, was partly wishful thinking, partly racism and partly an acknowledgment that, whatever else we did face, at least we did not have to contend with the legacy of slavery.

4   Yet we were not white. We were somehow borderline; we did not quite belong. Now, not only has the number of Asian-Americans in this country doubled in the last decade, we are growing faster than any other ethnic group. How meaningful it will ultimately prove to lump the Hmong with the Filipinos with the Japanese remains to be seen. Still, to be perceived as a significant minority is a development for which I, at least, am grateful.

5   There is a sense that to be perceived at all, a minority group must be plagued with problems—a problem in itself, to be sure. But what about our problems—were they significant enough to warrant attention? Who cared, for instance, that we did not see ourselves reflected on movie screens? Until recently, it did not occur to most of us that the absence of Asian and Asian-American images was symptomatic of a more profound invisibility.

6   Today, though, it is shocking to behold how little represented we have been, and in how blatantly distorted a manner. There has been some progress now that more Asian-Americans like David Henry Hwang and Philip Kan Gotanda have begun to write for stage and screen: also, some recent Caucasian-directed television shows, including *Shannon's Deal* and *Davis Rules*, are breaking new ground.

7   For the most part, however, film, television and theater, from *Miss Saigon* to *Teen-Age Mutant Ninja Turtles*, have persisted in perpetuating stereotypes. Mostly this has been through the portrayal of Asian characters; Asian-Americans have rarely been represented at all.

8   This invisibility is essentially linked to the process by which fanciful ideas are superimposed onto real human beings. How are everyday Asians transformed into mysterious "Orientals," after all, if not by distance? Americans can be led to believe anything about people living in a far-off land, or even a distinctly unfamiliar place like Chinatown. It is less easy with a kid next door who plays hockey and air guitar.

9   Over the years, Asians have been the form onto which white writers have freely projected their fears and desires. That this is a form of colonialism goes almost without saying; it can happen only when the people whose images are appropriated are in no position to object.

10   For certainly anyone would object to being identified with a figure as heartlessly evil and preternaturally cunning as Fu Manchu, a brilliant but diabolical force set on taking over the world. The character's prototype was invented in 1916, in a climate of hysteria over the "threat" that Asian workers

posed to native labor. We behold its likeness in figures like Odd Job in *Goldfinger* (1964); his influence can be seen in depictions of Chinatown as a den of iniquity in movies like *The Year of the Dragon* (1985) and *True Believer* (1988). *Chinatown* (1974) used it as a symbol of all that is rotten in the city of Los Angeles, despite the fact that no Chinese person had much to do with the evil turnings of the plot.

What fuels these images is xenophobia. In periods of heightened political   11
tension, they tend to recur; in more secure times, they are replaced by more benign images. Charlie Chan for example, arose in 1926, shortly after the last of a series of laws restricting Chinese immigration had been passed and the "Yellow Peril" seemed to be over.

The benign images, however, are typically no more tied to reality than   12
their malign counterparts; vilification is merely replaced by glorification. The aphorism-spouting Charlie Chan (played by Warner Oland, a white actor in yellow-face) is godlike in his intelligence, the original Asian whiz kid; you would not be surprised to hear he had won a Westinghouse prize in his youth. More message than human being, he recalls the ever-smiling black mammy that proliferated during Reconstruction: Don't worry, he seems to say, no one's going to go making any trouble.

One Good Guy, But He's a Rat

In today's social climate of multi-culturalism, movies like *Rambo*, which made   13
the Vietnamese out to be so much cannon fodder, seem to be behind us, at least temporarily. Instead, reflecting the American preoccupation with Japan, there is *Teen-Age Mutant Ninja Turtles*. Here the Japanese enemy gang leader is once again purely demonic and bestial, a hairless, barbaric figure who wears a metal claw for ornament. What gives the movie a more contemporary stamp is the fact that Master Splinter, the good-guy rodent leader of the Mutant Turtles, is also Japanese. It is as if Fu Manchu and Charlie Chan were cast into a single movie—seemingly presenting a balanced view of the Japanese as good and bad.

But the fact that the "good" Japanese is a rat means that slanty eyes belong   14
to the bad guy. And as individuals the Japanese are still portrayed as sub- or superhuman, possessing fabulous abilities and arcane knowledge that center on (another contemporary twist) martial arts.

Is it a sign of a fitness-crazed age that this single aspect of Asian culture is   15
so enthralling? So perennially popular are movies like *The Karate Kid* (1984) and this year's *Iron and Silk* that one begins to wonder whether Asian males pop out of the womb doing mid-air gyrations. The audience marvels: How fantastic, these people! Meanwhile, the non-Asian roles are the more recognizably human ones.

16   Real humanity similarly eludes the Asian characters in the Broadway play *Miss Saigon*. As in *Teen-Age Mutant Ninja Turtles*, they are either simply evil or simply good, with the possible exception of the Engineer (Jonathan Pryce) who, loathsome as he is, seems more self-interested than evil. Half-white, he seems to be, correspondingly, halfway human. In contrast, Thuy, the major Vietnamese character, is portrayed as so inhuman that he would kill a child in cold blood. Is this what Communists do? Asians? When Kim (Lea Salonga), the heroine, shoots her erstwhile loyal fiancé, the audience applauds, feeling no more for him than for Rambo's victims. The subhuman brute has got what he deserved.

17   At the same time, the audience does feel, horribly, for Kim, who has been forced to pull the trigger and now must live with blood on her hands. What a fate for a paragon of virtue! She is Madame Butterfly unpinned from her specimen board and let loose to flutter around the room again: abandoned, virtuous, she waits faithfully for her white lover, only to discover that he has married. He returns for his son (it's always a son); she kills herself.

    Isn't this a beautiful story? Annette Kolodny, a feminist critic, has observed that when the Western mind feels free to remake a place and people according to its liking, it conceives of that place and people as a woman. This has been nowhere so true as in the case of the "Orient," and correspondingly, no woman, it seems, has been portrayed as more exquisitely feminine than an Oriental.

18   Take any play in which both Oriental and Caucasian women appear—say, *South Pacific*—and it is immediately obvious which is more delicate, more willing to sacrifice for her man, more docile. Never mind that there are in the world real women who might object to having their image appropriated for such use.

19   But of course, women do object. I object, especially since the only possible end for this invented Butterfly is suicide. For how would the white characters go on with their lives?

20   It is an irony of stage history that a musical as conventional in its use of the Butterfly story should follow so closely on the heels of another play that turns the same narrative on its head. The 1988 Broadway play M. *Butterfly* offers not just the "beautiful story" itself, but also a white man who has been taken in by it. So enthralled is René Gallimard by the idea of his Butterfly, the projection of his own desire, that he forgets there is a real person—Song Liling, a man and a spy—upon which his notions are imposed.

21   Ultimately, M. *Butterfly* makes clear that for the "game" of Orientalism, there is a price to pay, not only by those whose images are appropriated, but by the appropriators.

22   Do stereotypes lurk even here? It might seem so, but would a stereotype wonder, as does Song Liling, whether he and Gallimard might not continue

on together, even after the truth has been revealed. When Song asks, "What do I do now?" he conveys how helpless he is too, how powerless. This is a human being. That he should be is maybe not so surprising, given that he was invented by David Henry Hwang, an Asian-American.

One Step Forward: Spoof the Stereotype

Are Asian-American writers the only hope for new forms of characterization?   23
Perhaps, when even directors as intelligent as Woody Allen portray China-town as having opium dens. In his most recent movie, *Alice*, Mr. Allen's recy-cling of an Asian sage is likewise problematic. Could he not have created a spoof of a sage—a character who winked at the stereotype even as he played it—without any damage to the plot?

Spoofing the stereotype was the strategy taken last spring in an episode of   24
the now-cancelled television series *Shannon's Deal* that featured a pony-tailed Korean immigrant. Here were clear signs for hope: the immigrant at first ap-peared to be an all-knowing Charlie Chan, but turned out to be at once less and more. At moments way ahead of the investigator Shannon, he proved to be way behind at others; he knew all the aphorisms but had trouble passing the bar exam, and discussed his own tendency to drop pronouns.

Other signs of change include a jeans-wearing, face-making, poker-playing   25
Japanese character in *Davis Rules*. Unexotic Mrs. Yamagami (Tamayo Otsuki) even shows a sense of humor, characterizing a coworker as "a rebel without a car." Similarly, in *Twin Peaks*, the figure of Jocelyn (Joan Chen), evil as she is, does not stand in contrast to the good, white characters the way a female Fu Manchu—a dragon lady—might. Neither, certainly, is she any Butterfly. She is, within the show's offbeat context, just one of the gang.

All these characters are heartening, since they are not simply unexamined   26
projections onto the Asian race. Still, as might be expected, directors like Wayne Wang and playwrights like Philip Kan Gotanda are not only more likely to present Asian-Americans in their work, but to present Asian-Ameri-cans who are not of the immigrant generation. In Mr. Wang's movie *Dim Sum* (1987) and Mr. Gotanda's film *The Wash* (1988), Asian-Americans are pre-sented in far greater complexity than is typical of the mainstream media; the characters seem more captured than constructed, more like flesh-and-blood than cartoons. This is partly a matter of their status as protagonists rather than peripheral figures.

And more images are needed if the few that exist now are not to become   27
new stereotypes. Since the much publicized success of Connie Chung, for ex-ample, Asian-American anchorwomen have become a staple in films like *Year of the Dragon* and *Moscow on the Hudson*. With real-life repercussions: the San Francisco newscaster Emerald Yeh tells of an interview with CNN, during

which she was more or less asked why she couldn't do her hair like Connie Chung's.

28   Ridiculous, right? And yet such is the power of image. We would not have to insist that images reflect life, except that all too often we ask life to reflect images.

Stephanie A. Crockett

"Haven't We Met . . . ?": The Pickup Line Just Goes On and On

"Picking up" a member of the opposite sex has never been easy. It's even harder in these times of political correctness, where a wrong move can be interpreted as a moral affront. In "Haven't We Met . . . ?" Stephanie Crockett, a reporter for the *Washington Post,* covers the basics of meeting people in today's extra-sensitive dating environment.

1   IT'S A PHENOMENON AS OLD AS THE BATTLE BETWEEN THE SEXES. The pickup line.

2   "What's up, sexy."

3   "I know my name, what's yours?"

4   Or the oldest line in the book—"Can I talk to you for a minute?"

5   Walter Cloud, "30-ish," divorced owner of a graphic design company in Arlington, has it down to a science. He enters the club, rakes his eyes over the crowd until he spots a subject, then moves in.

6   He chooses his words carefully, tailoring them to the way the woman is dressed, the event and the atmosphere. A woman in pearls or a business suit gets the gentle approach—polite conversation about the weather, the president, the O. J. trial.

7   "I would like to make them feel like the effort that they made to put that all together is well-deserved," explains Cloud.

8   But for sisters in sexier garb, no telling. "The base is the dress, that's how you decide what you're going to say to a woman," he says. "Believe it or not, people wear clothes that are appropriate for the event. If she's wearing something that is raunchy just to show off, you don't have as much respect for them."

9   Judson Tallandier, 22, a senior at Howard University majoring in telecom-

munications, says the key to his pickup lines is getting a woman to smile. "I say, 'Would you be offended if I ask you a personal question?' Then they have to tell me yes or no. Most girls say no, they wouldn't be offended," Tallandier says. Then he continues. "'Would you be offended if I asked you what your name was?' Then they smile. If they break a smile, a smile says so much."

Next thing, he says, he's buying her a drink or a hamburger and they're getting acquainted. Hopefully, he gets a telephone number. 10

Pickup lines are as varied as the people who deliver them. Some men and women looking to meet someone they have spotted across a room, in a grocery store aisle or along a trail in the park simply walk up, say hello and introduce themselves. 11

That's how Tony Mack, a 25-year-old administrative assistant at the National Institutes of Health, does it. He says pickup lines don't work. "Basically, I just say, 'How are you, what's your name, where are you from?' . . . stuff like that," says Mack. "Then I tell them a little about myself." 12

But for others, the pickup line is alive and well in an intricate series of verbal volleys and return shots that will either be entertaining enough to elicit a positive response or stupid enough to ensure rejection. 13

"Don't I know you from somewhere?" almost always results in an answer of "I don't think so," "I hope not," or "No, and you won't." 14

A typical response to "What's your sign?" is almost always "A stop sign." 15

"Can I go with you?" is sure to receive a curt "No." 16

Several pickup artists say the delivery is the key element to success in the introduction: "Everybody uses the same lines. It's like sex. Sex is sex, but lovers make it what it is," says Cloud, using a comparison to a familiar subject. 17

The general consensus, among several unscientifically polled people, is that men are more prone to use pickup lines than women, even in comparable social situations. "I have tried every trick in the book," says Cloud. "Guys have a whole head full of pickup lines." 18

Kimberly Turrentine, 24, an administrative assistant at Bolling Air Force Base, doesn't use lines on men in an effort to gain their affection. "Pickup lines are a last resort or desperate plea for attention for women," says Turrentine, turning up her nose at the thought of using one. 19

"Women should never put themselves in positions where they can be rejected," she goes on. "If a man approaches me or I see a man that I am attracted to, I will give him eye contact in the hope that he will notice that I am interested in him." 20

Men always are the ones who have to set themselves up for rejection, complains Dale Rudolph, a 28-year-old delivery driver. 21

"Girls want to look nice so guys can talk to them, then when we talk to them, they shove us away," he says. "You [women] shoot us down, but you can't do our job," he says. "Then you wonder why we get so mad." 22

23   Flattery, they say, will get you nowhere. But unabashed flattery is what Bernard Sumlin, a 30-year-old copyright technician, recommends.

24   "I say, 'Do you know that you are the most beautiful woman in the world?'" Sumlin says, lowering his voice seductively and moving closer, for a second assuming the pickup role.

25   Then he straightens up and his voice returns to its normal tone:

26   "And it works, I guarantee you, that works," he says.

Donald M. Murray

The Maker's Eye: Revising Your Own Manuscript

"My writing day begins about eleven-thirty in the morning when I turn off the computer and go out to lunch," says Donald Murray about his means of inspiration. "I have written and now I will allow the well to refill." He hasn't stopped writing—at least 500 words a day—since he got his first job at the *Boston Herald* in 1948. In the interim he's won the Pulitzer Prize, published two novels, and written a number of books about writing. He also founded the journalism program at the University of New Hampshire, where he is professor emeritus of English. In this essay, which first appeared in *The Writer* and was then rewritten for a different anthology, he analyzes the processes he and other great writers use to revise their work.

1   WHEN STUDENTS COMPLETE A FIRST DRAFT, they consider the job of writing done—and their teachers too often agree. When professional writers complete a first draft, they usually feel that they are at the start of the writing process. When a draft is completed, the job of writing can begin.

2   That difference in attitude is the difference between amateur and professional, inexperience and experience, journeyman and craftsman. Peter F. Drucker, the prolific business writer, calls his first draft the "zero draft"—after that he can start counting. Most writers share the feeling that the first draft, and all of those which follow, are opportunities to discover what they have to say and how best they can say it.

3   To produce a progression of drafts, each of which says more and says it more clearly, the writer has to develop a special kind of reading skill. In school we are taught to decode what appears on the page as finished writing. Writers, however, face a different category of possibility and responsibility when

they read their own drafts. To them the words on the page are never finished. Each can be changed and rearranged, can set off a chain reaction of confusion or clarified meaning. This is a different kind of reading which is possibly more difficult and certainly more exciting.

Writers must learn to be their own best enemy. They must accept the criticism of others and be suspicious of it; they must accept the praise of others and be even more suspicious of it. Writers cannot depend on others. They must detach themselves from their own pages so that they can apply both their caring and their craft to their own work. 4

Such detachment is not easy. Science fiction writer Ray Bradbury supposedly puts each manuscript away for a year to the day and then rereads it as a stranger. Not many writers have the discipline or the time to do this. We must read when our judgment may be at its worst, when we are close to the euphoric moment of creation. 5

Then the writer, counsels novelist Nancy Hale, "should be critical of everything that seems to him most delightful in his style. He should excise what he most admires, because he wouldn't thus admire it if he weren't . . . in a sense protecting it from criticism." John Ciardi, the poet, adds, "The last act of the writing must be to become one's own reader. It is, I suppose, a schizophrenic process, to begin passionately and to end critically, to begin hot and to end cold; and, more important, to be passion-hot and critic-cold at the same time." 6

Most people think that the principal problem is that writers are too proud of what they have written. Actually, a greater problem for most professional writers is one shared by the majority of students. They are overly critical, think everything is dreadful, tear up page after page, never complete a draft, see the task as hopeless. 7

The writer must learn to read critically but constructively, to cut what is bad, to reveal what is good. Eleanor Estes, the children's book author, explains: "The writer must survey his work critically, coolly, as though he were a stranger to it. He must be willing to prune, expertly and hard-heartedly. At the end of each revision, a manuscript may look . . . worked over, torn apart, pinned together, added to, deleted from, words changed and words changed back. Yet the book must maintain its original freshness and spontaneity." 8

Most readers underestimate the amount of rewriting it usually takes to produce spontaneous reading. This is a great disadvantage to the student writer, who sees only a finished product and never watches the craftsman who takes the necessary step back, studies the work carefully, returns to the task, steps back, returns, steps back, again and again. Anthony Burgess, one of the most prolific writers in the English-speaking world, admits, "I might revise a page twenty times." Roald Dahl, the popular children's writer, states, "By the time I'm nearing the end of a story, the first part will have been reread and al- 9 tered and corrected at least 150 times. . . . Good writing is essentially rewriting. I am positive of this."

10   Rewriting isn't virtuous. It isn't something that ought to be done. It is simply something that most writers find they have to do to discover what they have to say and how to say it. It is a condition of the writer's life.

11   There are, however, a few writers who do little formal rewriting, primarily because they have the capacity and experience to create and review a large number of invisible drafts in their minds before they approach the page. And some writers slowly produce finished pages, performing all the tasks of revision simultaneously, page by page, rather than draft by draft. But it is still possible to see the sequence followed by most writers most of the time in rereading their own work.

12   Most writers scan their drafts first, reading as quickly as possible to catch the larger problems of subject and form, then move in closer and closer as they read and write, reread and rewrite.

13   The first thing writers look for in their drafts is *information*. They know that a good piece of writing is built from specific, accurate, and interesting information. The writer must have an abundance of information from which to construct a readable piece of writing.

14   Next writers look for *meaning* in the information. The specifics must build to a pattern of significance. Each piece of specific information must carry the reader toward meaning.

15   Writers reading their own drafts are aware of *audience*. They put themselves in the reader's situation and make sure that they deliver information which a reader wants to know or needs to know in a manner which is easily digested. Writers try to be sure that they anticipate and answer the questions a critical reader will ask when reading the piece of writing.

16   Writers make sure that the *form* is appropriate to the subject and the audience. Form, or genre, is the vehicle which carries meaning to the reader, but form cannot be selected until the writer has adequate information to discover its significance and an audience which needs or wants that meaning.

17   Once writers are sure the form is appropriate, they must then look at the *structure*, the order of what they have written. Good writing is built on a solid framework of logic, argument, narrative, or motivation which runs through the entire piece of writing and holds it together. This is the time when many writers find it most effective to outline as a way of visualizing the hidden spine on which the piece of writing is supported.

18   The element on which writers may spend a majority of their time is *development*. Each section of a piece of writing must be adequately developed. It must give readers enough information so that they are satisfied. How much information is enough? That's as difficult as asking how much garlic belongs in a salad. It must be done to taste, but most beginning writers underdevelop, underestimating the reader's hunger for information.

As writers solve development problems, they often have to consider questions of *dimension*. There must be a pleasing and effective proportion among all the parts of the piece of writing. There is a continual process of subtracting and adding to keep the piece of writing in balance. 19

Finally, writers have to listen to their own voices. *Voice* is the force which drives a piece of writing forward. It is an expression of the writer's authority and concern. It is what is between the words on the page, what glues the piece of writing together. A good piece of writing is always marked by a consistent, individual voice. 20

As writers read and reread, write and rewrite, they move closer and closer to the page until they are doing line-by-line editing. Writers read their own pages with infinite care. Each sentence, each line, each clause, each phrase, each word, each mark of punctuation, each section of white space between the type has to contribute to the clarification of meaning. 21

Slowly the writer moves from word to word, looking through language to see the subject. As a word is changed, cut, or added, as a construction is rearranged, all the words used before that moment and all those that follow that moment must be considered and reconsidered. 22

Writers often read aloud at this stage of the editing process muttering or whispering to themselves, calling on the ear's experience with language. Does this sound right—or that? Writers edit, shifting back and forth from eye to page to ear to page. I find I must do this careful editing in short runs, no more than fifteen or twenty minutes at a stretch, or I become too kind with myself. I begin to see what I hope is on the page, not what actually is on the page. 23

This sounds tedious if you haven't done it, but actually it is fun. Making something right is immensely satisfying, for writers begin to learn what they are writing about by writing. Language leads them to meaning, and there is the joy of discovery, of understanding, of making meaning clear as the writer employs the technical skills of language. 24

Words have double meanings, even triple and quadruple meanings. Each word has its own potential for connotation and denotation. And when writers rub one word against the other, they are often rewarded with a sudden insight, an unexpected clarification. 25

The maker's eye moves back and forth from word to phrase to sentence to paragraph to sentence to phrase to word. The maker's eye sees the need for variety and balance, for a firmer structure, for a more appropriate form. It peers into the interior of the paragraph, looking for coherence, unity, and emphasis, which make meaning clear. 26

I learned something about this process when my first bifocals were prescribed. I had ordered a larger section of the reading portion of the glass because of my work, but even so, I could not contain my eyes within this new limit of vision. And I still find myself taking off my glasses and bending my 27 nose towards the page, for my eyes unconsciously flick back and forth across the page, back to another page, forward to still another, as I try to see each evolving line in relation to every other line.

28   When does this process end? Most writers agree with the great Russian writer Tolstoy, who said, "I scarcely ever reread my published writing. If by chance I come across a page, it always strikes me: all this must be rewritten; this is how I should have written it."

29   The maker's eye is never satisfied, for each word has the potential to ignite new meaning. This article has been twice written all the way through the writing process, and it was published four years ago. Now it is to be republished in a book. The editors made a few small suggestions, and then I read it with my maker's eye. Now it has been re-edited, revised, re-read, re-re-edited, for each piece of writing is to the writer full of potential and alternatives.

30   A piece of writing is never finished. It is delivered to a deadline, torn out of the typewriter on demand, sent off with a sense of accomplishment and shame and pride and frustration. If only there were a couple more days, time for just another run at it, perhaps then . . .

Alleen Pace Nilsen

Sexism and Language

Profoundly affected by the overt sexism she saw during a stay in Afghanistan in 1967, Alleen Pace Nilsen has since built a career out of examining the subtle ways the English language responds to and defines sexual roles and stereotypes. She is now a professor at the University of Arizona, and continues her work studying gender and language as it applies to literature for young adults.

1   OVER THE LAST HUNDRED YEARS, American anthropologists have travelled to the corners of the earth to study primitive cultures. They either became linguists themselves or they took linguists with them to help in learning and analyzing languages. Even if the culture was one that no longer existed, they were interested in learning its language because besides being tools of communication, the vocabulary and structure of a language tell much about the values held by its speakers.

2   However, the culture need not be primitive, nor do the people making observations need to be anthropologists and linguists. Anyone living in the United States who listens with a keen ear or reads with a perceptive eye can

come up with startling new insights about the way American English reflects our values.

Animal Terms for People—Mirrors of the Double Standard

If we look at just one semantic area of English, that of animal terms in rela- 3
tion to people, we can uncover some interesting insights into how our culture views males and females. References to identical animals can have negative connotations when related to a female, but positive or neutral connotations when related to a male. For example, a *shrew* has come to mean "a scolding, nagging, evil-tempered woman," while *shrewd* means "keen-witted, clever, or sharp in practical affairs; astute . . . businessman, etc." (*Webster's New World Dictionary of the American Language*, 1964).

A *lucky dog* or a *gay dog* may be a very interesting fellow, but when a 4
woman is a *dog*, she is unattractive, and when she's a *bitch* she's the personification of whatever is undesirable in the mind of the speaker. When a man is self-confident, he may be described as *cocksure* or even *cocky*, but in a woman this same self-confidence is likely to result in her being called a *cocky bitch*, which is not only a mixed metaphor, but also probably the most insulting animal metaphor we have. *Bitch* has taken on such negative connotations—children are taught it is a swear word—that in everyday American English, speakers are hesitant to call a female dog a *bitch*. Most of us feel that we would be insulting the dog. When we want to insult a man by comparing him to a dog, we call him a *son of a bitch*, which quite literally is an insult to his mother rather than to him.

If the female is called a *vixen* (a female fox), the dictionary says this means 5
she is "an ill-tempered, shrewish, or malicious woman." The female seems both to attract and to hold on longer to animal metaphors with negative connotations. A *vampire* was originally a corpse that came alive to suck the blood of living persons. The word acquired the general meaning of an unscrupulous person such as a blackmailer and then, the specialized meaning of "a beautiful but unscrupulous woman who seduces men and leads them to their ruin." From this latter meaning we get the word *vamp*. The popularity of this term and of the name *vampire bat* may contribute to the idea that a female being is referred to in a phrase such as *the old bat*.

Other animal metaphors do not have definitely derogatory connotations 6
for the female, but they do seem to indicate frivolity or unimportance, as in *social butterfly* and *flapper*. Look at the differences between the connotations of participating in a *hen party* and in a *bull session*. Male metaphors, even when they are negative in connotation, still relate to strength and conquest. Metaphors related to aggressive sex roles, for example, *buck, stag, wolf,* and *stud,* will undoubtedly remain attached to males. Perhaps one of the reasons that in the late sixties it was so shocking to hear policemen called *pigs* was that the con-

notations of *pig* are very different from the other animal metaphors we usually apply to males.

7   When I was living in Afghanistan, I was surprised at the cruelty and unfairness of a proverb that said, "When you see an old man, sit down and take a lesson; when you see an old woman, throw a stone." In looking at Afghan folk literature, I found that young girls were pictured as delightful and enticing, middle-aged women were sometimes interesting but more often just tolerable, while old women were always grotesque and villainous. Probably the reason for the negative connotation of old age in women is that women are valued for their bodies while men are valued for their accomplishments and their wisdom. Bodies deteriorate with age but wisdom and accomplishments grow greater.

8   When we returned home from Afghanistan, I was shocked to discover that we have remnants of this same attitude in America. We see it in our animal metaphors. If both the animal and the woman are young, the connotation is positive, but if the animal and the woman are old, the connotation is negative. Hugh Hefner might never have made it to the big time if he had called his girls *rabbits* instead of *bunnies*. He probably chose *bunny* because he wanted something close to, but not quite so obvious as *kitten* or *cat*—the all-time winners for connoting female sexuality. Also *bunny*, as in the skiers' *snow bunny*, already had some of the connotations Hefner wanted. Compare the connotations of *filly* to *old nag; bird* to *old crow* or *old bat*; and *lamb* to *crone* (apparently related to the early modern Dutch *kronje*, old ewe but now *withered old woman*).

9   Probably the most striking examples of the contrast between young and old women are animal metaphors relating to cats and chickens. A young girl is encouraged to be *kittenish*, but not *catty*. And though most of us wouldn't mind living next door to a *sex kitten*, we wouldn't want to live next door to a *cat house*. Parents might name their daughter *Kitty* but not *Puss* or *Pussy*, which used to be a fairly common nickname for girls. It has now developed such sexual connotations that it is used mostly for humor, as in the James Bond movie featuring Pussy Galore and her flying felines.

10   In the chicken metaphors, a young girl is a *chick*. When she gets old enough she marries and soon begins feeling *cooped up*. To relieve the boredom she goes to *hen parties* and *cackles* with her friends. Eventually she has her *brood*, begins to *henpeck* her husband, and finally turns into an *old biddy*.

How English Glorifies Maleness

11   Throughout the ages physical strength has been very important, and because men are physically stronger than women, they have been valued more. Only now in the machine age, when the difference in strength between males and females pales into insignificance in comparison to the

strength of earth-moving machinery, airplanes, and guns, males no longer have such an inherent advantage. Today a man of intellect is more valued than a physical laborer, and since women can compete intellectually with men, their value is on the rise. But language lags far behind cultural changes, so the language still reflects this emphasis on the importance of being male. For example, when we want to compliment a male, all we need to do is stress the fact that he is male by saying he is a *he-man*, or he is *manly*, or he is *virile*. Both *virile* and *virtuous* come from the Latin *vir*, meaning *man*.

The command or encouragement that males receive in sentences like "Be 12 a man!" implies that *to be a man* is to be honorable, strong, righteous, and whatever else the speaker thinks desirable. But in contrast to this, a girl is never told to be a *woman*. And when she is told to be a *lady*, she is simply being encouraged to "act feminine," which means sitting with her knees together, walking gracefully, and talking softly.

The armed forces, particularly the Marines, use the positive masculine 13 connotation as part of their recruitment psychology. They promote the idea that to join the Marines (or the Army, Navy, or Air Force) guarantees that you will become a man. But this brings up a problem, because much of the work that is necessary to keep a large organization running is what is traditionally thought of as *women's work*. Now, how can the Marines ask someone who has signed up for a *man-sized job* to do *women's work?* Since they can't, they euphemize and give the jobs titles that either are more prestigious or, at least, don't make people think of females. Waitresses are called *orderlies*, secretaries are called *clerk-typists*, nurses are called *medics*, assistants are called *adjutants*, and cleaning up an area is called *policing* the area. The same kind of word glorification is used in civilian life to bolster a man's ego when he is doing such tasks as cooking and sewing. For example, a *chef* has higher prestige than a *cook* and a *tailor* has higher prestige than a *seamstress*.

Little girls learn early in life that the boy's role is one to be envied and 14 emulated. Child psychologists have pointed out that experimenting with the role of the opposite sex is much more acceptable for little girls than it is for little boys. For example, girls are free to dress in boys' clothes, but certainly not the other way around. Most parents are amused if they have a daughter who is a *tomboy*, but they are genuinely distressed if they have a son who is a *sissy*. The names we give to young children reflect this same attitude. It is all right for girls to have boys' names, but pity the boy who has a girl's name! Because parents keep giving boys' names to girls, the number of acceptable boys' names keeps shrinking. Currently popular names for girls include *Jo, Kelly, Teri, Chris, Pat, Shawn, Toni*, and *Sam* (short for *Samantha*). *Evelyn, Carroll, Gayle, Hazel, Lynn, Beverley, Marion, Francis*, and *Shirley* once were acceptable names for males. But as they were given to females, they became less and less acceptable. Today, men who are stuck with them self-consciously go by their initials or by abbreviated forms such as *Haze, Shirl, Frank,* or *Ev.* And they seldom pass these names on to their sons.

15   Many common words have come into the language from people's names. These lexical items again show the importance of maleness compared to the triviality of the feminine activities being described. Words derived from the names of women include *Melba toast,* named for the Australian singer Dame Nellie Melba; *Sally Lunn cakes,* named after an eighteenth-century woman who first made them; *pompadour,* a hair style named after Madame Pompadour; and the word *maudlin,* as in *maudlin sentiment,* from Mary Magdalene, who was often portrayed by artists as displaying exaggerated sorrow.

16   There are trivial items named after men—*teddy bear* after Theodore Roosevelt and *sideburns* after General Burnside—but most words that come from men's names relate to significant inventions or developments. These include *pasteurization* after Louis Pasteur, *sousaphone* after John Philip Sousa, *mason jar* after John L. Mason, *boysenberry* after Rudolph Boysen, *pullman car* after George M. Pullman, *braille* after Louis Braille, *franklin stove* after Benjamin Franklin, *diesel engine* after Rudolf Diesel, *ferris wheel* after George W. G. Ferris, and the verb *to lynch* after William Lynch, who was a vigilante captain in Virginia in 1780.

17   The latter is an example of a whole set of English words dealing with violence. These words have strongly negative connotations. From research using free association and semantic differentials, with university students as subjects, James Ney concluded that English reflects both an anti-male and an anti-female bias because these biases exist in the culture (*Etc.: A Review of General Semantics,* March 1976, pp. 67–76). The students consistently marked as masculine such words as *killer, murderer, robber, attacker, fighter, stabber, rapist, assassin, gang, hood, arsonist, criminal, hijacker, villain,* and *bully,* even though most of these words contain nothing to specify that they are masculine. An example of bias against males, Ney observed, is the absence in English of a pejorative term for women equivalent to *rapist.* Outcomes of his free association test indicated that if "English speakers want to call a man something bad, there seems to be a large vocabulary available to them but if they want to use a term which is good to describe a male, there is a small vocabulary available. The reverse is true for women."

18   Certainly we do not always think positively about males; witness such words as *jerk, creep, crumb, slob, fink,* and *jackass.* But much of what deter-

mines our positive and negative feelings relates to the roles people play. We have very negative feelings toward someone who is hurting us or threatening us or in some way making our lives miserable. To be able to do this, the person has to have power over us and this power usually belongs to males.

On the other hand, when someone helps us or makes our life more pleasant, we have positive feelings toward that person or that role. *Mother* is one of the positive female terms in English, and we see such extensions of it as *Mother Nature*, *Mother Earth*, *mother lode*, *mother superior*, etc. But even though a word like *mother* is positive, it is still not a word of power. In the minds of English speakers being female and being powerless or passive are so closely related that we use the terms *feminine* and *lady* either to mean female or to describe a certain kind of quiet and unobtrusive behavior. 19

Words Labeling Women as Things

Because of our expectations of passivity, we like to compare females to items that people acquire for their pleasure. For example, in a . . . commercial for the television show "Happy Days," one of the characters announced that in the coming season, they were going to have not only "cars, motorcycles, and girls," but also a band. Another example of this kind of thinking is the comparison of females to food since food is something we all enjoy, even though it is extremely passive. We describe females as such delectable morsels as a *dish*, a *cookie*, a *tart*, *cheesecake*, *sugar and spice*, a *cute tomato*, *honey*, a *sharp cookie*, and *sweetie pie*. We say a particular girl has a *peaches and cream complexion* or "she looks good enough to eat." And parents give their daughters such names as *Candy* and *Cherry*. 20

Other pleasurable items that we compare females to are toys. Young girls are called *little dolls* or *China dolls*, while older girls—if they are attractive—are simply called *dolls*. We might say about a woman, "She's pretty as a picture," or "She's a fashion plate." And we might compare a girl to a plant by saying she is a *clinging vine*, a *shrinking violet*, or a *wallflower*. And we might name our daughters after plants such as *Rose*, *Lily*, *Ivy*, *Daisy*, *Iris*, and *Petunia*. Compare these names to boys' names such as *Martin* which means warlike, *Ernest* which means resolute fighter, *Nicholas* which means victory, *Val* which means strong or valiant, and *Leo* which means lion. We would be very hesitant to give a boy the name of something as passive as a flower although we might say about a man that he is a *late-bloomer*. This is making a comparison between a man and the most active thing a plant can do, which is to bloom. The only other familiar plant metaphor used for a man is the insulting *pansy*, implying that he is like a woman. 21

Student Essay

Eleanor Belgin

Pets and Their Humans

For this essay, Eleanor's assignment asked her to respond to Alleen Pace Nilsen's essay on sexism using a strategy employing many examples. Eleanor chose to imitate Nilsen's style, but give it a humorous twist.

1   IN HER ESSAY "SEXISM AND LANGUAGE," ALLEEN PACE NILSEN examines the biases inherent in the English language. When animal words, for example, are applied to humans, men are typically favorably compared to animals ("he's a stud") while females are unfavorably compared ("she's a dog"). Nilsen subtly demonstrates that our language reflects our biases—thus showing that the road to gender equality is fraught not only with the prejudices that tradition hands down from generation to generation, but also the slant implicit in every word we speak.

2   Perhaps even more frightening than the biases Nilsen observes, however, are the misdeeds of that most dastardly group of Americans—pet owners. Pet owners regularly and voluntarily compare their animals to humans, and the animals nearly always come out on top. At least people who use biased terms like "stud" and "dog" have the defense that these terms are ingrained in our language. Pet owners, through their words and actions, believe that animals are superior to humans.

3   For example, many dog owners clothe their animals in such human apparel as coats, hats, and even shoes. You'll see a well-dressed woman strolling down the street with her corgi—and the dog is dressed in a beautiful wool coat and matching Timberland moccasins. Meanwhile homeless people shiver on the street wearing only plastic bags.

4   Another hypocrisy of pet owners is the idea that their pets have the right to use any human's lawn as their own personal bathroom. While this practice is both disgusting and unhealthy, pet owners act like public restroom privileges for their animals is some sort of sacred freedom. If a human behaved this way in public, he or she would be fined, if not jailed. Pets, it seems, have more rights than humans.

5   If you listen to their owners, pets are also smarter than humans. According to its owner, a dog that can't be restrained from barking at a stranger isn't simply stupid, it's endowed with supernatural powers that enable it to sense when a stranger is afraid. When a human couple tells a charming story about

their baby's first word, the pet owners inevitably chime in with similar stories about their *animals:* "Fido understands every word I say," or "Spot can walk on her hind legs!"

Pet owners believe their pets experience the same emotions as humans. For example, pets are "depressed" when their owners leave town for a few days. There are even animal psychiatrists to help pets deal with such traumas as pet sibling rivalry, anxiety, and a death in the family. No doubt this service is covered by the many pet HMOs springing up across the country. 6

On television, pets now have their own game shows, athletic competitions, and yes, emergency room dramas. There is even an entire cable channel devoted to animals. What more evidence is necessary to show that pet owners have elevated their animals to superhuman importance? Perhaps only this— one of the worst insults you can level at a dog is to say that it "acts like a baby"! 7

4

Comparison & Contrast

Comparison & Contrast

1. **Identify an appropriate topic.** When writing a comparison and contrast essay, the topic is critical. Some topics beg to be covered using this strategy; others simply won't work at all. Essay exams often ask you quite directly to use this strategy: "Compare and contrast the reigns of Elizabeth I and Victoria." Other times, the assignment may be more subtle. You may be asked to simply "compare" two things, to examine the "similarities and differences," or you may simply want to evaluate two choices, such as books, college courses, or physical items like cars or computers. Comparison and contrast is an effective strategy for evaluating, analyzing, or assessing two things that have similarities and differences. It's not effective if the subjects you're comparing have little in common. Unless you're feeling very clever, don't try to compare and contrast milk with the Milky Way.

2. **Write a strong thesis.** Nothing is more dull than a simple list of similarities and differences. Unless you're making a point, your readers will quickly lose interest. Of course, as you write your essay, you may decide to modify your thesis or change it entirely. Remember that if you change your thesis, you'll also need to reassess your essay as a whole to make sure it's supporting your point.

3. **Narrow your comparison to the points that support your thesis.** Any comparison and contrast essay can easily be expanded to fill pages, even volumes. To be effective, you need to emphasize the examples that make your point best. Depending on your thesis, you could compare Elizabeth and Victoria's religious, political, and foreign policies, or you could compare their clothing, hairstyles, and love lives. Then make sure you cover these points using plenty of clear examples (see Chapter 3).

4. **Select the organization that fits your topic best.** Comparison and contrast usually follows either a point-by-point comparison model or a block pattern:

Point-by-point	Block	
Kennedy's clothes	Kennedy	Clinton
Clinton's clothes	clothes	clothes
Kennedy's hair	hair	hair
Clinton's hair	love life	love life
Kennedy's love life		
Clinton's love life		

Point-by-point usually works better for longer essays when you're concerned readers might not remember your earlier points. Block can be more effective for shorter essays or when you're comparing more than two items.

Bill McKibben

Nature and Televised Nature

Bill McKibben is an environmental writer who has tackled some of the most controversial issues our world has faced in the last ten years. He was one of the first people to warn of global warming in his 1989 book *The End of Nature*. He does not merely sound the alarm however; he also entreats us to help ease the problem by leading a simpler life. His concern about overpopulation is the topic of his latest book *Maybe One* which suggests that society needs to reconsider the stereotypes of "the only child" for the sake of the environment. McKibben has also written books on biking in his home area of the Adirondacks. *The Age of Missing Information*, from which this reading is taken, addresses the emphasis of quantity over quality in today's media.

UNABLE THOUGH I WAS TO FORECAST THE WEATHER, I retained sufficient 1
mother wit to recognize that it had turned into a gorgeous day, and so I set
out to climb Blackberry Mountain, Crow's smaller neighbor.

From the pond I followed a brook down to the valley between the peaks— 2
it is a mossy cool trickle in the summer, and instead of clambering over dead-
fall along the banks you can hop easily from rock to rock down the creek. I
stopped occasionally at the small clear pools to admire the water striders, their
legs dimpling the tense surface, their small bodies casting impressive shadows
on the creek bottom as they went about their inscrutable business.

When I reached the valley between the mountains, I could look up at the 3
open cliffs at the top of Blackberry. Since there's no trail to the summit, I just
hit out along a compass bearing through the woods. The bottom slopes have
been logged in the last couple of decades—the sun pours into the clearings,
which of course are luxuriant with thorny berry cane. I fought my way
through, and after twenty minutes or so, as the slope steepened, rock patches
began to appear—the trees were fewer and bigger, and in the shade of one hemlock I lay down to rest. After about ten minutes, at least a dozen small birds
began to resume the activity I had interrupted with my noisy arrival. They
were mostly small thrushes, and they flew in and out of the branches in what
looked like a high-speed game of tag, over and over, lighting now on a sway-
ing bough, then launching themselves off into the air once more.

After my rest I climbed the remaining distance to Blackberry's long sum- 4
mit ridge, and walked out along the top of the steep cliffs that faced back to
Crow. The wind was blowing below—I could hear it rush like white water and
see where it was riffling the maple tops in the mountain valley—but up on top
it was still, and the sun baked the fragrant pine needles. I was sitting, drinking from my canteen, when I saw a vulture appear way below in the draw be-

tween the mountains. He circled slowly and methodically up, holding his wings in a stiff, lacquered bow, never flapping, always soaring. Eventually, after perhaps a half hour, he was directly above me on the cliffs, perhaps a hundred feet in the air, still circling. He was joined there by four, then five, finally six others, circling so close I could count feathers. When they passed directly overhead it was nearly unbearable—almost erotic—this feeling of being watched. At moments I felt small and vulnerable, like prey; if they disappeared from view for a minute I wanted to know where they were. But by the time I finally rose to go back to my tent on Crow, I felt almost protected, watched over. It had been thrilling—my heart was beating hard.

5   Still and all, by the standards of television nature, the water striders and the thrushes and even the vultures were hardly worth mentioning. I had not been gored, chased, or even roared at. I had failed to tranquilize anything with a dart; no creature had inflated stupendous air sacs in a curious and ancient mating ritual, or eaten its young, or done any of the other prodigious tricks that happen around the clock on nature television. You could spend nearly the whole day watching nothing but nature documentaries, and if you did you would emerge exhausted. Nature on TV is the job) of a man named Graham or Ian or Nigel who makes every announcement ("Using his incisors like a comb, the marmot attends to his thick underfleece") sound like Churchill in wartime. The point of the show can be that, say, elephants are all but exterminated in a certain African refuge, but you can be sure that our host will find one. Not one—dozens. "I think there's a jolly good chance of sketching this lot," the host is saying as he piles out of his Land-Rover. "There's the matriarch—she's the one to watch. I'd be crazy to get too close to her. If I can reach that anthill I can get some good sketches. She's accompanied by uncles and aunties of all ages—the young males get kicked out because they get stroppy." On the voiceover, the narrator may be confessing the boring truth: "Lions are lazy—the males are the worst. They'll sleep twenty hours a day if they get the chance." But on the screen the lions are training their young by chasing jackals and other exotic game—Oooh, so much for that zebra. The man in the jeep, obligatory spare tire on the hood, tracks the lion pack toward a watering hole, never losing sight of them. He spies some ostriches: "Ostriches mean water, and water means life—and the lion feels an ancient urge. Perhaps she's come upon a place to start a pride." Oooh—lion sex! Cubs come tumbling out after a two- or three-minute gestation, full of play, and the timeless predatory cycle repeats—and someone is releasing a seal from a California aquarium. He starts to travel north, but suddenly a killer whale is on his tail. A brief respite in a kelp bed ("It's the life of Riley, lying on your back and eating crab so fresh it tries to walk away") and then our seal resumes his trip up the coast to the Pribilofs, where the breeding beach is a great heaving mass of flippers. At the precise moment our hero washes ashore, the men appear with the baseball

bats for the annual fur harvest; fortunately he retreats to the safety of the ocean before they can get him, still alive for the documentaries that will surely follow.

It would be churlish to complain about these gorgeous films. It would be even more churlish to quote from a recent interview in *Entertainment Weekly* with Wolfgang Bayer. An acclaimed nature photographer who's made dozens of TV films, he tells of hoisting tame, declawed jaguars into trees for action scenes, and spray-painting pet-shop ferrets till they're ringers for the nearly extinct black-footed variety, and starving piranhas so they'll attack with more ferocity. He once did a show on an Amazonian tarantula that occasionally eats birds. How often does it eat birds, asked the reporter? "As often as you throw them to him," he says. It would be churlish because TV nature films have without any question done an immense amount of good—species exist today that would be fossil records if Philo Farnsworth hadn't invented the picture tube. Your can of tuna has a little "dolphin-safe" symbol on it because in 1963 Chuck Connors starred in a film called *Flipper*, which gave birth to a TV show of the same name. The movie version was shown on May 3—in the month of May alone it was on the Disney Channel five times and on Cinemax twice, so presumably each new generation sees the boy battle his stern; old-fashioned father, who actually believes dolphins are a threat to his fishery. "If they come, we'll kill them. We have no choice," the father says. The rise of environmental consciousness over the intervening three decades can be felt in just how shocking this attitude now seems. Some fishermen still kill dolphins, but they try to hide their work because nearly everyone agrees it is a sick waste; in 1963, obviously, *not* killing dolphins was regarded as revolutionary, and *Flipper* is a key reason for the change.

In 1963, too, the sperm-whale kill reached its peak, claiming about thirty thousand of the great beasts. We think of whaling as being at its height in the last century, when Nantucket men and Gloucester men and Mystic men and the men of a dozen other ports that are now pricy tourist attractions sailed the globe in search of lamp oil. But the slaughter continued, except of those species that were already reduced below commercial levels, until about the time that a slight Frenchman took to the TV screens. On any given time that day you can see Jacques Cousteau, the John Muir of the deep, two or three times—here he is in the sea grass beds of Australia, a safe pasture for sea cows now threatened by sandmining; here he is working to "cweate a weef, shimmawing with life." His son Michel is apparently taking over the family trade, and has perfected the sad Gallic intonations of his dad. He is swimming next to a giant grouper—"I hardly ever see a fish so large anymore, which were my constant companions when I began diving. I cannot resist reaching out to this veteran of living, as if to touch the past, the time when big fish were nothing more than that." Cousteau's success can be measured in the sea, where rem-

nant populations of some species survive because of great human efforts, and
even more in the popular mind—a four-year-old boy just spent the weekend
with us, and his conversation rarely strayed from the topic of killer whales, a
species that until quite recently stirred loathing and not love.

8   Still, measured in the largest terms, such appeals aren't working. That is,
virtually everyone in the industrialized world has a television and has presumably, if only by accident, seen many hours of gorgeous nature films—seen
a more diverse and wondrous natural world than man could ever have seen
before. And yet we're still not willing to do anything very drastic to save that
world. We'll buy dolphin-safe tuna if it doesn't cost much extra, but we won't
cut back on driving and consuming electricity and doing the other things that
lead to global warming, even though the world now loses as much as 5 percent of its coral reefs annually due to higher water temperatures likely caused
by the greenhouse effect. Species continue to disappear, and at an accelerat-
ing rate; presidents continue to propose, say, drilling for oil in the Arctic National Wildlife Refuge, square in the middle of an enormous caribou herd.
Why can't Graham and Ian and Nigel stop this?

9   They can't, I think, because for all their dart guns and millions of feet of
film they actually get across remarkably little information—much less than
you'd acquire almost unconsciously from a good long hike. Half the time they
specialize in misinformation, undercutting their message with their pictures.
The Englishman is telling you that this great flightless bird is on the edge of
extinction, but for half an hour he is showing you endless pictures of this great
flightless bird, so how bad could it be? The actual numbers of surviving big
mammals are astoundingly small—grizzly bears in the lower forty-eight states
can be counted in the hundreds. In fact, you've probably seen a large fraction
of them at one time or another, wandering slowly through the telephoto field
of a Yellowstone camera. But they appear so often they seem numerous. No
one shows film of the weeks in camp waiting for the damned gorillas to appear—a documentary of trees that used to be inhabited by the ancient manlike
primates but no longer are is a documentary people wouldn't watch, though
that void is the true revelation about an awful lot of the world.

10   Something even more insidious happens when you get most of your nature through television, though—the "real" nature around you, even when it's
intact, begins to seem dull. Mr. Bayer, the man with the spray-painted ferrets,
said, "If we showed viewers only natural, unadulterated filmmaking, wildlife
filmmakers would be out of business in a year, it'd be so boring." So, instead,
nature films are like the highlight clips they show on the evening sportscast,
all rim-bending slam dunks and bleachers—clearing home runs and knee-
crumpling knockout punches. If you'd been raised on a steady diet of such
footage and then you went to a game, you'd feel cheated—what is all this business with singles and pop flies? Why do the hockey players skate around for

so long between fights? The highlights films erode appreciation for the various beauties of the game, some of which are small and patient.

The problem is even more severe with the natural world, where the ratio 11
of observable high drama is much lower. A movie like *Benji the Hunted*, which was on the Disney Channel, presents the forest as a place where, in the space of a day, you encounter and must vanquish mountain lions, wolves, grizzlies, badgers, and so on right down Noah's list—it is a car-chase flick with animals. (And as impossible in its outcome as most car chases—Benji, a domesticated dog, has somehow retained the instinct necessary to outwit every predatory mammal of the North American continent, while acquiring a remarkably un-Darwinian compassion for the young of other species.) How disappointing, then, to go for a walk in a healthy Eastern woods and see so few bared claws. In many years hiking in the East I've happened across bears twice. Once, in Maine, I rounded a corner in a trail and there, three feet away, as lost in thought as I had been, sat a black bear. One look at me and she dived for the bushes—total contact time perhaps four seconds. A few years later, walking near my house with my wife, I heard a noise in a treetop and all of a sudden another black bear, roughly the size and shape of a large sofa, dropped to the ground a few yards away. She glowered in our direction and then lit out the opposite way. Time of engagement: maybe seven seconds. Those were grand encounters, and they've spiced every other day I've spent in the woods—on the way up Blackberry Mountain, for instance, I sang as I waded through the berry bushes, aware that this is where any bear with a stomach would be. But if I counted as dramatic only those days when I actually saw a big fierce mammal, I would think the forest a boring place indeed.

Big animals are fairly scarce in the best of conditions, and understandably 12
shy—an Adirondack hunter last fall shot a bear that biologists, studying his teeth, determined was forty-three years old. That is, he'd been hiding out up here since before Truman beat Dewey. When you do see large animals it's usually at a pretty good distance, not right up close as on TV—you can rarely sneak up on, say, a heron the way you can with a zoom lens. (On the other hand, you need a big, natural field of vision to get a sense of the graceful spookiness with which they glide.) But even if you did see a rare animal, and somehow managed to creep up real close, chances are it wouldn't be doing anything all that amazing. Chances are it would be lying in the sun, or perhaps grooming itself, or maybe, like the duck on the pond, swimming back and forth. A lot of animals are remarkably good at sitting still (especially when they suspect they're under surveillance), and this is something TV never captures. The nature documentaries are as absurdly action-packed as the soap operas, where a life's worth of divorce, adultery, and sudden death are crammed into a week's worth of watching—trying to understand "nature" from watching *Wild Kingdom* is as tough as trying to understand "life" from watching *Dynasty*.

13   This is particularly true because, even at its best, TV covers only a small slice of the natural world. There are perhaps ten million (some say thirty million) species on earth; of those that we know about and have catalogued, only a few meet the requirements for extensive television coverage—cuteness (or grotesqueness so complete it borders on the cute), great amiability or ferocity, accessibility (it lives on grassland plains or beaches, not in the deep ocean, badly lit caves, or rainforest canopies), correct size to show up well on camera, and so on. Species with these characteristics seem to exist in roughly the same ratio as human television actors to the general population, and they are as consistently overexposed. But even the most unengaging, hard-to-get-at, drab little animal has a great advantage over any plant except a Venus's flytrap, and that is mobility. In its immense fear that we might grow bored, TV has not yet acquired the courage necessary to show an unmoving picture for very long, and so the only hope of star-struck vegetation is time-lapse photography, which works okay for orchids but doesn't do much for, say, evergreens. Someone sent me a "working treatment" recently for a television program celebrating trees that is being made by a leading wildlife filmmaker. The "tease opening" features, "intercutting of striking tree images with interview characters expressing

Wonder

Concern

Reverence

14 followed by opening credits over breathtaking images of trees and forests" against an "engaging mix of forest sounds, rain, and music." The film covers rain forest, swamps, and the autumn blaze of color; it looks at furniture and at musical instruments made from wood; it covers bonsai and the Yellowstone fires, all in forty-seven and a half minutes, leaving twelve and a half for commercials. Beautiful, no doubt, but perhaps the wrong way to nurture appreciation for trees, whose most glorious characteristic is that they stay in the same place forever. Any time spent in a real forest gives you this information: a tree is of a piece with the soil from which it grows and the sky it rises into, part and parcel of the insect that eats at its middle and the bird that eats the insect, inseparable from the forest of other trees and yet perfect in its humped and gnarly isolation. And yet this is so hard to show—much easier to flash a sequoia on the screen and say this counts because it's big.

15   The upshot of a nature education by television is a deep fondness for certain species and a deep lack of understanding of systems, or of the policies that destroy those systems. For instance, one of the ads that may come on during this celebration of trees, as it did several times on May 3, is paid for by the

Forest Products Council. "Today we have more trees than we did back in 1920," it says, "thanks in part to something our forest products companies do three million times a day—plant a tree." The visuals accompanying this reassuring voice are stunning—from the air we see a bend in a wilderness river with a rich and exuberant old forest spilling forth to the bank. There's a lot less of this kind of forest than there was in 1920, thanks in part (in whole, really) to something else the forest products companies do every day, which is cut down virgin stands of climax forest, the biologically diverse, marvelously complex ancient forest that covered much of this country when Europeans arrived. The forest products companies *do* plant trees. They plant them in nice straight rows, every sapling the same age and the same height and the same species, and then they drop herbicides from helicopters to keep down undesirable varieties; they create, in other words, sterile plantations for growing timber and pulp. And the forest products companies often perform this public service on public lands, under the guidance of government employees. The great national forests, which cover so much of the western part of the nation, are mostly managed as timber farms; the trees, in many cases old-growth forests, are sold to lumber companies and then cut down. One of these public servants is Smokey Bear, whose commercials run all day and night. We all grew up believing Smokey hated forest fires because they fried Bambi's kin, but the truth is Smokey doesn't want you to burn the forest down because his employer, the Forest Service, wants to cut it down instead. You don't see this when you drive through a national forest, because the government employs an enormous corps of landscape architects whose whole job is to make sure the clearcuts are invisible. And you don't see it on TV because it's political, and a tree is a tree, and it's time to look at the fur seals again.

In 1990, according to the *New York Times*, the not-to-be-lived-without accessory was the "personal meadow, a mini-expanse of green grass growing ever-so-sweetly out of a gently rusticated plywood box." "They couldn't walk by without coming in to touch it," said one florist. "It's such a fresh look. People have very strong reactions to it." An interior designer who changes the sod in his foyer every two weeks when it begins to yellow says, "I see it as Eastern in its concept." 16

Like urban living, TV cuts us off from context—stops us from understanding plants and animals as parts of systems, from grounding them in ideas larger than "fresh" or fierce or cute. And so we don't know what to make of them. We are still pulled toward this natural world, with a tug so strong it must be primal, but TV helps turn it into a zoo; hence most of our responses are artificial. Animals amble across the screen all day and night—I saw the same squad of marching flamingos twice during the day on different networks. ("They're stupid," said the handler on one of the programs. "It took me six months to 17 get them to walk in formation.") CNN, in just a few hours, reported on a new virus that was spreading among macaws, parrots, and cockatoos; an orphanage that had been established for African elephants whose mothers had been killed by poachers; a group of manatees in the waterways of Florida who were being gouged by outboard propellers; a white tiger being born in a zoo; some home videos of dolphins dying in the tuna nets that a man had risked his life to take; a debate about whether people should be permitted to swim in tanks with dolphins; some "doomsday dolphins" that might be trained for ordnance work; and a Navy plan to kill thirty-five thousand feral goats on San Clemente island. The day's main animal feature was a constantly repeated story on the abuses of puppy breeders, a story that also appeared on virtually every network's broadcast. The Humane Society had issued a report that morning—most pet store dogs, it turns out, come from breeders in six Midwestern states, who in many cases raise them in such horrid conditions that they sicken and die after purchase. Two big dogs and their owner came on the *Today* show to chat with Bryant Gumbel about the problem; other networks aired film of puppies crowded together in wire cages. "Her ear canal has been inflamed so long there's no longer any hole in there," said one vet. "Her skin is dry, cracking, bleeding in spots. Boy—I can imagine how uncomfortable she is."

18   We all can. That's the marvelous thing about pets—our visceral and natural affection for them offers an easy door for human minds to enter into a larger than normal world, a world where our preoccupations count for less. A dog or a cat or a rabbit is a constant reminder that there is more than us out there—our love for them is a healthy recognition of that more. But when that love lacks a larger context, the relationship turns mawkish. Everyone knows about pet cemeteries, but CNN carried the story of a cemetery where people could be buried *with* their pets. The Fox affiliate offered news of a New York company that will freeze-dry your dead pet so you can keep him in your living room. A twenty-pound dog will run you $1,200—"We charge by the pound, but on birds we've got a flat price"—and take four months to prepare. "After we got him back, we'd just put him in his normal position, and people would walk up to him, pet him, joke with him, and then notice he was dead," said one satisfied owner. "Archie was our whole life. Everything we did was for Archie. . . . Even though he wasn't going to be living, we could still stroke him, still tell him how much we loved him."

19   The healthier relationships always had some content to them—one of the local channels, for instance, carried a fine report about the members of the Fairfax County police K-9 squad, German shepherds who live at the homes of their handlers. "You get very used to grabbing the dog and loving him up," said one cop. But it's a relationship based more on respect—on an appreciation of a dog's nature, his gifts—than on sentiment. "When he gets in the cruiser his personality changes. You can actually see the transition. He has a

little dance he does—a twirl like 'Let's get rolling.'" One of the German shepherds, Jake, was stabbed seven times but kept on going—he collared the criminal despite his fatal wounds. "They become such a part of you—it's like losing
an arm or a leg or a baby," said his distraught handler. But there was no suggestion that Jake should be freeze-dried—he was too real for that.

In somewhat the same way, the men on a few of the angling programs   20
showed some real connection with their catch—they were both competitors
and, in a strange sense, colleagues. "This fish is exhausted beyond any of our
beliefs, it's fought so hard," said one hip-booted host of *Fish'n Canada*. "It's
your duty as an angler to wait till she's fully revived before releasing her." Don
Meissner, the host of *Rod 'n' Reel Streamside*, caught a big old brookie: "I tell
you, my heart's just a poundin'. Holy cow, oh, oh, holy cow, look at that fish.
. . . Since I got older, my feelings on fishing have changed tremendously. It's
just to be out there. Not to kill something. Oh my—I'm shaking like a leaf."
Now, you could argue that there's something perverse about catching a fish
and letting him go, and you could argue that if people really *admired* a fish
they wouldn't stick a barb through its lip and pull on it for a quarter of an
hour. And if you argued any of those things you might be right. Still, there is
an echo of something here, of the traditional respectful relationship between
hunters and their quarry.

Even in the most civilized, that tug remains. A Cousteau special on the   21
Turner Broadcasting System showed crowds of Australians climbing off buses
to wade along a beach where dolphins lolled in the surf. Some of the people
were painfully stupid—sticking their fingers down the dolphin's blowhole. But
most seemed genuinely filled with

Wonder

Concern

Reverence

"In ze welcome of ze dolphins lies ze test of human wisdom," said Cousteau,   22
right as usual. Do we appreciate dolphins for the tricks they can perform, for
being like limited humans?—the trainer at a Hawaii dolphin show said that she
knew her charge was "smart" because "he wants something for nothing." Do
we appreciate them as an economic and recreational "resource," like the
striped bass described by a hatchery director on *Virginia Wildlife*? (Captured
fish are weighed to determine how much hormone, collected from the pitu-
itaries of pregnant women, to inject them with—"Fish in captivity tend to hold
back on their eggs, but this overrides that.") Or do we begin to understand
again what once was common knowledge—that they're marvelous for their
own reasons, that they matter independently of us?

23   That piece of information can come only when you accept nature and its component parts on their own terms—small and placid and dull and parts of systems, as well as big and flashy and fierce and soulful. Alone on a mountain you do start slowly to learn this lesson—it's inevitable if you lie on your back for hours and watch the hawks just circle, or lie on your stomach and watch the ducks just swim. They are not there for you—they are there because the world belongs to them too. Learn this lesson too well and you are in trouble, for in our current world it will mostly bring pain, mostly breed hysteria. Even on television this pain occasionally surfaces. HBO was showing Diane Fossey's story, *Gorillas in the Mist*—it is the story of a kook, driven mad by her understanding of what was happening around her. On paper her actions look insane—she kidnaps poachers, imprisons them. But watching the gorillas, tugged by that old tug, you know why she did what she did. The gorillas so clearly *belong*. An even better film, and more remarkable considering it was made way back in 1958, is John Huston's *The Roots of Heaven*, an elephant story starring Errol Flynn that aired on the American Movie Channel. "Anyone who's seen the great herds on the march across the last free spaces knows it is something the world can't afford to lose," says the Flynn character, and of course he is right.

24   But the world *is* losing them—CNN is filled with the pictures of dying elephants and of a dozen other creatures. This is perhaps the ultimate loss of information—too sophisticated to burn books, we burn the planet. Each day information leaks away—some branch of life that evolved for millions of years is gone, and the next day two more, and six the day after that. The world grows stupider, less substantial. And those of us who would fight have little ground on which to stand, for the tug at our hearts from the sad picture on the screen is no substitute for the deep and lifelong understandings we've let slip away.

Mark Twain

Two Views of the Mississippi

Mark Twain was born in 1835, the year of the appearance of Halley's comet, and foresaw his own death with the return of that comet in 1910. Like the comet that framed his life, Mark Twain's writing lurks as a shadow behind all of American literature, and then occasionally, inevitably, bursts onto the scene in a fire of relevance. This unusual essay, excerpted from *Life on the Mississippi*, reveals none of the wry wit usually associated with Mark Twain. It is, instead, a lyrical, pensive reflection on his view of the river before and after he was trained as a riverboat pilot.

THE FACE OF THE WATER, IN TIME, BECAME A WONDERFUL BOOK—a book that was a dead language to the uneducated passenger, but which told its mind to me without reserve, delivering its most cherished secrets as clearly as if it uttered them with a voice. And it was not a book to be read once and thrown aside, for it had a new story to tell every day. Throughout the long twelve hundred miles there was never a page that was void of interest, never one that you could leave unread without loss, never one that you would want to skip, thinking you could find higher enjoyment in some other thing. There never was so wonderful a book written by man; never one whose interest was so absorbing, so unflagging, so sparklingly renewed with every reperusal. The passenger who could not read it was charmed with a peculiar sort of faint dimple on its surface (on the rare occasions when he did not overlook it altogether); but to the pilot that was an *italicized* passage; indeed, it was more than that, it was a legend of the largest capitals, with a string of shouting exclamation points at the end of it; for it meant that a wreck or a rock was buried there that could tear the life out of the strongest vessel that ever floated. It is the faintest and simplest expression the water ever makes, and the most hideous to a pilot's eye. In truth, the passenger who could not read this book saw nothing but all manner of pretty pictures in it, painted by the sun and shaded by the clouds, whereas to the trained eye these were not pictures at all, but the grimmest and most dead-earnest of reading matter.

Now when I had mastered the language of this water and had come to know every trifling feature that bordered the great river as familiarly as I knew the letters of the alphabet, I had made a valuable acquisition. But I had lost something, too. I had lost something which could never be restored to me while I lived. All the grace, the beauty, the poetry had gone out of the majestic river! I still keep in mind a certain wonderful sunset which I witnessed when steamboating was new to me. A broad expanse of the river was turned to blood; in the middle distance the red hue brightened into gold, through which a solitary log came floating, black and conspicuous; in one place a long, slanting mark lay sparkling upon the water; in another the surface was broken by boiling, tumbling rings, that were as many-tinted as an opal; where the ruddy flush was faintest, was a smooth spot that was covered with graceful circles and radiating lines, ever so delicately traced; the shore on our left was densely wooded, and the somber shadow that fell from this forest was broken in one place by a long, ruffled trail that shone like silver; and high above the forest wall a clean-stemmed dead tree waved a single leafy bough that glowed like a flame in the unobstructed splendor that was flowing from the sun. There were graceful curves, reflected images, woody heights, soft distances; and over the whole scene, far and near, the dissolving lights drifted steadily, enriching it, every passing moment, with new marvels of coloring.

I stood like one bewitched. I drank it in, in a speechless rapture. The world was new to me, and I had never seen anything like this at home. But as I have said, a day came when I began to cease from noting the glories and the charms which the moon and the sun and the twilight wrought upon the river's face; another day came when I ceased altogether to note them. Then, if that sunset scene had been repeated, I should have looked upon it without rapture, and should have commented upon it, inwardly, after this fashion: This sun means that we are going to have wind tomorrow; that floating log means that the river is rising, small thanks to it; that slanting mark on the water refers to a bluff reef which is going to kill somebody's steamboat one of these nights, if it keeps on stretching out like that; those tumbling "boils" show a dissolving bar and a changing channel there; the lines and circles in the slick water over yonder are a warning that that troublesome place is shoaling up dangerously; that silver streak in the shadow of the forest is the "break" from a new snag, and he has located himself in the very best place he could have found to fish for steamboats; that tall dead tree, with a single living branch, is not going to last long, and then how is a body ever going to get through this blind place at night without the friendly landmark?

4   No, the romance and the beauty were all gone from the river. All the value any feature of it had for me now was the amount of usefulness it could furnish toward compassing the safe piloting of a steamboat. Since those days, I have pitied doctors from my heart. What does the lovely flush in a beauty's cheek mean to a doctor but a "break" that rippled above some deadly disease? Are not all her visible charms sown thick with what are to him the signs and symbols of hidden decay? Does he ever see her beauty at all, or doesn't he simply view her professionally, and comment upon her unwholesome condition all to himself? And doesn't he sometimes wonder whether he had gained most or lost most by learning his trade?

David M. Kennedy

Can We Still Afford to Be a Nation of Immigrants?

Comparing yesterday's immigration with today's, a historian is struck by the unprecedented nature of our present situation

A professor of history at Stanford University, David Kennedy has received awards both for his teaching and his writing. When asked to provide some tips to aspiring young history teachers, Kennedy characteristically quoted Theodore Roosevelt: "make it a cartoon, not a portrait." His point was that simpler points are easier for listeners (and readers) to comprehend. Kennedy has spent a lifetime making history easier for thousands to comprehend—he has written a popular history textbook, *The American Portrait*, helped with PBS historical documentaries, and penned articles appearing in the *New York Times* and *The Atlantic Monthly*, from which this selection was taken.

THE QUESTION IN MY TITLE IMPLIES A PREMISE: that historically the United States has well afforded to be a nation of immigrants—indeed, has benefited handsomely from its good fortune as an immigrant destination. That proposition was once so deeply embedded in our national mythology as to be axiomatic. More than a century ago, for example, in the proclamation that made Thanksgiving Day a national holiday, Abraham Lincoln gave thanks to God for having "largely augmented our free population by emancipation and by immigration."

Lincoln spoke those words when there were but 34 million Americans and half a continent remained to be settled. Today, however, the United States is a nation of some 264 million souls on a continent developed beyond Lincoln's imagination. It is also a nation experiencing immigration on a scale never before seen. In the past three decades, since the passage of the Immigration and Nationality Act Amendments of 1965, the first major revision in American immigration statutes since the historic closure of immigration in the 1920s, some 20 million immigrants have entered the United States. To put those numbers in perspective: prior to 1965 the period of heaviest immigration to the United States was the quarter century preceding the First World War, when some 17 million people entered the country—roughly half the total number of Europeans who migrated to the United States in the century after 1820 (along with several hundred thousand Asians). The last pre-war census, in 1910, counted about 13.5 million foreign-born people in the American population, in contrast to about 22.5 million in 1994. Historians know a great deal about those earlier immigrants—why they came, how they ended up, what their impact was on the America of their day. Whether America's historical experience with immigration provides a useful guide to thinking about the present case is the principal question I want to address. I want not only to explore the substantive issue of immigration but also to test the proposition that the discipline of history has some value as a way of knowing and thinking about the world.

With respect to immigration itself, I intend to explore two sets of questions.

- Why did people migrate to America in the past, and what were the consequences, for them and for American society, once they landed?
- Why are people migrating to America today, and what might be the con-

sequences, for them and for American society, of their presence in such numbers?

The Pull of America

6 A generation or two ago upbeat answers to the first pair of questions so pervaded the culture that they cropped up in the most exotic places—in Tunisia, for example, on July 9, 1943. The occasion was the eve of the invasion of Sicily, and General George S. Patton Jr. was addressing his troops, who were about to embark for the battle. He urged, "When we land, we will meet German and Italian soldiers whom it is our honor and privilege to attack and destroy. Many of you have in your veins German and Italian blood, but remember that these ancestors of yours so loved freedom that they gave up home and country to cross the ocean in search of liberty. The ancestors of the people we shall kill lacked the courage to make such a sacrifice and continued as slaves."

7   In his own inimitable idiom Patton was invoking what for most Americans was—and still is—the standard explanation of who their immigrant forebears were, why they left their old countries, and what was their effect on American society. In this explanation immigrants were the main-chance-seeking and most energetic, entrepreneurial, and freedom-loving members of their Old World societies. They were drawn out of Europe by the irresistible magnet of American opportunity and liberty, and their galvanizing influence on American society made this country the greatest in the world.

8   A radically different explanation of immigration has also historically been at work in the American mind. As the noted social scientist Edward Alsworth Ross put it in 1914:

9   Observe immigrants not as they come travel-wan up the gang-plank, nor as they issue toil-begrimed from pit's mouth or mill-gate, but in their gatherings, washed, combed, and in their Sunday best. . . . [They] are hirsute, low-browed, big-faced persons of obviously low mentality. . . . They simply look out of place in black clothes and stiff collar, since clearly they belong in skins, in wattled huts at the close of the Great Ice Age. These ox-like men are descendants of those who always stayed behind.

10 Ross was describing in these invidious terms what he and his turn-of-the-century contemporaries called the "new" immigrants—new because they came predominantly from eastern and southern Europe, as distinct from the "old," early-and-mid-nineteenth-century immigrants, who had come mainly from northern and western Europe. Ironically, Ross was also talking about the parents of those very troops (at least the Italian-American troops) whom Patton addressed in 1943.

Between those two poles of explanation American views of immigration 11
have oscillated. On the one hand, as Patton reminds us, immigrants were
judged to be noble souls, tugged by the lodestone of American opportunity,
whose talents and genius and love of liberty account for the magnificent
American character. On the other hand, as in Ross's view, especially if they
had the misfortune to arrive on a more recent boat, immigrants were thought
to be degraded, freeloading louts, a blight on the national character and a
drain on the economy—the kind of people described all too literally, so the argument goes, by Emma Lazarus's famous inscription on the base of the Statue
of Liberty: "your tired, your poor . . . the wretched refuse of your teeming
shore."

Yet for all their differences, the two views have several things in common. 12
Both explain immigration in terms of the moral character of immigrants.
Both understand immigration as a matter of individual choice. And both implicitly invoke the American magnet as the irresistible force that put people in
motion, drawing them either to opportunity or to dependency.

Those concepts do not bear close analysis as adequate explanations for the 13
movement of some 35 million human beings over the course of a century. This
was a historical phenomenon too huge and too specific in time to be sufficiently
accounted for by summing 35 million decisions supposedly stimulated by the
suddenly irresistible gravitational attraction of a far-off continent.

The Push of Europe

For the first three centuries or so after the European discovery of the New 14
World the principal source of immigrants to the two American continents
and the Caribbean was not Europe but Africa. Only in the early nineteenth century did the accumulated total of European settlers in the New
World exceed the approximately 10 million Africans who had made the
trans-Atlantic voyage in the years since 1492. To explain the African dias-
pora by citing entrepreneurial instincts, the love of democracy, or the
freely chosen decisions of migrants to follow the lodestar of American
promise would be a mockery. Clearly, the involuntary movement of those
10 million Africans is best explained not in terms of their individual characters and choices but in terms of the catastrophically disruptive expansion of large-scale plantation agriculture and its accursed corollary, large-
scale commercial slavery.

A comparable—though, to be sure, not identical—element of involuntari- 15
ness characterized emigration from nineteenth-century Europe. Any generalization about what prompted a phenomenon as long-lived and complicated as
the great European migration must, of course, be subject to many qualifications. All discussions of the migration process recognize both push and pull
factors. But at bottom the evidence convincingly supports the argument that

disruption is essential to the movement of people on such a scale. And, as in the African case, the best, most comprehensive explanation for a process that eventually put some 35 million people in motion is to be found in two convulsively disruptive developments that lay far beyond the control of individual Europeans. Those developments had their historical dynamic within the context of European, not American, history.

16   The first of these needs little elaboration. It was, quite simply, population growth. In the nineteenth century the population of Europe more than doubled, from some 200 million to more than 400 million, even after about 70 million people had left Europe altogether. (Only half of these, it should be noted, went to the United States—one among many clues that the American-magnet explanation is inadequate.) That population boom was the indispensable precondition for Europe to export people on the scale that it did. And the boom owed little to American stimulus; rather, it was a product of aspects of European historical evolution, especially improvements in diet, sanitation, and disease control.

17   The second development was more complex, but we know it by a familiar name: the Industrial Revolution. It includes the closely associated revolution in agricultural productivity. Wherever it occurred, the Industrial Revolution shook people loose from traditional ways of life. It made factory workers out of artisans and, even more dramatically, turned millions of rural farmers into urban wage-laborers. Most of those migrants from countryside to city, from agriculture to industry, remained within their country of origin, or at least within Europe. But in the early stages of industrialization the movement of people, like the investment of capital during the unbridled early days of industrialism, was often more than what the market could bear. In time most European societies reached a kind of equilibrium, absorbing their own workers into their own wage markets. But in the typical transitional phase some workers who had left artisanal or agricultural employments could not be reabsorbed domestically in European cities. They thus migrated overseas.

18   The large scholarly literature documenting this process might be summarized as follows: Imagine a map of Europe. Across this map a time line traces the evolution of the Industrial Revolution. From a point in the British Isles in the late eighteenth century the line crosses to the Low Countries and Germany in the early and mid nineteenth century and to eastern and southern Europe in the late nineteenth and early twentieth centuries. Across the same map a second line traces the chronological evolution of migration to the United States. As it happens, the two lines are almost precisely congruent—migration came principally from the British Isles in the eighteenth and early nineteenth centuries, then mainly from Germany, and finally from the great watersheds of the Vistula and the Danube and the mountain ranges of the Apennines and Carpathians to the south and east.

The congruence of those lines is not coincidental. Industrialization, in   19
this view, is *the* root cause and the most powerful single variable explaining
the timing, the scale, the geographic evolution, and the composition of the
great European migration.

For another perspective on the importance of understanding the Eu-   20
ropean migration from a European point of view, consider the lyrics of a
nineteenth-century Italian folk song called "The Wives of the Americans."
In this case, the "Americans" were men who had gone off to America and
left their wives behind in Italy—specifically, the southern region of Cam-
pania. In fact, men, young men in particular, predominated in the nineteenth-century migratory stream, and their predominance constitutes a reliable indicator of their purposes. Many of them never intended to settle
permanently elsewhere but hoped to work abroad for a time and eventually return to the old country. Repatriation rates for European immigrants
averaged nearly 40 percent. Only the Jews and the Irish did not go home
again in significant numbers. For some later, "new" immigrant groups, especially from the southern Danube regions, repatriation rates ran as high
as 80 percent.

The song describes the wives of the Americans going to church and pray-   21
ing, "Send money, my husband. Send more money. The money you sent earlier I have already spent. I spent it on my lover. I spent it with pleasure. Send
more money, you *cornuto fottuto* [damnable cuckold]." Those lyrics conjure an
image of immigration quite different from the one General Patton urged on
his Italian-American troops in 1943. Together with the figures on repatriation, they offer a strong corrective to uncritical reliance on the American-magnet explanation for the past century's European migration.

The Immigrants in America

What happened to European immigrants, and to American society, once they   22
arrived? Much historical inquiry on this point focuses on immigrant hardship
and on recurrent episodes of nativism, anti-Semitism, anti-Catholicism, and
anti-foreign-radicalism, from the Know-Nothing movement of the 1850s to
the American Protective Association of the late nineteenth century and the
revived Ku Klux Klan of the early twentieth century, culminating in the highly
restrictive immigration legislation of the 1920s. Those are important elements
in the history of American immigration, and we would forget them at our
peril. But getting the question right is the most challenging part of any historical investigation, and there is an analytically richer question to be asked
than Why did immigrants meet sometimes nasty difficulties?

An even more intriguing question is How did tens of millions of new-   23
comers manage to accommodate themselves to America, and America to
them, without more social disruption? How can we explain this society's rela-

tive success—and success I believe it was—in making space so rapidly for so many people?

24   The explanation is surely not wise social policy. Beyond minimal monitoring at the ports of entry, no public policy addressed the condition of immigrants once they were cleared off Castle Garden or Ellis Island. But three specific historical circumstances, taken together, go a long way toward composing an answer to the question.

25   First, somewhat surprisingly, for all their numbers, immigrants—even the 17 million who arrived from 1890 to 1914—never made up a very large component of the already enormous society that was turn-of-the-century America. The census of 1910 records the highest percentage of foreign-born people ever resident in the United States: 14.7 percent. Now, 14.7 percent is not a trivial proportion, but it is a decided minority, and relative to other societies that have received large numbers of immigrants, a small minority. The comparable figures in Australia and Canada at approximately the same time were 17 percent and more than 20 percent, and even higher in Argentina. So here is one circumstance accounting for the relative lack of social conflict surrounding immigration a century ago: at any given moment immigrants were a relatively small presence in the larger society.

26   A second circumstance was economic. Immigrants supplied the labor that a growing economy urgently demanded. What is more, economic growth allowed the accommodation of newcomers without forcing thorny questions of redistribution—always the occasion for social contest and upheaval. Here, as so often in American history, especially during the period of heavy immigration before the First World War, economic growth worked as a pre-emptive solution to potential social conflict.

27   The third circumstance was more complicated than sheer numbers or economic growth. I call this circumstance "pluralism"—by which I mean simply that the European immigrant stream was remarkably variegated in its cultural, religious, national, and linguistic origins. These many subcurrents also distributed themselves over an enormous geographic region—virtually the entire northeastern quadrant of the United States—and through several political jurisdictions. By the 1920s immigrants were distributed widely across the great industrial belt that stretched from New England through New York, New Jersey, Pennsylvania, and beyond: Ohio, Indiana, Illinois, Michigan, Wisconsin, and Minnesota. The states with the most immigrants, not incidentally, also had per capita incomes higher than the national average—an important fact pertinent to understanding the relationship between immigration and economic vitality.

28   The varied composition and broad dispersal of the immigrant stream carried certain crucial implications, one being that no immigrant group could realistically aspire to preserve its Old World culture intact for more than a few

generations at best. To be sure, many groups made strenuous efforts to do just that. Legend to the contrary, last century's immigrants did not cast their Old World habits and languages overboard before their ship steamed into New York Harbor. In fact, many groups heroically exerted themselves to sustain their religions, tongues, and ways of life. The Catholic school system, which for a generation or two in some American cities educated nearly as many students as the public school system, eloquently testified to the commitment of some immigrant communities to resist assimilation. But circumstances weighed heavily against the success of such efforts. The virtual extinction of the parochial school system in the past generation—the empty schools and dilapidated parish buildings that litter the inner cores of the old immigrant cities—bears mute witness both to the ambition and to the ultimate failure of those efforts to maintain cultural distinctiveness.

A second and no less important implication of pluralism was that neither 29 any single immigrant group nor immigrants as a whole could realistically mount any kind of effective challenge to the existing society's way of doing things. No single group had sufficient weight in any jurisdiction larger than a municipality to dictate a new political order. And there was little likelihood that Polish Jews and Italian Catholics and Orthodox Greeks could find a common language, much less common ground for political action.

To recapitulate: The most comprehensive explanation of the causes of im- 30 migration a century ago is to be found in the disruptions visited on European society by population growth and the Industrial Revolution. The United States was, to use the language of the law, the incidental beneficiary of that upheaval. The swelling immigrant neighborhoods in turn-of-the-century American cities were, in effect, by-products of the urbanization of Europe. And once landed in America, immigrants accommodated themselves to the larger society—not always easily assimilating, but at least working out a modus vivendi—without the kinds of conflicts that have afflicted other multinational societies. That mostly peaceful process of accommodation came about because of the relatively small numbers of immigrants at any given time, because of the health of the economy, and because of the constraints on alternatives to accommodation inherent in the plural and dispersed character of the immigrant stream.

Having lit this little lamp of historical learning, I would like to carry it for- 31 ward and see if it can illuminate the present.

Today's Immigration

The biggest apparent novelty in current immigration is its source, or sources. 32 Well over half of the immigration of the past thirty years has come from just seven countries: Mexico, the Philippines, China (I am including Taiwan), Vietnam, Korea, India, and the Dominican Republic.

33   Not a single European country is on that list. Here, it would seem, is something new under the historical sun. Europe has dried up as a source of immigration and been replaced by new sources in Latin America and Asia.

34   And yet if we remember what caused the great European migration, the novelty of the current immigration stream is significantly diminished. Though particular circumstances vary, most of the countries now sending large numbers of immigrants to the United States are undergoing the same convulsive demographic and economic disruptions that made migrants out of so many nineteenth-century Europeans: population growth and the relatively early stages of their own industrial revolutions.

35   Mexico, by far the leading supplier of immigrants to the United States, conforms precisely to that pattern. Since the Second World War the Mexican population has more than tripled—a rate of growth that recollects, indeed exceeds, that of nineteenth-century Europe. And as in Europe a century ago, population explosion has touched off heavy internal migration, from rural to urban areas. By some reckonings, Mexico City has become the largest city in the world, with 20 million inhabitants and an in-migration from the Mexican countryside estimated at 1,000 people a day.

36   Also since the Second World War the Mexican economy, despite periodic problems, has grown at double the average rate of the U.S. economy. Rapid industrialization has been accompanied by the swift and widespread commercialization of Mexican agriculture. A Mexican "green revolution," flowing from improvements in mechanical processing, fertilizers, and insecticides, has in fact exacerbated the usual disruptions attendant on rapid industrialization: depopulation of the countryside, urban in-migration, and movement across the national border. But as in nineteenth-century Europe, most of the movement has been within Mexico itself. Since 1970 some five million Mexicans have entered the United States to stay; probably more than 10 million have moved to Mexico City alone.

37   Thus we are in the presence of a familiar historical phenomenon, impelled by developments that are for all practical purposes identical to those that ignited the great European migration of a century ago.

What Does the Future Hold?

38   If the causes of present-day immigration are familiar, what will be the consequences for today's immigrants and tomorrow's America?

39   I have suggested that three historical circumstances eased the accommodation between immigrants and the American society of a century ago—the relatively small number of immigrants present at any given time, the needs and vitality of the economy, and the plural and distributed character of the immigrant stream. How do those factors weigh in an analysis of immigration today?

40   With respect to numbers, the historical comparison gives a basis for con-

fidence that the answer to our original question—Can we still afford to be a nation of immigrants?—is yes. The U.S. Census Bureau reports that as of 1994 foreign-born people represented 8.7 percent of the American population, or just a bit more than half the proportion they made up in the census of 1910. (Comparable recent numbers for Canada and Australia, incidentally, are approximately 16 percent and 22 percent.) So, with reference to both American historical experience and contemporary experience in other countries, the *relative* incidence of current immigration to the United States is rather modest. Surely the United States at the end of the twentieth century is resourceful enough to deal with an immigrant inflow proportionally half what American society managed to deal with quite successfully in the early years of this century.

With reference to the needs and vitality of the economy, the historical   41 comparison is more complicated. Economic theory suggests that immigration is a bargain for any receiving society, because it augments the labor supply, one of the three principal factors of production (along with land and capital), essentially free of cost. The sending society bears the burden of feeding and raising a worker to the age when he or she can enter the labor market. If at that point the person emigrates and finds productive employment elsewhere, the source society has in effect subsidized the economy of the host society. That scenario essentially describes the historical American case, in which fresh supplies of immigrant labor underwrote the nation's phenomenal industrial surge in the half century after the Civil War.

The theory is subject to many qualifications. Unskilled immigrant work-   42 ers may indeed increase gross economic output, as they did from the Pittsburgh blast furnaces to the Chicago packinghouses a century ago, and as they do today in garment shops and electronic assembly plants from Los Angeles to Houston. But as productivity has become more dependent on knowledge and skill, the net value of unskilled immigrant labor has decreased, a point that informs much of the current case for restricting immigration. Yet it is important to note that argument on this point turns on the *relative* contribution of low-skill workers to overall output; the theory is still unimpeachable in its insistence on the *absolute* value of an additional worker, from whatever source, immigrant or native. Nevertheless, large numbers of unskilled immigrants may in the long run retard still higher potential outputs, because the inexpensive labor supply that they provide diminishes incentives to substitute capital and improved technology for labor, and thus inhibits productivity gains. On the other hand, just to complicate the calculation further, insofar as the host society continues to need a certain amount of low-skill work done, the availability of unskilled immigrants may *increase* the economy's overall efficiency by freeing significant numbers of better-educated native workers to pursue higher-productivity employment. And overhanging all this part of the immigration debate is the question of whose ox is gored. Low-skill immigrants may benefit the economy as a whole, but may at the same time impose substantial hardships on the low-skill native workers with whom they are in direct competition for jobs and wages.

43   Of course, the theory that immigration subsidizes the host economy is true only insofar as the immigrant in question is indeed a worker, a positive contributor to the productive apparatus of the destination society. Even the crude American immigration-control system of the nineteenth century recognized that fact, when it barred people likely to become social dependents, such as the chronically ill or known criminals. The issue of dependency is particularly vexatious in the United States today for two reasons. First, the 1965 legislation contained generous clauses providing for "family reunification," under the terms of which a significant portion of current immigrants are admitted not as workers but as the spouses, children, parents, and siblings of citizens or legally resident aliens. In 1993, a typical year, fewer than 20 percent of immigrants entered under "employment-based" criteria.

44   Because of family-reunification provisions, the current immigrant population differs from previous immigrant groups in at least two ways: it is no longer predominantly male and, even more strikingly, it is older. The percentage of immigrants over sixty-five exceeds the percentage of natives in that age group, and immigrants over sixty-five are two and a half times as likely as natives to be dependent on Supplemental Security Income, the principal federal program making cash payments to the indigent elderly. Newspaper accounts suggest that some families have brought their relatives here under the family-reunification provisions in the law expressly for the purpose of gaining access to SSI. Thus it appears that the availability of welfare programs—programs that did not exist a century ago—has combined with the family-reunification provisions to create new incentives for immigration that complicate comparisons of the economics of immigration today with that in the nineteenth century.

45   But on balance, though today's low-skill immigrants may not contribute as weightily to the economy as did their European counterparts a hundred years ago, and though some do indeed end up dependent on public assistance, as a group they make a positive economic contribution nevertheless. It is no accident that today's immigrants are concentrated in the richest states, among them California (home to fully one third of the country's immigrant population), just as those of the 1920s were. And just as in that earlier era, immigrants are not parasitic on the "native" economy but productive participants in it. The principal motivation for immigration remains what it was in the past: the search for productive employment. Most immigrants come in search of work, and most find it. Among working-age males, immigrant labor-force-participation rates and unemployment rates are statistically indistinguishable from those for native workers. The ancient wisdom still holds: *Ubi est pane, ibi*

est patria ("Where there is bread, there is my country"). Not simply geography but also that powerful economic logic explains why Mexico is the principal contributor of immigrants to the United States today: the income gap between the United States and Mexico is the largest between any two contiguous countries in the world.

One study, by the Stanford economist Clark W. Reynolds, estimated the 46 future labor-market characteristics and prospects for economic growth in Mexico and the United States. For Mexico to absorb all the new potential entrants into its own labor markets, Reynolds concluded, its economy would have to grow at the improbably high rate of some seven percent a year. The United States, in contrast, if its economy is to grow at a rate of three percent a year, must find somewhere between five million and 15 million more workers than can be supplied by domestic sources. Reynolds's conclusion was obvious: Mexico and the United States need each other, the one to ease pressure on its employment markets, the other to find sufficient labor to sustain acceptable levels of economic growth. If Reynolds is right, the question with which I began—Can we still afford to be a nation of immigrants?—may be wrongly put. The proper question may be Can we afford *not* to be? (For another perspective on this question see this month's article by George J. Borjas.)

The Reconquista

But if economic necessity requires that the United States be a nation of im- 47 migrants into the indefinite future, as it has been for so much of its past, some important questions remain. Neither men nor societies live by bread alone, and present-day immigration raises historically unprecedented issues in the cultural and political realms.

Pluralism—the variety and dispersal of the immigrant stream—made it eas- 48 ier for millions of European immigrants to accommodate themselves to American society. Today, however, one large immigrant stream is flowing into a defined region from a single cultural, linguistic, religious, and national source: Mexico. Mexican immigration is concentrated heavily in the Southwest, particularly in the two largest and most economically and politically influential states—California and Texas. Hispanics, including Central and South Americans but predominantly Mexicans, today compose 28 percent of the population of Texas and about 31 percent of the population of California. More than a million Texans and more than three million Californians were born in Mexico. California alone holds nearly half of the Hispanic population, and well over half of the Mexican-origin population, of the entire country.

This Hispanicization of the American Southwest is sometimes called the 49 Reconquista, a poetic reminder that the territory in question was, after all, incorporated into the United States in the first place by force of arms, in the Mexican War of the 1840s. There is a certain charm in this turn of the wheel of history, with its reminder that in the long term the drama of armed conquest may be less consequential than the prosaic effects of human migration and birth rates and wage differentials. But the sobering fact is that the United States has had no experience comparable to what is now taking shape in the Southwest.

50   Mexican-Americans will have open to them possibilities closed to previous immigrant groups. They will have sufficient coherence and critical mass in a defined region so that, if they choose, they can preserve their distinctive culture indefinitely. They could also eventually undertake to do what no previous immigrant group could have dreamed of doing: challenge the existing cultural, political, legal, commercial, and educational systems to change fundamentally not only the language but also the very institutions in which they do business. They could even precipitate a debate over a "special relationship" with Mexico that would make the controversy over the North American Free Trade Agreement look like a college bull session. In the process, Americans could be pitched into a soul-searching redefinition of fundamental ideas such as the meaning of citizenship and national identity.

51   All prognostications about these possibilities are complicated by another circumstance that has no precedent in American immigration history: the region of Mexican immigrant settlement in the southwestern United States is contiguous with Mexico itself. That proximity may continuously replenish the immigrant community, sustaining its distinctiveness and encouraging its assertiveness. Alternatively, the nearness of Mexico may weaken the community's coherence and limit its political and cultural clout by chronically attenuating its members' permanence in the United States, as the accessibility of the mother country makes for a kind of perpetual repatriation process.

52   In any case, there is no precedent in American history for these possibilities. No previous immigrant group had the size and concentration and easy access to its original culture that the Mexican immigrant group in the Southwest has today. If we seek historical guidance, the closest example we have to hand is in the diagonally opposite corner of the North American continent, in Quebec. The possibility looms that in the next generation or so we will see a kind of Chicano Quebec take shape in the American Southwest, as a group emerges with strong cultural cohesiveness and sufficient economic and political strength to insist on changes in the overall society's ways of organizing itself and conducting its affairs.

53   Public debate over immigration has already registered this prospect, however faintly. How else to explain the drive in Congress, and in several states, to make English the "official" language for conducting civil business? In previous eras no such legislative muscle was thought necessary to expedite the process of immigrant acculturation, because alternatives to eventual acculturation were simply unimaginable. Less certain now that the traditional incen-

tives are likely to do the work of assimilation, we seem bent on trying a *ukase*—a ham-handed and provocative device that may prove to be the opening chapter of a script for prolonged cultural warfare. Surely our goal should be to help our newest immigrants, those from Mexico especially, to become as well integrated in the larger American society as were those European "new" immigrants whom E. A. Ross scorned but whose children's patriotism George Patton could take for granted. To reach that goal we will have to be not only more clever than our ancestors were but also less confrontational, more generous, and more welcoming than our current anxieties sometimes incline us to be.

The present may echo the past, but will not replicate it. Yet the fact that 54 events have moved us into *terra nova et incognita* does not mean that history is useless as a way of coming to grips with our situation. To the contrary, the only way we can know with certainty as we move along time's path that we have come to a genuinely new place is to know something of where we have been. "What's new in the starry sky, dear Argelander?" Kaiser Wilhelm I is said to have asked his state astronomer, to which Argelander replied, "And does Your Majesty already know the old?" Knowing the old is the project of historical scholarship, and only that knowledge can reliably point us toward the new. As Lincoln also said, "As our case is new, so we must think anew, and act anew. We must disenthrall ourselves, and then we shall save our country."

Patricia Kean

Blowing Up the Tracks

Patricia Kean is a writer whose works have appeared in *Lingua Franca,* the *New York Times,* and the *Washington Monthly,* where this essay was first printed. She received her B.A. from Georgetown University, and an M.A. from the University of Wisconsin at Madison. She now writes on education issues for a variety of publications. In this essay, she focuses on the effects of "tracking" students into separate courses based on ability.

IT'S MORNING IN NEW YORK, and some seventh graders are more equal than 1
others.

Class 7–16 files slowly into the room, prodded by hard-faced men whose 2
walkie-talkies crackle with static. A pleasant looking woman shouts over the
din, "What's rule number one?" No reply. She writes on the board. "Rule
One: Sit down."

Rule number two seems to be an unwritten law: Speak slowly. Each of 3

Mrs. H's syllables hangs in the air a second longer than necessary. In fact, the entire class seems to be conducted at 16 RPM. Books come out gradually. Kids wander about the room aimlessly. Twelve minutes into class, we settle down and begin to play "O. Henry Jeopardy," a game which requires students to supply one-word answers to questions like: "'O. Henry moved from North Carolina to what state—Andy? Find the word on the page.'"

4   The class takes out a vocabulary sheet. Some of the words they are expected to find difficult include: popular, ranch, suitcase, arrested, recipe, tricky, ordinary, humorous, and grand jury.

5   Thirty minutes pass. Bells ring, doors slam.

6   Class 7-1 marches in unescorted, mindful of rule number one. Paperbacks of Poe smack sharply on desks, notebooks rustle, and kids lean forward expectantly, waiting for Mrs. H. to fire the first question. What did we learn about the writer?

7   Hands shoot into the air. Though Edgar Allan Poe ends up sounding a lot like Jerry Lee Lewis—a booze-hound who married his 13-year-old cousin—these kids speak confidently, in paragraphs. Absolutely no looking at the book allowed.

8   We also have a vocabulary sheet, drawn from "The Tell-Tale Heart," containing words like: audacity, dissimulation, sagacity, stealthy, anxiety, derision, agony, and supposition.

9   As I sit in the back of the classroom watching these two very different groups of seventh graders, my previous life as an English teacher allows me to make an educated guess and a chilling prediction. With the best of intentions, Mrs. H. is teaching the first group, otherwise known as the "slow kids," as though they are fourth graders, and the second, the honors group, as though they are high school freshmen. Given the odds of finding a word like "ordinary" on the SAT's, the children of 7-16 have a better chance of standing before a "grand jury" than making it to college.

10   Tracking, the practice of placing students in "ability groups" based on a host of ill-defined criteria—everything from test scores to behavior to how much of a fuss a mother can be counted on to make—encourages even well-meaning teachers and administrators to turn out generation after generation of self-fulfilling prophecies. "These kids know they're no Einsteins," Mrs. H. said of her low-track class when we sat together in the teacher's lounge. "They know they don't read well. This way I can go really slowly with them."

11   With his grades, however, young Albert would probably be hanging right here with the rest of lunch table 7-16. That's where I discover that while their school may think they're dumb, these kids are anything but stupid. "That teacher," sniffs a pretty girl wearing lots of purple lipstick. "She talks so slow. She thinks we're babies. She takes a year to do anything." "What about that other one?" a girl named Ingrid asks, referring to their once-a-

week student teacher. "He comes in and goes like this: Rail (pauses) road. Rail (pauses) road. Like we don't know what railroad means!" The table breaks up laughing.

Outside the walls of schools across the country, it's slowly become an open secret that enforced homogeneity benefits no one. The work of researchers like Jeannie Oakes of UCLA and Robert Slavin of Johns Hopkins has proven that tracking does not merely reflect differences—it causes them. Over time, slow kids get slower, while those in the middle and in the so-called "gifted and talented" top tracks fail to gain from isolation. Along the way, the practice re-segregates the nation's schools, dividing the middle from the lower classes, white from black and brown. As the evidence piles up, everyone from the Carnegie Corporation to the National Governors Association has called for change. 12

Though some fashionably progressive schools have begun to reform, tracking persists. Parent groups, school boards, teachers, and administrators who hold the power within schools cling to the myths and wax apocalyptic about the horrors of heterogeneity. On their side is the most potent force known to man: bureaucratic inertia. Because tracking puts kids in boxes, keeps the lid on, and shifts responsibility for mediocrity and failure away from the schools themselves, there is little incentive to change a nearly-century old tradition. "Research is research," the principal told me that day, "This is practice." 13

Back Track

Tracking has been around since just after the turn of the century. It was then, as cities teemed with immigrants and industry, that education reformers like John Franklin Bobbitt began to argue that the school and the factory shared a common mission, to "work up the raw material into that finished product for which it was best adapted." By the twenties, the scientific principles that ruled the factory floor had been applied to the classroom. They believed the IQ test—which had just become popular—allowed pure science, not the whims of birth or class, to determine whether a child received the type of education appropriate for a future manager or a future laborer. 14

It hasn't quite worked out that way. Driven by standardized tests, the descendants of the old IQ tests, tracking has evolved into a kind of educational triage premised on the notion that only the least wounded can be saved. Yet when the classroom operates like a battleground, society's casualties mount, and the results begin to seem absurd: Kids who enter school needing more get less, while the already enriched get, well, enricher. Then, too, the low-track graduates of 70 years ago held a distinct advantage over their modern counterparts: If tracking prepared them for mindless jobs, at least those jobs existed. 15

16   The sifting and winnowing starts as early as pre-K. Three-year-old Ebony and her classmates have won the highly prized "gifted and talented" label after enduring a battery of IQ and psychological tests. There's nothing wrong with the "regular" class in this Harlem public school. But high expectations for Ebony and her new friends bring tangible rewards like a weekly field trip and music and computer lessons.

17   Meanwhile, regular kids move on to regular kindergartens where they too will be tested, and where it will be determined that some children need more help, perhaps a "pre-first grade" developmental year. So by the time they're ready for first grade reading groups, certain six-year-olds have already been marked as "sparrows"—the low performers in the class.

18   In the beginning, it doesn't seem to matter so much, because the other reading groups—the robins and the eagles—are just a few feet away and the class is together for most of the day. Trouble is, as they toil over basic drill sheets, the sparrows are slipping farther behind. The robins are gathering more challenging vocabulary words, and the eagles soaring on to critical thinking skills.

19   Though policies vary, by fourth grade many of these groups have flown into completely separate classrooms, turning an innocent three-tier reading system into three increasingly rigid academic tracks—honors, regular, and remedial—by middle school.

20   Unless middle school principals take heroic measures like buying expensive software or crafting daily schedules by hand, it often becomes a lot easier to sort everybody by reading scores. So kids who do well on reading tests can land in the high track for math, science, social studies, even lunch, and move together as a self-contained unit all day. Friendships form, attitudes harden. Kids on top study together, kids in the middle console themselves by making fun of the "nerds" above and the "dummies" below, and kids on the bottom develop behavioral problems and get plenty of negative reinforcement.

21   By high school, many low-track students are locked out of what Jeannie Oakes calls "gatekeeper courses," the science, math, and foreign language classes that hold the key to life after twelfth grade. Doors to college are slamming shut, though the kids themselves are often the last to know. When researcher Anne Wheelock interviewed students in Boston's public schools, they'd all insist they were going to become architects, teachers, and the like. What courses were they taking? "Oh, Keyboarding II, Earth Science, Consumer Math. This would be junior year and I'd ask, 'Are you taking Algebra?' and they'd say no."

Black Marks

22   A funny thing can happen to minority students on the way to being tracked. Even when minority children score high, they often find themselves placed in lower tracks where counselors and principals assume they belong.

In Paula Hart's travels for The Achievement Council, a Los Angeles-based   23
educational advocacy group, she comes across district after district where
black and Latino kids score in the 75th percentile for math, yet never quite
make it into Algebra I, the classic gatekeeper course. A strange phenomenon
occurs in inner city areas with large minority populations—high track classes
shrink, and low track classes expand to fit humble expectations for the entire
school population.

A few years ago, Dr. Norward Roussell's curiosity got the best of him. As   24
Selma, Alabama's first black school superintendent, he couldn't help but notice that "gifted and talented" tracks were nearly lily white in a district that
was 70 percent black. When he looked for answers in the files of high school
students, he discovered that a surprising number of low track minority kids
had actually scored higher than their white top track counterparts.

Parents of gifted and talented students staged a full-scale revolt against   25
Roussell's subsequent efforts to establish logical standards for placement. In
four days of public hearings, speaker after speaker said the same thing: We're
going to lose a lot of our students to other schools. To Roussell, their meaning was clear: Put black kids in the high tracks and we pull white kids out of
the system. More blacks and more low-income whites did make it to the top
under the new criteria, but Roussell himself was left behind. The majority-
white school board chose not to renew his contract, and he's now superintendent in Macon County, Alabama, a district that is overwhelmingly black.

Race and class divisions usually play themselves out in a more subtle fash-   26
ion. Talk to teachers about how their high track kids differ from their low
track kids and most speak not of intelligence, but of motivation and "family."
It seems that being gifted and talented is hereditary after all, largely a matter
of having parents who read to you, who take you to museums and concerts,
and who know how to work the system. Placement is often a matter of who's
connected. Jennifer P., a teacher in a Brooklyn elementary school saw a pattern in her class. "The principal put all the kids whose parents were in the
PTA in the top tracks no matter what their scores were. He figures that if his
PTA's happy, he's happy."

Once the offspring of the brightest and the best connected have been   27
skimmed off in honors or regular tracks, low tracks begin to fill up with children whose parents are not likely to complain. These kids get less homework,
spend less class time learning, and are often taught by the least experienced
teachers, because avoiding them can become a reward for seniority in a profession where perks are few.

With the courts reluctant to get involved, even when tracking leads to racial   28
segregation and at least the appearance of civil rights violations, changing the
system becomes an arduous local battle fought school by school. Those who
undertake the delicate process of untracking need nerves of steel and should

be prepared to find resistance from every quarter, since, as Slavin notes, parents of high-achieving kids will fight this to the death. One-time guidance counselor Hart learned this lesson more than a decade ago when she and two colleagues struggled to introduce a now-thriving college curriculum program at Los Angeles' Banning High. Their efforts to open top-track classes to all students prompted death threats from an unlikely source—their fellow teachers.

Off Track Betting

29   Anne Wheelock's new book, *Crossing the Tracks*, tells the stories of schools that have successfully untracked or never tracked at all. Schools that make the transition often achieve dramatic results. True to its name, Pioneer Valley Regional school in Northfield, Massachusetts was one of the first in the nation to untrack. Since 1983, the number of Pioneer Valley seniors going on to higher education jumped from 37 to 80 percent. But, the author says, urban schools continue to lag behind. "We're talking about unequal distribution of reform," Wheelock declares. "Change is taking place in areas like Wellesley, Massachusetts and Jericho, Long Island. It's easier to untrack when kids are closer to one another to begin with."

30   It's also easier for educators to tinker with programs and make cosmetic adjustments than it is to ask them to do what bureaucrats hate most: give up one method of doing things without having another to put in its place. Tracking is a system; untracking is a leap of faith. When difficult kids can no longer be dumped in low tracks, new ways must be found to deal with disruptive behavior: early intervention, intensive work with families, and lots of tutoring. Untracking may also entail new instructional techniques like cooperative group learning and peer tutoring, but what it really demands is flexibility and improvisation.

31   It also demands that schools—and the rest of us—admit that some kids will be so disruptive or violent that a solution for dealing with them must be found *outside* of the regular public school system. New York City seems close to such a conclusion. Schools Chancellor Joseph Fernandez is moving forward with a voluntary "academy" program, planning separate schools designed to meet the needs of chronic troublemakers. One of them, the Wildcat Academy, run by a non-profit group of the same name, plans to enroll 150 students by the end of the year. Wildcat kids will attend classes from nine to five, wear uniforms, hold part-time jobs, and be matched with mentors from professional fields. Districts in Florida and California are conducting similar experiments.

32   Moving away from tracking is not about taking away from the gifted and talented and giving to the poor. That, as Wheelock notes, is "political suicide." It's not even about placing more black and Latino kids in their midst, a kind of pre-K affirmative action. Rather, it's about raising expectations for

everyone. Or, as Slavin puts it: "You can maintain your tracking system. Just put everyone into the top track."

That's not as quixotic as it sounds. In fact, it's long been standard practice 33
in the nation's Catholic schools, a system so backward it's actually progressive. When I taught in an untracked parochial high school, one size fit all—with the exception of the few we expelled for poor grades or behavior. My students, who differed widely in ability, interest, and background, nevertheless got Shakespeare, Thoreau, and Langston Hughes at the same pace, at the same time—and lived to tell the tale. Their survival came, in part, because my colleagues and I could decide if the cost of keeping a certain student around was too high and we had the option of sending him or her elsewhere if expulsion was warranted.

The result was that my honor students wrote elegant essays and made it to 34
Ivy League schools, right on schedule. And far from being held back by their "regular" and "irregular" counterparts, straight-A students were more likely to be challenged by questions they would never dream of asking. "Why are we studying this?" a big-haired girl snapping gum in the back of the room wondered aloud one day. Her question led to a discussion that turned into the best class I ever taught.

In four years, I never saw a single standardized test score. But time after 35
time I watched my students climb out of whatever mental category I had put them in. Tracking sees to it that they never get that chance. Flying directly in the face of Yogi Berra's rule Number One, it tells kids it's over before it's even begun. For ultimately, tracking stunts the opportunity for growth, the one area in which all children are naturally gifted.

Judith Ortiz Cofer

Advanced Biology

Born in 1952 in Puerto Rico, Judith Cofer moved to the U.S. with her family in 1956. Her poems and stories reflect her Hispanic heritage and her own struggle to live in two cultures. A collection of her personal essays and memoirs was published in 1990 as *Silent Dancing*, and the title essay was chosen for inclusion in *The Best American Essays of 1991*.

AS I LAY OUT CLOTHES FOR THE TRIP to Miami to do a reading from my recently 1
published novel, then on to Puerto Rico to see my mother, I take a close look at my travel wardrobe—the tailored skirts in basic colors easily coordinated

with my silk blouses—I have to smile to myself remembering what my mother had said about my conservative outfits when I visited her the last time—that I looked like the Jehovah's Witnesses who went from door to door in her pueblo trying to sell tickets to heaven to the die-hard Catholics. I would scare people she said. They would bolt their doors if they saw me approaching with my briefcase. As for her, she dresses in tropical colors—a red skirt and parakeet-yellow blouse look good on her tan skin, and she still has a good enough figure that she can wear a tight, black cocktail dress to go dancing at her favorite club, *El Palacio*, on Saturday nights. And, she emphasizes, still make it to the 10 o'clock mass on Sunday. Catholics can have fun and still be saved, she has often pointed out to me, but only if you pay your respects to God and all His Court with the necessary rituals. She has never accepted my gradual slipping out of the faith in which I was so strictly brought up.

2   As I pack my clothes into the suitcase, I recall our early days in Paterson, New Jersey, where we lived for most of my adolescence while my father was alive and stationed in Brooklyn Yard in New York. At that time, my mother's views on everything from clothing to (the forbidden subject) sex were ruled by the religious fervor that she had developed as a shield against the cold foreign city. These days we have traded places in a couple of areas since she has "gone home" after my father's death, and "gone native." I chose to attend college in the United States and make a living as an English teacher and, lately, on the lecture circuit as a novelist and poet. But, though our lives are on the surface radically different, my mother and I have affected each other reciprocally over the past twenty years; she has managed to liberate herself from the rituals, mores, and traditions that "cramp" her style, while retaining her femininity and "Puertoricanness," while I struggle daily to consolidate my opposing cultural identities. In my adolescence, divided into my New Jersey years and my Georgia years, I received an education in the art of cultural compromise.

3   In Paterson in the 1960s I attended a public school in our neighborhood. Still predominantly white and Jewish, it was rated very well academically in a city where the educational system was in chaos, deteriorating rapidly as the best teachers moved on to suburban schools following the black and Puerto Rican migration into, and the white exodus from, the city proper.

4   The Jewish community had too much at stake to make a fast retreat; many of the small businesses and apartment buildings in the city's core were owned by Jewish families of the World War II generation. They had seen worse things happen than the influx of black and brown people that was scaring away the Italians and the Irish. But they too would gradually move their families out of the best apartments in their buildings and into houses in East Paterson, Fairlawn, and other places with *lawns*. It was how I saw the world then; either you lived without your square of grass or you bought a house to go with it. But for

most of my adolescence, I lived among the Jewish people of Paterson. We rented an apartment owned by the Milsteins, proprietors also of the deli on the bottom floor. I went to school with their children. My father took his business to the Jewish establishments, perhaps because these men symbolized "dignified survival" to him. He was obsessed with privacy, and could not stand the personal turns conversations almost always took when two or more Puerto Ricans met casually over a store counter. The Jewish men talked too, but they concentrated on externals. They asked my father about his job, politics, his opinion on Vietnam, Lyndon Johnson. And my father, in his quiet voice, answered their questions knowledgeably. Sometimes before we entered a store, the cleaners, or a shoe-repair shop, he would tell me to look for the blue-inked numbers on the owner's left forearm. I would stare at these numbers, now usually faded enough to look like veins in the wrong place. I would try to make them out. They were a telegram from the past, I later decided, informing the future of the deaths of millions. My father discussed the Holocaust with me in the same hushed tones my mother used to talk about God's Mysterious Ways. I could not reconcile both in my mind. This conflict eventually led to my first serious clash with my mother over irreconcilable differences between the "real world" and religious doctrine.

It had to do with the Virgin Birth.   5

And it had to do with my best friend and study partner, Ira Nathan, the   6
acknowledged scientific genius at school. In junior high school it was almost a requirement to be "in love" with an older boy. I was an eighth grader and Ira was in the ninth grade that year and preparing to be sent away to some prep school in New England. I chose him as my boyfriend (in the eyes of my classmates, if a girl spent time with a boy that meant they were "going together") because I needed tutoring in biology—one of his best subjects. I ended up having a crush on him after our first Saturday morning meeting at the library. Ira was my first exposure to the wonders of an analytical mind.

The problem was the subject. Biology is a dangerous topic for young   7
teenagers who are themselves walking laboratories, experimenting with interesting combinations of chemicals every time they make a choice. In my basic biology class, we were looking at single-cell organisms under the microscope, and watching them reproduce in slow-motion films in a darkened classroom. Though the process was as unexciting as watching a little kid blow bubbles, we were aroused by the concept itself. Ira's advanced class was dissecting fetal pigs. He brought me a photograph of his project, inner organs labeled neatly on the paper the picture had been glued to. My eyes refused to budge from the line drawn from "genitals" to a part of the pig it pertained to. I felt a wave of heat rising from my chest to my scalp. Ira must have seen my discomfort, though I tried to keep my face behind the black curtain of my hair, but as the boy-scientist, he was relentless. He actually traced the line from label to pig with his pencil.

8   "All mammals reproduce sexually," he said in a teacherly monotone.

9   The librarian, far off on the other side of the room, looked up at us and frowned. Logically, it was not possible that she could have heard Ira's pronouncement, but I was convinced that the mention of sex enhanced the hearing capabilities of parents, teachers and librarians by one hundred percent. I blushed more intensely, and peeked through my hair at Ira.

10   He was holding the eraser of his pencil on the pig's blurry sexual parts and smiling at me. His features were distinctly Eastern European. I had recently seen the young singer Barbra Streisand on the Red Skelton show and had been amazed at how much similarity there was in their appearances. She could have been his sister. I was particularly attracted to the wide mouth and strong nose. No one that I knew in school thought that Ira was attractive, but his brains had long ago overshadowed his looks as his most impressive attribute. Like Ira, I was also a straight A student and also considered odd because I was one of the few Puerto Ricans on the honor roll. So it didn't surprise anyone that Ira and I had drifted toward each other. Though I could not have articulated it then, Ira was seducing me with his No. 2 pencil and the laboratory photograph of his fetal pig. The following Saturday, Ira brought in his advanced biology book and showed me the transparencies of the human anatomy in full color that I was not meant to see for a couple more years. I was shocked. The cosmic jump between paramecium and the human body was almost too much for me to take in. These were the first grown people I had ever seen naked and they revealed too much.

11   "Human sexual reproduction can only take place when the male's sperm is introduced into the female womb and fertilization of the egg takes place," Ira stated flatly.

12   The book was open to the page labeled "The Human Reproductive System." Feeling that my maturity was being tested, as well as my intelligence, I found my voice long enough to contradict Ira.

13   "There has been one exception to this, Ira." I was feeling a little smug about knowing something that Ira obviously did not.

14   "Judith, there are no exceptions in biology, only mutations, and adaptations through evolution." He was smiling in a superior way.

15   "The Virgin Mary had a baby without . . ." I couldn't say *having sex* in the same breath as the name of the Mother of God. I was totally unprepared for the explosion of laughter that followed my timid statement. Ira had crumpled in his chair and was laughing so hard that his thin shoulders shook. I could hear the librarian approaching. Feeling humiliated, I started to put my books together. Ira grabbed my arm.

16   "Wait, don't go," he was still giggling uncontrollably, "I'm sorry. Let's talk a little more. Wait, give me a chance to explain."

17   Reluctantly, I sat down again mainly because the librarian was already at

our table, hands on hips, whispering angrily: "If you *children* cannot behave in this *study area,* I will have to ask you to leave." Ira and I both apologized, though she gave him a nasty look because his mouth was still stretched from ear to ear in a hysterical grin.

"Listen, listen. I'm sorry that I laughed like that. I know you're Catholic 18 and you believe in the Virgin Birth (he bit his lower lip trying to regain his composure), but it's just not biologically possible to have a baby without . . . (he struggled for control) . . . losing your virginity."

I sank down on my hard chair. "Virginity." He had said another of the for- 19 bidden words. I glanced back at the librarian who was keeping her eye on us. I was both offended and excited by Ira's blasphemy. How could he deny a doctrine that people had believed in for 2,000 years? It was part of my prayers every night. My mother talked about La Virgen as if she were our most important relative.

Recovering from his fit of laughter, Ira kept his hand discreetly on my 20 elbow as he explained in the seductive language of the scientific laboratory how babies were made, and how it was impossible to violate certain natural laws.

"Unless God wills it," I argued feebly. 21

"There is no God," said Ira, and the last shred of my innocence fell away 22 as I listened to his arguments backed up by irrefutable scientific evidence.

Our meetings continued all that year, becoming more exciting with every 23 chapter in his biology book. My grades improved dramatically since one-celled organisms were no mystery to a student of advanced biology. Ira's warm, moist hand often brushed against mine under the table at the library, and walking home one bitter cold day, he asked me if I would wear his Beta Club pin. I nodded and when we stepped inside the hallway of my building where he removed his thick mittens which his mother had knitted, he pinned the blue enamel B to my collar. And to the hissing of the steam heaters, I received a serious kiss from Ira. We separated abruptly when we heard Mrs. Milstein's door open.

"Hello, Ira." 24

"Hello, Mrs. Milstein." 25

"And how is your mother? I haven't seen Fritzie all week. She's not sick, is 26 she?"

"She's had a mild cold, Mrs. Milstein. But she is steadily improving." Ira's 27 diction became extremely precise and formal when he was in the presence of adults. As an only child and a prodigy, he had to live up to very high standards.

"I'll call her today," Mrs. Milstein said, finally looking over at me. Her eyes 28 fixed on the collar of my blouse which was, I later saw in our hall mirror, sticking straight up with Ira's pin attached crookedly to the edge.

29   "Good-bye, Mrs. Milstein."

30   "Nice to see you, Ira."

31   Ira waved awkwardly to me as he left. Mrs. Milstein stood in the humid hallway of her building watching me run up the stairs.

32   Our "romance" lasted only a week; long enough for Mrs. Milstein to call Ira's mother, and for Mrs. Nathan to call my mother. I was subjected to a lecture on moral behavior by my mother, who, carried away by her anger and embarrassed that I had been seen kissing a boy (understood: a boy who was not even Catholic), had begun a chain of metaphors for the loss of virtue that was on the verge of the tragi/comical:

33   "A *perdida*, a cheap item," she said trembling before me as I sat on the edge of my bed, facing her accusations, "a girl begins to look like one when she allows herself to be *handled* by men."

34   "Mother . . ." I wanted her to lower her voice so that my father, sitting at the kitchen table reading, would not hear. I had already promised her that I would confess my sin that Saturday and take communion with a sparkling clean soul. I had not been successful at keeping the sarcasm out of my voice. Her fury was fueled by her own bitter litany.

35   "A dirty joke, a burden to her family . . ." She was rolling with her Spanish now; soon the Holy Mother would enter into the picture for good measure. "It's not as if I had not taught you better. Don't you know that those people do not have the example of the Holy Virgin Mary and her Son to follow and that is why they do things for the wrong reasons. Mrs. Nathan said she did not want her son messing around with you—not because of the wrongness of it—but because it would interfere with his studies!" She was yelling now. "She's afraid that he will (she crossed herself at the horror of the thought) make you pregnant!"

36   "We could say an angel came down and put a baby in my stomach, Mother." She had succeeded in dragging me into her field of hysteria. She grabbed my arm and pulled me to my feet.

37   "I do not want you associating any more than necessary with people who do not have God, do you hear me?"

38   "They have a god!" I was screaming now too, trying to get away from her suffocating grasp: "They have an intelligent god who doesn't ask you to believe that a woman can get pregnant without having sex!" That's when she slapped me. She looked horrified at what she had instinctively done.

39   "Nazi," I hissed, out of control by then too, "I bet you'd like to send Ira and his family to a concentration camp!" At that time I thought that was the harshest thing I could have said to anyone. I was certain that I had sentenced my soul to eternal damnation the minute the words came out of my mouth; but my cheek was burning from the slap and I wanted to hurt her. Father walked into my room at that moment looking shocked at the sight of the two of us entangled in mortal combat.

"Please, please," his voice sounded agonized. I ran to him and he held me   40
in his arms while I cried my heart out on his starched white shirt. My mother,
also weeping quietly, tried to walk past us, but he pulled her into the circle.
After a few moments, she put her trembling hand on my head.

"We are a family," my father said, "there is only the three of us against the   41
world. Please, please . . ." But he did not follow the "please" with any suggestions as to what we could do to make things right in a world that was as con-
fusing to my mother as it was to me.

I finished the eighth grade in Paterson, but Ira and I never got together to   42
study again. I sent his Beta club pin back to him via a mutual friend. Once in
a while I saw him in the hall or the playground. But he seemed to be in the
clouds, where he belonged. In the fall, I was enrolled at St. Joseph's Catholic
High School where everyone believed in the Virgin Birth, and I never had to
take a test on the human reproductive system. It was a chapter that was not
emphasized.

In 1968, the year Paterson, like many U.S. cities, exploded in racial vio-   43
lence, my father moved us to Augusta, Georgia, where two of his brothers had
retired from the army at Fort Gordon. They had convinced him that it was a
healthier place to rear teenagers. For me it was a shock to the senses, like moving from one planet to another: where Paterson had concrete to walk on and
gray skies, bitter winters, and a smorgasbord of an ethnic population, Georgia
was red like Mars, and Augusta was green—exploding in colors in more gardens of azaleas and dogwood and magnolia trees—more vegetation than I
imagined was possible anywhere not tropical like Puerto Rico. People seemed
to come in two basic colors: black and blond. And I could barely understand
my teachers when they talked in a slowed-down version of English like one of
those old 78-speed recordings played at 33. But I was placed in all advanced
classes and one of them was biology. This is where I got to see my first real
fetal pig which my assigned lab partner had chosen. She picked it up gingerly
by the ends of the plastic bag in which it was stored: "Ain't he cute?" she asked.
I nodded, nearly fainting from the overwhelming combination of the smell of
formaldehyde and my sudden flashback to my brief but intense romance with
Ira Nathan.

"What you want to call him?" My partner unwrapped our specimen on the   44
table, and I surprised myself by my instant recall of Ira's chart. I knew all the
parts. In my mind's eye I saw the pencil lines, the labeled photograph. I had
had an excellent teacher.

"Let's call him Ira."   45

"That's a funny name, but OK." My lab partner, a smart girl destined to be-   46
come my mentor in things Southern, then gave me a conspiratorial wink and
pulled out a little perfume atomizer from her purse. She sprayed Ira from snout
to tail with it. I noticed this operation was taking place at other tables too. The

teacher had conveniently left the room a few minutes before. I was once again stunned—almost literally knocked out by a fist of smell: "What is it?"

47   "*Intimate,*" my advanced biology partner replied smiling.

48   And by the time our instructor came back to the room, we were ready to delve into this mystery of muscle and bone; eager to discover the secrets that lie just beyond fear a little past loathing; of acknowledging the corruptibility of the flesh, and our own fascination with the subject.

49   As I finish packing, the telephone rings and it's my mother. She is reminding me to be ready to visit relatives, to go to a dance with her, and, of course, to attend a couple of the services at the church. It is the feast of the Black Virgin, revered patron saint of our home town in Puerto Rico. I agree to everything, and find myself anticipating the eclectic itinerary. Why not allow Evolution and Eve, Biology and the Virgin Birth? Why not take a vacation from logic? I will not be away for too long, I will not let myself be tempted to remain in the sealed garden of blind faith; I'll stay just long enough to rest myself from the exhausting enterprise of leading the examined life.

Student Essay

Benjamin James

Complaining Through College

Assigned to write an essay comparing two different periods in life, Benjamin took some inspiration from Judith Cofer's "Advanced Biology." However, unlike Cofer, Benjamin chose to show how his changing family situation affected his school life. The result is a simple but strong statement about the evolution of his own attitude toward his education.

1   ALL COLLEGE STUDENTS COMPLAIN: complaining is the unique feature that binds all of us through all of our many differences. As a college student, I complain too—but my complaints now take much different shape from the first time I went to college.

2   Then, I complained about homework, about how professors just didn't seem to understand that students are enrolled in four classes, that we couldn't

center our lives around just one class. Professors would inevitably coordinate their assignments so I had a paper due in each of my classes on the same day. When you combine the pressures of a work study job, having a decent social life, and participating in the school newspaper, it's simply unreasonable to ask students to write four papers in a week.

I complained about my social life. All the best looking females were dating 3 juniors and seniors, sometimes even graduate students. How's a freshman guy going to compete with that? Certainly there was no way the older women were going to give me the time of day. Parties were no place to meet people. Sure, you could dance and have fun with your friends, but no one would give a stranger a second look.

I complained about my job. I had the most boring job on campus—data 4 entry in the Accounts Payable Department. Everyone who worked there was so bored by their job that they simply went through the motions. There was certainly no opportunity to do homework. The work was so boring that the boss made an unwritten rule that everyone could leave at 4:45 (even though we were paid to work until 5:00). Anyone who stayed even a few minutes late to finish up a task was branded a workaholic.

So I quit school.   5

Now, four years later, I'm back in school, but I'm married with a 6-month- 6 old baby. My wife works during the day, so I'm taking care of the baby then. I go to night school while she feeds and bathes the baby and puts her to bed. I'm still complaining, but my complaints are entirely different from when I was a single college student.

I don't complain about my homework—homework is the one thing in my 7 life I have the most control over. It's amazing how much studying you can do in three hours a day—when you know that's the only three hours you'll get. I don't complain about my social life. What social life do you need when you're happily married with a beautiful baby, and family and friends constantly drop by to coo? I don't complain about my job. What work I do I enjoy—freelance typesetting for a local printer, while the baby naps.

So what do I complain about now? Well, the price of baby formula, for 8 one. And how my baby just doesn't seem to understand that she shouldn't stay up all night crying when Daddy has a big exam the next day. I can't stand it when people aren't open-minded about our nonconventional lifestyle. I cringe when people suggest that I can't take care of a baby as well as her mother does. I seethe when they call me "Mr. Mom." In fact, the people who seem to understand my unusual life best of all are my fellow college students. They, like me, are juggling an entirely unreasonable assortment of seemingly incompatible responsibilities. They, like me, have a great, big, long, wonderful life ahead of them—if only they can first finish those two papers that are due next Friday!

Suzanne Britt

Neat People vs. Sloppy People

Suzanne Britt graduated from Salem Academy in college and earned her Master's degree in English from Washington University in St. Louis. She is now teaching at Meredith College. Her essays and articles have appeared in various newspapers and magazines, including *Newsweek,* the *New York Times,* and the *Boston Globe.* She is the author of several books, including *Skinny People Are Dull and Crunchy Like Carrots* and *Show and Tell,* from which this essay is taken. She now writes regularly for the *Authors Ink* and has completed a novel.

1   I'VE FINALLY FIGURED OUT THE DIFFERENCE between neat people and sloppy people. The distinction is, as always, moral. Neat people are lazier and meaner than sloppy people.

2   Sloppy people, you see, are not really sloppy. Their sloppiness is merely the unfortunate consequence of their extreme moral rectitude. Sloppy people carry in their mind's eye a heavenly vision, a precise plan, that is so stupendous, so perfect, it can't be achieved in this world or the next.

3   Sloppy people live in Never-Never Land. Someday is their métier. Someday they are planning to alphabetize all their books and set up home catalogs. Someday they will go through their wardrobes and mark certain items for tentative mending and certain items for passing on to relatives of similar shape and size. Someday sloppy people will make family scrapbooks into which they will put newspaper clippings, postcards, locks of hair, and the dried corsage from their senior prom. Someday they will file everything on the surface of their desks, including the cash receipts from coffee purchases at the snack shop. Someday they will sit down and read all the back issues of *The New Yorker.*

4   For all these noble reasons and more, sloppy people never get neat. They aim too high and wide. They save everything, planning someday to file, order, and straighten out the world. But while these ambitious plans take clearer and clearer shape in their heads, the books spill from the shelves onto the floor, the clothes pile up in the hamper and closet, the family mementos accumulate in every drawer, the surface of the desk is buried under mounds of paper and the unread magazines threaten to reach the ceiling.

5   Sloppy people can't bear to part with anything. They give loving attention to every detail. When sloppy people say they're going to tackle the surface of the desk, they really mean it. Not a paper will go unturned; not a rubber band will go unboxed. Four hours or two weeks into the excavation, the desk looks exactly the same, primarily because the sloppy person is meticulously creating new piles of papers with new headings and scrupulously stopping to read all

the old book catalogs before he throws them away. A neat person would just bulldoze the desk.

Neat people are bums and clods at heart. They have cavalier attitudes to- 6 ward possessions, including family heirlooms. Everything is just another dust-catcher to them. If anything collects dust, it's got to go and that's that. Neat people will toy with the idea of throwing the children out of the house just to cut down on the clutter.

Neat people don't care about process. They like results. What they want to 7 do is get the whole thing over with so they can sit down and watch the rasslin' on TV. Neat people operate on two unvarying principles: Never handle any item twice, and throw everything away.

The only thing messy in a neat person's house is the trash can. The minute 8 something comes to a neat person's hand, he will look at it, try to decide if it has immediate use and, finding none, throw it in the trash.

Neat people are especially vicious with mail. They never go through their 9 mail unless they are standing directly over a trash can. If the trash can is be-side the mailbox, even better. All ads, catalogs, pleas for charitable contribu-tions, church bulletins and money-saving coupons go straight into the trash can without being opened. All letters from home, postcards from Europe, bills and paychecks are opened, immediately responded to, then dropped in the trash can. Neat people keep their receipts only for tax purposes. That's it. No sentimental salvaging of birthday cards or the last letter a dying relative ever wrote. Into the trash it goes.

Neat people place neatness above everything, even economics. They are in- 10 credibly wasteful. Neat people throw away several toys every time they walk through the den. I knew a neat person once who threw away a perfectly good dish drainer because it had mold on it. The drainer was too much trouble to wash. And neat people sell their furniture when they move. They will sell a La-Z-Boy recliner while you are reclining in it.

Neat people are no good to borrow from. Neat people buy everything in 11 expensive little single portions. They get their flour and sugar in two-pound bags. They wouldn't consider clipping a coupon, saving a leftover, reusing plas-tic nondairy whipped cream containers or rinsing off tin foil and draping it over the unmoldy dish drainer. You can never borrow a neat person's news-paper to see what's playing at the movies. Neat people have the paper all wadded up and in the trash by 7:05 A.M.

Neat people cut a clean swath through the organic as well as the inorganic 12 world. People, animals, and things are all one to them. They are so insensitive. After they've finished with the pantry, the medicine cabinet, and the attic, they will throw out the red geranium (too many leaves), sell the dog (too many fleas), and send the children off to boarding school (too many scuff-marks on the hardwood floors).

5

Process Analysis

Process Analysis

1. **Know the process.** This guideline may seem obvious, but it's especially important when you're describing a procedure you expect others to follow. In that case, a good rule of thumb is never to write a procedure for a process you haven't performed yourself. Of course, you could analyze a process that people don't perform at all, such as the annual salmon run or the workings of an internal combustion engine. In such cases it still remains true that the clearer your understanding of the process, the better your process analysis is likely to be.

2. **Determine the type of analysis to write.** There are two major types of process analyses: *procedures* you expect someone to follow, and *descriptions* you offer simply to inform your readers. The distinction is critical: in a procedure, you need to give enough information for your readers to complete the process themselves; in an informative analysis, too much detail will likely only bore your audience.

3. **Break the process into steps.** Whether your goal is to instruct or to inform, to analyze a process you'll need to determine what the major steps of the process are. In many cases, the steps will follow a chronological sequence—as when building or repairing a physical object. Other processes—like the workings of a car engine—occur simultaneously, so you'll need to create your own divisions based on your opinion of what aspects of the process are most important. You can see this technique applied in "How to Write with Style": while the writing process is simply too complex to proceed in the same manner every time, Kurt Vonnegut makes the topic more approachable by breaking it into component parts. He doesn't suggest that the parts must always be followed in the same manner; they are simply guidelines to writing more effectively.

4. **Adjust the level of detail to match your audience.** Think about describing how a car engine works to an engineer, a mechanic, or a layperson. Naturally you'd adjust your description depending on your audience's level of expertise. Not only would the steps you describe be different, but so would the terms you use. You'd expect a mechanic to know the difference between a carburetor and a fuel pump, but you'd need to define these terms for a layperson.

Student Essay

Sarah Pennington Doud

Changing Kyle

This essay offers a very matter-of-fact description of one of the realities of raising a child. You might be a bit shocked by the blunt, to-the-point, but completely accurate description of changing a diaper in this essay, but you shouldn't be—it's something everyone needs to know how to do.

FIRST, I HAVE TO CATCH HIM. Kyle runs with the discombobulated gait of a   1
paraplegic wearing artificial limbs for the first time. On the Rosslyn Children's Center playground, Kyle weaves between tricycles and hides in spaces my left leg couldn't fit through, let alone my entire body. Our game of chase is played out daily; providing primary day care for Kyle means changing his dirty diapers even if I have to drag him off the Hippity Hop.

At twenty months of age, Kyle knows when he has had a bowel movement,   2
but he is not self-conscious about the portable toilet smell that wafts around him like Pigpen's dust cloud. He would rather ride in the Cozy Coupe or go down the Little Tikes slide—anything but have his diaper changed. When I have him cornered, I scoop him up in my arms and promise I'll be as quick as I can.

Changing Kyle's diaper can be more exciting than Monday night football   3
and a bag of chips: he is my "talker." Kyle started to speak in two-word phrases at fourteen months and adds at least three new words to his vocabulary every day. Once, upon hearing a caregiver remark that he'd been spoiled by my constant doting, Kyle responded, "I'm not spoiled. I'm *handsome.*" Kyle's delightfully healthy self-image results in part from the phenomenon Russell Baker describes: "When you're the only pea in the pod, your parents are likely to get you confused with the Hope Diamond."

Kyle's mother, Angela, a Dubliner, is genetically responsible for Kyle's red   4
hair and his Irish forehead (thin skin, thick skull). Angela blames her husband, Paul, a Polish-Italian, for Kyle's fiery temper. Kyle's temper tantrums on the changing table are insufferable—a caregiver's version of Chinese water torture.

The diapering procedure at a licensed day care center has more steps than   5
the pre-flight check for the Space Shuttle. When fifteen children share the same Formica changing table, every bacterial infection within fifty feet comes looking for a host. A roll of changing paper rests at one end of the table, and

pulling it down creates a protective layer between the table and Kyle's bottom. For huge bowel movements, "BMs," I wear two rubber gloves on each hand. I lay Kyle on the table, perpendicular to me, and give him something to hold in his hands. In my experience, boys *need* something to occupy their hands while I play with their favorite toy. During a blizzard last winter, I filled soda bottles with colored water, vegetable oil, and confetti, then glued the caps on. Now my staff stores the bottles in the changing room to keep their babies' idle hands busy. Toys are essential to the success of changing Kyle's diaper. He is *always* poopy.

6   I change Kyle's disposable diapers with wanton disregard for the environment. I use antibacterial wipes, three or four at a time, and when my gloves get dirty, I rip them off and put on new ones. Thank God for trash cans with step-on lids, and further thanks to the genius who left a window in the door to the changing room. When the smell becomes so bad I can't breathe, I put a hand on Kyle's stomach to keep him from rolling over and I lean out the window, sucking in fresh air.

7   Kyle's skin is so sensitive that sometimes I avoid using diaper wipes; instead, I moisten a handful of paper towels with warm water and use those to clean him. Kyle's blessed with a pharmacist father; Paul keeps his son's diaper shelf stocked with Nystatin, Desitin, A&D ointment, and sulfa oxide creams. Nystatin is our favorite—when Kyle's bottom bleeds with open sores and I still have to change him every hour, we spread the Nystatin over every inch of his rear end. Kyle understands that the "keem," as he calls it, is going to make his diaper rash "all better."

8   Kyle is a difficult child to change—in keeping with common European practice, Angela refused to let Kyle be circumcised, calling the surgery "barbaric" and "insensitive." I pull the foreskin back, exposing the tip of the penis, and wipe it clean. Bacteria thrive in unclean, uncircumcised penises. Regularly spraying the table with bleach solution reduces the risk of infection from Coxsackie (better known as hand, foot, and mouth disease), streptococcus, Fifth's Disease, and a host of other predatory viruses.

9   The rule for wiping is front to back for girls, back to front for boys. I pry open the folds of wrinkled pink skin over Kyle's testicles, his scrotum, which can trap stray flecks of excrement. I check his upper thighs, double-check his bottom, and apply diaper cream.

10   Putting the fresh diaper on is the easiest step: bottom up, diaper under, bottom down, the front of the diaper comes up and over his genitals and fastens to the back with adhesive tape. After changing sixty diapers a week for fourteen months, I can complete the process in less than two minutes. It's simple, if not easy. Difficult, but worth it. Like a red-haired toddler I know.

Kurt Vonnegut

How to Write with Style

Kurt Vonnegut's writing has often focused on the conundrum of a technological world—the profusion of technology that makes it so simple for government propaganda machines to inject their version of reality into society. Perhaps it is ironic that his work, especially after the publication and subsequent film of his novel *Slaughterhouse Five,* has acquired something of a cult following, particularly among the technological elite: there are more references to Vonnegut on the Internet than to any of the other writers appearing in this book. What has Vonnegut himself to say about all this? "The Internet stuff is spooky," Vonnegut commented after someone sent him a printed copy of the Alt.books.kurt-vonnegut FAQ World Wide Web page. "I am of course not on line. I do remember ham radio operators though, usually in attics or basements, pallid, unsociable, and obsessed, inhabiting a spirit world, and harmless." A writer could do worse than imitate Vonnegut's highly readable, impeccably precise style.

NEWSPAPER REPORTERS AND TECHNICAL WRITERS ARE TRAINED to reveal almost   1
nothing about themselves in their writings. This makes them freaks in the world of writers, since almost all of the other ink-stained wretches in that world reveal a lot about themselves to readers. We call these revelations, accidental and intentional, elements of style.

These revelations tell us as readers what sort of person it is with whom we   2
are spending time. Does the writer sound ignorant or informed, stupid or bright, crooked or honest, humorless or playful—? And on and on.

Why should you examine your writing style with the idea of improving it?   3
Do so as a mark of respect for your readers, whatever you're writing. If you scribble your thoughts any which way, your readers will surely feel that you care nothing about them. They will mark you down as an egomaniac or a chowderhead—or worse, they will stop reading you.

The most damning revelation you can make about yourself is that you do   4
not know what is interesting and what is not. Don't you yourself like or dislike writers mainly for what they choose to show you or make you think about? Did you ever admire an empty-headed writer for his or her mastery of the language? No.

So your own winning style must begin with ideas in your head.   5

1. Find a Subject You Care About

Find a subject you care about and which you in your heart feel others   6
should care about. It is this genuine caring, and not your games with language, which will be the most compelling and seductive element in your style.

7   I am not urging you to write a novel, by the way—although I would not be sorry if you wrote one, provided you genuinely cared about something. A petition to the mayor about a pothole in front of your house or a love letter to the girl next door will do.

2. Do Not Ramble, Though

8   I won't ramble on about that.

3. Keep It Simple

9   As for your use of language: Remember that two great masters of language, William Shakespeare and James Joyce, wrote sentences which were almost childlike when their subjects were most profound. "To be or not to be?" asks Shakespeare's Hamlet. The longest word is three letters long. Joyce, when he was frisky, could put together a sentence as intricate and as glittering as a necklace for Cleopatra, but my favorite sentence in his short story "Eveline" is this one: "She was tired." At that point in the story, no other words could break the heart of a reader as those three words do.

10   Simplicity of language is not only reputable, but perhaps even sacred. The Bible opens with a sentence well within the writing skills of a lively fourteen-year-old: "In the beginning God created the heaven and the earth."

4. Have the Guts to Cut

11   It may be that you, too, are capable of making necklaces for Cleopatra, so to speak. But your eloquence should be the servant of the ideas in your head. Your rule might be this: If a sentence, no matter how excellent, does not illuminate your subject in some new and useful way, scratch it out.

5. Sound Like Yourself

12   The writing style which is most natural for you is bound to echo the speech you heard when a child. English was the novelist Joseph Conrad's third language, and much that seems piquant in his use of English was no doubt colored by his first language, which was Polish. And lucky indeed is the writer who has grown up in Ireland, for the English spoken there is so amusing and musical. I myself grew up in Indianapolis, where common speech sounds like a band saw cutting galvanized tin, and employs a vocabulary as unornamental as a monkey wrench.

13   In some of the more remote hollows of Appalachia, children still grow up hearing songs and locutions of Elizabethan times. Yes, and many Americans grow up hearing a language other than English, or an English dialect a majority of Americans cannot understand.

14   All these varieties of speech are beautiful, just as the varieties of butterflies are beautiful. No matter what your first language, you should treasure it all

your life. If it happens not to be standard English, and if it shows itself when you write standard English, the result is usually delightful, like a very pretty girl with one eye that is green and one that is blue.

I myself find that I trust my own writing most, and others seem to trust it   15 most, too, when I sound most like a person from Indianapolis, which is what I am. What alternatives do I have? The one most vehemently recommended by teachers has no doubt been pressed on you, as well: to write like cultivated Englishmen of a century or more ago.

6. Say What You Mean to Say

I used to be exasperated by such teachers, but am no more. I understand   16 now that all those antique essays and stories with which I was to compare my own work were not magnificent for their datedness or foreignness, but for saying precisely what their authors meant them to say. My teachers wished me to write accurately, always selecting the most effective words, and relating the words to one another unambiguously, rigidly, like parts of a machine. The teachers did not want to turn me into an Englishman after all. They hoped that I would become understandable—and therefore understood. And there went my dream of doing with words what Pablo Picasso did with paint or what any number of jazz idols did with music. If I broke all the rules of punctuation, had words mean whatever I wanted them to mean, and strung them together higgledy-piggledy, I would simply not be understood. So you, too, had better avoid Picasso-style or jazz-style writing, if you have something worth saying and wish to be understood.

Readers want our pages to look very much like pages they have seen be   17 fore. Why? This is because they themselves have a tough job to do, and they need all the help they can get from us.

7. Pity the Readers

They have to identify thousands of little marks on paper, and make sense   18 of them immediately. They have to *read*, an art so difficult that most people don't really master it even after having studied it all through grade school and high school—twelve long years.

So this discussion must finally acknowledge that our stylistic options as   19 writers are neither numerous nor glamorous, since our readers are bound to be such imperfect artists. Our audience requires us to be sympathetic and patient teachers, even willing to simplify and clarify—whereas we would rather soar high above the crowd, singing like nightingales.

That is the bad news. The good news is that we Americans are governed   20 under a unique Constitution, which allows us to write whatever we please without fear of punishment. So the most meaningful aspect of our styles, which is what we choose to write about, is utterly unlimited.

8. For Really Detailed Advice

21   For a discussion of literary style in a narrower sense, in a more technical sense, I commend to your attention *The Elements of Style,* by William Strunk Jr., and E. B. White (Macmillan, 1979). E. B. White is, of course, one of the most admirable literary stylists this country has so far produced.

22   You should realize, too, that no one would care how well or badly Mr. White expressed himself, if he did not have perfectly enchanting things to say.

John O'Hayre

A First Look at Gobbledygook

This essay is taken from a United States Department of the Interior, Bureau of Land Management, publication *Gobbledygook Has Gotta Go.* The author, John O'Hayre, is an employee of the Bureau. In his preface, O'Hayre says, "If we are to succeed in these times of new technologies, new demands, and new attitudes, we must improve our communications radically. We must abandon soggy formality and incoherence in favor of modern personal communications. No longer can gobbledygook be allowed to clog communication lines." This work was published in 1966. If we can believe what we read about the proliferation of "officialese," we can only conclude that O'Hayre's crusade has made little progress in more than thirty years.

1   A DISGRUNTLED STATE DIRECTOR tossed a copy of a memo on our desk some time back. "Here's a lusty sample of what good writing ain't," he said. "Maybe you can use it to show some of our staff how not to write."

2   He picked up the memo and rattled it, saying: "All I did was write this solicitor a short memo. I told him I thought we could solve a nasty trespass case we'd both been working on. We suggested we give this trespasser a special-use permit and make him legal. That way we'd all get off the hook. All I asked the solicitor was, 'is this okay with you?'"

3   He threw the memo on the desk and scowled. "Cripes! All he had to do was say 'yes' or 'no.' But look what he sends me!"

4   Properly meek by this time, I asked: "Did the solicitor say 'yes' or 'no'?"

5   The state director whirled: "How the heck do I know! I've only read it twice!"

6   There was no doubt about it, that state director had a problem; he simply couldn't get readable writing out of his staff, or, more important this day, his solicitor.

7   Our distressed state director wasn't alone in his sweat over unreadable writing. Leaders in government, business, and industry have had the same

feverish feeling for years. One chemical company executive put it this way: "If our antifreeze had the same quality as our writing, we'd rust out half the radiators in the country in six months."

A study showed executives in one company used 200 words to write 125-word memos, eight paragraphs for four-paragraph letters, and nearly 200 pages for 100-page reports. Another corporation finally got so frustrated it quit trying to hire writers and started training the ones it already had. Most big corporations are doing this now; they have to. This way they get good writing and save good money—lots of it. An average letter's cost varies from $6 for top executives to $2 at lower levels.   8

Let's read the memo that shook up the state director: 9

To: State Director
From: John Lawbook, Solicitor
Subject: Roland Occupancy Trespass

This responds to your memorandum dated February 21,1964, requesting that we review and comment concerning the subject Roland trespass on certain lands under reclamation withdrawal.   10

We appreciate your apprising us of this matter and we certainly concur that appropriate action is in order to protect the interests of the United States.   11

We readily recognize the difficult problem presented by this situation, and if it can be otherwise satisfactorily resolved, we would prefer to avoid trespass action. If you determine it permissible to legalize the Roland occupancy and hay production by issuance of a special use permit, as suggested in your memorandum, we have no objection to that procedure.   12

Any such permit should be subject to cancellation when the lands are actively required for reclamation purposes and should provide for the right of the officers, agents, and employees of the United States at all times to have unrestricted access and ingress to, passage over, and egress from all said lands, to make investigations of all kinds, dig test pits and drill test holes, to survey for reclamation and irrigation works, and to perform any and all necessary soil and moisture conservation work.   13

If we can be of any further assistance in this matter, please advise. We would appreciate being informed of the disposition of this problem.   14

Before we edit the solicitor's memo, let's look at two of its weak points: 15

1. *False Opening*: The solicitor starts his memo by telling the state director: "This is my memo to you, answering your memo to me." Who could care less? Openings like this tell nobody nothing. Yet many memos and letters start in this word-wasteful manner.   16

2. *Writer's Grade*: The solicitor's memo has 217 words, 44 difficult words, 3 syllables or over, and a writer's grade of 53; it should grade out at 70 or above to be reasonably readable. A high grade means that, even if you're not   17

saying what you mean, you're saying it readably well. Your sentences are short, your constructions simple, and your words are not painfully syllabic. A high writer's grade is a guarantee of readable writing. With it you're in business as a writer; without it you're in trouble with the reader.

18   A basic rule for all writing is: Have something to say; say it simply; quit! The next rule is: After you've quit, go over it again with a harsh pencil and a vengeance, crossing out everything that isn't necessary.

19   Let's see if the solicitor's memo takes well to the pencil. On our first trip through, in order to be fair to the solicitor, we won't change any of his words or word order.

20   Let's start penciling out:

21   ~~This responds to your memorandum dated February 21, 1964, requesting that we review and comment~~ concerning the ~~subject~~ Roland trespass ~~on certain lands under reclamation withdrawal.~~

22   ~~We appreciate your apprising us of this matter and~~ we ~~certainly~~ concur that ~~appropriate~~ action is in order ~~to protect the interests of the United States.~~

23   ~~We readily recognize the difficult problem presented by this situation, and if it can be otherwise satisfactorily resolved,~~ we would prefer to avoid trespass action. If you determine it permissible to legalize the Roland occupancy ~~and hay production~~ by issuance of a special use permit, ~~as suggested in your memorandum,~~ we have no objection ~~to that procedure.~~

24   Any such permit should be subject to cancellation ~~when the lands are actively required for reclamation purposes~~ and should provide for the right of ~~the officers, agents, and employees of the~~ United States at all times ~~to have unrestricted access and ingress to, passage over, and egress from all said lands, to make investigations of all kinds, dig test pits and drill test holes, to survey for reclamation and irrigation works, and~~ to perform any ~~and all~~ necessary ~~soil and moisture conservation~~ work.

25   ~~If we can be of any further assistance in this matter, please advise.~~ We would appreciate being informed of the disposition of this problem.

26   What did we accomplish in this quick trip? Well, let's see. We cut the number of words from 217 to 75, cut the difficult words from 44 to 10, and raised the writer's grade from 53 (difficult) to 60 (acceptable).

27   Can we cut more yet? Let's go over it again and see, still without changing the solicitor's words or word order.

28   First sentence: Concerning the Roland trespass case, we concur that action is in order.

29   We can throw this whole sentence out, because: (1) the subject heading of the memo clearly states what the memo concerns; and (2) both knew "action was in order." That's why they had been writing each other.

30   Second and third sentences: We would prefer to avoid trespass action. If you determine it permissible to legalize Roland's occupancy by issuance of a special use permit, we have no objection.

31   Let's leave this for now; it contains the essence of the memo; it's the answer.

Fourth sentence: Any such permit should be subject to cancellation and should provide 32
for the right of the United States at all times to perform all necessary work.

Let's throw this out, too. The state director and his staff issue special use 33
permits as a matter of routine. They know what cancellation clauses and special-use provisions these have to carry. Why tell them what they already know?

Fifth sentence: We would appreciate being informed of the disposition of this problem. 34

Let's leave this sentence as it is and see what we have left after two editings. 35

We would prefer to avoid trespass action. If you determine it permissible to legalize 36
Roland's occupancy by issuance of a special use permit, we have no objection.

We would appreciate being informed of the disposition of the problem. 37

A recount shows we're now down to 38 words, 8 difficult words, and have 38
a writer's grade of 68.

The question now is: Does the edited memo carry the essential message 39
and does it read easily? It does both pretty well. However, it could have a little
more clarity and a little less pretension if it said simply:

We'd like to avoid trespass action, if possible. So, if you can settle this case by issuing 40
Roland a special use permit, go ahead.

Please keep us informed. 41

This is the way we would have written the memo had we been in the so- 42
licitor's seat. The memo now has 28 words, 2 difficult words, and a writer's
grade of 70. That's good writing.

Let's go back to the original memo. What we did first was to concentrate 43
on axing out empty words and phrases. Note how they strain to sound unnatural—and succeed. Note how they can be replaced with simple, direct words.

First and second sentences: This responds to your memorandum dated February 21, 44
1964, requesting that we review and comment concerning the subject Roland trespass on certain
lands under reclamation withdrawal. We appreciate your apprising us of this matter, and we certainly concur that appropriate action is in order to protect the interests of the United States.

How much better had he said: "Got your memo on the Roland trespass 45
case. You're right; action is needed."

Third sentence: We readily recognize the difficult problem presented by this situation, 46
and if it can be otherwise satisfactorily resolved, we would prefer to avoid trespass action.

Why didn't he just say, "The problem is tough, and we'd like to avoid tres- 47
pass action if we can"?

Fourth sentence: If you determine it permissible to legalize Roland's occupancy by issuance 48
of a special use permit, as suggested in your memorandum, we have no objection to that procedure.

It's a lot clearer this way: "If you can solve this problem by issuing Roland 49
a special use permit, go ahead."

50   Fifth sentence: Any such permit should be subject to cancellation when the lands are actively required for reclamation purposes and should provide for the right of officers, agents and employees of the United States at all times to have unrestricted access and ingress to, passage over, and egress from all said lands, to make investigations of all kinds, dig test pits and drill test holes, to survey for reclamation and irrigation works, and to perform any and all necessary soil and moisture conservation work.

51   Such a lawyerish enumeration belongs, if it belongs at all, in a legal contract, not in an inter-office memo. If the solicitor felt an obligation to give the state director a reminder, he might have said: "Please spell out the Government's cancellation rights and right-to-use provisions in the permit."

52   Sixth and seventh sentences (adequate but somewhat high-blown): If we can be of any further assistance in this matter, please advise. We would appreciate being informed of the disposition of this problem.

53   It's somewhat better, at least shorter, this way: "If we can be of further help, please call. Keep us informed."

54   How does the whole, empty-word-less memo read now? Would it, too, be satisfactory? Let's look:

55   Got your memo on the Roland trespass case. You're right; action is needed. The problem *is* tough, and we'd like to avoid trespass action if we can. So, if you can settle this case by issuing Roland a special-use permit, go ahead. Please spell out the Government's cancellation rights and right-to-use provisions in the permit.

56   If we can be of further help, please call. Keep us informed.

57   In this version we have 70 words, only four difficult words, and a writer's grade of 69.

58   Moreover, we've said everything the solicitor said in his original memo, even the stuff that didn't need saying. The only difference is that we threw out the empty words, shortened the sentences, changed the passive to the active, and generally tried to say things simply, directly, and clearly. The gobbledygook is gone!

Peter Elbow

Desperation Writing

Peter Elbow has been teaching college writing since 1960 and has served as a consultant to several university writing centers. His books *Writing without Teachers* and *Writing with Power: Techniques of Mastering the Writing Process* are popular guides to clear, effective writing. He is a strong advocate of freewriting, stressing

that editing should be done after the ideas are down on paper. His interest in writing came from his "own difficulties with it" and this has inspired him not only to write, but also to help others learn to write. He has written many articles about the teaching of writing and is an active contributor to the National Council of Teachers of English.

I KNOW I AM NOT ALONE in my recurring twinges of panic that I won't be able   1
to write something when I need to, I won't be able to produce coherent speech
or thought. And that lingering doubt is a great hindrance to writing. It's a
constant fog or static that clouds the mind. I never got out of its clutches till
I discovered that it was possible to write something—not something great or
pleasing but at least something usable, workable—when my mind is out of
commission. The trick is that you have to do all your cooking out on the table:
Your mind is incapable of doing any inside. It means using symbols and pieces
of paper not as a crutch but as a wheelchair.

The first thing is to admit your condition: Because of some mood or event   2
or whatever, your mind is incapable of anything that could be called thought.
It can put out a babbling kind of speech utterance, it can put a simple feeling,
perception or sort-of-thought into understandable (though terrible) words.
But it is incapable of considering anything in relation to anything else. The
moment you try to hold that thought or feeling up against some other to see
the relationship, you simply lose the picture—you get nothing but buzzing
lines or waving colors.

So admit this. Avoid anything more than one feeling, perception, or   3
thought. Simply write as much as possible. Try simply to steer your mind in
the direction or general vicinity of the thing you are trying to write about and
start writing and keep writing.

Just write and keep writing. (Probably best to write on only one side of the   4
paper in case you should want to cut parts out with scissors—but you probably won't.) Just write and keep writing. It will probably come in waves. After a
flurry, stop and take a brief rest. But don't stop too long. Don't think about
what you are writing or what you have written or else you will overload the circuit again. Keep writing as though you are drugged or drunk. Keep doing this
till you feel you have a lot of material that might be useful; or, if necessary, till
you can't stand it any more—even if you doubt that there's anything useful
there.

Then take a pad of little pieces of paper—or perhaps 3 × 5 cards—and   5
simply start at the beginning of what you were writing, and as you read
over what you wrote, every time you come to any thought, feeling, perception, or image that could be gathered up into one sentence or one assertion, do so and write it by itself on a little sheet of paper. In short, you are
trying to turn, say, ten or twenty pages of wandering mush into twenty or

thirty hard little crab apples. Sometimes there won't be many on a page. But if it seems to you that there are none on a page, you are making a serious error—the same serious error that put you in this comatose state to start with. You are mistaking lousy, stupid, second-rate, wrong, childish, foolish, worthless ideas for no ideas at all. Your job is not to pick out *good* ideas but to pick out ideas. As long as you were conscious, your words will be full of things that could be called feelings, utterances, ideas—things that can be squeezed into one simple sentence. This is your job. Don't ask for too much.

6   After you have done this, take those little slips or cards, read through them a number of times—not struggling with them, simply wandering and mulling through them; perhaps shifting them around and looking through in various sequences. In a sense these are cards you are playing solitaire with, and the rules of this particular game permit shuffling the unused pile.

7   The goal of this procedure with the cards is to get them to distribute themselves in two or three or ten or fifteen different piles on your desk. You can get them to do this almost by themselves if you simply keep reading through them in different orders; certain cards will begin to feel like they go with other cards. I emphasize this passive, thoughtless mode because I want to talk about desperation writing in its pure state. In practice, almost invariably at some point in the procedure, your sanity begins to return. It is often at this point. You actually are moved to have thoughts or—and the difference between active and passive is crucial here—to *exert* thought; to hold two cards together and *build* or *assert* a relationship. It is a matter of bringing energy to bear.

8   So you may start to be able to do something active with these cards, and begin actually to think. But if not, just allow the cards to find their own piles with each other by feel, by drift, by intuition, by mindlessness.

9   You have now engaged in the two main activities that will permit you to get something cooked out on the table rather than in your brain: writing out into messy words, summing up into single assertions, and even sensing relationships between assertions. You can simply continue to deploy these two activities.

10   If, for example, after the first round of writing, assertion-making, and pile-making, your piles feel as though they are useful and satisfactory for what you are writing—paragraphs or sections or trains of thought—then you can carry on from there. See if you can gather each pile up into a single assertion. When you can, then put the subsidiary assertions of that pile into their best order to fit with that single unifying one. If you *can't* get the pile into one assertion, then take the pile as the basis for doing some more writing out into words. In the course of this writing, you may produce for yourself the single unifying assertion you were looking for; or

you may have to go through the cycle of turning the writing into assertions and piles and so forth. Perhaps more than once. The pile may turn out to want to be two or more piles itself; or it may want to become part of a pile you already have. This is natural. This kind of meshing into one configuration, then coming apart, then coming together and meshing into a different configuration—this is growing and cooking. It makes a terrible mess, but if you can't do it in your head, you have to put up with a cluttered desk and a lot of confusion.

If, on the other hand, all that writing *didn't* have useful material in it,   11 it means that your writing wasn't loose, drifting, quirky, jerky, associative enough. This time try especially to let things simply remind you of things that are seemingly crazy or unrelated. Follow these odd associations. Make as many metaphors as you can—be as nutty as possible—and explore the metaphors themselves—open them out. You may have all your energy tied up in some area of your experience that you are leaving out. Don't refrain from writing about whatever else is on your mind: how you feel at the moment, what you are losing your mind over, randomness that intrudes itself on your consciousness, the pattern on the wallpaper, what those people you see out the window have on their minds—though keep coming back to the whateveritis you are supposed to be writing about. Treat it, in short, like ten-minute writing exercises. Your best perceptions and thoughts are always going to be tied up in whatever is really occupying you, and that is also where your energy is. You may end up writing a love poem—or a hate poem—in one of those little piles while the other piles will finally turn into a lab report on data processing or whatever you have to write about. But you couldn't, in your present state of having your head shot off, have written that report without also writing the poem. And the report will have some of the juice of the poem in it and vice versa.

Mary Wollstonecraft Shelley

Introduction to *Frankenstein*

Mary Wollstonecraft Shelley (1797–1851), herself a great novelist, spent her life in the company of other great literary figures. Her mother, Mary Wollstonecraft (who died in childbirth), was a pioneer feminist; her husband, Percy Bysshe Shelley, a renowned poet. Though in this preface she is quite modest about the accomplishment of writing *Frankenstein,* giving much credit to her husband, the novel she wrote is today regarded as one of the greatest of all time. Here she describes the moment of inspiration that produced *Frankenstein.*

1   THE PUBLISHERS OF THE STANDARD NOVELS, in selecting "Frankenstein" for one of their series, expressed a wish that I should furnish them with some account of the origin of the story. I am the more willing to comply, because I shall thus give a general answer to the question, so very frequently asked me—"How I, then a young girl, came to think of, and to dilate upon, so very hideous an idea?" It is true that I am very averse to bringing myself forward in print; but as my account will only appear as an appendage to a former production, and as it will be confined to such topics as have connection with my authorship alone, I can scarcely accuse myself of a personal intrusion.

2   It is not singular that, as the daughter of two persons of distinguished literary celebrity, I should very early in life have thought of writing. As a child I scribbled; and my favourite pastime, during the hours given me for recreation, was to "write stories." Still I had a dearer pleasure than this, which was the formation of castles in the air—the indulging in waking dreams—the following up trains of thought, which had for their subject the formation of a succession of imaginary incidents. My dreams were at once more fantastic and agreeable than my writings. In the latter I was a close imitator—rather doing as others had done, than putting down the suggestions of my own mind. What I wrote was intended at least for one other eye—my childhood's companion and friend; but my dreams were all my own; I accounted for them to nobody; they were my refuge when annoyed—my dearest pleasure when free.

3   I lived principally in the country as a girl, and passed a considerable time in Scotland. I made occasional visits to the more picturesque parts; but my habitual residence was on the blank and dreary northern shores of the Tay, near Dundee. Blank and dreary on retrospection I call them; they were not so to me then. They were the eyry of freedom, and the pleasant region where unheeded I could commune with the creatures of my fancy. I wrote then—but in a most common-place style. It was beneath the trees of the grounds belonging to our house, or on the bleak sides of the woodless mountains near, that my true compositions, the airy flights of my imagination, were born and fostered. I did not make myself the heroine of my tales. Life appeared to me too common-place an affair as regarded myself. I could not figure to myself that romantic woes or wonderful events would ever be my lot; but I was not confined to my own identity; and I could people the hours with creations far more interesting to me at that age, than my own sensations.

4   After this my life became busier, and reality stood in place of fiction. My husband, however, was, from the first, very anxious that I should prove myself worthy of my parentage, and enroll myself on the page of fame. He was for ever inciting me to obtain literary reputation, which even on my own part I cared for then, though since I have become infinitely indifferent to it. At this time he desired that I should write, not so much with the

idea that I could produce any thing worthy of notice, but that he might himself judge how far I possessed the promise of better things hereafter. Still I did nothing. Travelling, and the cares of a family, occupied my time; and study, in the way of reading, or improving my ideas in communication with his far more cultivated mind, was all of literary employment that engaged my attention.

In the summer of 1816, we visited Switzerland, and became the neighbours of Lord Byron. At first we spent our pleasant hours on the lake, or wandering on its shores; and Lord Byron, who was writing the third canto of Childe Harold, was the only one among us who put his thoughts upon paper. These, as he brought them successively to us, clothed in all the light and harmony of poetry, seemed to stamp as divine the glories of heaven and earth, whose influences we partook with him.

But it proved a wet, ungenial summer, and incessant rain often confined us for days to the house. Some volumes of ghost stories, translated from the German into French, fell into our hands. There was the History of the Inconstant Lover, who, when he thought to clasp the bride to whom he had pledged his vows, found himself in the arms of the pale ghost of her whom he had deserted. There was the tale of the sinful founder of his race, whose miserable doom it was to bestow the kiss of death on all the younger sons of his fated house, just when they reached the age of promise. His gigantic, shadowy form, clothed like the ghost in Hamlet, in complete armour, but with the beaver up, was seen at midnight, by the moon's fitful beams, to advance slowly along the gloomy avenue. The shape was lost beneath the shadow of the castle walls; but soon a gate swung back, a step was heard, the door of the chamber opened, and he advanced to the couch of the blooming youths, cradled in healthy sleep. Eternal sorrow sat upon his face as he bent down and kissed the forehead of the boys, who from that hour withered like flowers snapt upon the stalk. I have not seen these stories since then; but their incidents are as fresh in my mind as if I had read them yesterday.

"We will each write a ghost story," said Lord Byron; and his proposition was acceded to. There were four of us. The noble author began a tale, a fragment of which he printed at the end of his poem of Mazeppa. Shelley, more apt to embody ideas and sentiments in the radiance of brilliant imagery, and in the music of the most melodious verse that adorns our language, than to invent the machinery of a story, commenced one founded on the experiences of his early life. Poor Polidori had some terrible idea about a skull-headed lady, who was so punished for peeping through a key-hole—what to see I forget—something very shocking and wrong of course; but when she was reduced to a worse condition than the renowned Tom of Coventry, he did not know what to do with her, and was obliged to despatch her to the tomb of the Capulets, the only place for which she was fitted. The illustrious poets also, annoyed by the platitude of prose, speedily relinquished their uncongenial task.

8   I busied myself to *think of a story,*—a story to rival those which had excited us to this task. One which would speak to the mysterious fears of our nature, and awaken thrilling horror—one to make the reader dread to look round, to curdle the blood, and quicken the beatings of the heart. If I did not accomplish these things, my ghost story would be unworthy of its name. I thought and pondered—vainly. I felt that blank incapability of invention which is the greatest misery of authorship, when dull Nothing replies to our anxious invocations. *Have you thought of a story?* I was asked each morning, and each morning I was forced to reply with a mortifying negative.

9   Every thing must have a beginning, to speak in Sanchean phrase, and that beginning must be linked to something that went before. The Hindoos give the world an elephant to support it, but they make the elephant stand upon a tortoise. Invention, it must be humbly admitted, does not consist in creating out of void, but out of chaos; the materials must, in the first place, be afforded: it can give form to dark, shapeless substances, but cannot bring into being the substance itself. In all matters of discovery and invention, even of those that appertain to the imagination, we are continually reminded of the story of Columbus and his egg. Invention consists in the capacity of seizing on the capabilities of a subject, and in the power of moulding and fashioning ideas suggested to it.

10   Many and long were the conversations between Lord Byron and Shelley, to which I was a devout but nearly silent listener. During one of these, various philosophical doctrines were discussed, and among others the nature of the principle of life, and whether there was any probability of its ever being discovered and communicated. They talked of the experiments of Dr. Darwin, (I speak not of what the Doctor really did, or said that he did, but, as more to my purpose, of what was then spoken of as having been done by him,) who preserved a piece of vermicelli in a glass case, till by some extraordinary means it began to move with voluntary motion. Not thus, after all, would life be given. Perhaps a corpse would be re-animated; galvanism had given token of such things: perhaps the component parts of a creature might be manufactured, brought together, and endued with vital warmth.

11   Night waned upon this talk, and even the witching hour had gone by, before we retired to rest. When I placed my head on my pillow, I did not sleep, nor could I be said to think. My imagination, unbidden, possessed and guided me, gifting the successive images that arose in my mind with a vividness far beyond the usual bounds of reverie. I saw—with shut eyes, but acute mental vision,—I saw the pale student of unhallowed arts kneeling beside the

thing he had put together. I saw the hideous phantasm of a man stretched out, and then, on the working of some powerful engine, show signs of life and stir with an uneasy, half vital motion. Frightful must it be; for supremely frightful would be the effect of any human endeavour to mock the stupendous mechanism of the Creator of the world. His success would terrify the artist; he would rush away from his odious handywork, horror-stricken. He would hope that, left to itself, the slight spark of life which he had communicated would fade; that this thing, which had received such imperfect animation, would subside into dead matter; and he might sleep in the belief that the silence of the grave would quench for ever the transient existence of the hideous corpse which he had looked upon as the cradle of life. He sleeps; but he is awakened; he opens his eyes; behold the horrid thing stands at his bedside, opening his curtains, and looking on him with yellow, watery, but speculative eyes.

I opened mine in terror. The idea so possessed my mind, that a thrill of 12 fear ran through me, and I wished to exchange the ghastly image of my fancy for the realities around. I see them still; the very room, the dark *parquet*, the closed shutters, with the moonlight struggling through, and the sense I had that the glassy lake and white high Alps were beyond. I could not so easily get rid of my hideous phantom; still it haunted me. I must try to think of something else. I recurred to my ghost story,—my tiresome unlucky ghost story! O! if I could only contrive one which would frighten my reader as I myself had been frightened that night!

Swift as light and as cheering was the idea that broke in upon me. "I have 13 found it! What terrified me will terrify others; and I need only describe the spectre which had haunted my midnight pillow." On the morrow I announced that I had *thought of a story*. I began that day with the words, *It was on a dreary night of November*, making only a transcript of the grim terrors of my waking dream.

At first I thought but of a few pages—of a short tale; but Shelley urged me 14 to develope the idea at greater length. I certainly did not owe the suggestion of one incident, nor scarcely of one train of feeling, to my husband, and yet but for his incitement, it would never have taken the form in which it was presented to the world. From this declaration I must except the preface. As far as I can recollect, it was entirely written by him.

And now, once again, I bid my hideous progeny go forth and prosper. I 15 have an affection for it, for it was the offspring of happy days, when death and grief were but words, which found no true echo in my heart. Its several pages speak of many a walk, many a drive, and many a conversation, when I was not alone; and my companion was one who, in this world, I shall never see more. But this is for myself; my readers have nothing to do with these associations.

Dave Barry

How to Watch the Super Bowl

Dave Barry became a newspaper columnist after several frustrating years teaching business writing—as he puts it, "trying to get his students to stop writing things like 'enclosed please find the enclosed enclosures.'" He has written for hundreds of newspapers, sold millions of books, won the Pulitzer Prize, and even had his life turned into a television series (for which he once quipped he had the ultimate contract: he did no writing, acting, or thinking—he just received a very large check). Called "one of the funniest writers alive" by novelist Carl Hiaasen, Barry never fails to point out the absurdity of everyday life, as he does in the following essay taken from his weekly column in the *Miami Herald*.

1   WE ARE COMING UP ON THE SUPER BOWL, which is by far the most important sporting event in the world as measured in total tons of free shrimp consumed by sportswriters.

2   This year, the Super Bowl will be broadcast to many foreign nations, which, almost by definition, contain numerous foreigners. These people are often puzzled by American football, a highly complex sport that requires a knowledge of many technical terms such as "run," "pass," "cornerbacker," "blitzkrieg," "Texas Leaguer," "ligament" and "Hank Stram." This complexity makes the game difficult for foreigners to grasp.

3   I know this because some years ago, while visiting Japan, I watched the Miami Dolphins and the Oakland Raiders play a demonstration game in a Tokyo stadium where, for a zesty snack, you could buy pieces of fried octopus on a stick. The fans were polite, but they had no clue what was going on. The only thing that aroused their interest was the Dolphins cheerleaders. The game would stop for a time out, and the cheerleaders would start jumping around, and immediately the fans would go WILD, cheering and thrusting their octopus nuggets into the air.

4   I'm not being critical here. I've been on the other side of this coin. While visiting Ireland, I watched an Irish sport called "hurling" (really) in which men who are not wearing helmets basically beat each other senseless with sticks. In terms of violence, this sport makes American football look like Pat the Bunny. I'd never seen this sport, so I relied on the fans around me to answer my questions ("Is that player dead?" "Did all that blood come out of his EAR?" etc.).

5   So I know how hard it can be to understand a foreign sport, which is why today, to help you foreign persons follow the Super Bowl, I am presenting:

The Rules of American Professional Football

Football is played on a field that is 100 yards (374 kilometers) long and   6
is covered with lines called "hash marks" to indicate where players have lost
their breakfasts. On either side of the field are the benches, where the 350
players who are not involved in the game sit and wave to their moms. Behind each bench is a big plastic jug of Gatorade. The object of the game is
to be the first team to dump this on the "coach," a very angry man who
hates everybody.

The game is divided into four 15-minute quarters, each of which lasts a   7
little over three hours. Time outs may be called by anybody at any time for
any reason, including political unrest in Guatemala. Between the second and
third quarters, there is a halftime musical extravaganza in which Neil Diamond, Toni Tennille, the Muppets and the late Al Hirt join with every
human being who has ever auditioned for Star Search to perform "A Tribute
to Medleys."

The game begins when a small man of foreign extraction kicks the pigskin,   8
or "ball," as far as possible, then wisely scuttles off the field. The referee then
places the ball on an imaginary "line of scrimmage," which is visible only to
the referee and his imaginary friend, Mr. Pootywinkle. On either side of this
line, the two teams form "huddles," where they decide who will perform the
traditional celebratory dance when the upcoming "play" is over.

The "play" itself happens very quickly, so you foreign persons must not   9
blink, or you'll miss it. Here's what happens:

1. A large player called the "center" squats over the ball, and then the   10
"quarterdeck" touches him in a way that would get them both executed in the
Middle East.

2. All the players run into each other and fall down.   11

3. Certain players leap to their feet and perform celebratory dances, while   12
referees add to the festivity by hurling brightly colored flags into the air.

Now comes the heart and soul of football: Watching slow-motion replays   13
of the players falling down. You'll see this from every possible point of reference, including the Hubble telescope. You'll see so many replays that at some
point you'll swear that, in the background, you can see Mr. Pootywinkle.

When the replays are finally over, the referee formally announces that the   14
play does not count. Then it's time for eight commercials featuring sport util-
ity vehicles climbing Mount Everest, and it's back to the huddles for more
nonstop action!

Yes, foreign persons, football is a complex sport, but you'll find that if you   15
take the time to watch this year's Super Bowl, you will soon discover why every
year, so many millions of Americans are glued to their television sets. Watching rental videos.

Jessica Mitford

Behind the Formaldehyde Curtain

Jessica Mitford's scathing exposé of the funeral industry in her 1963 book *The American Way of Death* was hardly her first act of protest against established morals and the staid way of life. The daughter of the proto-fascist Lord and Lady Redsdale, Mitford miffed her family by eloping with her left-wing activist second cousin (the nephew of Winston Churchill). They emigrated to the U.S. in 1939, but her husband, serving with the Royal Canadian Air Force, was killed in action over Germany in 1941. A political activist, Mitford joined the Communist party, and she and her second husband were active in the Civil Rights Congress. Her subsequent investigative books on the American prison system, obstetrics, and the trial of Dr. Spock fostered her reputation as "Queen of the Muckrakers." As a leader in investigative journalism, Mitford's writing set a standard that relied heavily on accurate process analysis, along with a good dose of her caustic wit.

Per her request, her memorial service was grand, with six black plumed horses pulling a carriage followed by a twelve-piece brass band. Her actual funeral, however, was a $475 cremation.

1   THE DRAMA BEGINS TO UNFOLD with the arrival of the corpse at the mortuary.

2   Alas, poor Yorick! How surprised he would be to see how his counterpart of today is whisked off to a funeral parlor and is in short order sprayed, sliced, pierced, pickled, trussed, trimmed, creamed, waxed, painted, rouged and neatly dressed—transformed from a common corpse into a Beautiful Memory Picture. This process is known in the trade as embalming and restorative art, and is so universally employed in the United States and Canada that the funeral director does it routinely, without consulting corpse or kin. He regards as eccentric those few who are hardy enough to suggest that it might be dispensed with. Yet no law requires embalming, no religious doctrine commends it, nor is it dictated by considerations of health, sanitation, or even of personal daintiness. In no part of the world but in Northern America is it widely used. The purpose of embalming is to make the corpse presentable for viewing in a suitably costly container; and here too the funeral director routinely, without first consulting the family, prepares the body for public display.

3   Is all this legal? The processes to which a dead body may be subjected are after all to some extent circumscribed by law. In most states, for instance, the signature of next of kin must be obtained before an autopsy may be performed, before the deceased may be cremated, before the body may be turned over to a medical school for research purposes; or such provision must be made in the decedent's will. In the case of embalming, no such permission is required nor is it ever sought. A textbook, *The Principles and Practices of Embalming*, comments on this: "There is some question regarding the legality of

much that is done within the preparation room." The author points out that it would be most unusual for a responsible member of a bereaved family to instruct the mortician, in so many words, to "embalm" the body of a deceased relative. The very term *embalming* is so seldom used that the mortician must rely upon custom in the matter. The author concludes that unless the family specifies otherwise, the act of entrusting the body to the care of a funeral establishment carries with it an implied permission to go ahead and embalm.

Embalming is indeed a most extraordinary procedure, and one must won-   4
der at the docility of Americans who each year pay hundreds of millions of dollars for its perpetuation, blissfully ignorant of what it is all about, what is done, how it is done. Not one in ten thousand has any idea of what actually takes place. Books on the subject are extremely hard to come by. They are not to be found in most libraries or bookshops.

In an era when huge television audiences watch surgical operations in the   5
comfort of their living rooms, when, thanks to the animated cartoon, the geography of the digestive system has become familiar territory even to the nursery school set, in a land where the satisfaction of curiosity about almost all matters is a national pastime, the secrecy surrounding embalming can, surely, hardly be attributed to the inherent gruesomeness of the subject. Custom in this regard has within this century suffered a complete reversal. In the early days of American embalming, when it was performed in the home of the deceased, it was almost mandatory for some relative to stay by the embalmer's side and witness the procedure. Today, family members who might wish to be in attendance would certainly be dissuaded by the funeral director. All others, except apprentices, are excluded by law from the preparation room.

A close look at what does actually take place may explain in large measure   6
the undertaker's intractable reticence concerning a procedure that has become his major *raison d'être*. Is it possible he fears that public information about embalming might lead patrons to wonder if they really want this service? If the funeral men are loath to discuss the subject outside the trade, the reader may, understandably, be equally loath to go on reading at this point. For those who have the stomach for it, let us part the formaldehyde curtain. . . .

The body is first laid out in the undertaker's morgue—or rather, Mr. Jones   7
is reposing in the preparation room—to be readied to bid the world farewell.

The preparation room in any of the better funeral establishments has the   8
tiled and sterile look of a surgery, and indeed the embalmer–restorative artist who does his chores there is beginning to adopt the term *dermasurgeon* (appropriately corrupted by some mortician-writers as "demi-surgeon") to describe his calling. His equipment, consisting of scalpels, scissors, augers, forceps, clamps, needles, pumps, tubes, bowls, and basins, is crudely imitative of the surgeon's, as is his technique, acquired in a nine- or twelve-month posthigh school course in an embalming school. He is supplied by an advanced

chemical industry with a bewildering array of fluids, sprays, pastes, oils, powders, creams, to fix or soften tissue, shrink or distend it as needed, dry it here, restore the moisture there. There are cosmetics, waxes, and paints to fill and cover features, even plaster of Paris to replace entire limbs. There are ingenious aids to prop and stabilize the cadaver: a Vari-Pose Head Rest, the Edwards Arm and Hand Positioner, the Repose Block (to support the shoulders during the embalming), and the Throop Foot Positioner, which resembles an old-fashioned stocks.

9   Mr. John H. Eckels, president of the Eckels College of Mortuary Science, thus describes the first part of the embalming procedure: "In the hands of a skilled practitioner, this work may be done in a comparatively short time and without mutilating the body other than by slight incision—so slight that it scarcely would cause serious inconvenience if made upon a living person. It is necessary to remove the blood, and doing this not only helps in the disinfecting, but removes the principal cause of disfigurements due to discoloration."

10   Another textbook discusses the all-important time element: "The earlier this is done, the better, for every hour that elapses between death and embalming will add to the problems and complications encountered. . . ." Just how soon should one get going on the embalming? The author tells us, "On the basis of such scanty information made available to this profession through its rudimentary and haphazard system of technical research, we must conclude that the best results are to be obtained if the subject is embalmed before life is completely extinct—that is, before cellular death has occurred. In the average case, this would mean within an hour after somatic death." For those who feel that there is something a little rudimentary, not to say haphazard, about this advice, a comforting thought is offered by another writer. Speaking of fears entertained in early days of premature burial, he points out, "One of the effects of embalming by chemical injection, however, has been to dispel fears of live burial." How true; once the blood is removed, chances of live burial are indeed remote.

11   To return to Mr. Jones, the blood is drained out through the veins and replaced by embalming fluid pumped in through the arteries. As noted in *The Principles and Practices of Embalming*, "every operator has a favorite injection and drainage point—a fact which becomes a handicap only if he fails or refuses to forsake his favorites when conditions demand it." Typical favorites are the carotid artery, femoral artery, jugular vein, subclavian vein. There are various choices of embalming fluid. If Flextone is used, it will produce a "mild, flexible rigidity. The skin retains a velvety softness, the tissues are rubbery and pliable. Ideal for women and children." It may be blended with B. and G. Products Company's Lyf-Lyk tint, which is guaranteed to reproduce "nature's own skin texture . . . the velvety appearance of living tissue." Suntone comes in

three separate tints: Suntan; Special Cosmetic Tint, a pink shade "especially indicated for female subjects"; and Regular Cosmetic Tint, moderately pink.

About three to six gallons of a dyed and perfumed solution of formalde- 12 hyde, glycerin, borax, phenol, alcohol; and water is soon circulating through Mr. Jones, whose mouth has been sewn together with a "needle directed upward between the upper lip and gum and brought out through the left nostril," with the corners raised slightly "for a more pleasant expression." If he should be bucktoothed, his teeth are cleaned with Bon Ami and coated with colorless nail polish. His eyes, meanwhile, are closed with flesh-tinted eye caps and eye cement.

The next step is to have at Mr. Jones with a thing called a trocar. This is a 13 long, hollow needle attached to a tube. It is jabbed into the abdomen, poked around the entrails and chest cavity, the contents of which are pumped out and replaced with "cavity fluid." This done, and the hole in the abdomen sewn up, Mr. Jones's face is heavily creamed (to protect the skin from burns which may be caused by leakage of the chemicals), and he is covered with a sheet and left unmolested for a while. But not for long—there is more, much more, in store for him. He has been embalmed, but not yet restored, and the best time to start the restorative work is eight to ten hours after embalming, when the tissues have become firm and dry.

The object of all this attention to the corpse, it must be remembered, is to 14 make it presentable for viewing in an attitude of healthy repose. "Our customs require the presentation of our dead in the semblance of normality . . . unmarred by the ravages of illness, disease, or mutilation," says Mr. J. Sheridan Mayer in his *Restorative Art*. This is rather a large order since few people die in the full bloom of health, unravaged by illness and unmarked by some disfigurement. The funeral industry is equal to the challenge: "In some cases the gruesome appearance of a mutilated or disease-ridden subject may be quite discouraging. The task of restoration may seem impossible and shake the confidence of the embalmer. This is the time for intestinal fortitude and determination. Once the formative work is begun and affected tissues are cleaned or removed, all doubts of success vanish. It is surprising and gratifying to discover the results which may be obtained."

The embalmer, having allowed an appropriate interval to elapse, returns 15 to the attack, but now he brings into play the skill and equipment of sculptor and cosmetician. Is a hand missing? Casting one in plaster of Paris is a simple matter. "For replacement purposes, only a cast of the back of the hand is necessary; this is within the ability of the average operator and is quite adequate." If a lip or two, a nose or an ear should be missing, the embalmer has at hand a variety of restorative waxes with which to model replacements. Pores and skin texture are simulated by stippling with a little brush, and over this cosmetics are laid on. Head off? Decapitation cases are rather routinely handled.

Ragged edges are trimmed, and head joined to torso with a series of splints, wires, and sutures. It is a good idea to have a little something at the neck—a scarf or a high collar—when time for viewing comes. Swollen mouth? Cut out tissue as needed from inside the lips. If too much is removed, the surface contour can easily be restored by padding with cotton. Swollen necks and cheeks are reduced by removing tissue through vertical incisions made down each side of the neck. "When the deceased is casketed, the pillow will hide the suture incisions . . . as an extra precaution against leakage, the suture may be painted with liquid sealer."

16   The opposite condition is more likely to present itself—that of emaciation. His hypodermic syringe now loaded with massage cream, the embalmer seeks out and fills the hollowed and sunken areas by injection. In this procedure the backs of the hands and fingers and the under-chin area should not be neglected.

17   Positioning the lips is a problem that recurrently challenges the ingenuity of the embalmer. Closed too tightly, they tend to give a stern, even disapproving expression. Ideally, embalmers feel, the lips should give the impression of being ever so slightly parted, the upper lip protruding slightly for a more youthful appearance. This takes some engineering, however, as the lips tend to drift apart. Lip drift can sometimes be remedied by pushing one or two straight pins through the inner margin of the lower lip and then inserting them between the two front upper teeth. If Mr. Jones happens to have no teeth, the pins can just as easily be anchored in his Armstrong Face Former and Denture Replacer. Another method to maintain lip closure is to dislocate the lower jaw, which is then held in its new position by a wire run through holes which have been drilled through the upper and lower jaws at the midline. As the French are fond of saying, *il faut souffrir pour être belle* (You have to suffer to be beautiful).

18   If Mr. Jones has died of jaundice, the embalming fluid will very likely turn him green. Does this deter the embalmer? Not if he has intestinal fortitude. Masking pastes and cosmetics are heavily laid on, burial garments and casket interiors are color-correlated with particular care, and Jones is displayed beneath rose-colored lights. Friends will say "How *well* he looks." Death by carbon monoxide, on the other hand, can be rather a good thing from the embalmer's viewpoint: "One advantage is the fact that this type of discoloration is an exaggerated form of a natural pink coloration." This is nice because the healthy glow is already present and needs but little attention.

19   The patching and filling completed, Mr. Jones is now shaved, washed, and dressed. Cream-based cosmetic, available in pink, flesh, suntan, brunette, and blond, is applied to his hands and face, his hair is shampooed and combed (and, in the case of Mrs. Jones, set), his hands manicured. For the horny-handed son of toil special care must be taken; cream should be applied to re-

move ingrained grime, and the nails cleaned. "If he were not in the habit of having them manicured in life, trimming and shaping is advised for better appearance—never questioned by kin."

Jones is now ready for casketing (this is the present participle of the verb "to casket"). In this operation his right shoulder should be depressed slightly "to turn the body a bit to the right and soften the appearance of lying flat on the back." Positioning the hands is a matter of importance, and special rubber positioning blocks may be used. The hands should be cupped slightly for a more lifelike, relaxed appearance. Proper placement of the body requires a delicate sense of balance. It should lie as high as possible in the casket, yet not so high that the lid, when lowered, will hit the nose. On the other hand, we are cautioned, placing the body too low "creates the impression that the body is in a box." 20

Jones is next wheeled into the appointed slumber room where a few last touches may be added—his favorite pipe placed in his hand or, if he was a great reader, a book propped into position. (In the case of little Master Jones a Teddy bear may be clutched.) Here he will hold open house for a few days, visiting hours 10 A.M. to 9 P.M. 21

All now being in readiness, the funeral director calls a staff conference to make sure that each assistant knows his precise duties. Mr. Wilber Kriege writes: "This makes your staff feel that they are a part of the team, with a definite assignment that must be properly carried out if the whole plan is to succeed. You never heard of a football coach who failed to talk to his entire team before they go on the field. They have drilled on the plays they are to execute for hours and days, and yet the successful coach knows the importance of making even the bench-warming third-string substitute feel that he is important if the game is to be won." The winning of *this* game is predicated upon glass-smooth handling of the logistics. The funeral director has notified the pallbearers whose names were furnished by the family, has arranged for the presence of clergyman, organist, and soloist, has provided transportation for everybody, has organized and listed the flowers sent by friends. In *Psychology of Funeral Service* Mr. Edward A. Martin points out: "He may not always do as much as the family thinks he is doing, but it is his helpful guidance that they appreciate in knowing they are proceeding as they should. . . . The important thing is how well his services can be used to make the family believe they are giving unlimited expression to their own sentiment." 22

The religious service may be held in a church or in the chapel of the funeral home; the funeral director vastly prefers the latter arrangement, for not only is it more convenient for him but it affords him the opportunity to show off his beautiful facilities to the gathered mourners. After the clergyman has had his say, the mourners queue up to file past the casket for a last look at the deceased. The family is *never* asked whether they want an open-casket cere- 23 mony; in the absence of their instruction to the contrary, this is taken for granted. Consequently well over 90 percent of all American funerals feature the open casket—a custom unknown in other parts of the world. Foreigners are astonished by it. An English woman living in San Francisco described her reaction in a letter to the writer:

24   I myself have attended only one funeral here—that of an elderly fellow worker of mine. After the service I could not understand why everyone was walking towards the coffin (sorry, I mean casket), but thought I had better follow the crowd. It shook me rigid to get there and find the casket open and poor old Oscar lying there in his brown tweed suit, wearing a suntan makeup and just the wrong shade of lipstick. If I had not been extremely fond of the old boy, I have a horrible feeling that I might have giggled. Then and there I decided that I could never face another American funeral—even dead.

25   The casket (which has been resting throughout the service on a Classic Beauty Ultra Metal Casket Bier) is now transferred by a hydraulically operated device called Porto-Lift to a balloon-tired, Glide Easy casket carriage which will wheel it to yet another conveyance, the Cadillac Funeral Coach. This may be lavender, cream, light green—anything but black. Interiors, of course, are color-correlated, "for the man who cannot stop short of perfection."

26   At graveside, the casket is lowered into the earth. This office, once the prerogative of friends of the deceased, is now performed by a patented mechanical lowering device. A "Lifetime Green" artificial grass mat is at the ready to conceal the sere earth, and overhead, to conceal the sky, is a portable Steril Chapel Tent ("resists the intense heat and humidity of summer and the terrific storms of winter . . . available in Silver Grey, Rose, or Evergreen"). Now is the time for the ritual scattering of earth over the coffin, as the solemn words "earth to earth, ashes to ashes, dust to dust" are pronounced by the officiating cleric. This can today be accomplished "with a mere flick of the wrist with the Gordon Leak-Proof Earth Dispenser. No grasping of a handful of dirt, no soiled fingers. Simple, dignified, beautiful, reverent! The modern way!" The Gordon Earth Dispenser (at $5) is of nickel-plated brass construction. It is not only "attractive to the eye and long wearing"; it is also "one of the 'tools' for building better public relations" if presented as "an appropriate non-commercial gift" to the clergyman. It is shaped something like a saltshaker.

27   Untouched by human hand, the coffin and the earth are now united.

28   It is in the function of directing the participants through this maze of gadgetry that the funeral director has assigned to himself his relatively new role of "grief therapist." He has relieved the family of every detail, he has revamped

the corpse to look like a living doll, he has arranged for it to nap for a few days in a slumber room, he has put on a well-oiled performance in which the concept of *death* has played no part whatsoever—unless it was inconsiderately mentioned by the clergyman who conducted the religious service. He has done everything in his power to make the funeral a real pleasure for everybody concerned. He and his team have given their all to score an upset victory over death.

6

Classification

Classification

1. **Develop a method of classification.** Classification is simply the organization of information into groups. You can classify using two methods: grouping similar items, such as types of poisonous snakes, and dividing parts of a larger item, such as components of a computer. In either case, you must decide how you'd like to classify the information: you could classify poisonous snakes according to their habitats, anatomical characteristics, or level of danger to humans. Depending on your audience, different methods will be more or less useful. Doctors (and campers) may be more interested in danger to humans, but biologists might prefer an arrangement according to habitat or anatomy.

2. **Make your classification consistent and complete.** While it's obvious that a classification of snakes that doesn't include rattlers wouldn't be very useful, some classification errors are subtler. It might seem unimportant to include the power cord in a classification of a computer, but if readers try to use your information to help buy the components for a computer, they won't have all the information they need. Consistency is also important. Don't start your discussion of pizza classifying by ingredients, then switch halfway through to an arrangement according to pizzeria locations.

3. **Use clear and specific examples.** Examples add life even to seemingly mundane topics. What's the most boring topic you can think of? Watching grass grow? Watching paint dry? In an essay classifying types of grass, examples make the difference between life and death (by boredom). Add a few examples—the neighbor whose Kentucky tall fescue grew so fast, he went through four lawnmower blades in a single summer; the obsessed gardener who was so driven to remove every blade of crabgrass from his lawn, he incinerated his front yard with a blowtorch—and suddenly even grass growing is exciting.

4. **Organize the essay to support your purpose.** Afraid your readers won't read past the first sentence in your grass-growing essay? Move the blowtorch example to the front. Want to leave your readers with a lasting final impression? Save your best category for last. You can organize your essay any way you want, as long as your readers are able to follow along. In order to hold readers' attention, classification essays need to make a point. Make sure your organization suits that purpose.

Judith Viorst

Friends, Good Friends—and Such Good Friends

Judith Viorst wanted to be a writer since she was a child; her first book was a collection of poems published in 1965. Her second collection, *It's Hard to Be Hip over Thirty and Other Tragedies of Married Life*, was published in 1968 and established Viorst as a best selling author of light verse. Her poems and also her children's books strike a chord with readers by shedding a humorous light on the little moments of everyday life–her inspiration frequently comes from her own marriage (to political reporter and journalist Milton Viorst) and her three children. Several of Viorst's articles in *Redbook* have won awards, and she won an Emmy in 1970 for her poetic monologues written for the CBS television special *Annie: The Women in the Life of a Man*. Although her writing has taken on deeper issues since she graduated from the Washington Psychoanalytic Institute, she still injects it with humor and compassion.

WOMEN ARE FRIENDS, I once would have said, when they totally love and support and trust each other, and bare to each other the secrets of their souls, and run—no questions asked—to help each other, and tell harsh truths to each other (no, you can't wear that dress unless you lose ten pounds first) when harsh truths must be told. 1

Women are friends, I once would have said, when they share the same affection for Ingmar Bergman, plus train rides, cats, warm rain, charades, Camus, and hate with equal ardor Newark and Brussels sprouts and Lawrence Welk and camping. 2

In other words, I once would have said that a friend is a friend all the way, but now I believe that's a narrow point of view. For the friendships I have and the friendships I see are conducted at many levels of intensity, serve many different functions, meet different needs and range from those as all-the-way as the friendship of the soul sisters mentioned above to that of the most nonchalant and casual playmates. 3

Consider these varieties of friendship: 4

1. Convenience friends. These are women with whom, if our paths weren't crossing all the time, we'd have no particular reason to be friends: a next-door neighbor, a woman in our car pool, the mother of one of our children's closest friends or maybe some mommy with whom we serve juice and cookies each week at the Glenwood Co-op Nursery. 5

Convenience friends are convenient indeed. They'll lend us their cups and silverware for a party. They'll drive our kids to soccer when we're sick. They'll take us to pick up our car when we need a lift to the garage. They'll even take our cats when we go on vacation. As we will for them. 6

7   But we don't, with convenience friends, ever come too close or tell too much; we maintain our public face and emotional distance. "Which means," says Elaine, "that I'll talk about being overweight but not about being depressed. Which means I'll admit being mad but not blind with rage. Which means that I might say that we're pinched this month but never that I'm worried sick over money."

8   But which doesn't mean that there isn't sufficient value to be found in these friendships of mutual aid, in convenience friends.

9   2. Special-interest friends. These friendships aren't intimate, and they needn't involve kids or silverware or cats. Their value lies in some interest jointly shared. And so we may have an office friend or a yoga friend or a tennis friend or a friend from the Women's Democratic Club.

10   "I've got one woman friend," says Joyce, "who likes, as I do, to take psychology courses. Which makes it nice for me—and nice for her. It's fun to go with someone you know and it's fun to discuss what you've learned, driving back from the classes." And for the most part, she says, that's all they discuss.

11   "I'd say that what we're doing is *doing* together, not being together," Suzanne says of her Tuesday-doubles friends. "It's mainly a tennis relationship, but we play together well. And I guess we all need to have a couple of playmates."

12   I agree.

13   My playmate is a shopping friend, a woman of marvelous taste, a woman who knows exactly *where* to buy *what,* and furthermore is a woman who always knows beyond a doubt what one ought to be buying. I don't have the time to keep up with what's new in eyeshadow, hemlines and shoes and whether the smock look is in or finished already. But since (oh, shame!) I care a lot about eyeshadow, hemlines and shoes, and since I don't *want* to wear smocks if the smock look is finished, I'm very glad to have a shopping friend.

14   3. Historical friends. We all have a friend who knew us when . . . maybe way back in Miss Meltzer's second grade, when our family lived in that three-room flat in Brooklyn, when our dad was out of work for seven months, when our brother Allie got in that fight where they had to call the police, when our sister married the endodontist from Yonkers and when, the morning after we lost our virginity, she was the first, the only, friend we told.

15   The years have gone by and we've gone separate ways and we've little in common now, but we're still an intimate part of each other's past. And so whenever we go to Detroit we always go to visit this friend of our girlhood. Who knows how we looked before our teeth were straightened. Who knows how we talked before our voice got un-Brooklyned. Who knows what we ate before we learned about artichokes. And who, by her presence, puts us in touch with an earlier part of ourself, a part of ourself it's important never to lose.

"What this friend means to me and what I mean to her," says Grace, "is having a sister without sibling rivalry. We know the texture of each other's lives. She remembers my grandmother's cabbage soup. I remember the way her uncle played the piano. There's simply no other friend who remembers those things." 16

4. Crossroads friends. Like historical friends, our crossroads friends are important for *what was*—for the friendship we shared at a crucial, now past, time of life. A time, perhaps, when we roomed in college together; or worked as eager young singles in the Big City together; or went together, as my friend Elizabeth and I did, through pregnancy, birth and that scary first year of new motherhood. 17

Crossroads friends forge powerful links, links strong enough to endure with not much more contact than once-a-year letters at Christmas. And out of respect for those crossroads years, for those dramas and dreams we once shared, we will always be friends. 18

5. Cross-generational friends. Historical friends and crossroads friends seem to maintain a special kind of intimacy—dormant but always ready to be revived—and though we may rarely meet, whenever we do connect, it's personal and intense. Another kind of intimacy exists in the friendships that form across generations in what one woman calls her daughter-mother and her mother-daughter relationships. 19

Evelyn's friend is her mother's age—"but I share so much more than I ever could with my mother"—a woman she talks to of music, of books and of life. "What I get from her is the benefit of her experience. What she gets—and enjoys—from me is a youthful perspective. It's a pleasure for both of us." 20

I have in my own life a precious friend, a woman of 65 who has lived very hard, who is wise, who listens well; who has been where I am and can help me understand it; and who represents not only an ultimate ideal mother to me but also the person I'd like to be when I grow up. 21

In our daughter role we tend to do more than our share of self-revelation; in our mother role we tend to receive what's revealed. It's another kind of pleasure—playing wise mother to a questing younger person. It's another very lovely kind of friendship. 22

6. Part-of-a-couple friends. Some of the women we call our friends we never see alone—we see them as part of a couple at couples' parties. And though we share interests in many things and respect each other's views, we aren't moved to deepen the relationship. Whatever the reason, a lack of time or—and this is more likely—a lack of chemistry, our friendship remains in the context of a group. But the fact that our feeling on seeing each other is always, "I'm *so* glad she's here" and the fact that we spend half the evening talking together says that this too, in its own way, counts as a friendship. 23

24   (Other part-of-a-couple friends are the friends that came with the marriage, and some of these are friends we could live without. But sometimes, alas, she married our husband's best friend; and sometimes, alas, she *is* our husband's best friend. And so we find ourself dealing with her, somewhat against our will, in a spirit of what I'll call *reluctant* friendship.)

25   7. Men who are friends. I wanted to write just of women friends, but the women I've talked to won't let me—they say I must mention man-woman friendships too. For these friendships can be just as close and as dear as those that we form with women. Listen to Lucy's description of one such friendship:

26   "We've found we have things to talk about that are different from what he talks about with my husband and different from what I talk about with his wife. So sometimes we call on the phone or meet for lunch. There are similar intellectual interests—we always pass on to each other the books that we love—but there's also something tender and caring too."

27   In a couple of crises, Lucy says, "he offered himself for talking and for helping. And when someone died in his family he wanted me there. The sexual, flirty part of our friendship is very small, but *some*—just enough to make it fun and different." She thinks—and I agree—that the sexual part, though small, is always *some*, is always there when a man and a woman are friends.

28   It's only in the past few years that I've made friends with men, in the sense of a friendship that's *mine*, not just part of two couples. And achieving with them the ease and the trust I've found with women friends has value indeed. Under the dryer at home last week, putting on mascara and rouge, I comfortably sat and talked with a fellow named Peter. Peter, I finally decided, could handle the shock of me minus mascara under the dryer. Because we care for each other. Because we're friends.

29   8. There are medium friends, and pretty good friends, and very good friends indeed, and these friendships are defined by their level of intimacy. And what we'll reveal at each of these levels of intimacy is calibrated with care. We might tell a medium friend, for example, that yesterday we had a fight with our husband. And we might tell a pretty good friend that this fight with our husband made us so mad that we slept on the couch. And we might tell a very good friend that the reason we got so mad in that fight that we slept on the couch had something to do with that girl who works in his office. But it's only to our very best friends that we're willing to tell all, to tell what's going on with that girl in his office.

30   The best of friends, I still believe, totally love and support and trust each other, and bare to each other the secrets of their souls, and run—no questions asked—to help each other, and tell harsh truths to each other when they must be told.

31   But we needn't agree about everything (only 12-year-old girl friends agree

about *everything)* to tolerate each other's point of view. To accept without judgment. To give and to take without ever keeping score. And to *be* there, as I am for them and as they are for me, to comfort our sorrows, to celebrate our joys.

Jane Austen

from *Pride and Prejudice*

A novelist and social critic, Jane Austen (1775–1817) wrote most often about society and marriage. Ironically, she never married, and kept herself quite removed from society. This excerpt from her novel, *Pride and Prejudice*, offers a penetrating description of the relationship between the Bennets, and the urgency which accompanied the custom of marriage.

IT IS A TRUTH UNIVERSALLY ACKNOWLEDGED that a single man in possession of   1
a good fortune must be in want of a wife.

However little known the feelings or views of such a man may be on his   2
first entering a neighbourhood, this truth is so well fixed in the minds of the surrounding families that he is considered as the rightful property of some one or other of their daughters.

"My dear Mr. Bennet," said his lady to him one day, "have you heard that   3
Netherfield Park is let at last?"

Mr. Bennet replied that he had not.   4

"But it is," returned she; "for Mrs. Long has just been here, and she told   5
me all about it."

Mr. Bennet made no answer.   6

"Do not you want to know who has taken it?" cried his wife impatiently.   7

"*You* want to tell me, and I have no objection to hearing it."   8

This was invitation enough.   9

"Why, my dear, you must know, Mrs. Long says that Netherfield is taken   10
by a young man of large fortune from the north of England; that he came down on Monday in a chaise and four to see the place, and was so much delighted with it that he agreed with Mr. Morris immediately; that he is to take possession before Michaelmas, and some of his servants are to be in the house by the end of next week."

"What is his name?"   11

"Bingley."   12

13   "Is he married or single?"

14   "Oh! single, my dear, to be sure! A single man of large fortune; four or five thousand a year. What a fine thing for our girls!"

15   "How so? How can it affect them?"

16   "My dear Mr. Bennet," replied his wife, "how can you be so tiresome! You must know that I am thinking of his marrying one of them."

17   "Is that his design in settling here?"

18   "Design! nonsense, how can you talk so! But it is very likely that he *may* fall in love with one of them, and therefore you must visit him as soon as he comes."

19   "I see no occasion for that. You and the girls may go, or you may send them by themselves, which perhaps will be still better, for as you are as handsome as any of them, Mr. Bingley might like you the best of the party."

20   "My dear, you flatter me. I certainly *have* had my share of beauty, but I do not pretend to be anything extraordinary now. When a woman has five grown up daughters, she ought to give over thinking of her own beauty."

21   "In such cases, a woman has not often much beauty to think of."

22   "But, my dear, you must indeed go and see Mr. Bingley when he comes into the neighbourhood."

23   "It is more than I engage for, I assure you."

24   "But consider your daughters. Only think what an establishment it would be for one of them. Sir William and Lady Lucas are determined to go, merely on that account, for in general you know they visit no newcomers. Indeed you must go, for it will be impossible for us to visit him if you do not."

25   "You are over scrupulous surely. I dare say Mr. Bingley will be very glad to see you; and I will send a few lines by you to assure him of my hearty consent to his marrying whichever he chooses of the girls; though I must throw in a good word for my little Lizzy."

26   "I desire you will do no such thing. Lizzy is not a bit better than the others; and I am sure she is not half so handsome as Jane, nor half so good-humoured as Lydia. But you are always giving *her* the preference."

27   "They have none of them much to recommend them," replied he; "they are all silly and ignorant like other girls; but Lizzy has something more of quickness than her sisters."

28   "Mr. Bennet, how can you abuse your own children in such a way? You take delight in vexing me. You have no compassion on my poor nerves."

29   "You mistake me, my dear. I have a high respect for your nerves. They are my old friends. I have heard you mention them with consideration these twenty years at least."

30   "Ah! you do not know what I suffer."

31   "But I hope you will get over it, and live to see many young men of four thousand a year come into the neighbourhood."

"It will be no use to us if twenty such should come since you will not visit   32
them."

"Depend upon it, my dear, that when there are twenty, I will visit them   33
all."

Mr. Bennet was so odd a mixture of quick parts, sarcastic humour, reserve,   34
and caprice, that the experience of three and twenty years had been insufficient to make his wife understand his character. *Her* mind was less difficult to
develop. She was a woman of mean understanding, little information, and uncertain temper. When she was discontented she fancied herself nervous. The
business of her life was to get her daughters married; its solace was visiting and
news.

William Zinsser

College Pressures

William Zinsser's knowledge of writing comes firsthand and started with his first job working at the *New York Herald Tribune* from 1946 to 1959. His experience with college pressures comes from not only his own school-ing at Princeton University, but also from his nine years of teaching English at Yale University. It was his popu-lar writing course that inspired his book *On Writing Well: An Informal Guide to Writing Nonfiction*, which has become a classic guide to writing. He has also written books about his other passions: baseball, jazz, and traveling.

Dear Carlos: I desperately need a dean's excuse for my chem midterm which will   1
begin in about 1 hour. All I can say is that I totally blew it this week. I've fallen
incredibly, inconceivably behind.

Carlos: Help! I'm anxious to hear from you. I'll be in my room and won't leave it   2
until I hear from you. Tomorrow is the last day for . . .

Carlos: I left town because I started bugging out again. I stayed up all night to fin-   3
ish a take-home make-up exam & am typing it to hand in on the 10th. It was due
on the 5th. P.S. I'm going to the dentist. Pain is pretty bad.

Carlos: Probably by Friday I'll be able to get back to my studies. Right now I'm   4
going to take a long walk. This whole thing has taken a lot out of me.

5   *Carlos: I'm really up the proverbial creek. The problem is I really bombed the history final. Since I need that course for my major I . . .*

6   *Carlos: Here follows a tale of woe. I went home this weekend, had to help my Mom, & caught a fever so didn't have much time to study. My professor . . .*

7   *Carlos: Aargh! Trouble. Nothing original but everything's piling up at once. To be brief, my job interview . . .*

8   *Hey Carlos, good news! I've got mononucleosis.*

9   Who are these wretched supplicants, scribbling notes so laden with anxiety, seeking such miracles of postponement and balm? They are men and women who belong to Branford College, one of the twelve residential colleges at Yale University, and the messages are just a few of the hundreds that they left for their dean, Carlos Hortas—often slipped under his door at 4 A.M.—last year.

10   But students like the ones who wrote those notes can also be found on campuses from coast to coast—especially in New England and at many other private colleges across the country that have high academic standards and highly motivated students. Nobody could doubt that the notes are real. In their urgency and their gallows humor they are authentic voices of a generation that is panicky to succeed.

11   My own connection with the message writers is that I am master of Branford College. I live in its Gothic quadrangle and know the students well. (We have 485 of them.) I am privy to their hopes and fears—and also to their stereo music and their piercing cries in the dead of the night ("Does anybody *ca-a-are?*"). If they went to Carlos to ask how to get through tomorrow, they come to me to ask how to get through the rest of their lives.

12   Mainly I try to remind them that the road ahead is a long one and that it will have more unexpected turns than they think. There will be plenty of time to change jobs, change careers, change whole attitudes and approaches. They don't want to hear such liberating news. They want a map—right now—that they can follow unswervingly to career security, financial security, Social Security and, presumably, a prepaid grave.

13   What I wish for all students is some release from the clammy grip of the future. I wish them a chance to savor each segment of their education as an experience in itself and not as a grim preparation for the next step. I wish them the right to experiment, to trip and fall, to learn that defeat is as instructive as victory and is not the end of the world.

14   My wish, of course, is naïve. One of the few rights that America does not proclaim is the right to fail. Achievement is the national god, venerated in our

media—the million-dollar athlete, the wealthy executive—and glorified in our praise of possessions. In the presence of such a potent state religion, the young are growing up old.

I see four kinds of pressure working on college students today: economic 15 pressure, parental pressure, peer pressure, and self-induced pressure. It is easy to look around for villains—to blame the colleges for charging too much money, the professors for assigning too much work, the parents for pushing their children too far, the students for driving themselves too hard. But there are no villains; only victims.

"In the late 1960s," one dean told me, "the typical question that I got from 16 students was 'Why is there so much suffering in the world?' or 'How can I make a contribution?' Today it's 'Do you think it would look better for getting into law school if I did a double major in history and political science, or just majored in one of them?'" Many other deans confirmed this pattern. One said: "They're trying to find an edge—the intangible something that will look better on paper if two students are about equal."

Note the emphasis on looking better. The transcript has become a sacred 17 document, the passport to security. How one appears on paper is more important than how one appears in person. A is for Admirable and B is for Borderline, even though, in Yale's official system of grading, A means "excellent" and B means "very good." Today, looking very good is no longer good enough, especially for students who hope to go on to law school or medical school. They know that entrance into the better schools will be an entrance into the better law firms and better medical practices where they will make a lot of money. They also know that the odds are harsh. Yale Law School, for instance, matriculates 170 students from an applicant pool of 3,700; Harvard enrolls 550 from a pool of 7,000.

It's all very well for those of us who write letters of recommendation for 18 our students to stress the qualities of humanity that will make them good lawyers or doctors. And it's nice to think that admission officers are really reading our letters and looking for the extra dimension of commitment or concern. Still, it would be hard for a student not to visualize these officers shuffling so many transcripts studded with As that they regard a B as positively shameful.

The pressure is almost as heavy on students who just want to graduate and 19 get a job. Long gone are the days of the "gentleman's C," when students journeyed through college with a certain relaxation, sampling a wide variety of courses—music, art, philosophy, classics, anthropology, poetry, religion—that would send them out as liberally educated men and women. If I were an employer I would rather employ graduates who have this range and curiosity than those who narrowly pursued safe subjects and high grades. I know countless students whose inquiring minds exhilarate me. I like to hear the play of their ideas. I don't know if they are getting As or Cs, and I don't care. I also like them as people. The country needs them, and they will find satisfying jobs. I tell them to relax. They can't.

20   Nor can I blame them. They live in a brutal economy. Tuition, room, and board at most private colleges now comes to at least $7,000 [in 1979], not counting books and fees. This might seem to suggest that the colleges are getting rich. But they are equally battered by inflation. Tuition covers only 60 percent of what it costs to educate a student, and ordinarily the remainder comes from what colleges receive in endowments, grants, and gifts. Now the remainder keeps being swallowed by the cruel costs—higher every year—of just opening the doors. Heating oil is up. Insurance is up. Postage is up. Health-premium costs are up. Everything is up. Deficits are up. We are witnessing in America the creation of a brotherhood of paupers—colleges, parents, and students, joined by the common bond of debt.

21   Today it is not unusual for a student, even if he works part time at college and full time during the summer, to accrue $5,000 in loans after four years—loans that he must start to repay within one year after graduation. Exhorted at commencement to go forth into the world, he is already behind as he goes forth. How could he not feel under pressure throughout college to prepare for this day of reckoning? I have used "he," incidentally, only for brevity. Women at Yale are under no less pressure to justify their expensive education to themselves, their parents, and society. In fact, they are probably under more pressure. For although they leave college superbly equipped to bring fresh leadership to traditionally male jobs, society hasn't yet caught up with this fact.

22   Along with economic pressure goes parental pressure. Inevitably, the two are deeply intertwined.

23   I see many students taking pre-medical courses with joyless tenacity. They go off to their labs as if they were going to the dentist. It saddens me because I know them in other corners of their life as cheerful people.

24   "Do you want to go to medical school?" I ask them.

25   "I guess so," they say, without conviction, or "Not really."

26   "Then why are you going?"

27   "Well, my parents want me to be a doctor. They're paying all this money and . . ."

28   Poor students, poor parents. They are caught in one of the oldest webs of love and duty and guilt. The parents mean well; they are trying to steer their sons and daughters toward a secure future. But the sons and daughters want to major in history or classics or philosophy—subjects with no "practical" value. Where's the payoff on the humanities? It's not easy to persuade such loving parents that the humanities do indeed pay off. The intellectual facul-

ties developed by studying subjects like history and classics—an ability to synthesize and relate, to weigh cause and effect, to see events in perspective—are just the faculties that make creative leaders in business or almost any general field. Still, many fathers would rather put their money on courses that point toward a specific profession—courses that are pre-law, pre-medical, pre-business, or, as I sometimes heard it put, "pre-rich."

But the pressure on students is severe. They are truly torn. One part of 29 them feels obligated to fulfill their parents' expectations; after all, their parents are older and presumably wiser. Another part tells them that the expectations that are right for their parents are not right for them.

I know a student who wants to be an artist. She is very obviously an artist 30 and will be a good one—she has already had several modest local exhibits. Meanwhile she is growing as a well-rounded person and taking humanistic subjects that will enrich the inner resources out of which her art will grow. But her father is strongly opposed. He thinks that an artist is a "dumb" thing to be. The student vacillates and tries to please everybody. She keeps up with her art somewhat furtively and takes some of the "dumb" courses her father wants her to take—at least they are dumb courses for her. She is a free spirit on a campus of tense students—no small achievement in itself—and she deserves to follow her muse.

Peer pressure and self-induced pressure are also intertwined, and they 31 begin almost at the beginning of freshman year.

"I had a freshman student I'll call Linda," one dean told me, "who came 32 in and said she was under terrible pressure because her roommate, Barbara, was much brighter and studied all the time. I couldn't tell her that Barbara had come in two hours earlier to say the same thing about Linda."

The story is almost funny—except that it's not. It's symptomatic of all the 33 pressures put together. When every student thinks every other student is working harder and doing better, the only solution is to study harder still. I see students going off to the library every night after dinner and coming back when it closes at midnight. I wish they would sometimes forget about their peers and go to a movie. I hear the clacking of typewriters in the hours before dawn. I see the tension in their eyes when exams are approaching and papers are due: *"Will I get everything done?"*

Probably they won't. They will get sick. They will get "blocked." They will 34 sleep. They will oversleep. They will bug out. *Hey, Carlos, help!*

Part of the problem is that they do more than they are expected to do. A 35 professor will assign five-page papers. Several students will start writing ten-page papers to impress him. Then more students will write ten-page papers, and a few will raise the ante to fifteen. Pity the poor student who is still just doing the assignment.

"Once you have twenty or thirty percent of the student population delib- 36 erately overexerting," one dean points out, "it's bad for everybody. When a teacher gets more and more effort from his class, the student who is doing normal work can be perceived as not doing well. The tactic works, psychologically."

37   Why can't the professor just cut back and not accept longer papers? He can, and he probably will. But by then the term will be half over and the damage done. Grade fever is highly contagious and not easily reversed. Besides, the professor's main concern is with his course. He knows his students only in relation to the course and doesn't know that they are also overexerting in their other courses. Nor is it really his business. He didn't sign up for dealing with the student as a whole person and with all the emotional baggage the student brought along from home. That's what deans, masters, chaplains, and psychiatrists are for.

38   To some extent this is nothing new: a certain number of professors have always been self-contained islands of scholarship and shyness, more comfortable with books than with people. But the new pauperism has widened the gap still further, for professors who actually like to spend time with students don't have as much time to spend. They are also overexerting. If they are young, they are busy trying to publish in order not to perish, hanging by their fingernails onto a shrinking profession. If they are old and tenured, they are buried under the duties of administering departments—as departmental chairmen or members of committees—that have been thinned out by the budgetary axe.

39   Ultimately it will be the students' own business to break the circles in which they are trapped. They are too young to be prisoners of their parents' dreams and their classmates' fears. They must be jolted into believing in themselves as unique men and women who have the power to shape their own future.

40   "Violence is being done to the undergraduate experience," says Carlos Hortas. "College should be open-ended: at the end it should open many, many roads. Instead, students are choosing their goal in advance, and their choices narrow as they go along. It's almost as if they think that the country has been codified in the type of jobs that exist—that they've got to fit into certain slots. Therefore, fit into the best-paying slot.

41   "They ought to take chances. Not taking chances will lead to a life of colorless mediocrity. They'll be comfortable. But something in the spirit will be missing."

42   I have painted too drab a portrait of today's students, making them seem a solemn lot. That is only half of their story; if they were so dreary I wouldn't so thoroughly enjoy their company. The other half is that they are easy to like. They are quick to laugh and to offer friendship. They are not introverts. They are unusually kind and are more considerate of one another than any student generation I have known.

Nor are they so obsessed with their studies that they avoid sports and ex-   43
tracurricular activities. On the contrary, they juggle their crowded hours to
play on a variety of teams, perform with musical and dramatic groups, and
write for campus publications. But this in turn is one more cause of anxiety.
There are too many choices. Academically, they have 1,300 courses to select
from; outside class they have to decide how much spare time they can spare
and how to spend it.

This means that they engage in fewer extracurricular pursuits than their   44
predecessors did. If they want to row on the crew and play in the symphony
they will eliminate one; in the '60s they would have done both. They also tend
to choose activities that are self-limiting. Drama, for instance, is flourishing in
all twelve of Yale's residential colleges as it never has before. Students hurl
themselves into these productions—as actors, directors, carpenters, and tech-
nicians—with a dedication to create the best possible play, knowing that the
day will come when the run will end and they can get back to their studies.

They also can't afford to be the willing slave of organizations like the *Yale*   45
Daily News. Last spring at the one-hundredth anniversary banquet of that
paper—whose past chairmen include such once and future kings as Potter
Stewart, Kingman Brewster, and William F. Buckley, Jr.—much was made of
the fact that the editorial staff used to be small and totally committed and that
"newsies" routinely worked fifty hours a week. In effect they belonged to a
club; Newsies is how they defined themselves at Yale. Today's student will
write one or two articles a week, when he can, and he defines himself as a student. I've never heard the word Newsie except at the banquet.

If I have described the modern undergraduate primarily as a driven crea-   46
ture who is largely ignoring the blithe spirit inside who keeps trying to come
out and play, it's because that's where the crunch is, not only at Yale but
throughout American education. It's why I think we should all be worried
about the values that are nurturing a generation so fearful of risk and so goal-
obsessed at such an early age.

I tell students that there is no one "right" way to get ahead—that each of them   47
is a different person, starting from a different point and bound for a different
destination. I tell them that change is a tonic and that all the slots are not codified nor the frontiers closed. One of my ways of telling them is to invite men and
women who have achieved success outside the academic world to come and talk
informally with my students during the year. They are heads of companies or ad
agencies, editors of magazines, politicians, public officials, television magnates,
labor leaders, business executives, Broadway producers, artists, writers, econo-
mists, photographers, scientists, historians—a mixed bag of achievers.

I ask them to say a few words about how they got started. The students as-   48
sume that they started in their present profession and knew all along that it

was what they wanted to do. Luckily for me, most of them got into their field by a circuitous route, to their surprise, after many detours. The students are startled. They can hardly conceive of a career that was not pre-planned. They can hardly imagine allowing the hand of God or chance to nudge them down some unforeseen trail.

Lewis Thomas

The Technology of Medicine

Lewis Thomas (1913–1993) had a distinguished career as a professor of medicine, working with several university hospitals and serving on countless advisory committees. In addition to contributing hundreds of articles to medical and scientific journals, he wrote the column "Notes of a Biology Watcher" in the *New England Journal of Medicine* for over 20 years. *The Lives of a Cell: Notes of a Biology Watcher*, a collection of these columns, received a National Book Award in 1974. His writings—scientifically precise, detailed, informative, but also poetic—always remind us of our place in the universe.

1   TECHNOLOGY ASSESSMENT HAS BECOME a routine exercise for the scientific enterprises on which the country is obliged to spend vast sums for its needs. Brainy committees are continually evaluating the effectiveness and cost of doing various things in space, defense, energy, transportation, and the like, to give advice about prudent investments for the future.

2   Somehow medicine, for all the $80-odd billion that it is said to cost the nation, has not yet come in for much of this analytical treatment. It seems taken for granted that the technology of medicine simply exists, take it or leave it, and the only major technologic problem which policy-makers are interested in is how to deliver today's kind of health care, with equity, to all the people.

3   When, as is bound to happen sooner or later, the analysts get around to the technology of medicine itself, they will have to face the problem of measuring the relative cost and effectiveness of all the things that are done in the management of disease. They make their living at this kind of thing, and I wish them well, but I imagine they will have a bewildering time. For one thing, our methods of managing disease are constantly changing—partly under the influence of new bits of information brought in from all corners of biologic science. At the same time, a great many things are done that are not so closely related to science, some not related at all.

In fact, there are three quite different levels of technology in medicine, so unlike each other as to seem altogether different undertakings. Practitioners of medicine and the analysts will be in trouble if they are not kept separate.

1. First of all, there is a large body of what might be termed "nontechnol-   4
ogy," impossible to measure in terms of its capacity to alter either the natural course of disease or its eventual outcome. A great deal of money is spent on this. It is valued highly by the professionals as well as the patients. It consists of what is sometimes called "supportive therapy." It tides patients over through diseases that are not, by and large, understood. It is what is meant by the phrases "caring for" and "standing by." It is indispensable. It is not, how-ever, a technology in any real sense, since it does not involve measures directed at the underlying mechanism of disease.

It includes the large part of any good doctor's time that is taken up with   5
simply providing reassurance, explaining to patients who fear that they have contracted one or another lethal disease that they are, in fact, quite healthy.

It is what physicians used to be engaged in at the bedside of patients with   6
diphtheria, meningitis, poliomyelitis, lobar pneumonia, and all the rest of the infectious diseases that have since come under control.

It is what physicians must now do for patients with intractable cancer, se-   7
vere rheumatoid arthritis, multiple sclerosis, stroke, and advanced cirrhosis. One can think of at least twenty major diseases that require this kind of sup-portive medical care because of the absence of an effective technology. I would include a large amount of what is called mental disease, and most va-rieties of cancer, in this category.

The cost of this nontechnology is very high, and getting higher all the   8
time. It requires not only a great deal of time but also very hard effort and skill on the part of physicians; only the very best of doctors are good at coping with this kind of defeat. It also involves long periods of hospitalization, lots of nurs-ing, lots of involvement of nonmedical professionals in and out of the hospi-tal. It represents, in short, a substantial segment of today's expenditures for health.

2. At the next level up is a kind of technology best termed "halfway tech-   9
nology." This represents the kinds of things that must be done after the fact, in efforts to compensate for the incapacitating effects of certain diseases whose course one is unable to do very much about. It is a technology designed to make up for disease, or to postpone death.

The outstanding examples in recent years are the transplantations of   10
hearts, kidneys, livers, and other organs, and the equally spectacular inventions of artificial organs. In the public mind, this kind of technology has come to seem like the equivalent of the high technologies of the physical sciences. The media tend to present each new procedure as though it represented a break-through and therapeutic triumph, instead of the makeshift that it really is.

11   In fact, this level of technology is, by its nature, at the same time highly so-phisticated and profoundly primitive. It is the kind of thing that one must continue to do until there is a genuine understanding of the mechanisms in-volved in disease. In chronic glomerulonephritis, for example, a much clearer insight will be needed into the events leading to the destruction of glomeruli by the immunologic reactants that now appear to govern this disease, before one will know how to intervene intelligently to prevent the process, or turn it around. But when this level of understanding has been reached, the technol-ogy of kidney replacement will not be much needed and should no longer pose the huge problem of logistics, cost, and ethics that it poses today.

12   An extremely complex and costly technology for the management of coro-nary heart disease has evolved—involving specialized ambulances and hospital units, all kinds of electronic gadgetry, and whole platoons of new professional personnel—to deal with the end results of coronary thrombosis. Almost every-thing offered today for the treatment of heart disease is at this level of tech-nology, with the transplanted and artificial hearts as ultimate examples. When enough has been learned to know what really goes wrong in heart dis-ease, one ought to be in a position to figure out ways to prevent or reverse the process, and when this happens the current elaborate technology will proba-bly be set to one side.

13   Much of what is done in the treatment of cancer, by surgery, irradiation, and chemotherapy, represents halfway technology, in the sense that these mea-sures are directed at the existence of already established cancer cells, but not at the mechanisms by which cells become neoplastic.

14   It is a characteristic of this kind of technology that it costs an enormous amount of money and requires a continuing expansion of hospital facilities. There is no end to the need for new, highly trained people to run the enter-prise. And there is really no way out of this, at the present state of knowledge. If the installation of specialized coronary-care units can result in the extension of life for only a few patients with coronary disease (and there is no question that this technology is effective in a few cases), it seems to me an inevitable fact of life that as many of these as can be will be put together, and as much money as can be found will be spent. I do not see that anyone has much choice in this. The only thing that can move medicine away from this level of technology is new information, and the only imaginable source of this infor-mation is research.

15   3. The third type of technology is the kind that is so effective that it seems to attract the least public notice; it has come to be taken for granted. This is the genuinely decisive technology of modern medicine, exemplified best by modern methods for immunization against diphtheria, pertussis, and the childhood virus diseases, and the contemporary use of antibiotics and chemotherapy for bacterial infections. The capacity to deal effectively with

syphilis and tuberculosis represents a milestone in human endeavor, even though full use of this potential has not yet been made. And there are, of course, other examples: the treatment of endocrinologic disorders with appropriate hormones, the prevention of hemolytic disease of the newborn, the treatment and prevention of various nutritional disorders, and perhaps just around the corner the management of Parkinsonism and sickle-cell anemia. There are other examples, and everyone will have his favorite candidates for the list, but the truth is that there are nothing like as many as the public has been led to believe.

The point to be made about this kind of technology—the real high technology of medicine—is that it comes as the result of a genuine understanding of disease mechanisms, and when it becomes available, it is relatively inexpensive, and relatively easy to deliver. 16

Offhand, I cannot think of any important human disease for which medicine possesses the outright capacity to prevent or cure where the cost of the technology is itself a major problem. The price is never as high as the cost of managing the same diseases during the earlier stages of no-technology or halfway technology. If a case of typhoid fever had to be managed today by the best methods of 1935, it would run to a staggering expense. At, say, around fifty days of hospitalization, requiring the most demanding kind of nursing care, with the obsessive concern for details of diet that characterized the therapy of that time, with daily laboratory monitoring, and, on occasion, surgical intervention for abdominal catastrophe, I should think $10,000 would be a conservative estimate for the illness, as contrasted with today's cost of a bottle of chloramphenicol and a day or two of fever. The halfway technology that was evolving for poliomyelitis in the early 1950s, just before the emergence of the basic research that made the vaccine possible, provides another illustration of the point. Do you remember Sister Kenny, and the cost of those institutes for rehabilitation, with all those ceremonially applied hot fomentations, and the debates about whether the affected limbs should be totally immobilized or kept in passive motion as frequently as possible, and the masses of statistically tormented data mobilized to support one view or the other? It is the cost of that kind of technology, and its relative effectiveness, that must be compared with the cost and effectiveness of the vaccine. 17

Pulmonary tuberculosis had similar episodes in its history. There was a sudden enthusiasm for the surgical removal of infected lung tissue in the early 1950s, and elaborate plans were being made for new and expensive installations for major pulmonary surgery in tuberculosis hospitals, and the INH and streptomycin came along and the hospitals themselves were closed up. 18

It is when physicians are bogged down by their incomplete technologies, by the innumerable things they are obliged to do in medicine when they lack a clear understanding of disease mechanisms, that the deficiencies of the 19 health-care system are most conspicuous. If I were a policy-maker, interested in saving money for health care over the long haul, I would regard it as an act of high prudence to give high priority to a lot more basic research in biologic science. This is the only way to get the full mileage that biology owes to the science of medicine, even though it seems, as used to be said in the days when the phrase still had some meaning, like asking for the moon.

Mary Austin

Water Trails of the Ceriso

Though her books sometimes barely covered their own expenses, Mary Austin's fame in the West was made secure by her intense personality and her association with the literary and cultural elite of the region: she had ties with Jack London, Bret Harte, Ansel Adams, and Willa Cather, to name a few. Her many books, including _Land of Little Rain, Earth Horizon_, and _Taos Pueblo_, were recognized as great works by the literary community of the time. Yet her work has only recently begun to be accepted into the larger "canon" of American literature. In "Water Trails of the Ceriso," which originally appeared in _Land of Little Rain_, Mary Austin (1868–1934) offers a unique perspective on the lives of the inhabitants of the desert.

1   BY THE END OF THE DRY SEASON the water trails of the Ceriso are worn to a white ribbon in the leaning grass, spread out faint and fanwise toward the homes of gopher and ground rat and squirrel. But however faint to man-sight, they are sufficiently plain to the furred and feathered folk who travel them. Getting down to the eye level of rat and squirrel kind, one perceives what might easily be wide and winding roads to us if they occurred in thick plantations of trees three times the height of a man. It needs but a slender thread of barrenness to make a mouse trail in the forest of the sod. To the little people the water trails are as country roads, with scents as signboards.

2   It seems that man-height is the least fortunate of all heights from which to study trails. It is better to go up the front of some tall hill, say the spur of Black Mountain, looking back and down across the hollow of the Ceriso. Strange how long the soil keeps the impression of any continuous treading, even after grass has overgrown it. Twenty years since, a brief heyday of mining at Black Mountain made a stage road across the Ceriso, yet the parallel lines that are the wheel traces show from the height dark and well defined. Afoot in the Ceriso one looks in vain for any sign of it. So all the paths that wild creatures

use going down to the Lone Tree Spring are mapped out whitely from this level, which is also the level of the hawks.

There is little water in the Ceriso at the best of times, and that little brack- 3 ish and smelling vilely, but by a lone juniper where the rim of the Ceriso breaks away to the lower country, there is a perpetual rill of fresh sweet drink in the midst of lush grass and watercress. In the dry season there is no water else for a man's long journey of a day. East to the foot of the Black Mountain, and north and south without counting, are the burrows of small rodents, rat and squirrel kind. Under the sage are the shallow forms of the jack-rabbits, and in the dry banks of washes, and among the strewn fragments of black rock, lairs of bobcat, fox, and coyote.

The coyote is your true water-witch, one who snuffs and paws, snuffs and 4 paws again at the smallest spot of moisture-scented earth until he has freed the blind water from the soil. Many water-holes are no more than this detected by the lean hobo of the hills in localities where not even an Indian would look for it.

It is the opinion of many wise and busy people that the hill-folk pass the 5 ten-month interval between the end and renewal of winter rains, with no drink; but your true idler, with days and nights to spend beside the water trails, will not subscribe to it. The trails begin, as I said, very far back in the Ceriso, faintly, and converge in one span broad, white, hard-trodden way in the gully of the spring. And why trails if there are no travelers in that direction?

I have yet to find the land not scarred by the thin, far roadways of rabbits 6 and what not of furry folks that run in them. Venture to look for some sel-dom-touched water-hole, and so long as the trails run with your general di-rection make sure you are right, but if they begin to cross yours at never so slight an angle, to converge toward a point left or right of your objective, no matter what the maps say, or your memory, trust them; they *know*.

It is very still in the Ceriso by day, so that were it not for the evidence of 7 those white beaten ways, it might be the desert it looks. The sun is hot in the dry season, and the days are filled with the glare of it. Now and again some unseen coyote signals his pack in a long-drawn, dolorous whine that comes from no determinate point, but nothing stirs much before mid-afternoon. It is a sign when there begin to be hawks skimming above the sage that the lit-tle people are going about their business.

We have fallen on a very careless usage, speaking of wild creatures as if 8 they were bound by some such limitation as hampers clockwork. When we say of one and another, they are night prowlers, it is perhaps true only as the things they feed upon are more easily come by in the dark, and they know well how to adjust themselves to conditions wherein food is more plentiful by day. And their accustomed performance is very much a matter of keen eye, keener scent, quick ear, and a better memory of sights and sounds than man dares boast. Watch a coyote come out of his lair and cast about in his mind where he will go for his daily killing. You cannot very well tell what decides him, but very easily that he has decided. He trots or breaks into short gallops, with very perceptible pauses to look up and about at landmarks, alters his tack a little, looking forward and back to steer his proper course. I am persuaded that the coyotes in my valley, which is narrow and beset with steep, sharp hills, in long passages steer by the pinnacles of the sky-line, going with head cocked to one side to keep to the left or right of such and such a promontory.

9   I have trailed a coyote often, going across country, perhaps to where some slant-winged scavenger hanging in the air signaled prospect of a dinner, and found his track such as a man, a very intelligent man accustomed to a hill country, and a little cautious, would make to the same point. Here a detour to avoid a stretch of too little cover, there a pause on the rim of gully to pick the better way,—and it is usually the best way,—and making his point with the greatest economy of effort. Since the time of Seyavi the deer have shifted their feeding ground across the valley at the beginning of deep snows, by way of the Black Rock, fording the river at Charley's Butte, and making straight for the mouth of the cañon that is the easiest going to the winter pastures on Waban. So they still cross, though whatever trail they had has been long broken by ploughed ground; but from the mouth of Tinpah Creek, where the deer come out of the Sierras, it is easily seen that the creek, the point of Black Rock, and Charley's Butte are in line with the wide bulk of shade that is the foot of Waban Pass. And along with this the deer have learned that Charley's Butte is almost the only possible ford, and all the shortest crossing of the valley. It seems that the wild creatures have learned all that is important to their way of life except the changes of the moon. I have seen some prowling fox or coyote, surprised by its sudden rising from behind the mountain wall, slink in its increasing glow, watch it furtively from the cover of near-by brush, unprepared and half uncertain of its identity until it rode clear of the peaks, and finally make off with all the air of one caught napping by an ancient joke. The moon in its wanderings must be a sort of exasperation to cunning beasts, likely to spoil by untimely risings some fore-planned mischief.

10   But to take the trail again; the coyotes that are astir in the Ceriso of late afternoons, harrying the rabbits from their shallow forms, and the hawks that sweep and swing above them, are not there from any mechanical promptings of instinct, but because they know of old experience that the small fry are about to take to seed gathering and the water trails. The rabbits begin it, taking the trail with long, light leaps, one eye and ear cocked to the hills from whence a coyote might descend upon them at any moment. Rabbits are a foolish people. They do not fight except with their own kind, nor use their paws except for feet, and appear to have no reason for existence but to furnish meals for meat-eaters. In flight they seem to rebound from the earth of their

own elasticity, but keep a sober pace going to the spring. It is the young watercress that tempts them and the pleasures of society, for they seldom drink.
Even in localities where there are flowing streams they seem to prefer the
moisture that collects on herbage, and after rains may be seen rising on their
haunches to drink delicately the clear drops caught in the tops of the young
sage. But drink they must, as I have often seen them mornings and evenings
at the rill that goes by my door. Wait long enough at the Lone Tree Spring
and sooner or later they will all come in. But here their matings are accomplished, and though they are fearful of so little as a cloud shadow or blown
leaf, they contrive to have some playful hours. At the spring the bobcat drops
down upon them from the black rock, and the red fox picks them up returning in the dark. By day the hawk and eagle overshadow them, and the coyote
has all times and seasons for his own.

Cattle, when there are any in the Ceriso, drink morning and evening,   11
spending the night on the warm last lighted slopes of neighboring hills, stirring with the peep o' day. In these half wild spotted steers the habits of an earlier lineage persist. It must be long since they have made beds for themselves,
but before lying down they turn themselves round and round as dogs do.
They choose bare and stony ground, exposed fronts of westward facing hills,
and lie down in companies. Usually by the end of the summer the cattle have
been driven or gone of their own choosing to the mountain meadows. One
year a maverick yearling, strayed or overlooked by the vaqueros, kept on until
the season's end, and so betrayed another visitor to the spring that else I
might have missed. On a certain morning the half-eaten carcass lay at the foot
of the black rock, and in moist earth by the rill of the spring, the foot-pads of
a cougar, puma, mountain lion, or whatever the beast is rightly called. The kill
must have been made early in the evening, for it appeared that the cougar had
been twice to the spring; and since the meat-eater drinks little until he has
eaten, he must have fed and drunk, and after an interval of lying up in the
black rock, had eaten and drunk again. There was no knowing how far he had
come, but if he came again the second night he found that the coyotes had
left him very little of his kill.

Nobody ventures to say how infrequently and at what hour the small fry   12
visit the spring. There are such numbers of them that if each came once between the last of spring and the first of winter rains, there would still be water
trails. I have seen badgers drinking about the hour when the light takes on the
yellow tinge it has from coming slantwise through the hills. They find out
shallow places, and are loath to wet their feet. Rats and chipmunks have been
observed visiting the spring as late as nine o'clock mornings. The larger sper-
mophiles that live near the spring and keep awake to work all day, come and
go at no particular hour, drinking sparingly. At long intervals on half-lighted
days, meadow and field mice steal delicately along the trail. These visitors are

all too small to be watched carefully at night, but for evidence of their frequent coming there are the trails that may be traced miles out among the crisping grasses. On rare nights, in the places where no grass grows between the shrubs, and the sand silvers whitely to the moon, one sees them whisking to and fro on innumerable errands of seed gathering, but the chief witnesses of their presence near the spring are the elf owls. Those burrow-haunting, speckled fluffs of greediness begin a twilight flitting toward the spring, feeding as they go on grasshoppers, lizards, and small, swift creatures, diving into burrows to catch field mice asleep, battling with chipmunks at their own doors, and getting down in great numbers toward the lone juniper. Now owls do not love water greatly on its own account. Not to my knowledge have I caught one drinking or bathing, though on night wanderings across the mesa they flit up from under the horse's feet along stream borders. Their presence near the spring in great numbers would indicate the presence of the things they feed upon. All night the rustle and soft hooting keeps on in the neighborhood of the spring, with seldom small shrieks of mortal agony. It is clear day before they have all gotten back to their particular hummocks, and if one follows cautiously, not to frighten them into some near-by burrow, it is possible to trail them far up the slope.

13   The crested quail that troop in the Ceriso are the happiest frequenters of the water trails. There is no furtiveness about their morning drink. About the time the burrowers and all that feed upon them are addressing themselves to sleep, great flocks pour down the trails with that peculiar melting motion of moving quail, twittering, shoving, and shouldering. They splatter into the shallows, drink daintily, shake out small showers over their perfect coats, and melt away again into the scrub, preening and pranking, with soft contented noises.

14   After the quail, sparrows and ground-inhabiting birds bathe with the utmost frankness and a great deal of splutter; and here in the heart of noon hawks resort, sitting panting, with wings aslant, and a truce to all hostilities because of the heat. One summer there came a road-runner up from the lower valley, peeking and prying, and he had never any patience with the water baths of the sparrows. His own ablutions were performed in the clean, hopeful dust of the chaparral; and whenever he happened on their morning splatterings, he would depress his glossy crest, slant his shining tail to the level of his body, until he looked most like some bright venomous snake, daunting them with shrill abuse and feint of battle. Then suddenly he would go tilting and balancing down the gully in fine disdain, only to return in a day or two to make sure the foolish bodies were still at it.

15   Out on the Ceriso about five miles, and wholly out of sight of it, near where the immemorial foot trail goes up from Saline Flat toward Black Mountain, is a water sign worth turning out of the trail to see. It is a laid circle of

stones large enough not to be disturbed by any ordinary hap, with an opening flanked by two parallel rows of similar stones, between which were an arrow placed, touching the opposite rim of the circle, it would point as the crow flies to the spring. It is the old, indubitable water mark of the Shoshones. One still finds it in the desert ranges in Salt Wells and Mesquite valleys, and along the slopes of Waban. On the other side of Ceriso, where the black rock begins, about a mile from the spring, is the work of an older, forgotten people. The rock hereabout is all volcanic, fracturing with a crystalline whitish surface, but weathered outside to furnace blackness. Around the spring, where must have been a gathering place of the tribes, it is scored over with strange pictures and symbols that have no meaning to the Indians of the present day; but out where the rock begins, there is carved into the white heart of it a pointing arrow over the symbol for distance and a circle full of wavy lines reading thus: "In this direction three [units of measurement unknown] is a spring of sweet water; look for it."

Student Essay

Diana Peck

The Shellfish of Arey's Pond

The quintessential *bad* essay topic is "What I did during my summer vacation." It has acquired such a negative reputation that few students are even assigned it anymore, leaving elementary school teachers across the nation struggling to come up with adequate lesson plans for the first day of school. Yet even topics like this one can be turned into great essays if the recollections are described with a fond realism and the whole piece makes a good point. Diana Peck does precisely that in this essay, progressing in a careful manner from descriptions of the most common shellfish of her pond to the most coveted. A simple description becomes a quest, and in the end becomes a comment on the relationship of humanity and nature.

THE ATLANTIC OCEAN POUNDING THE CAPE COD SHORELINE finds a break in the dunes just north of Monomoy Point. Here, it can enter the calm, shallow waters of Pleasant Bay, separated from the ocean's surf by the outsized sand dune named Nauset. Continuing a tidal journey, some ocean water finds its way to the northern reaches of the bay and sidetracks into a small channel called Namequoit. Twice a day, every day, ocean water completes its journey down this channel and fills Arey's Pond, one of the many ponds that terminate similar channels. Nursed by this fresh supply of nutrient-rich waters, Arey's Pond, small though it is, has until recently provided the spawning grounds for a rich variety of marine fauna. When I was a child, many a summer day's activities revolved around the shellfish life of the pond.

2   The periwinkle was both the most common and the most useless shellfish in the pond. Hundreds of these small black snails, the size of lima beans, littered our tiny beach at low tide. As we stepped on them, unable to avoid them, they squashed into the wet sand, emerging undaunted a moment later. Although edible, they were useless as food since it would have taken a dozen of their soft black insides to produce a thimbleful of escargots. Adults ignored periwinkles, and even children quickly tired of picking them up, waiting for them to stick their bodies out of the shells, then poking them to watch them disappear inside their shells. Sometimes, picking up these shells, we were surprised to find the tiniest fiddler crab had made an empty shell its home. Struggling to pull its right claw, equal in size to the rest of its body, inside the borrowed shell, the crab entertained us for a few moments. We enjoyed it far more, however, when an adult fiddler crab, accidentally shell-less, would run frantically around the beach, terrorized by its vulnerability.

3   Less common were the horseshoe crabs which the tide brought to our beach. Often they were paired, the male glued to the back of the female, and it thrilled us to pick up one spiny tail and lift up the two helpless, heavy bodies, their dozens of small underlegs thrashing in the air. The dark brown armored semicircles of their bodies, often about ten inches in width, were too heavy for us to hold for long, and so they would usually be freed within a half-minute. Meatless, they had only one use: sometimes my father split a female horseshoe crab with one blow of his axe, put each of her halves in an eel pot, and attracted eels for miles around with her roe.

4   An animal which was not particularly common but could be found accidentally was the blue crab. The big brother of the Maryland soft-shell crab, this species offered little meat and was therefore usually ignored except at a clambake where the joy of cracking open the shells excused the meager store of meat. The only aggressive variety of shellfish we encountered, this type of crab would endlessly surprise us, pinching our toes as we waded in the water, gripping our drop lines as we pulled up what we thought was a flounder, staring at us through the wires as we hauled up our eel pots.

5   But hiding in the mud of the pond were the rare bivalves with edible meat, especially sought-after by adults who, aided by curious children, spent whole afternoons searching for them, spurred on by my father's enthusiasm. The most common of the bivalves were clams, called soft-shell clams by the tourists but just plain clams by Cape Codders. My father led the expeditions at dead-low tide, armed with a shovel and a bucket. In the sand near the water, he looked for telltale air holes, then dug a shovelful of mud and dumped it

out on the beach. The children, responsible for combing the mud with their fingers to find the smooth, oval bodies of the clams, usually squeezed each clam, watching it squirt a last stream of water through its long, thick neck, then tossed it unceremoniously into the waiting bucket. We worked our way down the shoreline until, as the tide started in, we stood in a few inches of water. Over and over, my father dug into the muck, sending swirls of black grit into the water, raising the pungent smell of disturbed compost, dumping shovelfuls of oozing mud into the shallow water for us to search. Over and over we gushed the mud through our fingers, plucked out the clams, and moved on to the next shovelful, often stepping into the soft warm muck up to our ankles, hearing the "pop" of the suction as we pulled out our feet. The clams, hard-won from the mud, would provide a feast of steamers for all the relatives, as well as bait for the next day's fishing.

More difficult to find were the quahogs, and not until we were older did   6 my father teach us, one by one, how to find them. Adults considered them more of a delicacy than the clams and either ate the meat raw or ground it for chowder. A hard-shelled clam, quahogs have no necks and keep their mantles inside their tightly closed shells. They, too, burrow in the mud, but they keep a ridge of shell just above the surface. To find quahogs, my father, in goggles and bathing suit, floated face down along the shoreline where the water was about a foot deep. The water being too murky to see through, he pulled himself along, feeling the mud with his hands for the telltale ridge. When he found one, he loosened the surrounding mud with his fingers and pulled the quahog out of its hiding place. This was a slow, arduous process, demanding too much patience for most of us children. But my father was motivated by his love for the result of his labors, especially enjoying the sweet flavor of the small quahogs' meat, called cherrystones, as he swallowed them raw.

Even more treasured than quahogs and more difficult to find were the   7 jewels of Arey's Pond: the oysters. Even my father, experienced shellfisherman as he was, had a special smile as he emerged from the water with an oyster. Hiding in their sharp, blotchy, irregularly shaped shells amidst the roots of the eel grass at the shore's edge, oysters were impossible to see. Feeling for them was difficult, because the edges of the eel grass felt similar to the layered edges of the oyster's shell. The grass eventually yielded to pressure, while the oyster remained firm, but anyone pressing hard enough to distinguish the difference was sure to cut his fingers on the reedy edge of the grass or the sharp edge of a shell. Wearing gloves made the hands too clumsy to detect the difference. For my father it was a labor of love. The scores of tiny cuts on his fingers were small payment for the joy of eating a raw oyster, captured only minutes before. Children were never offered oysters, and those adults fortunate enough to be present when my father caught some usually mirrored his sublime expression as they swallowed the fresh meat. Even the oyster's shell had value, serving as bureau-top catch-alls, ash trays, or a decorative border for the garden.

8   We still visit Arey's Pond whenever we can, my father still digging for clams and searching for quahogs. But some years ago, the channel to the bay was deepened to provide access for pleasure boats. The shellfish never recovered. After two or three years some of the clams came back and a few quahogs can still be found, but the oysters are gone and none of the crabs can negotiate the channel. Only the periwinkles remain in abundance to remind us of how it once was.

7

Cause & Effect

Cause & Effect

1. **Understand the problem.** Cause and effect analysis requires an in-depth understanding of a process or event. It's an analysis often applied by historians, engineers and anyone interested in how or why something happens. Historians typically immerse themselves in information—letters, newspaper reports, census data—before attempting to assess a historical event. Your professors may ask you to do a cause and effect analysis in an essay exam for a different reason—to make sure *you* understand the material.

2. **Be careful in attributing causes.** Although timing of events is essential to causal analysis, just because one event precedes another doesn't mean it caused it. As a rule, the more remote the possible cause, the less likely it was to have precipitated a given effect. More immediate causes are easier to prove, but they often reveal only trivial insights: "He was caught speeding because he pressed too hard on the accelerator," is not as relevant as "He was caught speeding because he didn't notice he was in a school zone," or better still, "He didn't notice he was in a school zone because he was talking on his cell phone."

3. **Support your analysis with evidence.** In cause-effect analysis, because causes are often so difficult to pinpoint, evidence becomes very important. Well-selected evidence can make the difference between an insightful essay and speculative garbage. Even Barbara Carton's humorous story on quotation marks still makes its point by offering many examples, offering several different perspectives on the issue. Cathy Young makes her point about the causes of sexism by citing examples both from the United States and her native Soviet Union.

4. **Organize your analysis to make your point.** The most obvious strategy for organizing a cause-effect essay is chronological. However, unless you're writing a humorous essay like Suzanne Scarbek's "Monkey See, Monkey Do," this strategy is often ineffective—the improbable chain of events depicted in Suzanne's essay may make you laugh, but it probably doesn't convince that there's a single cause of bad writing. More effective organization strategies place the most convincing cause last, or lead the reader through the logic of a complex cause and effect.

Abraham Lincoln

Gettysburg Address

President Abraham Lincoln (1809–1865) gave this speech in 1863 after the most crucial Union victory of the Civil War. If the Confederate army had won at Gettysburg, it would have had the potential to deal severe damage to the North, if not win the war outright. Perhaps the reason that this speech is so memorable is in its allusion to the great works of our nation's history—the Declaration of Independence, the Constitution—and also those of the world—the Bible, Pericles' Funeral Oration. Yet all these ideas are integrated into a work of just a few paragraphs, constituting a speech less than two minutes long.

FOUR SCORE AND SEVEN YEARS AGO our fathers brought forth on this continent, a new nation, conceived in Liberty, and dedicated to the proposition that all men are created equal.

Now we are engaged in a great civil war, testing whether that nation, or any nation so conceived and so dedicated, can long endure. We are met on a great battle-field of that war. We have come to dedicate a portion of that field, as a final resting place for those who here gave their lives that that nation might live. It is altogether fitting and proper that we should do this.

But, in a larger sense, we can not dedicate—we can not consecrate—we can not hallow—this ground. The brave men, living and dead, who struggled here, have consecrated it, far above our poor power to add or detract. The world will little note, nor long remember what we say here, but it can never forget what they did here. It is for us the living, rather, to be dedicated here to the unfinished work which they who fought here have thus far so nobly advanced. It is rather for us to be here dedicated to the great task remaining before us—that from these honored dead we take increased devotion to that cause for which they gave the last full measure of devotion—that we here highly resolve that these dead shall not have died in vain—that this nation, under God, shall have a new birth of freedom—and that government of the people, by the people, for the people, shall not perish from the earth.

Chief Seattle

Address

Chief Seattle (1786?–1866) was chief of the Duwamish and other tribes when the United States took possession of what are now the states of Washington and Oregon. His tribes' situation when he made this speech was similar to what had already been the fate of hundreds of tribes across America: faced with the overwhelming might and numbers of Americans, they were forced into signing disadvantageous treaties—eventually losing almost everything they had. Seattle's speech was made in response to Governor Isaac Stevens' offer to purchase two million acres of Duwampo territory. As Seattle's speech implies, his tribe in fact had little choice in the matter. There has been speculation in recent years that the text of this speech was largely fabricated, that Seattle's words were appropriated by white men after the fact. Nonetheless, whatever the source of these words, they remain a profound statement of Native American philosophy, which has been used by whites and Indians alike to better understand the Indian world.

1   THE GOVERNOR MADE A FINE SPEECH, but he was outranged and outclassed that day. Chief Seattle, who answered on behalf of the Indians, towered a foot above the Governor. He wore his blanket like the toga of a Roman senator, and he did not have to strain his famous voice, which everyone agreed was audible and distinct at a distance of half a mile. Seattle's oration was in Duwamish. Doctor Smith, who had learned the language, wrote it down; under the flowery garlands of his translation the speech rolls like an articulate iron engine, grim with meanings that outlasted his generation and may outlast all the generations of men. As the amiable follies of the white race become less amiable, the iron rumble of old Seattle's speech sounds louder and more ominous. Standing in front of Doctor Maynard's office in the stumpy clearing, with his hand on the little Governor's head, the white invaders about him and his people before him, Chief Seattle said:

2   "Yonder sky that has wept tears of compassion upon my people for centuries untold, and which to us appears changeless and eternal, may change. Today is fair. Tomorrow may be overcast with clouds. My words are like the stars that never change. Whatever Seattle says the great chief at Washington can rely upon with as much certainty as he can upon the return of the sun or the seasons. The White Chief says that Big Chief at Washington sends us greetings of friendship and goodwill. That is kind of him for we know he has little need of our friendship in return. His people are many. They are like the grass that covers vast prairies. My people are few. They resemble the scattering trees of a storm-swept plain. The great, and—I presume—good, White Chief sends us word that he wishes to buy our lands but is willing to allow us enough to live

comfortably. This indeed appears just, even generous, for the Red Man no longer has rights that he need respect, and the offer may be wise also, as we are no longer in need of an extensive country. . . . I will not dwell on, nor mourn over, our untimely decay, nor reproach our paleface brothers with hastening it, as we too may have been somewhat to blame.

"Youth is impulsive. When our young men grow angry at some real or 3 imaginary wrong, and disfigure their faces with black paint, it denotes that their hearts are black, and then they are often cruel and relentless, and our old men and old women are unable to restrain them. Thus it has ever been. Thus it was when the white men first began to push our forefathers further westward. But let us hope that the hostilities between us may never return. We would have everything to lose and nothing to gain. Revenge by young men is considered gain, even at the cost of their own lives, but old men who stay at home in times of war, and mothers who have sons to lose, know better.

"Our good father at Washington—for I presume he is now our father as 4 well as yours, since King George has moved his boundaries further north—our great good father, I say, sends us word that if we do as he desires he will pro- tect us. His brave warriors will be to us a bristling wall of strength, and his wonderful ships of war will fill our harbors so that our ancient enemies far to the northward—the Hydas and Tsimpsians—will cease to frighten our women, children, and old men. Then in reality will he be our father and we his chil- dren. But can that ever be? Your God is not our God! Your God loves your people and hates mine. He folds his strong and protecting arms lovingly about the paleface and leads him by the hand as a father leads his infant son—but He has forsaken His red children—if they really are his. Our God, the Great Spirit, seems also to have forsaken us. Your God makes your people wax strong every day. Soon they will fill the land. Our people are ebbing away like a rapidly receding tide that will never return. The white man's God cannot love our people or He would protect them. They seem to be orphans who can look nowhere for help. How then can we be brothers? How can your God be- come our God and renew our prosperity and awaken in us dreams of return- ing greatness? If we have a common heavenly father He must be partial—for He came to his paleface children. We never saw Him. He gave you laws but He had no word for His red children whose teeming multitudes once filled this vast continent as stars fill the firmament. No; we are two distinct races with separate origins and separate destinies. There is little in common be- tween us.

"To us the ashes of our ancestors are sacred and their resting place is hal- 5 lowed ground. You wander far from the graves of your ancestors and seemingly without regret. Your religion was written upon tables of stone by the iron finger of your God so that you could not forget. The Red Man could never comprehend nor remember it. Our religion is the traditions of our ancestors—the dreams of our old men, given them in solemn hours of night by the Great Spirit; and the visions of our sachems; and it is written in the hearts of our people.

6   "Your dead cease to love you and the land of their nativity as soon as they pass the portals of the tomb and wander way beyond the stars. They are soon forgotten and never return. Our dead never forget the beautiful world that gave them being.

7   "Day and night cannot dwell together. The Red Man has ever fled the approach of the White Man, as the morning mist flees before the morning sun. However, your proposition seems fair and I think that my people will accept it and will retire to the reservation you offer them. Then we will dwell apart in peace, for the words of the Great White Chief seem to be the words of nature speaking to my people out of dense darkness.

8   "It matters little where we pass the remnant of our days. They will not be many. A few more moons; a few more winters—and not one of the descendants of the mighty hosts that once moved over this broad land or lived in happy homes, protected by the Great Spirit, will remain to mourn over the graves of a people once more powerful and hopeful than yours. But why should I mourn at the untimely fate of my people? Tribe follows tribe, and nation follows nation, like the waves of the sea. It is the order of nature, and regret is useless. Your time of decay may be distant, but it will surely come, for even the White Man whose God walked and talked with him as friend with friend, cannot be exempt from the common destiny. We may be brothers after all. We will see.

9   "We will ponder your proposition, and when we decide we will let you know. But should we accept it, I here and now make this condition that we will not be denied the privilege without molestation of visiting at any time the tombs of our ancestors, friends and children. Every part of this soil is sacred in the estimation of my people. Every hillside, every valley, every plain and grove, has been hallowed by some sad or happy event in days long vanished. . . . The very dust upon which you now stand responds more lovingly to their footsteps than to yours, because it is rich with the blood of our ancestors and our bare feet are conscious of the sympathetic touch. . . . Even the little children who lived here and rejoiced here for a brief season will love these somber solitudes and at eventide they greet shadowy returning spirits. And when the last Red Man shall have perished, and the memory of my tribe shall have become a myth among the White Men, these shores will swarm with the invisible dead of my tribe, and when your children's children think themselves alone in the field, the store, the shop, upon the highway, or in the silence of the pathless woods, they will not be alone. . . . At night when the streets of your cities and villages are silent and you think them deserted, they will throng with the returning hosts that once filled and still love this beautiful land. The White Man will never be alone.

10   "Let him be just and deal kindly with my people, for the dead are not powerless."

W. E. B. DuBois

The Souls of White Folk

William Edgar Burghardt DuBois was a descendant of a French Huguenot and an African slave. He received B.A. degrees from both Fisk and Harvard Universities and a Ph.D. from the University of Berlin. He taught, at various times, at Wilberforce, the University of Pennsylvania, and Atlanta University, holding professorships in Greek, Latin, Sociology, Economics, and History. In addition, he edited many publications, including *Crisis*, the journal of the National Association for the Advancement of Colored People, from 1910 to 1934. One of his most famous works was *The Souls of Black Folk*—both a fine piece of English prose and a plea for greater understanding of blacks by whites. Seven years later, in 1910, he wrote this essay as a plea to whites to understand themselves.

HIGH IN THE TOWER WHERE I SIT beside the loud complaining of the human   1
sea I know many souls that toss and whirl and pass, but none there are that
puzzle me more than the Souls of White Folk. Not, mind you, the souls of
them that are white, but souls of them that have become painfully conscious
of their whiteness; those in whose minds the paleness of their bodily skins is
fraught with tremendous and eternal significance.

Forgetting (as I can at times forget) the meaning of this singular obsession   2
to me and my folk, I become the more acutely sensitive to the marvelous part
this thought is playing today, and to the way it is developing the Souls of
White Folk, and I wonder what the end will be.

The discovery of personal whiteness among the world's people is a very   3
modern thing—a nineteenth- and twentieth-century matter, indeed. The ancient world would have laughed at such a distinction. The Middle Ages regarded it with mild curiosity, and even up into the eighteenth century we were
hammering our national manikins into one great Universal Man with fine
frenzy, which ignored color and race as well as birth. Today we have changed
all that, and the world, in sudden emotional conversation, has discovered that
it is white, and, by that token, wonderful.

When I seek to explain this, to me, inexplicable phenomenon, there al-   4
ways creeps first to my mind the analogy of the child and his candy. To every
child there comes a time when the toothsomeness of his sweets is strangely enhanced by the thought that his playmate has none. Further than this, however, the analogy fails, for with one accord the mother world seeks to teach
this child the third new joy of sharing. Any thought, however, of sharing their
color is to white folk not simply unthinkable, but its mention is liable to lead
to violent explosions of anger and vituperation. Not only is there this unre-

buked and vociferously applauded greediness, but something that sounds like: "I shall keep my candy and you shall not have yours." Or, in other words, it is not the obvious proposition: "I am white and you are black," but the astonishing declaration, "I am white and you are nothing."

5   This assumption that of all the hues of God, whiteness alone is candy to the world child—is inherently and obviously better than brownness or tan— leads to curious acts; even the sweeter souls of the dominant world, as they discourse with me on weather, weal and woe, are continually playing above their actual words an obligato of turn and tone, saying:

6   "My poor unwhite thing! Weep not nor rage. I know, too well, that the curse of God lies heavy on you. Why? That is not for me to say; but be brave! Do your work in your lowly sphere, praying the good Lord that into heaven above, where all is love, you may one day, be born—white!"

7   At such times I have an unholy desire to laugh, and to ask with seemingly irrelevance and certain irreverence: "But what on earth is whiteness, that one should so desire it?"

8   Then always somehow, some way, silently but clearly, I am given to understand that whiteness is the ownership of the earth, forever and ever, Amen!

9   Now, what is the effect on a man or a nation when it comes passionately to believe such an extraordinary dictum as this? That nations are coming to believe it is manifest daily. Wave on wave, each with increasing virulence, is dashing this new religion of whiteness on the shores of our time. Its first effects are funny; the strut of the Southerner, the arrogance of the Englishman amuck, the whoop of the hoodlum who vicariously leads your mob. Next it appears dampening generous enthusiasm in what we once counted glorious: To free the slave is discovered to be tolerable only insofar as it freed his master. Do we sense somnolent writhings in black Africa, or angry groans in India, or triumphant "banzais" in Japan? "To your tents, O Israel!" These nations are not white. Build warships and heft the Big Stick.

10   After the more comic manifestations and chilling of generous enthusiasm, come subtler, darker deeds. Everything considered, the title to the universe claimed by white folk is faulty. It ought at least to look plausible. How easy, then, by emphasis and omission, to make every child believe that every great soul the world ever saw was a white man's soul; that every great thought the world ever knew was a white man's thought; that every great deed the world ever did was a white man's deed; that every great dream the world ever sang was a white man's dream. In fine, that if from the world were dropped everything that could not fairly be attributed to white folk the world would, if anything, be even greater, truer, better than now. And if all this be a lie, is it not a lie in a great cause?

11   Here it is that the comedy verges to tragedy. The first minor note is struck all unconsciously by those worthy souls in whom consciousness of high descent

brings burning desire to spread the gift abroad—the obligation of nobility to the ignoble. Such sense of duty assumes two things: A real possession of the heritage and its frank appreciation by the humbly born. So long, then, as humble black folk, voluble with thanks, receive barrels of old clothes from lordly and generous whites, there is much mental peace and moral satisfaction. But when the black man begins to dispute the white man's title to certain alleged bequests of the Father's in wage and position, authority and training; and when his attitude toward charity is sullen anger rather than humble jollity; when he insists on his human rights to swagger and swear and waste—then the spell is suddenly broken and the philanthropist is apt to be ready to believe that Negroes are impudent, that the South is right, and that Japan wants to fight us.

Mentally the blight has fallen on American science. The race problem is 12 not insoluble if the correct answer is sought. It is insoluble if the wrong answer is insisted upon as it has been insisted upon for thrice a hundred years. A very moderate brain can show that two and two is four. But no human ingenuity can make that sum three or five. This American science has long attempted to do. It has made itself the handmaid of a miserable prejudice. In its attempt to justify the treatment of black folk it has repeatedly suppressed evidence, misquoted authority, distorted fact and deliberately lied. It is wonderful that in the very lines of social study, where America should shine, it has done nothing.

Worse than this is our moral and religious plight. We profess a religion of 13 high ethical advancement, a spiritual faith, of respect for truth, despising of personal riches, a reverence for humility, and not simply justice to our fellows, but personal sacrifice of our good for theirs. It is a high aim, so high that we ought not utterly to be condemned for not reaching it, so long as we strive bravely toward it. Do we, as a people? On the contrary, we have injected into our creed a gospel of human hatred and prejudice, a despising of our less fortunate fellows, not to speak of our reverence for wealth, which flatly contradicts the Christian ideal. Granting all that American Christianity has done to educate and uplift black men, it must be frankly admitted that there is absolutely no logical method by which the treatment of black folk by white folk in this land can be squared with any reasonable statement or practice of the Christian ideal.

What is the result? It is either the abandonment of the Christian ideal or 14 hypocrisy. Some frankly abandon Christianity when it comes to the race problem and say: Religion does not enter here. They then retire to some more primitive paganism and live there, enlightened by such prejudices as they adopt or inherit. This is retrogression toward barbarism, but it is at least honest. It is infinitely better than its widely accepted alternative, which attempts to reconcile color caste and Christianity, and sees or affects to see no incongruity. What ails the religion of a land when its strongholds of orthodoxy are to be found in those regions where race prejudice is most uncompromising, vindictive, and cruel; where human brotherhood is a lie?

15   The one great moral issue of America upon which the Church of Christ comes nearest being dumb is the question as to the application of the golden rule between white and black folk.

16   All this I see and hear up in my tower above the thunder of the seven seas. From my narrowed windows I stare into the night that looms beneath the cloud-swept stars. Eastward and westward storms are brewing great, ugly whirlwinds of hatred and blood and cruelty. I will not believe them inevitable. I will not believe that all that was must be—that all the shameful drama of the past must be done again today before the sunlight sweeps the silver seas.

17   If I cry amid this roar of elemental forces, must my cry be vain because it is but a cry—a small and human cry amid Promethean gloom?

18   Back beyond the world and swept by these wild white faces of the awful dead, why will this Soul of the White Folk, this modern Prometheus, hang bound by his own binding, tethered by a labor of the past? I hear his mighty cry reverberating through the world, "I am white!" Well and good, O Prometheus, divine thief! The world is wide enough for two colors, two little shinings of the sun; why then devour your own vitals when I answer, "I am black"?

Student Essay

Susan Scarbek

Monkey See, Monkey Do

Though this essay seems mostly to complain about writing instructors, it also has a good point to make about writing: there is no one way to write well. Sometimes "I am going bananas" is just the right sentence for the situation.

1   DURING A RECENT WORKSHOP ON GRAMMAR, a sentence—"I am going bananas"—was introduced for comment. A short poll of this class has rendered some suggestions about the kinds of responses a teacher would give if a student dared to write such a sentence.

2   "I am going bananas." The teacher will write "Slang. Please rewrite" in the margin. The student will obviously know what's slangy about the sentence, so no further comment is needed. This approach avoids the sticky question of verbs altogether and especially avoids discussion of intransitive, transitive, and linking verbs.

3   The teacher will probably get "I am going crazy" as the rewritten sentence.

If this does indeed occur, the teacher can choose between two attacks: (1) Ignore it and go on, or (2) Mark "Too colloquial for Standard English models. Please rewrite." The latter is the more common, and certainly the preferred teacher response, since it affords her the opportunity to explain what colloquialisms are and why Standard English is *so* much better. After she has explained how "crazy" can be improved upon, she'll probably get the following rewrite: "I am losing my mind."

This sentence will really allow the teacher to deliver the *coup de grace* to the   4
student! She'll simply write "Idiom" next to the sentence. After all, everyone knows you don't *really* lose your mind unless you have a particularly leaky cranium. If people really could lose their minds, others of us would find them lying around, wouldn't we? The student, of course, will believe this to be another error, and take one of two courses. He'll either give up, or produce an unsolicited rewrite.

The result might look like this: "As a response to certain unfavorable   5
stimuli in an increasingly complex and hostile environment, this subject is developing a labile personality and is rapidly approaching an irrational state of mind." This, fellow writers, is a teacher's gold mine. She might begin with wordiness and jargon, but the majority of students polled (99.9%) felt that the following teacher comment would be most fitting and would help the student understand the intricacies of the English language more fully: "Jargon. Be concise and clear. Why don't you just write, 'I'm going bananas'?"

Barbara Carton

Why Does "Everybody" Now Put "Everything" in Quotation Marks?

Because It Moves Merchandise and Lends That Bit of Stress That the Occasion Calls For

Though she is a staff reporter for the *Wall Street Journal,* Barbara Carton's stories focus on the whimsical side of life. Writing about ordinary topics like turkey stuffing, Carton injects much-needed humor into the staid business newspaper. In this selection, which appeared in 1999, Carton comments on the random quotation marks that seem to be popping up almost everywhere.

1   OUR 'GOAL' IS TO HELP OUR CUSTOMERS CONSERVE ENERGY.

—Letter from Atlas Oil Co., Westwood, Mass.

2   Thank you for . . . keeping your 'health' club as clean as possible.

—Locker-room sign, World Trade Center, New York

3   Call it overzealous marketing. Or pretentiousness. Maybe it's the work of those who might charitably be called 'challenged, punctuationwise.'

4   Whatever the reason, an 'epidemic' of runaway 'quotation marks' is raging in the world of words.

5   'I've seen it in letters I get from my brother,' says Michael Pemberton, an assistant professor of English at the University of Illinois. 'Quotation marks around words that seem so amazingly commonplace I can't understand why he's doing it.'

6   'I've seen it a lot in Yellow Pages advertising,' adds Richard Dowis, president of the Society for the Preservation of English Language and Literature, in Waleska, Ga. He has also noticed signs such as the ones in diners that say, 'Please pay the 'cashier.'' They will have cashier in quotation marks as if to suggest the person behind the counter isn't really up to snuff.

7   The 'Doonesbury' cartoon that ran Friday in the New York Daily News, among other newspapers, contained this bit of conversation:

8   'You think he'll be 'impressed' by quotation marks?'

9   'Sure—he's a college boy.'

10   Tom McArthur, who edits the Oxford Companion to the English Language in Cambridge, England, sees errant quotes popping up throughout Britain. 'I have a colleague on a committee here who is a structural engineer,' he says. 'His writing is peppered with this kind of quotation.'

11   As any of our academic experts could explain, the rightful job of quotation marks is to denote words first uttered elsewhere, or titles of books and other works. They are also used to enclose nicknames or unfamiliar terms.

12   In its proper place, the quotation mark keeps company with timeless and noble utterances. Misplaced, as it is with growing frequency, it surrounds commonly understood words. But why?

13   Modern-day stress is one reason.

14   A lot of these quotation marks are stress-related. Marvin Owen, general manager of Automated Church Systems Inc. of Florence, S.C., says his six staff writers employ quotes for added punch. 'If something's really important,' Mr. Owen says, 'you've got to do whatever you can to get it in front of them.' Really important, following this precept, is the Sunday-offerings tally that the software firm compiles for churches across the country. Parishioners at these churches receive their 'Record of Contributions' in quotes.

15   At the Fitness Co., New York-area manager Bonnie Patrick had irony as well as stress in mind when she wrote the World Trade Center sign thanking members for keeping the health club clean. 'Our point was, if you leave your

sneakers out, as everybody does, on top of the lockers, they smell and it's an unhealthy situation and we belong to a health club,' says Ms. Patrick. 'We were trying to do a play on words and, at the same time, get the point across.'

For some reason, stores (among other users of English) find quotation   16
marks irresistible when the word 'all' comes up. According to a sign at the Souper Salad deli in downtown Boston, 'One hot lid fits 'all' size coffee cups.' Super Stop & Shop grocery stores in the same city advertise "All Natural' Jumbo Sea Scallops.' Similarly, the Appalachian Mountain Club lists various services in a letter to members, noting that membership entitles them to discounts on 'all of the above.'

Mary N. Bruder of Pittsburgh, a former English teacher who operates the   17
'Grammar Lady' Web site, has noticed people using the apostrophe to form plurals, 'tomato's,' for example, and figures it's part of the same trend affecting quotation marks.

It would seem to be. Indeed, the 'trend' appears to have had its 'origins'   18
long ago. Witness this bit from a 1985 Dave Barry column:

'Dear Mr. Language Person: What is the purpose of the apostrophe?   19

'The apostrophe is used mainly in hand-lettered small-business signs to   20
alert the reader that an 'S' is coming up at the end of a word, as in: WE DO NOT ACCEPT PERSONAL CHECK'S. Another important grammar concept to bear in mind when creating hand-lettered small-business signs is that you should put quotation marks around random words for decoration, as in 'TRY' OUR HOT DOG'S, or even TRY 'OUR' HOT DOG'S.

John Broderick, author of 'The Able Writer: A Rhetoric and Handbook,'   21
suspects that many people have a 'vague feeling' about quotation marks, but 'are not literate enough—literally, widely and well-read enough—fully to have grasped the subtleties involved.'

Consider this sign placed on three stores in the Boston area: 'Join Our   22
Team. Economy Hardware. 'Hiring.''

'The writer seems to try to disassociate himself or herself from taking full   23
responsibility for the word,' says Prof. Broderick, who teaches English at Old Dominion University in Norfolk, Va. 'Maybe they're only 'hiring' until the job is filled.' Similarly, in the case of the Atlas letter about conservation, 'Maybe the oil company doesn't want to be forced actually to achieve their 'goal.''

Dr. Broderick adds: 'I'm trying to be kind in finding interpretations.'   24

Rob Renaud, general manager of the hardware stores that are 'hiring,'   25
blames the sign company. 'It wasn't our idea to put the quotation marks there,' he says. 'We just wanted to stress hiring, and maybe that's their style of stressing something. We wanted a sign that stood out, not a regular old help-wanted sign.'

26   Sign painter Rick Hammar, of Pelham, N.H., installed the quotation marks for Mr. Renaud, but he usually prefers stars. 'Like, we did some bumper stickers and on the very top line we had a star, then it said, 'Think Women' and then another star, and then in big bold letters, it said, 'Think Republican.''

27   In any case, Mr. Hammar says, sign painters don't call these kinds of punctuation 'quotation marks'—they call them 'slashes.' Besides, he says, 'We have a license in art to do what we want.'

John F. Kennedy

Inaugural Address

John F. Kennedy (1917–1963) set forth a tall agenda as he began his short presidency in 1961. He had been a war hero, a best-selling historian, and a popular senator. Nonetheless, his margin of victory in the election had been one of the smallest in history, and he needed to begin his term of office by bringing popular sentiment to his side. He needed to allay fears from the right that he would not be tough enough in the middle of the Cold War, and fears from the left that he would not be aggressive enough in gaining civil rights for all. The result was a highly patriotic, highly allusive speech, which includes some lines which are still quoted today.

1   WE OBSERVE TODAY NOT A VICTORY OF PARTY but a celebration of freedom— symbolizing an end as well as a beginning—signifying renewal as well as change. For I have sworn before you and Almighty God the same solemn oath our forebears prescribed nearly a century and three quarters ago.

2   The world is very different now. For man holds in his mortal hands the power to abolish all forms of human poverty and all forms of human life. And yet the same revolutionary beliefs for which our forebears fought are still at issue around the globe—the belief that the rights of man come not from the generosity of the state but from the hand of God.

3   We dare not forget today that we are the heirs of that first revolution. Let the word go forth from this time and place, to friend and foe alike, that the torch has been passed to a new generation of Americans—born in this century, tempered by war, disciplined by a hard and bitter peace, proud of our ancient heritage—and unwilling to witness or permit the slow undoing of those human rights to which this nation has always been committed, and to which we are committed today at home and around the world.

Let every nation know, whether it wishes us well or ill, that we shall pay   4
any price, bear any burden, meet any hardship, support any friend, oppose any
foe, to assure the survival and the success of liberty.

This much we pledge—and more.   5

To those old allies whose cultural and spiritual origins we share, we pledge   6
the loyalty of faithful friends. United, there is little we cannot do in a host of
cooperative ventures. Divided, there is little we can do—for we dare not meet
a powerful challenge at odds and split asunder.

To those new states whom we welcome to the ranks of the free, we pledge   7
our word that one form of colonial control shall not have passed away merely
to be replaced by a far more iron tyranny. We shall not always expect to find
them supporting our view. But we shall always hope to find them strongly supporting their own freedom—and to remember that in the past, those who foolishly sought power by riding the back of the tiger ended up inside.

To those peoples in the huts and villages of half the globe struggling to   8
break the bonds of mass misery, we pledge our best efforts to help them help
themselves, for whatever period is required—not because the Communists
may be doing it, not because we seek their votes, but because it is right. If a
free society cannot help the many who are poor, it cannot save the few who
are rich.

To our sister republics south of our border, we offer a special pledge—to   9
convert our good words into good deeds—in a new alliance for progress—to as-
sist free men and free governments in casting off the chains of poverty. But
this peaceful revolution of hope cannot become the prey of hostile powers.
Let all our neighbors know that we shall join with them to oppose aggression
or subversion anywhere in the Americas. And let every other power know that
this hemisphere intends to remain the master of its own house.

To that world assembly of sovereign states, the United Nations, our last   10
best hope in an age where the instruments of war have far outpaced the instruments of peace, we renew our pledge of support—to prevent it from becoming merely a forum for invective—to strengthen its shield of the new and
the weak—and to enlarge the area in which its writ may run.

Finally, to those nations who would make themselves our adversary, we   11
offer not a pledge but a request: that both sides begin anew the quest for
peace, before the dark powers of destruction unleashed by science engulf all
humanity in planned or accidental self-destruction.

We dare not tempt them with weakness. For only when our arms are suf-   12
ficient beyond doubt can we be certain beyond doubt that they will never be
employed.

But neither can two great and powerful groups of nations take comfort   13
from our present course—both sides overburdened by the cost of modern
weapons, both rightly alarmed by the steady spread of the deadly atom, yet

both racing to alter that uncertain balance of terror that stays the hand of mankind's final war.

14　So let us begin anew—remembering on both sides that civility is not a sign of weakness, and sincerity is always subject to proof. Let us never negotiate out of fear. But let us never fear to negotiate.

15　Let both sides explore what problems unite us instead of belaboring those problems which divide us.

16　Let both sides, for the first time, formulate serious and precise proposals for the inspection and control of arms—and bring the absolute power to destroy other nations under the absolute control of all nations.

17　Let both sides seek to invoke the wonders of science instead of its terrors. Together let us explore the stars, conquer the deserts, eradicate disease, tap the ocean depths, and encourage the arts and commerce.

18　Let both sides unite to heed in all corners of the earth the command of Isaiah—to "undo the heavy burdens [and] let the oppressed go free."

19　And if a beachhead of cooperation may push back the jungle of suspicion, let both sides join in creating a new endeavor, not a new balance of power, but a new world of law, where the strong are just and the weak secure and the peace preserved.

20　All this will not be finished in the first one hundred days. Nor will it be finished in the first one thousand days, nor in the life of this administration, nor even perhaps in our lifetime on this planet. But let us begin.

21　In your hands, my fellow citizens, more than mine, will rest the final success or failure of our course. Since this country was founded, each generation of Americans has been summoned to give testimony to its national loyalty. The graves of young Americans who answered the call to service surround the globe.

22　Now the trumpet summons us again—not as a call to bear arms, though arms we need—not as a call to battle, though embattled we are—but as a call to bear the burden of a long twilight struggle, year in and year out, "rejoicing in hope, patient in tribulation"—a struggle against the common enemies of man: tyranny, poverty, disease, and war itself.

23　Can we forge against these enemies a grand and global alliance, North and South, East and West, that can assure a more fruitful life for all mankind? Will you join in that historic effort?

24　In the long history of the world, only a few generations have been granted the role of defending freedom in its hour of maximum danger. I do not shrink from this responsibility—I welcome it. I do not believe that any of us would exchange places with any other people or any other generation. The energy, the faith, the devotion which we bring to this endeavor will light our country and all who serve it—and the glow from that fire can truly light the world.

And so, my fellow Americans: ask not what your country can do for you— 25
ask what you can do for your country.

My fellow citizens of the world: ask not what America will do for you, but 26
what together we can do for the freedom of man.

Finally, whether you are citizens of America or citizens of the world, ask 27
of us here the same high standards of strength and sacrifice which we ask of
you. With a good conscience our only sure reward, with history the final
judge of our deeds, let us go forth to lead the land we love, asking His blessing and His help, but knowing that here on earth God's work must truly be
our own.

Cathy Young

Keeping Women Weak

Born in the Soviet Union in 1963, Cathy Young emigrated to the United States in 1980. After graduating from
Rutgers University, she began a successful career as a writer, publishing several books including the autobio-
graphical *Growing up in Moscow*. Building on her unique perspective, Young's works on racism, feminism, and
Generation X have appeared in the *American Spectator*, the *Detroit Free Press*, and the *Wall Street Journal*.

NOT LONG AGO, I attended a conference on women's research and activism in 1
the nineties, attended by dozens of feminist academics, writers, and public figures. At the wrap-up session, a middle-aged history professor from the Mid-
west introduced a discordant note into the spirit of celebration. "The fact,"
she said, "is that young women just aren't interested in feminism or feminist
ideas, even though they are leading feminist lives—planning to become lawyers,
doctors, professionals. What is it about feminism, and about our approach,
that puts young women off?"

In response, some blamed "the backlash," others "homophobia." One 2
woman protested that there *were* young feminists out there, citing sexual harassment lawsuits filed by high-school girls—apparently a greater accomplishment
than merely preparing for a career. Another declared that what feminist educators needed to give their students was "an understanding of the power dynamic,"
not "quote-unquote objectivity." (Could it be something about comments like
these that turns female students off?) Missing from this picture was any serious
discussion of what modern feminism has to offer modern young women.

Feminism meant a great deal to me when I came to the United States thir- 3 teen years ago, after a childhood spent in the Soviet Union. Indeed, one of the things that elated me the most about America was women's liberation.

4   The society in which I had grown up was one that officially proclaimed sexual equality and made it a point of great pride yet stereotyped men and women in ways reminiscent of the American fifties. At school, we had mandatory home economics for girls and shop for boys, a practice no one thought of challenging. At the music school for the gifted where my mother taught piano, to say that someone played "like a girl"—pleasantly, neatly, and without substance—was a commonly used putdown; in literary reviews, the highest compliment to be paid a woman writer or poet was that she wrote like a man.

5   As I approached college age, I learned that there was tacit but widely known discrimination against women in the college-entrance exams, on the assumption that a less-capable male would in the end be a more valuable asset than a bright female, who would have boys and makeup and marriage on her mind. And all too many smart, ambitious girls seemed to accept this injustice as inevitable, assuming simply that they had to be twice as good as the boys to prove themselves.

6   It was just as unquestioningly accepted that housework, including the arduous task of Soviet shopping, was women's work; when the problem of women's excessive double burden at home and on the job was mentioned at all, the proposed solution was always for men to be paid more and for women to spend more time at home, not for men to pitch in with domestic chores. And although my parents' relationship was an uncommonly equal one, my father still quoted to me the dictum (coming from Karl Marx, a thinker he generally did not regard as much of an authority) that "woman's greatest strength is her weakness."

7   My discovery of America was also a discovery of feminism—not only Ms. magazine and The Feminine Mystique but also the open and straightforward manner of young American women I met. This was in stark contrast to the style that so many Russian women reverently equated with "femininity"—a more-or-less affected air of capriciousness and frailty, a flirtatious deference to men. I admired the easy camaraderie between boys and girls on American college campuses, the independence and self-confidence of young women who invited guys on dates and picked up the tab, drove when they were out with male companions, and wouldn't let anyone treat them like frail, helpless little things.

8   Those early impressions may have been too optimistic, perhaps somewhat superficial, perhaps incomplete. But I don't think they were wrong.

9   Becoming an American as a teenager in 1980, I joined the first generation of American women who had grown up assuming not only that they would work most of their lives but also that they were the equals of men and that they could be anything they wanted to be (except maybe a full-time home-

maker). This was also the first generation, really, to have grown up after the sexual revolution—at a time when, at least among the educated, the nice-girls-don't sexual standard vanished almost completely. In a somewhat dizzying reversal of traditional norms, many girls felt embarrassed telling their first lovers that they were virgins (at least that's how I felt).

Of course new choices meant new pressures. I never thought a world of sexual equality would be a utopia of peace and harmony. I did believe that our generation of women, and men, was on its way to achieving a world in which people were judged as individuals and not on the basis of their gender; a world in which men and women worked and loved in equal partnership—even if, inevitably, they continued every so often to make each other miserable and furious. 10

And then something funny happened on the way to that feminist future. We were told that we were victims, with little control over our lives and our choices; we were told that we needed to be protected. 11

When the right said that women were victimized by career opportunities and sexual freedom, it didn't matter much—at least to the middle-class, college-educated women who were the main beneficiaries of these new opportunities. Who, in those social circles, was going to listen to people who said that wives should obey their husbands and stick to the kitchen and nursery—to Phyllis Schlafly or Jerry Falwell, notorious reactionaries with little impact on mass culture? 12

But the message of victimhood also came from the feminist left. Everywhere around us, we were told, was a backlash seeking to snatch from us the freedoms we had gained. We were told that we were the targets of a hidden war and had better start acting like one, searching for subtle signs of enemy forays everywhere. If we believed that we had never experienced gender-based injustice and had never felt particularly restricted by our gender, we were not just naive but dangerous: we were turning our backs on feminism and fostering the myth that its major battles had been won. 13

Whenever a campus study has shown that young people of both sexes increasingly share the same values and aspirations and that most college women are quite confident of their ability to succeed in the workplace and to combine family and career, older feminists seem far from pleased. Their warnings—oh, just wait until these young women get a taste of the real world and find that they still face prejudice and discrimination—can sound almost gleeful. 14

Older feminists talk a good line about empowering young women and letting them speak in their own voices; but that goes only as long as these voices say all the approved things. At a university workshop on peer sexual harassment in schools I attended in the spring of 1993, some of the panelists complained that many girls didn't seem to understand what sexual harassment 15 was; when boys made passes or teased them sexually they just shrugged it off, or they thought it was funny and actually liked it. "They need to be educated," one speaker said earnestly, "that the boys aren't just joking around with you, that it's harassment."

16   Ignored in all this discussion was intriguing evidence of the assertive, even aggressive sexuality of many of today's teenage girls, who apparently do a bit of harassing of their own. If girls seemed to revel in sexual attention, that could only be a sign of "low self-esteem" or inability to say no.

17   Judging by all those complaints about the unraised consciousness of the young, the preoccupation with the sexual and other victimization of high-school and college females is not coming, by and large, from young women themselves. Most of them, I believe, tend to regard all the extreme rhetoric as a sort of background noise; if they think about feminism at all, they often decide that they want no part of it—even if they're all for equal rights. The kind of feminists they usually see in their midst may further contribute to this alienation.

18   When I was still in college, I began to notice, alongside the spirited, independent, ambitious young women I admired, a different product of the feminist age: the ever-vigilant watchdog on the alert for signs of sexism. Occasionally, she made a good point; when our environmental science professor blamed overpopulation in part on Third World women "choosing" to have lots of babies, a student spoke up to note that for most Third World women, childbearing was hardly a matter of choice.

19   More typical, alas, was the young woman in my human sexuality class who was constantly pouncing on the professor for saying something like "People who suffer from premature ejaculation . . ." ("Are you implying that only men are people?"). When he had the audacity to cite data indicating that some rapists were motivated primarily by hatred of women and the desire to dominate them but others were driven primarily by sexual impulses, she went ballistic: "The ONLY thing that causes rape is men wanting to control and terrorize women, and you're trying to make it SEXY!" Later, this person bragged about having caused the poor prof "a lot of trouble" by filing a complaint with the dean.

20   Paranoid is a red-flag word to many feminists—understandably so, since it has been used all too often to dismiss women's rightful concerns about sexism. But what other word can come to mind when a woman claims that her writing instructor's selection of a sample of bad writing—a conservative Christian screed linking pornography and communism—was a personal insult directed at her, since she had sometimes worn a Women Against Pornography button in school?

21   And what can one expect when Naomi Wolf, a writer hailed as a trailblazer of a new "Third Wave" of feminism for the younger generation, urges

women to undertake—and men, to gracefully (and gratefully) second—"the arduous, often boring, nonnegotiable *daily chore of calling attention to sexism*" (emphasis mine)? In the essay "Radical Heterosexuality, or, How to Love a Man and Save Your Feminist Soul" (published in the twentieth-anniversary issue of Ms.), Wolf describes how even well-intentioned men tend to be blind to the horrific things women have to put up with:

> Recently, I walked down a New York City avenue with a woman friend, X,   22
> and a man friend, Y. I pointed out to Y the leers, hisses, and invitations to sit
> on faces. Each woman saw clearly what the other woman saw, but Y was baf-
> fled. . . . A passerby makes kissy-noises with his tongue while Y is scrutinizing
> the menu of the nearest bistro. "There, there! Look! Listen!" we cried. "What?
> Where? Who?" wailed poor Y, valiantly, uselessly spinning.

Like poor Y, I am baffled. God knows, I've been taking walks in Manhat-   23
tan at least once or twice a week for nearly thirteen years now, and not a single invitation to sit on a face, not even a single hiss as far as I recall—nothing
more dramatic than the occasional "You look gorgeous today" or "That's a
pretty outfit," and certainly nothing like the constant barrage Wolf describes.
Even the time I wore a new dress that exposed much more cleavage than I realized, all it cost me was one fairly tame remark (as I was stepping into a subway car, a man who was stepping off stared at my bosom and muttered, "Very
nice"). Applied to everyday life and interpersonal relations, "eternal vigilance
is the price of liberty" strikes me as a rather disastrous motto to adopt.

Like all would-be revolutionaries, the radical feminists seek to subordinate   24
private life to ideology—an endeavor that I find, quite simply, frightening. You
don't have to spend part of your life under a totalitarian system (though
maybe it helps) to realize that social and political movements that subordinate
life to ideology have a nasty way of turning coercive, whether it's the mass violence of communism or the neo-Puritan controls of "P.C."

This is not to say that there is no room for rethinking traditional attitudes,   25
on things ranging from who picks up the check in the restaurant to who takes
care of the baby. Millions of women and men are grappling with these issues
at home and in the workplace, some more successfully than others. But that
doesn't mean they have to walk around with their eyes glued to a microscope.

Eternal vigilance is a tempting trap for post-baby-boomer feminists. It has   26
been often remarked that women of earlier generations had to struggle against
visible and overt barriers, such as being denied admission to law school, or told
that only men need apply for certain jobs or that married women shouldn't
work. It seemed that once such barriers dropped, equality would come
quickly. It didn't quite turn out that way; there were other, more insidious
roadblocks, from a working mother's guilt over taking a business trip to a pro-

fessor's unconscious tendency to call on the boys in the class. The problem, however, is that subtle sexism is an elusive target, with plenty of room for error and misinterpretation. If you complain to your professor that you find the course work too difficult and he says, "Well, I've always thought girls didn't belong in this class anyway," there's not a shadow of a doubt that he's a sexist pig. But suppose he says, "Hey, start working harder or drop the class, but don't come whining to me." Is he being insensitive to you as a woman? (An incident of this sort figured in a recent sex-discrimination suit at the University of Minnesota.) Or is he simply a blunt fellow who believes people should stand on their own two feet and who would have treated a male student exactly the same? And if he had been tough on a man but sensitive and solicitous toward a woman student, wouldn't that have been exactly the kind of paternalism feminists used to oppose?

27   But then, certain aspects of cutting-edge feminism do smack of a very old-fashioned paternalism, a sort of chivalry without the charm. At some campus meetings, it is considered P.C. for men who are first in line for the microphone to cede their place to a woman in order to ensure that female speakers—apparently too timid to just get up and get in line—get a proper hearing. Ladies first?

28   Definitions of "hostile environment" sexual harassment often seem like a throwback to prefeminist, if not positively Victorian, standards of how to treat a lady: no off-color jokes, no sexual remarks, no swearing and, God forbid, no improper advances. Surveys purporting to gauge the prevalence of harassment lump together sexual blackmail—demands for sex as a condition of promotion, good grades, or other rewards—with noncoercive advances from coworkers or fellow students, with sexual jokes or innuendo, "improper staring" or "winking."

29   Well, guess what: women too make off-color jokes and risqué comments, and even sexual advances. Sure, many women at one time or another also have to deal with obnoxious, lecherous, and/or sexist jerks. But in most cases, especially if the man is not a superior, they're perfectly capable of putting a jerk back in his place. Of course, radical feminists such as Catharine MacKinnon tell us that there is *always* an imbalance of power between a man and a woman: even if you're studying for an MBA and have a prestigious job lined up, you're still powerless. Now there's a message guaranteed to build up self-confidence and self-esteem.

30   A video on sexual harassment, broadcast on public television twice in January 1993 and available free through an 800 number, includes a segment on a university experiment in which unwitting male students are assigned to supervise the computer work of an attractive girl. Before leaving them alone, the male research assistant pretends to take small liberties with the young woman (putting a hand on her shoulder, bending closely over her) while explaining

the work process, and in most cases the male student proceeds to imitate this behavior or even push it a little further.

Then, the young woman—who, of course, has known what's been going on 31 the whole time—talks on camera about how the experience has helped her understand what it's like to feel powerless. But doesn't this powerlessness have at least something to do with the fact that she was undoubtedly instructed not to show displeasure? Is it such a good idea to teach young women that, short of legal intervention, they have no way of dealing with such annoyances?

I don't believe that our views or our allegiances are determined solely or 32 primarily by age. Still, one might have expected our generation to articulate a feminism rooted in the experience of women who have never felt subordinated to men, have never felt that their options were limited by gender in any significant way or that being treated as sexual beings diminished their personhood. This is not, of course, the experience of all young women; but it is the experience of many, and an experience that should be taken as a model. Perhaps those of us who have this positive view of our lives and our relationships with men have not lived up to our responsibility to translate that view into a new feminist vision.

In an *Esquire* article about sexual politics and romantic love on campus in 33 the nineties, Janet Viggiani, then-assistant dean for coeducation at Harvard, was quoted as saying, "I think young women now are very confused. . . . They don't have many models for how to be strong females and feminine. Many of their models are victim models—passive, weak, endangered." In recent years, feminist activism has focused almost entirely on negatives, from eating disorders to sexual violence and abuse. Sadly, these problems are all too real, and they certainly should be confronted; what they should not be is the central metaphor for the female condition or for relations between women and men, or for feminism. What does it mean when the only time young women and girls think of feminism is not when they think of achievement but when they think of victimization?

The emphasis on victimhood has had an especially dramatic effect on at- 34 titudes toward sexuality. We didn't revel in our sexual freedom for too long; as if the shadow of AIDS weren't bad enough, sex was suddenly fraught with danger and violence as much as possibilities of pleasure, or even more so. A cartoon in the *Nation* shows a girl grooming herself before a mirror, with the caption, "Preparing for a date"—and in the next frame, a boy doing the same, with the caption, "Preparing for a date rape." Pamphlets on sexual assault warn that one out of every five dates ends in a rape, and that up to 25 percent of college women become victims: "Since you can't tell who has the potential for rape by simply looking, be on your guard with every man."

If these numbers are true, women would be well advised either to forswear 35 dating altogether or to carry a can of Mace on every date. But what about these numbers? When one looks at how they are obtained, and how rape is defined, it becomes clear that the acquaintance-rape hysteria not only gives young women an exaggerated picture of the dangers they face in the company of men but essentially demeans women, absolving or stripping them of all responsibility for their behavior.

36   The question is not whether a woman's provocative dress, flirtatious behavior, or drinking justifies sexual assault; that attitude is now on the wane, for which the women's movement certainly deserves credit. It's not even a question of whether a woman should have to fight back and risk injury to prove that she did not consent to sex. The latest crusade makes a woman a victim of rape if she did not rebuff a man's sexual advances because she was too shy or didn't want to hurt his feelings, or if she had sex while drunk (not passed out, just sufficiently intoxicated so that her inhibitions were loosened) and felt bad about it afterwards. In a typical scenario, a couple is making out and then the woman pulls back and says, "I really think we shouldn't," and the man draws her back toward him, *nonforcibly*, and continues to fondle her, or says, "Oh come on, you know you want it," and eventually they end up having sex. If the woman feels that the intercourse was "unwanted," she can—according to the anti-date-rape activists—claim to be a victim, no different from the woman who's attacked at knifepoint in a dark, empty parking lot.

37   A few years ago, I was at the apartment of an ex-boyfriend with whom I was still on friendly terms; after a couple of beers, we started kissing. When his hand crept under my skirt, I suddenly sobered up and thought of several good reasons why I should not go to bed with the guy. I wriggled out of his arms, got up, and said, "That's enough." Undaunted, he came up from behind and squeezed my breasts. I rammed my elbow into his chest, forcefully enough to make the point, and snapped, "Didn't you hear me? I said, enough."

38   Some people might say that I overreacted (my ex-boyfriend felt that way), but the logic of modern-day radical feminists suggests the opposite: that I displayed a heroism that cannot be required of any woman in a situation like that because she could expect the guy to beat her up, to maim her, even if he hadn't made any threats or shown any violent tendencies. A "reasonable" woman would have passively submitted and then cried rape.

39   Even "no means no" is no longer enough; some activists want to say that yes means no, or at least the absence of an explicit yes means no. Feminist legal theorist MacKinnon suggests that much of what our society regards as consensual sex hardly differs from rape and that, given women's oppression, it is doubtful "whether consent is a meaningful concept" at all. Which is to say that, like underage children and the mentally retarded, women are to be presumed incapable of valid consent. MacKinnon's frequent ally, polemicist Andrea Dworkin, states bluntly that all intercourse is rape.

This reasoning is still very far from mainstream acceptance. Even Mac-   40
Kinnon only expresses such views when addressing fairly narrow and con-
verted audiences, not when she's interviewed on TV. Yet a 1992 report by the
Harvard Date Rape Task Force recommended that university guidelines define rape as "any act of sexual intercourse that occurs without the expressed
consent of the person." What does this mean—that a consent form must be
signed before a date? Or that, as a couple moves toward the bed after passionate and mutual heavy petting, the man should ask the woman if she's
quite sure she wants to? (A friend who just graduated from college tells me
that some men are actually beginning to act that way.) And perhaps he has to
keep asking every time: the couple's prior sexual relationship, the advocates
say, makes no difference whatsoever.

Clearly, this vision leaves no room for spontaneity, for ambiguity, for pas-   41
sionate, wordless, animal sex. What's more, it is, in the end, deeply belittling
to women, who apparently cannot be expected to convey their wishes clearly
or to show a minimum of assertiveness. It also perpetuates a view of woman
as the passive and reticent partner who may or may not want sex and man as
the pursuer who is naturally presumed to want it: *she* is not required to ask for
his consent (even though, given some current definitions, plenty of women
must have committed rape at least a few times in their lives; I'm sure I have).
Sex is something men impose on women. We're back full circle to fragile,
chaste, nineteenth-century womanhood.

And some people think that's good. Recently, I got into a discussion with   42
a conservative Catholic male who vehemently argued that the campaign
against date rape was nothing more than a distorted expression of women's legitimate rejection of sexual freedom, a thing so contrary to their chaste na-
tures. Casual sex, he said, makes women (but not men) feel cheap and used,
and what they're doing now is using the extreme language of rape to describe
this exploitation; things were really better under the much-maligned double
standard, when women were expected to say no to sex, and thus accorded
more protection from male lust. To some conservatives, the outcry about sexual harassment confirms what conservatives have known all along: women
want to be put on a pedestal and treated like ladies; they find sexual advances
insulting because they are chaster than men.

I don't think that's true. Most young women have no wish to return to the   43
days when they were branded as sluts if they said yes. It may be, however, that
this generation's confusion over sexual boundaries has to do with the pains of
transition from one set of morals to another, of contradictory cultural messages: the traditional ones of chastity as the basis of female self-respect and reputation and the new ones of sexual liberation and female desire. Sometimes,
we may not think we're "cheap" if we go to bed with a man we just met—at
least, we're no worse than the guy is for going to bed with a woman he just

met—yet when we wake up the next morning we may find that *he* thinks less of us but not of himself. And we may find, to our chagrin, that feminine coyness is not quite as extinct as we might like to think. The other day, a very liberated fortysomething friend of mine breezily said, "Oh, of course no modern woman says no when she means yes." Alas, recent studies (done by feminist researchers) show that *by their own admission,* about half of college women sometimes do.

44   But there may be another reason, too, for this generation's susceptibility to the victim mentality: overconfidence in the perfectibility of life. The sexual-liberation rhetoric itself overlooked the complexity of human emotions and fostered the belief that sexual relationships could be free of all manipulation or unfair pressure. More generally, there is the idealistic arrogance of middle-class boys and girls who have grown up in a sheltered, affluent environment, accustomed to the notion that getting one's way is a basic right. The old cliché "Life isn't fair" is not only unpopular nowadays but profoundly suspect, seen as a smokescreen designed by the oppressors to keep the oppressed—women and minorities, in particular—in their place. Yes, it has been used for such purposes often enough. But often it happens to be true, and to disregard that is to invite disastrous consequences—like the belief that anyone, male or female, is entitled to an annoyance-free life.

45   The danger in the new radical feminism is not only that it legitimizes what is, deep down, an extremely retrograde view of women; it also seeks to regulate personal relationships to a degree unprecedented since the Puritans roamed the earth. If you feel that a man has enticed or pressured you into having unwanted sex, you don't confront him and call him a manipulative creep; you run to a campus grievance committee and demand redress. If you don't like the way a coworker has been putting his hand on your shoulder, you don't have to tell him to stop it—you can go and file a lawsuit instead. Courts and law-enforcement authorities are being asked to step into situations where, short of installing hidden cameras in every bedroom and every office hallway, they have no way of finding out on whose side the truth is. Of course, many millions of women and men remain relatively unaffected by this relentless politicization of the personal. Still, the damage is being done.

46   Again, it may be my Soviet background that makes me especially sensitive to the perils of this aggressive, paternalistic interventionism. In the Soviet *ancien régime,* it was not uncommon to report one's unfaithful spouse to the Communist party bureau at his (or, less commonly, her) workplace, and conflicts between husband and wife—particularly if both were party members—were often settled at public meetings that satisfied both the voyeuristic and the viciously moralistic impulses of the other comrades.

47   What are we going to be, then? Assertive, strong women (and sometimes, surely, also needy and vulnerable, because we *are* human), seeing ourselves as

no better or worse than men; aware of but not obsessed with sexism; interested in loving and equal relationships but with enough confidence in ourselves, and enough understanding of human foibles, to know better than to scrutinize every move we or our partners make for political incorrectness? Or full-time agents of the gender-crimes police?

Women's liberation is not yet a completed task. Sexism still lingers and injustice toward women still exists, particularly in the distribution of domestic tasks. We are still working on new standards and values to guide a new, equal relationship between men and women. But "Third Wave" feminism, which tries to fight gender bias by defining people almost entirely in terms of gender, is not the way to go.   48

We need a "Third Way" feminism that rejects the excesses of the gender fanatics *and* the sentimental traditionalism of the Phyllis Schlaflys; one that does not seek special protections for women and does not view us as too socially disadvantaged to take care of ourselves. Because on the path that feminism has taken in the past few years, we are allowing ourselves to be treated as frail, helpless little things—by our would-be liberators.   49

Student Essay

Felicia Andersen

Why I Am Not a Feminist

Growing up in the '70s and '80s means growing up *after* the '60s, when many of American society's attitudes were turned upside-down. Suddenly, it was OK for a man to stay home and raise children. Suddenly, it was OK for a woman to have a career. Felicia grew up in the '70s, and the result has been perhaps somewhat different than expected. As you read, consider how the times you grew up in have affected your politics.

I AM NOT A FEMINIST. Where I come from, I could get in big trouble saying that. My mother, while never exactly an agitator, was a divorced mother from about 1970 on, and she found herself in a position of "liberating" the men around her. She gender-integrated a men's exercise class, she learned (and taught) that women could pick up the check in a restaurant without castrating men, and she was a charter subscriber to Ms. magazine. Yet I am not a feminist—so where did she fail?   1

I guess she made the world too easy, too much better for her daughters.   2

Nobody could get away with telling me or my sister that we couldn't take shop or try out for the football team or join the Boy Scouts of America—but we never wanted those things. Nobody ever told my brother that he should be "manly" and avoid cooking or housework for more masculine activities like lawn-mowing and watching televised sports—he just ended up inept at all those skills. Without an atmosphere of denial, suppression, obviously unfair rules or social structures inhibiting us, my brother and sister and I grew up expecting the world to treat us fairly, or each as fairly as the others, and it always has.

3   Well, fair-to-middling. I have noticed that my sister and I, having followed my mother's wishes for *all* her children, became proficient typists and have been able to get secretarial jobs in a flash. My brother, on the other hand, graduated from college with a B.A. in English and no such manual skills, only intellectual ones, and was able to begin work immediately as a paralegal, earning $23,000 a year to start. He never had to type after that; all his typing was done by a secretary, also with a B.A., who earned $17,000 a year, probably because she had listened to her mother and excelled at typing.

4   Granted, both of those positions are dead-end. The difference between them is primarily status, and kind of work required. I don't point this out because I'm a feminist, because I'm not, merely because it's true.

5   On the other hand, my mother managed, over the course of 20 years, to parlay her typing skills and a B.A. in English into a career in city government, in which she earned $48,000 a year. My father, on the other hand, never much of a typist but armed with an M.S. in mathematics, plateaued at around $36,000 a year in software engineering. It's hard to see any systematic forces at work here. I see instead two personalities, two different lives lived differently. My mother likes work and my father doesn't. My mother raised three children (not without my father's help, but as primary caregiver), while my father began ten years ago to raise his fourth. My father is intensely involved in his leisure activities; my mother prefers work activity. Perhaps the discrepancy in my brother's office between his earnings and the earnings of a similarly qualified woman is due to an ambition discrepancy as well. I point this out because I'm not a feminist, because a feminist would never bother to point this out.

6   I'll bet you my brother will never be asked to take a typing test. And neither will my father. But though I try to, I can't begin to feel outraged at this. I have the same opportunity to go to college as my mother and her mother, the same as my father and brother and sister. I can take exercise classes with men (even at formerly all-male clubs), I can buy a man dinner, and I can get a job using my mind. I thank my mother for these opportunities, but I have always been secure that they will be there. No one has ever suggested otherwise to me. If anyone did, I'd black his eye—with my typing hand.

8

Analogy

Analogy

1. **Use analogy to clarify your main point.** An analogy is simply a comparison of two apparently different things. In "High Tide in Tucson," for example, Barbara Kingsolver compares her own life to that of a hermit crab she accidentally brought home from a vacation in the Caribbean. One of her points in the essay is that she has carried habits from her previous life in Kentucky to her new life in Arizona. By describing the dramatic shift in the crab's life—removal from the tropical beach to an arid desert—she illustrates how much her own life has changed. If Kingsolver had simply started by describing her move to Arizona, the point may still have been made, but it would have been neither as clear nor as powerful.

2. **Make sure your analogy is appropriate.** Writing a useful analogy requires care. If the connection between the subject of your analogy and your main point is either too close or too remote, the analogy will usually be ineffective. If Kingsolver had compared moving to Arizona with moving to New Mexico, it would have been difficult to understand how significant the move was in her life. Similarly, if she had compared moving to a bowl of fruit, the analogy would be nonsensical. You should also take care not to offend with your analogies—comparing nuns to Nazis, for example, is generally a bad idea.

3. **Support your analogy with details.** Careful use of detail can help your analogy come alive. Kingsolver describes the hermit crab for many pages before she makes the connection to her own life. John Muir, in "A Wind-Storm in the Forests," paints a vivid picture of wind-swept treetops roiling like a raging sea.

4. **Remember that analogy does not constitute proof.** An analogy can clarify your point, but it cannot prove it. In his essay "Modern-Day Mobsters," when Maurice Johnson compares banks to gangsters, his point relies on the fact that we've all had bad experiences with banks. If his point wasn't supported by both a general belief and the actual evidence he gives to support the idea that banks use predatory practices, using an analogy wouldn't be enough to save it.

Toni Morrison

Nobel Lecture 1993

Although now her list of novels is long, including *The Bluest Eye, Song of Solomon, Tar Baby, Beloved,* and *Jazz,* it wasn't until 1978 that Toni Morrison cut down her editorial work and decided to make a full commitment to writing. Born in 1931 into a poor but hard-working family in Cleveland, Ohio, Morrison was able to attend college and graduate school with the help of her parents. During her years as a professor at Howard University, she wrote in secret and did not let other people see her work. After divorcing her husband, she moved to New York and became an editor at Random House, where her gift as a writer was discovered. Morrison won the Pulitzer Prize for fiction in 1988, and in 1993 she won the Nobel Prize for literature, where she gave the speech reprinted here.

"ONCE UPON A TIME THERE WAS AN OLD WOMAN. Blind but wise." Or was it an 1
old man? A guru, perhaps. Or a griot soothing restless children. I have heard
this story, or one exactly like it, in the lore of several cultures.

"Once upon a time there was an old woman. Blind. Wise." 2

In the version I know the woman is the daughter of slaves, black, Ameri- 3
can, and lives alone in a small house outside of town. Her reputation for wisdom is without peer and without question. Among her people she is both the
law and its transgression. The honor she is paid and the awe in which she is
held reach beyond her neighborhood to places far away, to the city where the
intelligence of rural prophets is the source of much amusement.

One day the woman is visited by some young people who seem to be bent 4
on disproving her clairvoyance and showing her up for the fraud they believe
she is. Their plan is simple: they enter her house and ask the one question the
answer to which rides solely on her difference from them, a difference they regard as a profound disability: her blindness. They stand before her, and one
of them says, "Old woman, I hold in my hand a bird. Tell me whether it is living or dead."

She does not answer, and the question is repeated. "Is the bird I am hold- 5
ing living or dead?"

Still she doesn't answer. She is blind and cannot see her visitors, let alone 6
what is in their hands. She does not know their color, gender, or homeland.
She only knows their motive.

The old woman's silence is so long, the young people have trouble hold- 7
ing their laughter.

Finally she speaks and her voice is soft but stern. "I don't know," she says. 8

"I don't know whether the bird you are holding is dead or alive, but what I do know is that it is in your hands. It is in your hands."

9   Her answer can be taken to mean: if it is dead, you have either found it that way or you have killed it. If it is alive, you can still kill it. Whether it is to stay alive, it is your decision. Whatever the case, it is your responsibility.

10   For parading their power and her helplessness, the young visitors are reprimanded, told they are responsible not only for the act of mockery but also for the small bundle of life sacrificed to achieve its aims. The blind woman shifts attention away from assertions of power to the instrument through which that power is exercised.

11   Speculation on what (other than its own frail body) that bird-in-the-hand might signify has always been attractive to me, but especially so now, thinking, as I have been, about the work I do that has brought me to this company. So I choose to read the bird as language and the woman as a practiced writer. She is worried about how the language she dreams in, given to her at birth, is handled, put into service, even withheld from her for certain nefarious purposes. Being a writer, she thinks of language partly as a system, partly as a living thing over which one has control, but mostly as agency—as an act with consequences. So the question the children put to her—"Is it living or dead?"—is not unreal because she thinks of language as susceptible to death, erasure, certainly imperiled and salvageable only by an effort of the will. She believes that if the bird in the hands of her visitors is dead, the custodians are responsible for the corpse. For her a dead language is not only one no longer spoken or written; it is unyielding language content to admire its own paralysis. Like statist language, censored and censoring. Ruthless in its policing duties, it has no desire or purpose other than maintaining the free range of its own narcotic narcissism, its own exclusivity and dominance. However moribund, it is not without effect, for it actively thwarts the intellect, stalls conscience, suppresses human potential. Unreceptive to interrogation, it cannot form or tolerate new ideas, shape other thoughts, tell another story, fill baffling silences. Official language smitheryed to sanction ignorance and preserve privilege is a suit of armor, polished to shocking glitter, a husk from which the knight departed long ago. Yet there it is: dumb, predatory, sentimental. Exciting reverence in schoolchildren, providing shelter for despots, summoning false memories of stability, harmony among the public.

12   She is convinced that when language dies, out of carelessness, disuse, and absence of esteem, indifference or killed by fiat, not only she herself but all users and makers are accountable for its demise. In her country children have bitten their tongues off and use bullets instead to iterate the voice of speechlessness, of disabled and disabling language, of language adults have abandoned altogether as a device for grappling with meaning, providing guidance, or expressing love.

But she knows tongue-suicide is not only the choice of children. It is common among the infantile heads of state and power merchants whose evacuated language leaves them with no access to what is left of their human instincts, for they speak only to those who obey, or in order to force obedience.

The systematic looting of language can be recognized by the tendency of its 13 users to forgo its nuanced, complex, midwifery properties for menace and subjugation. Oppressive language does more than represent violence; it is violence; does more than represent the limits of knowledge; it limits knowledge. Whether it is obscuring state language or the faux-language of mindless media; whether it is the proud but calcified language of the academy or the commodity-driven language of science; whether it is the malign language of law-without-ethics, or language designed for the estrangement of minorities, hiding its racist plunder in its literary cheek—it must be rejected, altered, and exposed. It is the language that drinks blood, laps vulnerabilities, tucks its fascist boots under crinolines of respectability and patriotism as it moves relentlessly toward the bottom line and the bottomed-out mind. Sexist language, racist language, theistic language—all are typical of the policing languages of mastery, and cannot, do not permit new knowledge or encourage the mutual exchange of ideas.

The old woman is keenly aware that no intellectual mercenary, no insa- 14 tiable dictator, no paid-for politician or demagogue, no counterfeit journalist would be persuaded by her thoughts. There is and will be rousing language to keep citizens armed and arming, slaughtered and slaughtering in the malls, courthouses, post offices, playgrounds, bedrooms, and boulevards; stirring, memorializing language to mask the pity and waste of needless death. There will be more diplomatic language to countenance rape, torture, assassination. There is and will be more seductive, mutant language designed to throttle women, to pack their throats like paté-producing geese with their own unsayable, transgressive words; there will be more of the language of surveillance disguised as research; of politics and history calculated to render the suffering of millions mute; of language glamorized to thrill the dissatisfied and bereft into assaulting their neighbors; arrogant, pseudoempirical language crafted to lock creative people into cages of inferiority and hopelessness.

Underneath the eloquence, the glamour, the scholarly associations, how- 15 ever stirring or seductive, the heart of such language is languishing, or perhaps not beating at all—if the bird is already dead.

She has thought about what could have been the intellectual history of 16 any discipline if it had not insisted upon, or been forced into, the waste of time and life that rationalizations for and representations of dominance required—lethal discourses of exclusion blocking access to cognition for both the excluder and the excluded.

17   The conventional wisdom of the Tower of Babel story is that the collapse was a misfortune. That it was the distraction, or the weight of many languages that precipitated the tower's failed architecture. That one monolithic language would have expedited the building and heaven would have been reached. Whose heaven, she wonders? And what kind? Perhaps the achievement of Paradise was premature, a little hasty, if no one could take the time to understand other languages, other views, other narratives. Had they, the heaven they imagined might have been found at their feet. Complicated, demanding, yes, but a view of heaven as life, not heaven as postlife.

18   She would not want to leave her young visitors with the impression that language should be forced to stay alive merely to be. The vitality of language lies in its ability to limn the actual, imagined, and possible lives of its speakers, readers, writers. Although its poise is sometimes in displacing experience, it is not a substitute for it. It arcs toward the place where meaning may lie. When a President of the United States thought about the graveyard his country had become and said "The world will little note nor long remember what we say here. But it will never forget what they did here," his simple words were exhilarating in their life-sustaining properties because they refused to encapsulate the reality of 600,000 dead men in a cataclysmic race war. Refusing to monumentalize, disdaining the "final word," the precise "summing up," acknowledging their "poor power to add or detract," his words signal deference to the uncapturability of the life it mourns. It is the deference that moves her, that recognition that language can never live up to life once and for all. Nor should it. Language can never "pin down" slavery, genocide, war. Nor should it yearn for the arrogance to be able to do so. Its force, its felicity is in its reach toward the ineffable.

19   Be it grand or slender, burrowing, blasting, or refusing to sanctify, whether it laughs out loud or is a cry without an alphabet, the choice word, the chosen silence, unmolested language surges toward knowledge, not its destruction. But who does not know of literature banned because it is interrogative, discredited because it is critical, erased because alternate? And how many are outraged by the thought of a self-ravaged tongue?

20   Word-work is sublime, she thinks, because it is generative; it makes meaning that secures our difference, our human difference—the way in which we are like no other life.

21   We die. That may be the meaning of life. But we do language. That may be the measure of our lives.

22   "Once upon a time . . . ," visitors ask an old woman a question. Who are they, these children? What did they make of that encounter? What did they hear in those final words: "The bird is in your hands"? A sentence that gestures toward possibility or one that drops a latch? Perhaps what the children heard

was "It's not my problem. I am old, female, black, blind. What wisdom I have now is in knowing I cannot help you. The future of language is yours."

They stand there. Suppose nothing was in their hands? Suppose the visit 23
was only a ruse, a trick to get to be spoken to, taken seriously as they have not been before? A chance to interrupt, to violate the adult world, its miasma of discourse about them, for them, but never to them? Urgent questions are at stake, including the one they have asked: "Is the bird we hold living or dead?" Perhaps the question meant: "Could someone tell us what is life? What is death?" No trick at all; no silliness. A straightforward question worthy of the attention of a wise one. An old one. And if the old and wise who have lived life and faced death cannot describe either, who can?

But she does not; she keeps her secret, her good opinion of herself, her 24
gnomic pronouncements, her art without commitment. She keeps her distance, enforces it, and retreats into the singularity of isolation, in sophisticated, privileged space.

Nothing, no word follows her declarations of transfer. That silence is 25
deep, deeper than the meaning available in the words she has spoken. It shivers, this silence, and the children, annoyed, fill it with language invented on the spot.

"Is there no speech," they ask her, "no words you can give us that help us 26
break through your dossier of failures? Through the education you have just given us that is no education at all because we are paying close attention to what you have done as well as to what you have said? To the barrier you have erected between generosity and wisdom?

"We have no bird in our hands, living or dead. We have only you and our 27
important question. Is the nothing in our hands something you could not bear to contemplate, to even guess? Don't you remember being young when language was magic without meaning? When what you could say, could not mean? When the invisible was what imagination strove to see? When questions and demands for answers burned so brightly you trembled with fury at not knowing?

"Do we have to begin consciousness with a battle heroines and heroes like 28
you have already fought and lost, leaving us with nothing in our hands except what you have imagined is there? Your answer is artful, but its artiness embarrasses us and ought to embarrass you. Your answer is indecent in its self-congratulation. A made-for-television script that makes no sense if there is nothing in our hands.

"Why didn't you reach out, touch us with your soft fingers, delay the 29
sound bite, the lesson, until you knew who we were? Did you so despise our trick, our modus operandi, you could not see that we were baffled about how to get your attention? We are young. Unripe. We have heard all our short lives that we have to be responsible. What could that possibly mean in the cata-

strophe this world has become, where, as a poet said, 'nothing needs to be exposed since it is already barefaced'? Our inheritance is an affront. You want us to have your old, blank eyes and see only cruelty and mediocrity. Do you think we are stupid enough to perjure ourselves again and again with the fiction of nationhood? How dare you talk to us of duty when we stand waist deep in the toxin of your past?

30   "You trivialize us and trivialize the bird that is not in our hands. Is there no context for our lives? No song, no literature, no poem full of vitamins, no history connected to experience that you can pass along to help us start strong? You are an adult. The old one, the wise one. Stop thinking about saving your face. Think of our lives and tell us your particularized world. Make up a story. Narrative is radical, creating us at the very moment it is being created. We will not blame you if your reach exceeds your grasp, if love so ignites your words they go down in flames and nothing is left but their scald. Or if, with the reticence of a surgeon's hands, your words suture only the places where blood might flow. We know you can never do it properly—once and for all. Passion is never enough; neither is skill. But try. For our sake and yours, forget your name in the street; tell us what the world has been to you in the dark places and in the light. Don't tell us what to believe, what to fear. Show us belief's wide skirt and the stitch that unravels fear's caul. You, old woman, blessed with blindness, can speak the language that tells us what only language can: how to see without pictures. Language alone protects us from the scariness of things with no names. Language alone is meditation.

31   "Tell us what it is to be a woman so that we may know what it is to be a man. What moves at the margin. What it is to have no home on this place. To be set adrift from the one you knew. What it is to live at the edge of towns that cannot bear your company.

32   "Tell us about ships turned away from shorelines at Easter, placenta in a field. Tell us about a wagonload of slaves, how they sang so softly their breath was indistinguishable from the falling snow. How they knew from the hunch of the nearest shoulder that the next stop would be their last. How, with hands prayered in their sex they thought of heat, then suns. Lifting their faces as though it was there for the taking. Turning as though there for the taking. They stop at an inn. The driver and his mate go in with the lamp, leaving them humming in the dark. The horse's void steams into the snow beneath its hooves, and its hiss and melt is the envy of the freezing slaves.

33   "The inn door opens: a girl and a boy step away from its light. They climb into the wagon bed. The boy will have a gun in three years, but now he carries a lamp and a jug of warm cider. They pass it from mouth to mouth. The girl offers bread, pieces of meat, and something more: a glance into the eyes of the one she serves. One helping for each man, two for each woman. And a look. They look back. The next stop will be their last. But not this one. This one is warmed."

It's quiet again when the children finish speaking, until the woman breaks into the silence.

"Finally," she says, "I trust you now. I trust you with the bird that is not in   34
your hands because you have truly caught it. Look. How lovely it is, this thing we have done—together."

Stockholm, 8 December 1993

Peter Huber

Herod II
Human clones are closer than you think

Peter Huber was born in Toronto in 1952 and became a naturalized citizen of the United States in 1985.   With a background in engineering (a doctorate from M.I.T. in 1976) and law (J.D. from Harvard in 1982), he is well positioned to write informed articles dealing with science, technology, and the legal system. He is currently a senior fellow at the Manhattan Institute for Policy Research and is a regular columnist for *Forbes* magazine.

SOME TIME NEXT YEAR an embryo will be cloned from a human adult. It will   1
be implanted in the uterus of a young woman selected with some care for her wide pelvis and robust health. A son will be born at the dawn of the third millennium. Neither angels nor newswires are likely to herald the birth. The father—an Asian plutocrat, South American kleptocrat or aging Western rock star—won't be looking for publicity. He will be looking for everlasting life.

In the last few months the technological annunciations have become   2
quite clear. English scientists recently finished the first complete decoding of the genes of a multicelled animal, a roundworm. The decoding of the human genome will be completed within a few years, much earlier than expected only a short while ago. Researchers funded by Geron, a Menlo Park, Calif. company, have grown stem cells from human embryos and fetuses into neurons, muscle cells and other tissues. Medicine in general is being reduced to chemistry; reproductive medicine won't be the exception. December brought reports from Japan of the cloning of cows—the fourth mammal to be copied. What is biotechnically possible with a sheep or cow is readily possible with a man.

Genetic technology is headed down the same cost curve as silicon tech-   3 nology, just some decades behind it. Moving mountains of material or energy is inherently expensive. Moving electrons, atoms and molecules around is inherently cheap, once you learn the trick. Fifty years ago the world didn't have a single transistor; today it has trillions. Thirty years ago medicine had little idea how to turn off the biochemical chain reaction we call cancer. When they arrived, the first chemotherapies for cancer were clumsy and expensive. But recent advances have come fast. The clone wizards are now learning to turn on what the oncologists are learning to turn off. The key breakthroughs have already occurred; all the rest now is detail. It will be worked out terribly fast.

4   Cloning technology cannot be contained by pulpit or commission. The raw materials are ubiquitous; the processing tools are quite simple and inexpensive. Proliferation of the other technology of the atom—the nuclear bomb—has been limited mainly by the difficulty of extracting the key raw material, which is very rare. Enriching uranium requires an enormous capital and technological infrastructure. Replicating cellular protein doesn't.

5   The political incentives to block bioatomic power are far weaker, too. The specter of the double helix is not the specter of Hiroshima. There will be no global outcry on the cold and frosty morning that Saddam II draws his first breath in the bassinet of an ultraprivate hospital nestled somewhere in the hills above Zurich.

6   And if not Zurich, then Stockholm or Buenos Aires. New York won't be far behind. Harvard's legal academics are already busily explaining why self-procreation is as fundamental a right as abortion, which is, under current readings of the Constitution, very fundamental indeed. A society that not only accepts but openly admires the no-dad and two-dad family will find a way to get comfortable with the all-dad child.

7   The bio-industrial complex will copiously replicate the genes of only the rich and the powerful, for the first few rounds anyway, until the costs begin to fall. The politically correct among us insist that genes don't actually determine anything much at all. But as identical-twin studies already confirm, genes in fact determine a lot, including many basic facets of character. In all likelihood, the new progeny of old genes will turn out as self-absorbed and manipulative as their biological fathers.

8   Issuing as they will from the not-at-all meek or mild, the first generation of clonekids will inherit, along with their DNA, a rich legacy of economic and social power. They are likely to do very well for themselves, if not for society.

9   There was a day when even kings might put their hope and faith in a child of humble origin. In our narcissistic times, it will be Herod the Great who travels afar to gaze upon a biological copy of himself.

Barry Lopez

Encounter on the Tundra

Barry Lopez (b. 1945) has become one of the nation's most respected natural history writers. After a childhood spent in New York City and southern California, he returned to the West Coast in 1967 to live in the Cascade Mountains in Oregon with his wife, and has been there ever since. Somewhat paradoxically, both a sense of place and a thirst for travel motivate Lopez. He and his wife have spent more than twenty-five years mapping out their property in Oregon, getting to know intimately the land that they live on. But Lopez has also described himself as "a writer who travels," a fact which is evident in his work. "Encounter on the Tundra," an excerpt from *Arctic Dreams,* draws from his experience in Alaska, where he went first to study wolves, and later to study all the things other than wolves that he had missed before. He has also written about experiences in Kenya, the Northern Territory of Australia, and the Galápagos Islands.

IN CERTAIN PARTS OF THE ARCTIC—Lancaster Sound, the shores of Queen Maud Gulf, the Mackenzie River Delta, northern Bering Sea, the Yukon-Kuskokwin Delta—great concentrations of wildlife seem to belie violent fluctuations in this ecosystem. The Arctic seems resplendent with life. But these are summer concentrations, at well-known oases, widely separated over the land; and they consist largely of migratory creatures—geese, alcids, and marine mammals. When the rivers and seas freeze over in September they will all be gone. The winter visitor will find only caribou and muskoxen, and occasionally arctic hares, concentrated in any number, and again only in a few places. 1

All life, of course, cannot fly or swim or walk away to a warmer climate. When winter arrives, these animals must disperse to areas where they will have a good chance to find food and where there is some protection from the weather. A few hibernate for seven or eight months. Voles and lemmings go to ground too, but remain active all winter. Wolves shift their home ranges to places where caribou and moose are concentrated. Arctic foxes follow polar bears out onto the sea ice, where they scavenge the bear's winter kills. Arctic hares seek out windblown slopes where vegetation is exposed. All these resident animals have a measure of endurance about them. They expect to see you, as unlikely as it may seem, in the spring. 2

In my seasonal travels the collared lemming became prominent in my mind as a creature representative of winter endurance and resiliency. When you encounter it on the summer tundra, harvesting lichen or the roots of cotton grass, it rises on its back feet and strikes a posture of hostile alertness that urges you not to trifle. Its small size is not compromising; it displays a quality of heart, all the more striking in the spare terrain. 3

4   Lemmings are ordinarily sedentary, year-round residents of local tundra communities. They came into the central Arctic at the end of the Pleistocene some 8,000 years ago, crossing great stretches of open water and extensive rubble fields of barren sea ice to reach the places they live in today. In winter lemmings live under an insulating blanket of snow in a subnivean landscape, a dark, cool, humid world of quiet tunnels and windless corridors. They emerge in spring to a much brighter, warmer, and infinitely more open landscape—where they are spotted by hungry snowy owls and parasitic jaegers and are hunted adroitly by foxes and short-tailed weasels. In most years, in most places, there is not much perplexing about this single link in several arctic food chains. In some places, every three or four years, however, the lemming population explodes. Lemmings emerge from their subnivean haunts in extraordinary numbers and strike out—blindly is the guess—across the tundra.

5   The periodic boom in lemming populations—there are comparable, though more vaguely defined, cycles affecting the periodic rise and fall of snowshoe hare and lynx populations, and caribou and wolf populations—is apparently connected with the failure of the lemmings' food base. The supply of available forage reaches a peak and then collapses, and the lemmings move off smartly in all directions as soon as traveling conditions permit in the spring. Occasionally many thousands of them reach sea cliffs or a swift-moving river; those pushing in the rear force the vanguard into the water to perish.

6   Arctic scientist Laurence Irving, camped once on a gravel bar off the Alaska coast, wrote: "In the spring of a year of climaxing abundance, a lively and pugnacious lemming came into my camp . . . [more] tracks and a dead lemming were seen on the ice several kilometers from shore. The seaward direction of this mad movement was pointless, but it illustrates stamina that could lead to a far dispersal." Irving's regard, of course, is a regard for the animal itself, not for the abstract mechanisms of population biology of which it seems to merely be a part. Its apparently simple life on the tundra suggests it can be grasped, while its frantic migrations make it seem foolish. In the end, it is complex in its behavior, intricately fitted into its world, and mysterious.

7   Whenever I met a collared lemming on a summer day and took its stare I would think: Here is a tough animal. Here is a valuable life. In a heedless moment, years from now, will I remember more machinery here than mind? If it could tell me of its will to survive, would I think of biochemistry, or would I think of the analogous human desire? If it could speak of the time since the retreat of the ice, would I have the patience to listen?

8   One time I fell asleep on the tundra, a few miles from our camp. I was drowsy with sun and the weight of languid air. I nestled in the tussock heath,

in the warm envelope of my down parka; and was asleep in a few moments. When I awoke I did not rise, but slowly craned my head around to see what was going on. At a distance I saw a ground squirrel crouched behind a limestone slab that rose six or eight inches out of the ground like a wall. From its attitude I thought it was listening, confirming the presence of some threat on the other side of the rock, in a shallow draw. After a while it put its paws delicately to the stone and slowly rose up to peer over, breaking the outline of the rock with the crown of its head. Then, with its paws still flat at the rim, it lowered itself and rested its forehead on the rock between its forelegs. The feeling that it was waiting for something deadly to go away was even stronger. I thought: Well, there is a fox over there, or a wolverine. Maybe a bear. He'd better be careful.

I continued to stare at him from the warm crevice in the earth that concealed me. If it is a bear, I thought, I should be careful too, not move from here until the ground squirrel loses that tension in its body. Until it relaxes, and walks away.   9

I lay there knowing something eerie ties us to the world of animals. Sometimes the animals pull you backward into it. You share hunger and fear with them like salt in blood.   10

The ground squirrel left. I went over to the draw beyond the rock but could find no tracks. No sign. I went back to camp mulling the arrangements animals manage in space and in time—their migrations, their patience, their lairs. Did they have intentions as well as courage and caution?   11

Few things provoke like the presence of wild animals. They pull at us like tidal currents with questions of volition, of ethical involvement, of ancestry.   12

For some reason I brooded often about animal behavior and the threads of evolution in the Arctic. I do not know whether it was the reserves of space, the simplicity of the region's biology, its short biological history, striking encounters with lone animals, or the realization of my own capacity to annihilate life here. I wondered where the animals had come from; and where we had come from; and where each of us was going. The ecosystem itself is only 10,000 years old, the time since the retreat of the Wisconsin ice. The fact that it is the youngest ecosystem on earth gives it a certain freshness and urgency. (Curiously, historians refer to these same ten millennia as the time of civilized man, from his humble beginnings in northern Mesopotamia to the present. Arctic ecosystems and civilized man belong, therefore, to the same, short epoch, the Holocene. Mankind is, in fact, even older than the Arctic, if you consider his history to have begun with the emergence of Cro-Magnon people in Europe 40,000 years ago.)   13

Human beings dwell in the same biological systems that contain the other creatures but, to put the thought bluntly, they are not governed by   14 the same laws of evolution. With the development of various technologies—hunting weapons, protective clothing, firemaking tools; and then agriculture and herding—mankind has not only been able to take over the specific niches of other animals but has been able to move into regions that were formerly unavailable to him. The animals he found already occupying niches in these other areas he, again, either displaced or eliminated. The other creatures have had no choice. They are confined to certain niches—places of food (stored solar energy), water, and shelter—which they cannot leave without either speciating or developing tools. To finish the thought, the same technological advances and the enormous increase in his food base have largely exempted man from the effect of natural controls on the size of his population. Outside of some virulent disease, another ice age, or his own weapons technology, the only thing that promises to stem the continued increase in his population and the expansion of his food base (which now includes oil, exotic minerals, fossil ground water, huge tracts of forest, and so on, and entails the continuing, concomitant loss of species) is human wisdom.

15   Walking across the tundra, meeting the stare of a lemming, or coming on the tracks of a wolverine, it would be the frailty of our wisdom that would confound me. The pattern of our exploitation of the Arctic, our increasing utilization of its natural resources, our very desire to "put it to use," is clear. What is it that is missing, or tentative, in us, I would wonder, to make me so uncomfortable walking out here in a region of chirping birds, distant caribou, and redoubtable lemmings? It is restraint.

16   Because mankind can circumvent evolutionary law, it is incumbent upon him, say evolutionary biologists, to develop another law to abide by if he wishes to survive, to not outstrip his food base. He must learn restraint. He must derive some other, wiser way of behaving toward the land. He must be more attentive to the biological imperatives of the system of sun-driven protoplasm upon which he, too, is still dependent. Not because he must, because he lacks inventiveness, but because herein is the accomplishment of the wisdom that for centuries he has aspired to. Having taken on his own destiny, he must now think with critical intelligence about where to defer.

17   A Yup'ik hunter on Saint Lawrence Island once told me that what traditional Eskimos fear most about us is the extent of our power to alter the land, the scale of that power, and the fact that we can easily effect some of these changes electronically, from a distant city. Eskimos, who sometimes see themselves as still not quite separate from the animal world, regard us as a kind of people whose separation may have become too complete. They call us, with a mixture of incredulity and apprehension, "the people who change nature."

Barbara Kingsolver

High Tide in Tucson

Barbara Kingsolver's novels and poems reflect her own transition from the Kentucky of her childhood to the American Southwest where she now resides. Kingsolver's narrative is given depth by her background as a biologist (with a Master's Degree from the University of Arizona) and compassion by her unflinching belief in human rights and political activism. Her writing is often a curious blend of the southern accents of her youth and the Hispanic and Native American influences of her adopted home in the Southwest. She has won awards from the American Library Association and the United Nations National Council of Women, as well as the Edward Abbey Ecofiction Award. In this title selection from her first collection of essays, Kingsolver uses the metaphor of the natural world to muse on her common themes of family, community, and human nature.

A HERMIT CRAB LIVES IN MY HOUSE. Here in the desert he's hiding out from   1
local animal ordinances, at minimum, and maybe even the international laws
of native-species transport. For sure, he's an outlaw against nature. So be it.

He arrived as a stowaway two Octobers ago. I had spent a week in the Ba-   2
hamas, and while I was there, wishing my daughter could see those sparkling
blue bays and sandy covers, I did exactly what she would have done: I collected
shells. Spiky murexes, smooth purple moon shells, ancient-looking whelks
sand-blasted by the tide—I tucked them in the pockets of my shirt and shorts
until my lumpy, suspect hemlines gave me away, like a refugee smuggling the
family fortune. When it was time to go home, I rinsed my loot in the sink and
packed it carefully into a plastic carton, then nested it deep in my suitcase for
the journey to Arizona.

I got home in the middle of the night, but couldn't wait till morning to   3
show my hand. I set the carton on the coffee table for my daughter to open.
In the dark living room her face glowed, in the way of antique stories about
children and treasure. With perfect delicacy she laid the shells out on the
table, counting, sorting, designating scientific categories like yellow-striped
pinky, Barnacle Bill's pocketbook . . . Yeek! She let loose a sudden yelp,
dropped her booty, and ran to the far end of the room. The largest, knottiest
whelk had begun to move around. First it extended one long red talon of a
leg, tap-tap-tapping like a blind man's cane. Then came half a dozen more red
legs, plus a pair of eyes on stalks, and a purple claw that snapped open and
shut in a way that could not mean We come in Friendship.

Who could blame this creature? It had fallen asleep to the sound of the   4
Caribbean tide and awakened on a coffee table in Tucson, Arizona, where the

nearest standing water source of any real account was the municipal sewage-treatment plant.

5   With red stiletto legs splayed in all directions, it lunged and jerked its huge shell this way and that, reminding me of the scene I make whenever I'm moved to rearrange the living-room sofa by myself. Then, while we watched in stunned reverence, the strange beast found its bearings and began to reveal a determined, crabby grace. It felt its way to the edge of the table and eased itself over, not falling bang to the floor but hanging suspended underneath within the long grasp of its ice-tong legs, lifting any two or three at a time while many others still held in place. In this remarkable fashion it scrambled around the underside of the table's rim, swift and sure and fearless like a rock climber's dream.

6   If you ask me, when something extraordinary shows up in your life in the middle of the night, you give it a name and make it the best home you can.

7   The business of naming involved a grasp of hermit-crab gender that was way out of our league. But our household had a deficit of males, so my daughter and I chose Buster, for balance. We gave him a terrarium with clean gravel and a small cactus plant dug out of the yard and a big cockleshell full of tap water. All this seemed to suit him fine. To my astonishment our local pet store carried a product called Vitaminized Hermit Crab Cakes. Tempting enough (till you read the ingredients) but we passed, since our household leans more toward the recycling ethic. We give him leftovers. Buster's rapture is the day I drag the unidentifiable things in cottage cheese containers out of the back of the fridge.

8   We've also learned to give him a continually changing assortment of seashells, which he tries on and casts off like Cinderella's stepsisters preening for the ball. He'll sometimes try to squeeze into ludicrous outfits too small to contain him (who can't relate?). In other moods, he will disappear into a conch the size of my two fists and sit for a day, immobilized by the weight of upward mobility. He is in every way the perfect housemate: quiet, entertaining, and willing to eat up the trash. He went to school for first-grade show-and-tell, and was such a hit the principal called up to congratulate me (I think) for being a broad-minded mother.

9   It was a long time, though, before we began to understand the content of Buster's character. He required more patient observation than we were in the habit of giving to a small, cold-blooded life. As months went by, we would periodically notice with great disappointment that Buster seemed to be dead. Or not entirely dead, but ill, or maybe suffering the crab equivalent of the blues. He would burrow into a gravelly corner, shrink deep into his shell, and not move, for days and days. We'd take him out to play, dunk him in water, offer him a new frock—nothing. He wanted to be still.

10   Life being what it is, we'd eventually quit prodding our sick friend to cheer

up, and would move on to the next stage of a difficult friendship: neglect. We'd ignore him wholesale, only to realize at some point later on that he'd lapsed into hyperactivity. We'd find him ceaselessly patrolling the four corners of his world, turning over rocks, rooting out and dragging around truly disgusting pork-chop bones, digging up his cactus and replanting it on its head. At night when the household fell silent I would lie in bed listening to his methodical pebbly racket from the opposite end of the house. Buster was manic-depressive.

I wondered if he might be responding to the moon. I'm partial to lunar cycles, ever since I learned as a teenager that human females in their natural state—which is to say, sleeping outdoors—arrive at menses in synchrony and ovulate with the full moon. My imagination remains captive to that primordial village: the comradely grumpiness of new-moon days, when the entire world at once would go on PMS alert. And the compensation that would turn up two weeks later on a wild wind, under that great round headlamp, driving both men and women to distraction with the overt prospect of conception. The surface of the land literally rises and falls—as much as fifty centimeters!—as the moon passes over, and we clayfooted mortals fall like dominoes before the swell. It's no surprise at all if a full moon inspires lyricists to corny love songs, or inmates to slamming themselves against barred windows. A hermit crab hardly seems this impetuous, but animals are notoriously responsive to the full moon: wolves howl; roosters announce daybreak all night. Luna moths, Arctic loons, and lunatics have a sole inspiration in common. Buster's insomniac restlessness seemed likely to be a part of the worldwide full-moon fellowship. 11

But it wasn't, exactly. The full moon didn't shine on either end of his cycle, the high or the low. We tried to keep track, but it soon became clear: Buster marched to his own drum. The cyclic force that moved him remained as mysterious to us as his true gender and the workings of his crustacean soul. 12

Buster's aquarium occupies a spot on our kitchen counter right next to the coffeepot, and so it became my habit to begin mornings with chin in hands, pondering the oceanic mysteries while awaiting percolation. Finally, I remembered something. Years ago when I was a graduate student of animal behavior, I passed my days reading about the likes of animals' internal clocks. Temperature, photoperiod, the rise and fall of hormones—all these influences have been teased apart like so many threads from the rope that pulls every creature to its regulated destiny. But one story takes the cake. F. A. Brown, a researcher who is more or less the grandfather of the biological clock, set about in 1954 to track the cycles of intertidal oysters. He scooped his subjects from the clammy coast of Connecticut and moved them into the basement of a laboratory in landlocked Illinois. For the first fifteen days in their new aquariums, the oysters kept right up with their normal intertidal behavior: they spent time shut away in their shells, and time with their mouths wide 13 open, siphoning their briny bath for the plankton that sustained them, as the tides ebbed and flowed on the distant Connecticut shore. In the next two weeks, they made a mystifying shift. They still carried out their cycles in unison, and were regular as the tides, but their high-tide behavior didn't coincide with high tide in Connecticut, or for that matter California, or any other tidal charts known to science. It dawned on the researchers after some calculations that the oysters were responding to high tide in Chicago. Never mind that the gentle mollusks lived in glass boxes in the basement of a steel-and-cement building. Nor that Chicago has no ocean. In the circumstances, the oysters were doing their best.

14   When Buster is running around for all he's worth, I can only presume it's high tide in Tucson. With or without evidence, I'm romantic enough to believe it. This is the lesson of Buster, the poetry that camps outside the halls of science: Jump for joy, hallelujah. Even a desert has tides.

15   When I was twenty-two, I donned the shell of a tiny yellow Renault and drove with all I owned from Kentucky to Tucson. I was a typical young American, striking out. I had no earthly notion that I was bringing on myself a calamity of the magnitude of the one that befell poor Buster. I am the commonest kind of North American refugee: I believe I like it here, far-flung from my original home. I've come to love the desert that bristles and breathes and sleeps outside my windows. In the course of seventeen years I've embedded myself in a family here—neighbors, colleagues, friends I can't foresee living without, and a child who is native to this ground, with loves of her own. I'm here for good, it seems.

16   And yet I never cease to long in my bones for what I left behind. I open my eyes on every new day expecting that a creek will run through my backyard under broad-leafed maples, and that my mother will be whistling in the kitchen. Behind the howl of coyotes, I'm listening for meadowlarks, I sometimes ache to be rocked in the bosom of the blood relations and busybodies of my childhood. Particularly in my years as a mother without a mate, I have deeply missed the safety net of extended family.

17   In a city of half a million I still really look at every face, anticipating recognition, because I grew up in a town where every face meant something to me. I have trouble remembering to lock the doors. Wariness of strangers I learned the hard way. When I was new to the city, I let a man into my house one hot afternoon because he seemed in dire need of a drink of water; when I turned from the kitchen sink I found sharpened steel shoved against my belly. And so I know, I know. But I cultivate suspicion with as much difficulty as I force tomatoes to grow in the drought-stricken hardpan of my strange backyard. No creek runs here, but I'm still listening to secret tides, living as if I belonged to an earlier place: not Kentucky, necessarily, but a welcoming earth and a human family. A forest. A species.

In my life I've had frightening losses and unfathomable gifts: A knife in   18
my stomach. The death of an unborn child. Sunrise in a rain forest. A stupendous column of blue butterflies rising from a Greek monastery. A car that
spontaneously caught fire while I was driving it. The end of a marriage, followed by a year in which I could barely understand how to keep living. The
discovery, just weeks ago when I rose from my desk and walked into the
kitchen, of three strangers industriously relieving my house of its contents.

I persuaded the strangers to put down the things they were holding (what   19
a bizarre tableau of anti-Magi they made, these three unwise men, bearing a
camera, an electric guitar, and a Singer sewing machine), and to leave my
home, pronto. My daughter asked excitedly when she got home from school,
"Mom, did you say bad words?" (I told her this was the very occasion that bad
words exist for.) The police said, variously, that I was lucky, foolhardy, and "a
brave lady." But it's not good luck to be invaded, and neither foolish nor brave
to stand your ground. It's only the way life goes, and I did it, just as years ago
I fought off the knife; mourned the lost child; bore witness to the rain forest;
claimed the blue butterflies as Holy Spirit in my private pantheon; got out of
the burning car; survived the divorce by putting one foot in front of the other
and taking good care of my child. On most important occasions, I cannot
think how to respond, I simply do. What does it mean, anyway, to be an animal in human clothing? We carry around these big brains of ours like the
crown jewels, but mostly I find that millions of years of evolution have prepared me for one thing only: to follow internal rhythms. To walk upright, to
protect my loved ones, to cooperate with my family group—however broadly I
care to define it—to do whatever will help us thrive. Obviously, some habits
that saw us through the millennia are proving hazardous in a modern context:
for example, the yen to consume carbohydrates and fat whenever they cross
our path, or the proclivity for unchecked reproduction. But it's surely worth
forgiving ourselves these tendencies a little, in light of the fact that they are
what got us here. Like Buster, we are creatures of inexplicable cravings. Thinking isn't everything. The way I stock my refrigerator would amuse a levelheaded interplanetary observer, who would see I'm responding not to real necessity but to the dread of famine honed in the African savannah. I can laugh
at my Rhodesian Ridgeback as she furtively sniffs the houseplants for a place
to bury bones, and circles to beat down the grass before lying on my kitchen
floor. But she and I are exactly the same kind of hairpin.

We humans have to grant the presence of some past adaptations, even in   20
their unforgivable extremes, if only to admit they are permanent rocks in the
steam we're obliged to navigate. It's easy to speculate and hard to prove, ever,
that genes control our behaviors. Yet we are persistently, excruciatingly adept
at many things that seem no more useful to modern life than the tracking of
tides in a desert. At recognizing insider/outsider status, for example, starting

with white vs. black and grading straight into distinctions so fine as to baffle the bystander—Serb and Bosnian, Hutu and Tutsi, Crip and Blood. We hold that children learn discrimination from their parents, but they learn it fiercely and well, world without end. Recite it by rote like a multiplication table. Take it to heart, though it's neither helpful nor appropriate, anymore than it is to hire the taller of two men applying for a position as bank clerk, though statistically we're likely to do that too. Deference to the physical superlative, a preference for the scent of our own clan: a thousand anachronisms dance down the strands of our DNA from a hidebound tribal past, guiding us toward the glories of survival, and some vainglories as well. If we resent being bound by these ropes, the best hope is to seize them out like snakes, by the throat, look them in the eye and own up to their venom.

21   But we rarely do, silly egghead of a species that we are. We invent the most outlandish intellectual grounds to justify discrimination. We tap our toes to chaste love songs about the silvery moon without recognizing them as hymns to copulation. We can dress up our drives, put them in three-piece suits or ballet slippers, but still they drive us. The wonder of it is that our culture attaches almost unequivocal shame to our animal nature, believing brute urges must be hurtful, violent things. But it's no less an animal instinct that leads us to marry (species that benefit from monogamy tend to practice it); to organize a neighborhood cleanup campaign (rare and doomed is the creature that fouls its nest); to improvise and enforce morality (many primates socialize their young to be cooperative and ostracize adults who won't share food).

22   It's starting to look as if the most shameful tradition of Western civilization is our need to deny we are animals. In just a few centuries of setting ourselves apart as landlords of the Garden of Eden, exempt from the natural order and entitled to hold dominion, we have managed to behave like so-called animals anyway, and on top of it to wreck most of what took three billion years to assemble. Air, water, earth, and fire—so much of our own element so vastly contaminated, we endanger our own future. Apparently we never owned the place after all. Like every other animal, we're locked into our niche: the mercury in the ocean, the pesticides on the soybean fields, all comes home to our breastfed babies. In the silent spring we are learning it's easier to escape from a chain gang than a food chain. Possibly we will have the sense to begin a new century by renewing our membership in the Animal Kingdom.

23   Not long ago I went backpacking in the Eagle Tail Mountains. This range is a trackless wilderness in western Arizona that most people would call God-forsaken, taking for granted God's preference for loamy topsoil and regular precipitation. Whoever created the Eagle Tails had dry heat on the agenda, and a thing for volcanic rock. Also cactus, twisted mesquites, and five-alarm sunsets. The hiker's program in a desert like this is dire and blunt: carry in enough water to keep you alive till you can find a water source: then fill your

bottles and head for the next one, or straight back out. Experts warn adventurers in this region, without irony, to drink their water while they're still alive, as it won't help later.

Several canyons looked promising for springs on our topographical map, but turned up dry. Finally, at the top of a narrow, overgrown gorge we found a blessed tinaja, a deep, shaded hollow in the rock about the size of four or five claw-foot tubs, holding water. After we drank our fill, my friends struck out again, but I opted to stay and spend the day in the hospitable place that had slaked our thirst. On either side of the natural water tank, two shallow caves in the canyon wall faced each other, only a few dozen steps apart. By crossing from one to the other at noon, a person could spend the whole day here in shady comfort—or in colder weather, follow the winter sun. Anticipating a morning of reading, I pulled *Angle of Repose* out of my pack and looked for a place to settle on the flat, dusty floor of the west-facing shelter. Instead, my eyes were startled by a smooth corn-grinding stone. It sat in the exact center of its rock bowl, as if the Hohokam woman or man who used this mortar and pestle had walked off and left them there an hour ago. The Hohokam disappeared from the earth in A.D. 1450. It was inconceivable to me that no one had been here since then, but that may have been the case—that is the point of trackless wilderness. I picked up the grinding stone. The size and weight and smooth, balanced perfection of it in my hand filled me at once with a longing to possess it. In its time, this excellent stone was the most treasured thing in a life, a family, maybe the whole neighborhood. To whom it still belonged. I replaced it in the rock depression, which also felt smooth to my touch. Because my eyes now understood how to look at it, the ground under my feet came alive with worked flint chips and pottery shards. I walked across to the other cave and found its floor just as lively with historic debris. Hidden under brittlebush and catclaw I found another grinding stone, this one some distance from the depression in the cave floor that once answered its pressure daily, for the grinding of corn or mesquite beans.

For a whole day I marveled at this place, running my fingers over the knife edges of dark flint chips, trying to fit together thick red pieces of shattered clay jars, biting my lower lip like a child concentrating on a puzzle. I tried to guess the size of whole pots from the curve of the broken pieces: some seemed as small as my two cupped hands, and some maybe as big as a bucket. The sun scorched my neck, reminding me to follow the shade across to the other shelter. Bees hummed at the edge of the water hole, nosing up to the water, their abdomens pulsing like tiny hydraulic pumps; by late afternoon they rimmed the pool completely, a collar of busy lace. Off and on, the lazy hand of a hot breeze shuffled the white leaves of the brittlebush. Once I looked up to see a screaming pair of red-tailed hawks mating in midair, and once a clatter of hooves warned me to hold still. A bighorn ram emerged through the brush, his head bent low under his hefty cornice, and ambled by me with nothing on his mind so much as a cool drink.

26   How long can a pestle stone lie still in the center of its mortar? That long ago—that recently—people lived here. *Here,* exactly, and not one valley over, or two, or twelve, because this place had all a person needs: shelter, food, and permanent water. They organized their lives around a catchment basin in a granite boulder, conforming their desires to the earth's charities; they never expected the opposite. The stories I grew up with lauded Moses for striking the rock and bringing forth the bubbling stream. But the stories of the Hohokam—oh, how they must have praised that good rock.

27   At dusk my friends returned with wonderful tales of the ground they had covered. We camped for the night, refilled our canteens, and hiked back to the land of plumbing and a fair guarantee of longevity. But I treasure my memory of the day I lingered near water and covered no ground. I can't think of a day in my life in which I've had such a clear fix on what it means to be human.

28   *Want is* a thing that unfurls unbidden like fungus, opening large upon itself, stopless, filling the sky. But *needs,* from one day to the next, are few enough to fit in a bucket, with room enough left to rattle like brittlebush in a dry wind.

29   For each of us—furred, feathered, or skinned alive—the whole earth balances on the single precarious point of our own survival. In the best of times, I hold in mind the need to care for things beyond the self: poetry, humanity, grace. In other times, when it seems difficult merely to survive and be happy about it, the condition of my thought tastes as simple as this: let me be a good animal today. I've spent months at a stretch, even years, with that taste in my mouth, and have found that it serves.

30   But it seems a wide gulf to cross, from the raw, green passion for survival to the dispassionate, considered state of human grace. How does the animal mind construct a poetry for the modern artifice in which we now reside? Often I feel as disoriented as poor Buster, unprepared for the life that zooms headlong past my line of sight. This clutter of human paraphernalia and counterfeit necessities—what does it have to do with the genuine business of life on earth? It feels strange to me to be living in a box, hiding from the steadying influence of the moon; wearing the hide of a cow, which is supposed to be dyed to match God-knows-what, on my feet; making promises over the telephone about things I will do at a precise hour next *year.* (I always feel the urge to add, as my grandmother does, "Lord willing and the creeks don't rise!") I find it impossible to think, with a straight face, about what colors ought not to be worn after Labor Day. I can become hysterical over the fact that someone, somewhere, invented a thing called the mushroom scrubber, and that many other people undoubtedly feel they *need* to possess one. It's completely usual for me to get up in the morning, take a look around, and laugh out loud.

Strangest of all, I am carrying on with all of this in a desert, two thousand   31
miles from my verdant childhood home. I am disembodied. No one here remembers how I was before I grew to my present height. I'm called upon to
reinvent my own childhood time and again; in the process, I wonder how I
can ever know the truth about who I am. If someone had told me what I was
headed for in that little Renault—that I was stowing away in a shell, bound to
wake up to an alien life on a persistently foreign shore—I surely would not have
done it. But no one warned me. My culture, as I understand it, values independence above all things—in part to ensure a mobile labor force, grease for
the machine of a capitalist economy. Our fairy table commands: Little Pig, go
out and seek your fortune! So I did.

Many years ago I read that the Tohono O'odham, who dwell in the deserts   32
near here, traditionally bury the umbilicus of a newborn son or daughter
somewhere close to home and plant a tree over it, to hold the child in place.
In a sentimental frame of mind, I did the same when my own baby's cord fell
off. I'm staring at the tree right now, as I write—a lovely thing grown huge outside my window, home to woodpeckers, its boughs overarching the house, as
dissimilar from the sapling I planted seven years ago as my present life is from
the tidy future I'd mapped out for us all when my baby was born. She will
roam light-years from the base of that tree. I have no doubt of it. I can only
hope she's growing as the tree is, absorbing strength and rhythms and a trust
in the seasons, so she will always be able to listen for home.

I feel remorse about Buster's monumental relocation; it's a weighty re-   33
sponsibility to have thrown someone else's life into permanent chaos. But as for
my own, I can't be sorry I made the trip. Most of what I learned in the old place
seems to suffice for the new: if the seasons like Chicago tides come at ridiculous
times and I have to plant in September instead of May, and if I have to make up
family from scratch, what matters is that I do have sisters and tomato plants, the
essential things. Like Buster, I'm inclined to see the material backdrop of my life
as mostly immaterial, compared with what moves inside of me. I hold on to my
adopted shore, chanting private vows: wherever I am, let me never forget to distinguish *want* from *need*. Let me be a good animal today. Let me dance in the
waves of my private tide, the habits of survival and love.

Every one of us is called upon, probably many times, to start a new life. A   34
frightening diagnosis, a marriage, a move, loss of a job or a limb or a loved
one, a graduation, bringing a new baby home: it's impossible to think at first
how this all will be possible. Eventually, what moves it all forward is the sub-
terranean ebb and flow of being alive among the living.

In my own worst seasons I've come back from the colorless world of de-   35
spair by forcing myself to look hard, for a long time, at a single glorious thing:
a flame of red geranium outside my bedroom window. And then another: my
daughter in a yellow dress. And another: the perfect outline of a full, dark

sphere behind the crescent moon. Until I learned to be in love with my life again. Like a stroke victim retraining new parts of the brain to grasp lost skills, I have taught myself joy, over and over again.

36   It's not such a wide gulf to cross, then, from survival to poetry. We hold fast to the old passions of endurance that buckle and creak beneath us, dovetailed, tight as a good wooden boat to carry us onward. And onward full tilt we go, pitched and wrecked and absurdly resolute, driven in spite of everything to make good on a new shore. To be hopeful, to embrace one possibility after another—that is surely the basic instinct. Baser even than hate, the thing with teeth, which can be stilled with a tone of voice or stunned by beauty. If the whole world of the living has to turn on the single point of remaining alive, that pointed endurance is the poetry of hope. The thing with feathers.

37   What a stroke of luck. What a singular brute feat of outrageous fortune: to be born to citizenship in the Animal Kingdom. We love and we lose, go back to the start and do it right over again. For every heavy forebrain solemnly cataloging the facts of a harsh landscape, there's a rush of intuition behind it crying out: High tide! Time to move out into the glorious debris. Time to take this life for what it is.

John Muir

A Wind-Storm in the Forests

John Muir (1838–1914) has had so many mountains, trails, creeks, and lakes named for him that the U.S. Geological Survey has said it would refuse to approve naming any more landmarks after Muir, to avoid confusion on maps. In his zeal to see the great natural sites of North America, he has been burned by sulfur vents on Mt. Shasta (to avoid being frozen in a blizzard), lived on a crust of bread while hiking through the Alaskan wilderness (so as to see more, while traveling lightly), and survived bouts of malaria and typhoid fever in the swamps of Florida. A founder of the Sierra Club, which has been credited with preserving much of California's wilderness, Muir later in life began to write about some of the spectacular wild lands he so loved—the better for the rest of us to appreciate it. Though we may never experience a severe windstorm in an expansive forest, Muir can relate that experience from his own unconventional viewpoint, painting a picture so vivid that we almost feel like we *are* there, experiencing the storm with Muir.

1   THE MOUNTAIN WINDS, LIKE THE DEW AND RAIN, sunshine and snow, are measured and bestowed with love on the forests to develop their strength and beauty. However restricted the scope of other forest influences, that of the

winds is universal. The snow bends and trims the upper forests every winter, the lightning strikes a single tree here and there, while avalanches mow down thousands at a swoop as a gardener trims out a bed of flowers. But the winds go to every tree, fingering every leaf and branch and furrowed bole; not one is forgotten; the Mountain Pine towering with outstretched arms on the rugged buttresses of the icy peaks, the lowliest and most retiring tenant of the dells; they seek and find them all, caressing them tenderly, bending them in lusty exercise, stimulating their growth, plucking off a leaf or limb as required, or removing an entire tree or grove, now whispering and cooing through the branches like a sleepy child, now roaring like the ocean; the winds blessing the forests, the forests the winds, with ineffable beauty and harmony as the sure result.

After one has seen pines six feet in diameter bending like grasses before 2 a mountain gale, and ever and anon some giant falling with a crash that shakes the hills, it seems astonishing that any, save the lowest thickset trees, could ever have found a period sufficiently stormless to establish themselves; or, once established, that they should not, sooner or later, have been blown down. But when the storm is over, and we behold the same forests tranquil again, towering fresh and unscathed in erect majesty, and consider what centuries of storms have fallen upon them since they were first planted,—hail, to break the tender seedlings; lightning, to scorch and shatter; snow, winds, and avalanches, to crush and overwhelm,—while the manifest result of all this wild storm-culture is the glorious perfection we behold; then faith in Nature's forestry is established, and we cease to deplore the violence of her most destructive gales, or of any other storm-implement whatsoever.

There are two trees in the Sierra forests that are never blown down, so 3 long as they continue in sound health. These are the Juniper and the Dwarf Pine of the summit peaks. Their stiff, crooked roots grip the storm-beaten ledges like eagles' claws, while their lithe, cord-like branches bend round compliantly, offering but slight holds for winds, however violent. The other alpine conifers—the Needle Pine, Mountain Pine, Two-leaved Pine, and Hemlock Spruce—are never thinned out by this agent to any destructive extent, on account of their admirable toughness and the closeness of their growth. In general the same is true of the giants of the lower zones. The kingly Sugar Pine, towering aloft to a height of more than 200 feet, offers a fine mark to storm-winds; but it is not densely foliaged, and its long, horizontal arms swing round compliantly in the blast, like tresses of green, fluent algae in a brook; while the Silver Firs in most places keep their ranks well together in united strength. The Yellow or Silver Pine is more frequently overturned than any other tree on the Sierra, because its leaves and branches form a larger mass in proportion to its height, while in many places it is planted sparsely, leaving open lanes through which storms may enter with full force. Furthermore, because it is distributed along the lower portion of the range, which was the first to be left bare on the breaking up of the ice-sheet at the close of the glacial winter, the soil it is growing upon has been longer exposed to post-glacial weathering, and consequently is in a more crumbling, decayed condition than the fresher soils farther up the range, and therefore offers a less secure anchorage for the roots.

4   While exploring the forest zones of Mount Shasta, I discovered the path of a hurricane strewn with thousands of pines of this species. Great and small had been uprooted or wrenched off by sheer force, making a clean gap, like that made by a snow avalanche. But hurricanes capable of doing this class of work are rare in the Sierra, and when we have explored the forests from one extremity of the range to the other, we are compelled to believe that they are the most beautiful on the face of the earth, however we may regard the agents that have made them so.

5   There is always something deeply exciting, not only in the sounds of winds in the woods, which exert more or less influence over every mind, but in their varied waterlike flow as manifested by the movements of the trees, especially those of the conifers. By no other trees are they rendered so extensively and impressively visible, not even by the lordly tropic palms or tree-ferns responsive to the gentlest breeze. The waving of a forest of the giant Sequoias is indescribably impressive and sublime, but the pines seem to me the best interpreters of winds. They are mighty waving goldenrods, ever in tune, singing and writing wind-music all their long century lives. Little, however, of this noble tree-waving and tree-music will you see or hear in the strictly alpine portion of the forests. The burly Juniper, whose girth sometimes more than equals its height, is about as rigid as the rocks on which it grows. The slender lash-like sprays of the Dwarf Pine stream out in wavering ripples, but the tallest and slenderest are far too unyielding to wave even in the heaviest gales. They only shake in quick, short vibrations. The Hemlock Spruce, however, and the Mountain Pine, and some of the tallest thickets of the Two-leaved species bow in storms with considerable scope and gracefulness. But it is only in the lower and middle zones that the meeting of winds and woods is to be seen in all its grandeur.

6   One of the most beautiful and exhilarating storms I ever enjoyed in the Sierra occurred in December, 1874, when I happened to be exploring one of the tributary valleys of the Yuba River. The sky and the ground and the trees had been thoroughly rain-washed and were dry again. The day was intensely pure, one of those incomparable bits of California winter, warm and balmy and full of white sparkling sunshine, redolent of all the purest influences of the spring, and at the same time enlivened with one of the most bracing wind-storms conceivable. Instead of camping out, as I usually do, I then chanced to be stopping

at the house of a friend. But when the storm began to sound, I lost no time in pushing out into the woods to enjoy it. For on such occasions Nature has always something rare to show us, and the danger to life and limb is hardly greater than one would experience crouching deprecatingly beneath a roof.

It was still early morning when I found myself fairly adrift. Delicious sunshine came pouring over the hills, lighting the tops of the pines, and setting free a steam of summery fragrance that contrasted strangely with the wild tones of the storm. The air was mottled with pine-tassels and bright green plumes, that went flashing past in the sunlight like birds pursued. But there was not the slightest dustiness, nothing less pure than leaves, and ripe pollen, and flecks of withered bracken and moss. I heard trees falling for hours at the rate of one every two or three minutes; some uprooted, partly on account of the loose, water-soaked condition of the ground; others broken straight across, where some weakness caused by fire had determined the spot. The gestures of the various trees made a delightful study. Young Sugar Pines, light and feathery as squirrel-tails, were bowing almost to the ground; while the grand old patriarchs, whose massive boles had been tried in a hundred storms, waved solemnly above them, their long, arching branches streaming fluently on the gale, and every needle thrilling and ringing and shedding off keen lances of light like a diamond. The Douglas Spruces, with long sprays drawn out in level tresses, and needles massed in a gray, shimmering glow, presented a most striking appearance as they stood in bold relief along the hilltops. The madroños in the dells, with their red bark and large glossy leaves tilted every way, reflected the sunshine in throbbing spangles like those one so often sees on the rippled surface of a glacier lake. But the Silver Pines were now the most impressively beautiful of all. Colossal spires 200 feet in height waved like supple goldenrods chanting and bowing low as if in worship, while the whole mass of their long, tremulous foliage was kindled into one continuous blaze of white sun-fire. The force of the gale was such that the most steadfast monarch of them all rocked down to its roots with a motion plainly perceptible when one leaned against it. Nature was holding high festival, and every fiber of the most rigid giants thrilled with glad excitement.

I drifted on through the midst of this passionate music and motion, across many a glen, from ridge to ridge; often halting in the lee of a rock for shelter, or to gaze and listen. Even when the grand anthem had swelled to its highest pitch, I could distinctly hear the varying tones of individual trees;—Spruce, and Fir, and Pine, and leafless Oak,—and even the infinitely gentle rustle of the withered grasses at my feet. Each was expressing itself in its own way,— singing its own song, and making its own peculiar gestures,—manifesting a richness of variety to be found in no other forest I have yet seen. The coniferous woods of Canada, and the Carolinas, and Florida, are made up of trees that resemble one another about as nearly as blades of grass, and grow close together in much the same way. Coniferous trees, in general, seldom possess individual character, such as is manifest among Oaks and Elms. But the California forests are made up of a greater number of distinct species than any other in the world. And in them we find, not only a marked differentiation into special groups, but also a marked individuality in almost every tree, giving rise to storm effects indescribably glorious.

9   Toward midday, after a long, tingling scramble through copses of hazel and ceanothus, I gained the summit of the highest ridge in the neighborhood; and then it occurred to me that it would be a fine thing to climb one of the trees to obtain a wider outlook and get my ear close to the Æolian music of its topmost needles. But under the circumstances the choice of a tree was a serious matter. One whose instep was not very strong seemed in danger of being blown down, or of being struck by others in case they should fall; another was branchless to a considerable height above the ground, and at the same time too large to be grasped with arms and legs in climbing; while others were not favorably situated for clear views. After cautiously casting about, I made choice of the tallest of a group of Douglas Spruces that were growing close together like a tuft of grass, no one of which seemed likely to fall unless all the rest fell with it. Though comparatively young, they were about 100 feet high, and their lithe, brushy tops were rocking and swirling in wild ecstasy. Being accustomed to climb trees in making botanical studies, I experienced no difficulty in reaching the top of this one, and never before did I enjoy so noble an exhilaration of motion. The slender tops fairly flapped and swished in the passionate torrent, bending and swirling backward and forward, round and round, tracing indescribable combinations of vertical and horizontal curves, while I clung with muscles firm braced, like a bobolink on a reed.

10   In its widest sweeps my tree-top described an arc of from twenty to thirty degrees, but I felt sure of its elastic temper, having seen others of the same species still more severely tried—bent almost to the ground indeed, in heavy snows—without breaking a fiber. I was therefore safe, and free to take the wind into my pulses and enjoy the excited forest from my superb outlook. The view from here must be extremely beautiful in any weather. Now my eye roved over the piny hills and dales as over fields of waving grain, and felt the light running in ripples and broad swelling undulations across the valleys from ridge to ridge, as the shining foliage was stirred by corresponding waves of air. Oftentimes these waves of reflected light would break up suddenly into a kind of beaten foam, and again, after chasing one another in regular order, they would seem to bend forward in concentric curves, and disappear on some hillside, like sea-waves on a shelving shore. The quantity of light reflected from the bent needles was so great as to make whole groves appear as if covered with snow, while the black shadows beneath the trees greatly enhanced the effect of the silvery splendor.

Excepting only the shadows there was nothing somber in all this wild sea   11
of pines. On the contrary, notwithstanding this was the winter season, the colors were remarkably beautiful. The shafts of the pine and libocedrus were
brown and purple, and most of the foliage was well tinged with yellow; the laurel groves, with the pale undersides of their leaves turned upward, made
masses of gray; and then there was many a dash of chocolate color from
clumps of manzanita, and jet of vivid crimson from the bark of the madroños,
while the ground on the hillsides, appearing here and there through openings
between the groves, displayed masses of pale purple and brown.

The sounds of the storm corresponded gloriously with this wild exuber-   12
ance of light and motion. The profound bass of the naked branches and boles
booming like waterfalls; the quick, tense vibrations of the pine-needles, now
rising to a shrill, whistling hiss, now falling to a silky murmur; the rustling of
laurel groves in the dells, and the keen metallic click of leaf on leaf—all this
was heard in easy analysis when the attention was calmly bent.

The varied gestures of the multitude were seen to fine advantage, so that   13
one could recognize the different species at a distance of several miles by this
means alone, as well as by their forms and colors, and the way they reflected
the light. All seemed strong and comfortable, as if really enjoying the storm,
while responding to its most enthusiastic greetings. We hear much nowadays
concerning the universal struggle for existence, but no struggle in the common meaning of the word was manifest here; no recognition of danger by any
tree; no deprecation; but rather an invincible gladness as remote from exulta-
tion as from fear.

I kept my lofty perch for hours, frequently closing my eyes to enjoy the   14
music by itself, or to feast quietly on the delicious fragrance that was streaming
past. The fragrance of the woods was less marked than that produced during
warm rain, when so many balsamic buds and leaves are steeped like tea; but,
from the chafing of resiny branches against each other, and the incessant at-
trition of myriads of needles, the gale was spiced to a very tonic degree. And
besides the fragrance from these local sources there were traces of scents
brought from afar. For this wind came first from the sea, rubbing against its
fresh, briny waves, then distilled through the redwoods, threading rich ferny
gulches, and spreading itself in broad undulating currents over many a flower-
enameled ridge of the coast mountains, then across the golden plains, up the
purple foot-hills, and into these piny woods with the varied incense gathered
by the way.

Winds are advertisements of all they touch, however much or little we may   15
be able to read them; telling their wanderings even by their scents alone.
Mariners detect the flowery perfume of land-winds far at sea, and sea-winds
carry the fragrance of dulse and tangle far inland, where it is quickly recognized, though mingled with the scents of a thousand land-flowers. As an il-

lustration of this, I may tell here that I breathed sea-air on the Firth of Forth, in Scotland, while a boy; then was taken to Wisconsin, where I remained nineteen years; then, without in all this time having breathed one breath of the sea, I walked quietly, alone, from the middle of the Mississippi Valley to the Gulf of Mexico, on a botanical excursion, and while in Florida, far from the coast, my attention wholly bent on the splendid tropical vegetation about me, I suddenly recognized a sea-breeze, as it came sifting through the palmettos and blooming vine-tangles, which at once awakened and set free a thousand dormant associations, and made me a boy again in Scotland, as if all the intervening years had been annihilated.

16   Most people like to look at mountain rivers, and bear them in mind; but few care to look at the winds, though far more beautiful and sublime, and though they become at times about as visible as flowing water. When the north winds in winter are making upward sweeps over the curving summits of the High Sierra, the fact is sometimes published with flying snow-banners a mile long. Those portions of the winds thus embodied can scarce be wholly invisible, even to the darkest imagination. And when we look around over an agitated forest, we may see something of the wind that stirs it, by its effects upon the trees. Yonder it descends in a rush of water-like ripples, and sweeps over the bending pines from hill to hill. Nearer, we see detached plumes and leaves, now speeding by on level currents, now whirling in eddies, or, escaping over the edges of the whirls, soaring aloft on grand, upswelling domes of air, or tossing on flame-like crests. Smooth, deep currents, cascades, falls, and swirling eddies, sing around every tree and leaf, and over all the varied topography of the region with telling changes of form, like mountain rivers conforming to the features of their channels.

17   After tracing the Sierra streams from their fountains to the plains, marking where they bloom white in falls, glide in crystal plumes, surge gray and foam-filled in boulder-choked gorges, and slip through the woods in long, tranquil reaches—after thus learning their language and forms in detail, we may at length hear them chanting all together in one grand anthem, and comprehend them all in clear inner vision, covering the range like lace. But even this spectacle is far less sublime and not a whit more substantial than what we may behold of these storm-streams of air in the mountain woods.

18   We all travel the milky way together, trees and men; but it never occurred to me until this storm-day, while swinging in the wind, that trees are travelers, in the ordinary sense. They make many journeys, not extensive ones, it is true; but our own little journeys, away and back again, are only little more than tree-wavings—many of them not so much.

19   When the storm began to abate, I dismounted and sauntered down through the calming woods. The storm-tones died away, and, turning toward the east, I beheld the countless hosts of the forests hushed and tranquil, tow-

ering above one another on the slopes of the hills like a devout audience. The setting sun filled them with amber light, and seemed to say, while they listened, "My peace I give unto you."

As I gazed on the impressive scene, all the so-called ruin of the storm was   20
forgotten, and never before did these noble woods appear so fresh, so joyous, so immortal.

Olive Schreiner

Sex-Parasitism

South African novelist Olive Schreiner was the daughter of a missionary father and a stern and rigid Victorian mother who believed in the superiority of the British over native black Africans and the Boers. Schreiner's parents met any show of sympathy for those two groups with severe punishment. Rather than adopt the same views, Schreiner resolved to spend her life defending the weak against the strong. In 1889 she met and married a cattle rancher, Samuel Cronwright, another anti-imperialist who, at her request, took her name when they married. The first novel Schreiner published, *The Story of an African Farm,* was an immediate best-seller. Her 1911 work *Women and Labour* is the volume from which this selection is taken. In this work Schreiner outlines the history and fate of any nation in which prosperity, because of the subjugation of a slavery class, leads to its women becoming useless except as vessels in which to breed the next generation.

THERE NEVER HAS BEEN, AND AS FAR AS CAN BE SEEN, there never will be, a time   1
when the majority of the males in any society will be supported by the rest of the males in a condition of perfect mental and physical inactivity. "*Find labour or die,*" is the choice ultimately put before the human male today, as in the past; and *this* constitutes his labour problem.

The labour of the man may not always be useful in the highest sense to his   2
society, or it may even be distinctly harmful and antisocial, as in the case of the robber-barons of the Middle Ages, who lived by capturing and despoiling all who passed by their castles; or as in the case of the share speculators, stockjobbers, ring-and-corner capitalists, and monopolists of the present day, who feed upon the productive labours of society without contributing anything to its welfare. But even males so occupied are compelled to expend a vast amount of energy and even a low intelligence in their callings; and, however injurious to their societies, they run no personal risk of handing down effete and enervated constitutions to their race. Whether beneficially or unbeneficially, the human male must, generally speaking, employ his intellect, or his muscle, or die.

3   The position of the unemployed modern female is one wholly different. The choice before her, as her ancient fields of domestic labour slip from her, is not generally or often at the present day the choice between finding new fields of labour, or death; but one far more serious in its ultimate re-action on humanity as a whole—it is the choice between finding new forms of labour or sinking into a condition of more or less complete and passive *sex-parasitism!*

4   Again and again in the history of the past, when among human creatures a certain stage of material civilization has been reached, a curious tendency has manifested itself for the human female to become more or less parasitic; social conditions tend to rob her of all forms of active conscious social labour, and to reduce her, like the field-bug, to the passive exercise of her sex func-tions alone. And the result of this parasitism has invariably been the decay in vitality and intelligence of the female, followed after a longer or shorter period by that of her male descendants and her entire society.

5   Nevertheless, in the history of the past the dangers of the sex-parasitism have never threatened more than a small section of the females of the human race, those exclusively of some dominant race or class; the mass of women be-neath them being still compelled to assume many forms of strenuous activity. It is at the present day, and under the peculiar conditions of our modern civ-ilization, that for the first time sex-parasitism has become a danger, more or less remote, to the mass of civilized women, perhaps ultimately to all.

6   In the very early stages of human growth, the sexual parasitism and de-generation of the female formed no possible source of social danger. Where the conditions of life rendered it inevitable that all the labour of a commu-nity should be performed by the members of that community for themselves, without the assistance of slaves or machinery, the tendency has always been rather to throw an excessive amount of social labour on the female. Under no conditions, at no time, in no place, in the history of the world have the males of any period, of any nation, or of any class, shown the slightest inclination to allow their own females to become inactive or parasitic, so long as the actual muscular labour of feeding and clothing them would in that case have de-volved upon *themselves!*

7   The parasitism of the human female becomes a possibility only when a point in civilization is reached (such as that which was attained in the ancient civilizations of Greece, Rome, Persia, Assyria, India, and such as today exists in many of the civilizations of the East, such as those of China and Turkey), when, owing to the extensive employment of the labour of slaves, or of sub-ject races or classes, the dominant race or class has become so liberally sup-plied with the material goods of life that mere physical toil on the part of its own female members has become unnecessary.

8   It is when this point has been reached, and never before, that the symp-

toms of female parasitism have in the past almost invariably tended to manifest themselves, and have become a social danger. The males of the dominant class have almost always contrived to absorb to themselves the new intellectual occupations, which the absence of necessity for the old forms of physical toil made possible in their societies and the females of the dominant class or race, for whose muscular labours there was now also no longer any need, not succeeding grasping or attaining to these new forms of labour, have sunk into a state in which, performing no species of active social duty, they have existed through the passive performance of sexual functions alone, with how much or how little of discontent will now never be known, since no literary record has been made by the woman of the past, of her desires or sorrows. Then, in place of the active labouring woman, upholding society—by her toil, has come the effete wife, concubine or prostitute, clad in fine raiment, the work of others' fingers; fed on luxurious viands, the result of others' toil, waited on and tended by the labour of others. The need for her physical labour having gone, and mental industry not having taken its place, she bedecked and scented her person, or had it bedecked and scented for her, she lay upon her sofa, or drove or was carried out in her vehicle, and, loaded with jewels, she sought by dissipations and amusements to fill up the inordinate blank left by the lack of productive activity. And the hand whitened and frame softened, till, at last, the very duties of motherhood, which were all the constitution of her life left her, became distasteful, and, from the instant when her infant came damp from her womb, it passed into the hands of others, to be tended and reared by them; and from youth to age her offspring often owed nothing to her personal toil. In many cases so complete was her enervation, that at last the very joy of giving life, the glory and beatitude of a virile womanhood, became distasteful; and she sought to evade it, not because of its interference with more imperious duties to those already born of her, or to her society, but because her existence of inactivity had robbed her of all joy in strenuous exertion and endurance in any form. Finely clad, tenderly housed, life became for her merely the gratification of her own physical and sexual appetites, and the appetites of the male, through the stimulation of which she could maintain herself. And, whether as kept wife, kept mistress, or prostitute, she contributed nothing to the active and sustaining labours of her society. She had attained to the full development of that type which, whether in modern Paris or New York or London, or in ancient Greece, Assyria, or Rome, is essentially one in its features, its nature, and its results. She was the "fine lady," the human female parasite—the most deadly microbe which can make its appearance on the surface of any social organism.

Wherever in the history of the past this type has reached its full development and has comprised the bulk of the females belonging to any dominant class or race, it has heralded its decay. In Assyria, Greece, Rome, Persia, as in Turkey today, the same material conditions have produced the same social disease among wealthy and dominant races and again and again when the nation so affected has come into contact with nations more healthily constituted, the diseased condition has contributed to its destruction.

Henry David Thoreau

An Immoral Law

Henry David Thoreau (1817–1862) was known in his time as an odd sort of educated vagrant, rarely employed, who mostly kept to himself. He wrote voraciously in his journals at the suggestion of his most notable friend, Ralph Waldo Emerson. Occasionally, to earn extra money, he lectured about life in the backwoods, peppering his rather dry talks with folksy anecdotes. The one exception was when he spoke or wrote about slavery, when his laconic wit became an intense fire of emotion. In his most significant book, *Walden*, he expresses his seemingly contradictory individualist philosophy of civil responsibility. The following selection, from his journal entry of June 16, 1854, is an application of the principles expressed in *Walden* to an event which deeply affected Thoreau's community—the enforcement of the Fugitive Slave Act by the forcible returning of a black man (possibly not even an escaped slave) to the South. The Fugitive Slave Act was never again enforced in Massachusetts.

1   THE EFFECT OF A GOOD GOVERNMENT IS TO MAKE LIFE MORE VALUABLE,—of a bad government, to make it less valuable. We can afford that railroad and all merely material stock should depreciate, for that only compels us to live more simply and economically; but suppose the value of life itself should be depreciated. Every man in New England capable of the sentiment of patriotism must have lived the last three weeks with the sense of having suffered a vast, indefinite loss. I had never respected this government, but I had foolishly thought that I might manage to live here, attending to my private affairs, and forget it. For my part, my old and worthiest pursuits have lost I cannot say how much of their attraction, and I feel that my investment in life here is worth many per cent, less since Massachusetts last deliberately and forcibly restored an innocent man, Anthony Burns, to slavery. I dwelt before in the illusion that my life passed somewhere only between heaven and hell, but now I cannot persuade myself that I do not dwell wholly within hell. The sight of that political organization called Massachusetts is to me morally covered with scoriae and volcanic cinders, such as Milton imagined. If there is any hell more unprincipled than our

rulers and our people, I feel curious to visit it. Life itself being worthless, all things with it, that feed it, are worthless. Suppose you have a small library, with pictures to adorn the walls,—a garden laid out around—and contemplate scientific and literary pursuits, etc., etc., and discover suddenly that your villa, with all its contents, is located in hell, and that the justice of the peace is one of the devil's angels, has a cloven foot and forked tail,—do not these things suddenly lose their value in your eyes? Are you not disposed to sell at a great sacrifice?

I feel that, to some extent, the State has fatally interfered with my just and   2 proper business. It has not merely interrupted me in my passage through Court Street on errands of trade, but it has, to some extent, interrupted me and every man on his onward and upward path, on which he had trusted soon to leave Court Street far behind. I have found that hollow which I had relied on for solid.

I am surprised to see men going about their business as if nothing had   3 happened, and say to myself, "Unfortunates! they have not heard the news"; that the man whom I just met on horseback should be so earnest to overtake his newly bought cows running away,—since all property is insecure, and if they do not run away again, they may be taken away from him when he gets them. Fool! does he not know that his seed-corn is worth less this year,—that all beneficent harvests fail as he approaches the empire of hell? No prudent man will build a stone house under these circumstances, or engage in any peaceful enterprise which it requires a long time to accomplish. Art is as long as ever, but life is more interrupted and less available for a man's proper pursuits. It is time we had done referring to our ancestors. We have used up all our inherited freedom, like the young bird the albumen in the egg. It is not an era of repose. If we would save our lives, we must fight for them.

The discovery is what matter of men your countrymen are. They steadily   4 worship mammon—and on the seventh day curse God with a tintamarre from one end of the *Union* to the other. I heard the other day of a meek and sleek devil of a Bishop Somebody, who commended the law and order with which Burns was given up. I would like before I sit down to a table to inquire if there is one in the company who styles himself or is styled Bishop, and he or I should go out of it. I would have such a man wear his bishop's hat and his clerical bib and tucker, that we may know him.

Why will men be such fools as [to] trust to lawyers for a *moral* reform? I do   5 not believe that there is a judge in this country prepared to decide by the principle that a law is immoral and therefore of no force. They put themselves, or rather are by character, exactly on a level with the marine who discharges his musket in any direction in which he is ordered. They are just as much tools, and as little men.

Student Essay

Maurice Johnson

Modern-Day Mobsters

For this essay, Maurice was assigned to use analogy to compare something old with something new. The result, a lighthearted look at today's banking practices, is very effective.

1   IN THE MEAN STREETS OF THE GREAT OLD CITIES like Chicago and New York, gangsters once ruled. Instead of acting like petty thieves or burglars, the gangsters formed syndicates which devised more and more complex schemes to extract ever greater sums of money from their victims. The simplest of these schemes was the "protection racket." Gangsters forced individuals and businesses in their territories to make weekly or monthly payments in exchange for "protection" against crime from rival gangs—or more commonly, from the gangsters themselves. Another common scheme was to lend money for gambling—at extraordinary interest rates. If you didn't pay up, the gang's henchmen would burglarize your home or break your bones. Using schemes like the protection racket, gangsters became wealthy, but at the expense of ordinary working people.

2   Today gangs still exist, but they behave much differently from the gangsters of old—they devote most of their attention to more serious criminal activities like prostitution and trafficking drugs. The modern institution that behaves most like the organized crime syndicates of the early twentieth century is your friendly, neighborhood bank.

3   Surprised? Look at the evidence. What modern institution is more like a protection racket than an Automated Teller Machine? In exchange for "protecting" your money by keeping it safe in the bank, the ATM charges extravagant fees—up to $4.50—every time you need $20 to go to the movies. If you dare let your bank balance fall below $3,000, the fees get higher, and you're charged an extra $20 a month! Just like Al Capone and his buddies, the bank makes money from you because you're frightened to carry around too much cash.

4   Credit cards, too, aren't much different from good old-fashioned loan sharks. Banks make the cards seem like easy money, just like gangsters used to do. They send them free in the mail, burying in fine print all the details about the 21 percent interest rates, the $15 late fees, and the $50 annual fee. And just like gangsters, if you don't pay, the banks will send their thugs to repos-

sess your furniture, your car, and even your home. Short of breaking your legs, the new loan sharks act just like the old ones.

Banks are now even getting into the gambling racket. It's almost impossible these days to open a simple bank account—the banker won't let you leave the building until you've set up a brokerage account so you can buy into the latest stock market fad. Don't have the money to invest? How about handing over your pension plan? You can even borrow money to invest. If the stock market crashes, it's no different from losing at the racetrack—just don't expect any sympathy from your banker. 5

Today's banks do everything yesterday's gangster did, but cloaked under the authority of "FDIC" and "FNMA." Just like the gangsters, the bankers are getting rich at your expense. The only real difference is in the old days the gangsters came to you. Now you have to wait in line to get robbed. 6

9

Definition

Definition

1. **Use the type of definition that suits your purpose.** There are two types of definitions: concise "dictionary" or sentence definitions, and essay or extended definitions. Any essay may require a sentence definition if you introduce a specialized or technical term with which your readers may not be familiar. In those cases, simply define the word in a sentence or two and move on. This chapter mostly concerns itself with extended definitions, which not only provide a concise definition of a term or concept, but also build a fuller explanation of its object, using any of the other strategies in this book—example, description, analogy, and so on. When writing an extended definition, you may begin with dictionary definition, as D. H. Lawrence does in "Pornography," but the remainder of the essay should add something to, or even, as Lawrence does, completely contradict the standard definition.

2. **Select a writing strategy to develop your definition.** Depending on your purpose, any writing strategy can be effective in developing an extended definition. William Raspberry makes a powerful point about the word "black" by using examples. Margaret Atwood explains the term "pornography" largely by using narration. Because it can employ any writing strategy, definition is less of a strategy in itself than it is a goal. When writing an extended definition, you can use any strategy or combination of strategies to help you achieve your goal.

3. **Make your definition clear and unique.** Both dictionary and extended definitions must be clear enough for readers to understand, and precise enough to make a term or concept clearly different from all others. Defining "dog" as "an animal" is not unique because many other animals exist.

4. **Make sure your definition essay makes a point.** Like any other essay, definition essays should make a point. Usually this means you need a thesis sentence and a conclusion. For example, Marie Winn's point is that TV is as addictive as drugs or cigarettes, and Jason Gray suggests that intelligence is a complicated concept that can't be measured by a single number. Don't settle for the obvious definition of a term—that, after all, is what dictionaries are for.

D. H. Lawrence

Pornography

D. H. Lawrence (1885–1930) was a controversial figure in English literature because of the vivid descriptions of sex in his novels. His most famous work, *Lady Chatterley's Lover,* was banned in both England and the United States when it was published in 1928. In fact, the version published in 1928 was actually toned down by Lawrence in an attempt to elude censorship. After a widely publicized trial in 1960, the work was finally allowed to be published in unexpurgated form. Though the passages in question are actually quite tame by today's standards, some have even credited the re-release of *Lady Chatterley's Lover* in 1961 with causing the "free-love" movement of the 1960s. Here Lawrence defends his work by constructing a definition of pornography which carefully excludes his novels.

WHAT IS PORNOGRAPHY TO ONE MAN is the laughter of genius to another. The 1 word itself, we are told, means "pertaining to harlots"—the graph of the harlot. But nowadays, what is a harlot? If she was a woman who took money from a man in return for going to bed with him—really, most wives sold themselves, in the past, and plenty of harlots gave themselves, when they felt like it, for nothing. If a woman hasn't got a tiny streak of harlot in her, she's a dry stick as a rule. And probably most harlots had somewhere a streak of womanly generosity. Why be so cut and dried? The law is a dreary thing, and its judgments have nothing to do with life. . . .

One essay on pornography, I remember, comes to the conclusion that 2 pornography in art is that which is calculated to arouse sexual desire, or sexual excitement. And stress is laid on the fact, whether the author or artist *intended* to arouse sexual feelings. It is the old vexed question of intention, become so dull today, when we know how strong and influential our unconscious intentions are. And why a man should be held guilty of his conscious intentions, and innocent of his unconscious intentions, I don't know, since every man is more made up of unconscious intentions than of conscious ones. I am what I am, not merely what I think I am.

However! We take it, I assume, that *pornography* is something base, some- 3 thing unpleasant. In short, we don't like it. And why don't we like it? Because it arouses sexual feelings?

I think not. No matter how hard we may pretend otherwise, most of us 4 rather like a moderate rousing of our sex. It warms us, stimulates us like sunshine on a grey day. After a century or two of Puritanism, this is still true of most people. Only the mob-habit of condemning any form of sex is too strong to let us admit it naturally. And there are, of course, many people who are genuinely repelled by the simplest and most natural stirrings of sexual feeling. But these people are perverts who have fallen into hatred of their fellow men; thwarted, disappointed, unfulfilled people, of whom, alas, our civilisation contains so many. And they nearly always enjoy some unsimple and unnatural form of sex excitement, secretly.

5   Even quite advanced art critics would try to make us believe that any picture or book which had "sex appeal" was *ipso facto* a bad book or picture. This is just canting hypocrisy. Half the great poems, pictures, music, stories, of the whole world are great by virtue of the beauty of their sex appeal. Titian or Renoir, the Song of Solomon or *Jane Eyre*, Mozart or "Annie Laurie," the loveliness is all interwoven with sex appeal, sex stimulus, call it what you will. Even Michelangelo, who rather hated sex, can't help filling the Cornucopia with phallic acorns. Sex is a very powerful, beneficial and necessary stimulus in human life, and we are all grateful when we feel its warm, natural flow through us, like a form of sunshine. . . .

6   Then what is pornography, after all this? It isn't sex appeal or sex stimulus in art. It isn't even a deliberate intention on the part of the artist to arouse or excite sexual feelings. There's nothing wrong with sexual feelings in themselves, so long as they are straightforward and not sneaking or sly. The right sort of sex stimulus is invaluable to human daily life. Without it the world grows grey. I would give everybody the gay Renaissance stories to read; they would help to shake off a lot of grey self-importance, which is our modern civilised disease.

7   But even I would censor genuine pornography, rigorously. It would not be very difficult. In the first place, genuine pornography is almost always underworld, it doesn't come into the open. In the second, you can recognise it by the insult it offers, invariably, to sex and to the human spirit.

8   Pornography is the attempt to insult sex, to do dirt on it. This is unpardonable. Take the very lowest instance, the picture postcard sold underhand, by the underworld, in most cities. What I have seen of them have been of an ugliness to make you cry. The insult to the human body, the insult to a vital human relationship! Ugly and cheap they make the human nudity, ugly and degraded they make the sexual act, trivial and cheap and nasty.

9   It is the same with the books they sell in the underworld. They are either so ugly they make you ill, or so fatuous you can't imagine anybody but a cretin or a moron reading them, or writing them.

10   It is the same with the dirty limericks that people tell after dinner, or the dirty stories one hears commercial travellers telling each other in a smoke-room. Occasionally there is a really funny one, that redeems a great deal. But usually they are just ugly and repellent, and the so-called "humour" is just a trick of doing dirt on sex.

11   Now the human nudity of a great many modern people is just ugly and de-

graded, and the sexual act between modern people is just the same, merely ugly and degrading. But this is nothing to be proud of. It is the catastrophe of our civilisation. I am sure no other civilisation, not even the Roman, has showed such a vast proportion of ignominious and degraded nudity, and ugly, squalid dirty sex. Because no other civilisation has given sex into the underworld, and nudity to the w.c.

The intelligent young, thank heaven, seem determined to alter in these two respects. They are rescuing their young nudity from the stuffy, pornographical hole-and-corner underworld of their elders, and they refuse to sneak about the sexual relation. This is a change the elderly grey ones of course deplore, but it is in fact a very great change for the better, and a real revolution.   12

But it is amazing how strong is the will in ordinary, vulgar people, to do dirt on sex. It was one of my fond illusions, when I was young, that the ordinary healthy-seeming sort of men in railway carriages, or the smoke-room of an hotel or a pullman, were healthy in their feelings and had a wholesome, rough devil-may-care attitude towards sex. All wrong! All wrong! Experience teaches that common individuals of this sort have a disgusting attitude towards sex, a disgusting contempt of it, a disgusting desire to insult it. If such fellows have intercourse with a woman, they triumphantly feel that they have done her dirt, and now she is lower, cheaper, more contemptible than she was before.   13

It is individuals of this sort that tell dirty stories, carry indecent picture postcards, and know the indecent books. This is the great pornographical class—the really common men-in-the-street and women-in-the-street. They have as great a hate and contempt of sex as the greyest Puritan, and when an appeal is made to them, they are always on the side of the angels. They insist that a film heroine shall be a neuter, a sexless thing of washed-out purity. They insist that real sex-feeling shall only be shown by the villain or villainess, low lust. They find a Titian or a Renoir really indecent, and they don't want their wives and daughters to see it.   14

Why? Because they have the grey disease of sex-hatred, coupled with the yellow disease of dirt-lust. The sex functions and the excrementory functions in the human body work so close together, yet they are, so to speak, utterly different in direction. Sex is a creative flow, the excrementory flow is towards dissolution, decreation, if we may use such a word. In the really healthy human being the distinction between the two is instant, our profoundest instincts are perhaps our instincts of opposition between the two flows. But in the degraded human being the deep instincts have gone dead, and then the two flows become identical. *This* is the secret of really vulgar and of pornographical people: the sex flow and the excrement flow is the same to them. It happens when the psyche deteriorates, and the profound controlling instincts col-   15 lapse. Then sex is dirt and dirt is sex, and sexual excitement becomes a playing with dirt, and any sign of sex in a woman becomes a show of her dirt. This is the condition of the common, vulgar human being whose name is legion, and who lifts his voice, and it is the *Vox populi, vox Dei*. And this is the source of all pornography.

Margaret Atwood

Pornography

Margaret Atwood (b. 1939), a novelist, poet, and essayist, is best known as the author of novels such as *The Handmaid's Tale* (1986) and *Cat's Eye* (1989). In this essay, Atwood clearly has a much narrower definition of pornography than D. H. Lawrence. Instead of merely defining pornography, however, she is more interested in determining how to regulate it. The issues she brings up are not without consequence: how can we balance the need for freedom of expression against the rights of potential victims of rape or incest? If pornography incites people to violence, shouldn't it be banned? Should we define a movie depicting the horrible consequences of rape as "pornography" or "education"?

1   WHEN I WAS IN FINLAND A FEW YEARS AGO for an international writers' conference, I had occasion to say a few paragraphs in public on the subject of pornography. The context was a discussion of political repression, and I was suggesting the possibility of a link between the two. The immediate result was that a male journalist took several large bites out of me. Prudery and pornography are two halves of the same coin, said he, and I was clearly a prude. What could you expect from an Anglo-Canadian? Afterward, a couple of pleasant Scandinavian men asked me what I had been so worked up about. All "pornography" means, they said, is graphic depictions of whores, and what was the harm in that?

2   Not until then did it strike me that the male journalist and I had two entirely different things in mind. By "pornography," he meant naked bodies and sex. I, on the other hand, had recently been doing the research for my novel *Bodily Harm*, and was still in a state of shock from some of the material I had seen, including the Ontario Board of Film Censors' "outtakes." By "pornography," I meant women getting their nipples snipped off with garden shears, having meat hooks stuck into their vaginas, being disemboweled; little girls being raped; men (yes, there are some men) being smashed to a pulp and forcibly sodomized. The cutting edge of pornography, as far as I could see, was

no longer simple old copulation, hanging from the chandelier or otherwise: it was death, messy, explicit and highly sadistic. I explained this to the nice Scandinavian men. "Oh, but that's just the United States," they said. "Everyone knows they're sick." In their country, they said, violent "pornography" of that kind was not permitted on television or in movies; indeed, excessive violence of any kind was not permitted. They had drawn a clear line between erotica, which earlier studies had shown did not incite men to more aggressive and brutal behavior toward women, and violence, which later studies indicated did.

Some time after that I was in Saskatchewan, where, because of the scenes 3
in *Bodily Harm*, I found myself on an open-line radio show answering questions about "pornography." Almost no one who phoned in was in favor of it, but again they weren't talking about the same stuff I was, because they hadn't seen it. Some of them were all set to stamp out bathing suits and negligees, and, if possible, any depictions of the female body whatsoever. God, it was implied, did not approve of female bodies, and sex of any kind, including that practised by bumblebees, should be shoved back into the dark, where it belonged. I had more than a suspicion that *Lady Chatterley's Lover*, Margaret Laurence's *The Diviners*, and indeed most books by most serious modern authors would have ended up as confetti if left in the hands of these callers.

For me, these two experiences illustrate the two poles of the emotionally 4
heated debate that is now thundering around this issue. They also underline the desirability and even the necessity of defining the terms. "Pornography" is now one of those catchalls, like "Marxism" and "feminism," that have become so broad they can mean almost anything, ranging from certain verses in the Bible, ads for skin lotion and sex tests for children to the contents of *Penthouse*, Naughty '90s postcards and films with titles containing the word *Nazi* that show vicious scenes of torture and killing. It's easy to say that sensible people can tell the difference. Unfortunately, opinions on what constitutes a sensible person vary.

But even sensible people tend to lose their cool when they start talking 5
about this subject. They soon stop talking and start yelling, and the name calling begins. Those in favor of censorship (which may include groups not noticeably in agreement on other issues, such as some feminists and religious fundamentalists) accuse the others of exploiting women through the use of degrading images, contributing to the corruption of children, and adding to the general climate of violence and threat in which both women and children live in this society; or, though they may not give much of a hoot about actual women and children, they invoke moral standards and God's supposed aversion to "filth," "smut" and deviated *preversion*, which may mean ankles.

The camp in favor of total "freedom of expression" often comes out howl- 6
ing as loud as the Romans would have if told they could no longer have inno-

cent fun watching the lions eat up Christians. It too may include segments of the population who are not natural bedfellows: those who proclaim their God-given right to freedom, including the freedom to tote guns, drive when drunk, drool over chicken porn and get off on videotapes of women being raped and beaten, may be waving the same anticensorship banner as responsible liberals who fear the return of Mrs. Grundy, or gay groups for whom sexual emanci-pation involves the concept of "sexual theatre." *Whatever turns you on* is a handy motto, as is *A man's home is his castle* (and if it includes a dungeon with beau-tiful maidens strung up in chains and bleeding from every pore, that's his business).

7   Meanwhile, theoreticians theorize and speculators speculate. Is today's pornography yet another indication of the hatred of the body, the deep mind-body split, which is supposed to pervade Western Christian society? Is it a backlash against the women's movement by men who are threatened by up-pity female behavior in real life, so like to fantasize about women done up like outsize parcels, being turned into hamburger, kneeling at their feet in slave-like adoration or sucking off guns? Is it a sign of collective impotence, of a gen-eration of men who can't relate to real women at all but have to make do with bits of celluloid and paper? Is the current flood just a result of smart market-ing and aggressive promotion by the money men in what has now become a multi-billion dollar industry? If they were selling movies about men getting their testicles stuck full of knitting needles by women with swastikas on their sleeves, would they do as well, or is this penchant somehow peculiarly male? If so, why? Is pornography a power trip rather than a sex one? Some say that those ropes, chains, muzzles and other restraining devices are an argument for the immense power female sexuality still wields in the male imagination: you don't put these things on dogs unless you're afraid of them. Others, more lit-erary, wonder about the shift from the 19th-century Magic Woman or Femme Fatale image to the lollipop-licker, airhead or turkey-carcass treatment of women in porn today. The proporners don't care much about theory; they merely demand product. The antiporners don't care about it in the final analysis either; there's dirt on the street, and they want it cleaned up, now.

8   It seems to me that this conversation, with its *You're-a-prude/You're-a-pervert* dialectic, will never get anywhere as long as we continue to think of this ma-terial as just "entertainment." Possibly we're deluded by the packaging, the for-mat: magazine, book, movie, theatrical presentation. We're used to thinking of these things as part of the "entertainment industry," and we're used to thinking of ourselves as free adult people who ought to be able to see any kind of "entertainment" we want to. That was what the First Choice pay-TV debate was all about. After all, it's only entertainment, right? Entertainment means fun, and only a killjoy would be antifun. What's the harm?

9   This is obviously the central question: *What's the harm?* If there isn't any

real harm to any real people, then the antiporners can tsk-tsk and/or throw up as much as they like, but they can't rightfully expect more legal controls or sanctions. However, the no harm position is far from being proven.

(For instance, there's a clear-cut case for banning—as the federal govern- 10 ment has proposed—movies, photos and videos that depict children engaging in sex with adults: real children are used to make the movies, and hardly anybody thinks this is ethical. The possibilities for coercion are too great.)

To shift the viewpoint, I'd like to suggest three other models for looking 11 at "pornography"—and here I mean the violent kind.

Those who find the idea of regulating pornographic materials repugnant 12 because they think it's Fascist or Communist or otherwise not in accordance with the principles of an open democratic society should consider that Canada has made it illegal to disseminate material that may lead to hatred toward any group because of race or religion. I suggest that if pornography of the violent kind depicted these acts being done predominantly to Chinese, to blacks, to Catholics, it would be off the market immediately, under the present laws. Why is hate literature illegal? Because whoever made the law thought that such material might incite real people to do real awful things to other real people. The human brain is to a certain extent a computer: garbage in, garbage out. We only hear about the extreme cases (like that of American multimurderer Ted Bundy) in which pornography has contributed to the death and/or mutilation of women and/or men. Although pornography is not the only factor involved in the creation of such deviance, it certainly has upped the ante by suggesting both a variety of techniques and the social acceptability of such actions. Nobody knows yet what effect this stuff is having on the less psychotic.

Studies have shown that a large part of the market for all kinds of porn, soft 13 and hard, is drawn from the 16-to-21-year-old population of young men. Boys used to learn about sex on the street, or (in Italy, according to Fellini movies) from friendly whores, or, in more genteel surroundings, from girls, their parents, or, once upon a time, in school, more or less. Now porn has been added, and sex education in the schools is rapidly being phased out. The buck has been passed, and boys are being taught that all women secretly like to be raped and that real men get high on scooping out women's digestive tracts.

Boys learn their concept of masculinity from other men: is this what most 14 men want them to be learning? If word gets around that rapists are "normal" and even admirable men, will boys feel that in order to be normal, admirable and masculine they will have to be rapists? Human beings are enormously flexible, and how they turn out depends a lot on how they're educated, by the society in which they're immersed as well as by their teachers. In a society that advertises and glorifies rape or even implicitly condones it, more women get raped. It becomes socially acceptable. And at a time when men and the traditional male role have taken a lot of flak and men are confused and casting around for an acceptable way of being male (and, in some cases, not getting much comfort from women on that score), this must be at times a pleasing thought.

15   It would be naïve to think of violent pornography as just harmless entertainment. It's also an educational tool and a powerful propaganda device. What happens when boy educated on porn meets girl brought up on Harlequin romances? The clash of expectations can be heard around the block. She wants him to get down on his knees with a ring, he wants her to get down on all fours with a ring in her nose. Can this marriage be saved?

16   Pornography has certain things in common with such addictive substances as alcohol and drugs: for some, though by no means for all, it induces chemical changes in the body, which the user finds exciting and pleasurable. It also appears to attract a "hard core" of habitual users and a penumbra of those who use it occasionally but aren't dependent on it in any way. There are also significant numbers of men who aren't much interested in it, not because they're undersexed but because real life is satisfying their needs, which may not require as many appliances as those of users.

17   For the "hard core," pornography may function as alcohol does for the alcoholic: tolerance develops, and a little is no longer enough. This may account for the short viewing time and fast turnover in porn theatres. Mary Brown, chairwoman of the Ontario Board of Film Censors, estimates that for every one mainstream movie requesting entrance to Ontario, there is one porno flick. Not only the quantity consumed but the quality of explicitness must escalate, which may account for the growing violence: once the big deal was breasts, then it was genitals, then copulation, then that was no longer enough and the hard users had to have more. The ultimate kick is death, and after that, as the Marquis de Sade so boringly demonstrated, multiple death.

18   The existence of alcoholism has not led us to ban social drinking. On the other hand, we do have laws about drinking and driving, excessive drunkenness and other abuses of alcohol that may result in injury or death to others.

19   This leads us back to the key question: what's the harm? Nobody knows, but this society should find out fast, before the saturation point is reached. The Scandinavian studies that showed a connection between depictions of sexual violence and increased impulse toward it on the part of male viewers would be a starting point, but many more questions remain to be raised as well as answered. What, for instance, is the crucial difference between men who are users and men who are not? Does using affect a man's relationship with actual women, and, if so, adversely? Is there a clear line between erotica and violent pornography, or are they on an escalating continuum? Is this a "men versus women" issue, with all men secretly siding with the pro-

porners and all women secretly siding against? (I think not; there *are* lots of men who don't think that running their true love through the Cuisinart is the best way they can think of to spend a Saturday night, and they're just as nauseated by films of someone else doing it as women are.) Is pornography merely an expression of the sexual confusion of this age or an active contributor to it?

Nobody wants to go back to the age of official repression, when even 20 piano legs were referred to as "limbs" and had to wear pantaloons to be decent. Neither do we want to end up in George Orwell's 1984, in which pornography is turned out by the State to keep the proles in a state of torpor, sex itself is considered dirty and the approved practise it only for reproduction. But Rome under the emperors isn't such a good model either.

If all men and women respected each other, if sex were considered joyful 21 and life-enhancing instead of a wallow in germ-filled glop, if everyone were in love all the time, if, in other words, many people's lives were more satisfactory for them than they appear to be now, pornography might just go away on its own. But since this is obviously not happening, we as a society are going to have to make some informed and responsible decisions about how to deal with it.

Mark Gerzon

Manhood: The Elusive Goal

Mark Gerzon, journalist, activist, consultant, lecturer, and writer, has spent much of his life trying to reconcile differences between groups with different beliefs. His journey started with the publication in 1969 of *The Whole World is Watching: A Young Man Looks at Youth's Dissent*, which explored the conflict between the baby-boom generation and their parents' generation. He spent the seventies cofounding and editing *World-Paper*, a "global newspaper" with contributing editors from the cultures of four continents. In *A Choice of Heroes: The Changing Faces of American Manhood*, published in 1982, Gerzon tried to connect the feminist movement with the emerging men's movement. In this excerpt from *A Choice of Heroes*, Gerzon recounts an episode from his own youth and contrasts it with modern expectations for men.

There is no steady unretracing progress in this life. . . . Once gone 1 through, we trace the round again; and are infants, boys, and men, and Ifs eternally.

HERMAN MELVILLE, *MOBY DICK*

2   IT WAS NOT COINCIDENCE THAT WHEN LOVE ENTERED MY LIFE so did violence. I fell in love for the first time with a high school classmate, Diana. She was a cheerleader, the most feminine of all roles. Even now, almost twenty years later, I think of her when I see cheerleaders practicing. In one cheer, they would shout each letter of each member of the starting line-up's name as they ran onto the basketball court heralding them as if they were heroes. They had mastered the art of feminine support: they remained on the sidelines while acclaiming the men who played the game.

3   In this, Diana was wholehearted. In winter, her face would glow when the ball swished through the hoop; she would look crestfallen when it fell short. In autumn, chanting "Hit 'em again, hit 'em again, harder, harder," her body pulsed to the rhythm of her words. Even if she was not the most beautiful cheerleader, she was certainly the most magnetic. She made us feel like men.

4   Before she and I started dating, she went with a fellow two years my senior, a leading figure in one of the male clubs known for its toughness. Since he and Diana had broken up (or so she said), I felt no qualms when our study dates became romantic. Soon she and I were together almost constantly. When she invited me to a party sponsored by her club, I accepted. After all, she was "mine."

5   Midway through the evening, however, her former beau arrived with several of his hefty club brothers behind him. "They want you," a friend warned me, then quickly disappeared. My strategy, which was to pretend that I had not noticed their arrival, became impractical when three of them had me cornered. And I had no club brothers to back me up.

6   "Let's go outside," said Diana's old beau.

7   "What for?" I was still playing dumb.

8   The purpose of our outing was to settle with our fists who Diana belonged to. He obviously felt that he had staked his claim first and that I was trespassing on his territory. I believed that she had the right to choose for herself to whom she wanted to belong. Neither of us, perhaps not even Diana herself, considered it odd that at the age of sixteen she should belong to anyone.

9   As it turned out, the other boyfriend and I didn't fight, at least not that night. "Why'd you let him talk you out of it?" one of his buddies asked him. He was outraged at being deprived of what was to be the high point of his evening.

10   A few weeks later, after a basketball game, my adversary and I passed each other under the bleachers. Without warning, he punched me hard in my right eye. My fist was raised to return the blow when several arms pressed me back against the wall.

11   "Whatsa matter?" he shouted at me contemptuously. "Are you gonna cry?"

12   The impatient crowd pushed us in opposite directions. Stunned, I felt my eye to check if it was bleeding. Only then did I feel the tell-tale moistness. Al-

though no tears trickled down my cheeks, they were still evidence against my manliness. First, I had weaseled out of a fight. Next, I let him hit me without ever returning the blow. But the most damaging evidence of all were my barely averted tears. To be hit and to cry was the ultimate violation of the code of masculine conduct.

That happened half a lifetime ago. I no longer see my unwillingness to fight   13
as an indictment of my character. Had I been as old and as tough as my adversary, perhaps I would have handled our conflict differently. Perhaps I would have fought. Perhaps I even might have won. Instead, aware of my relative weakness and inexperience, I chose not to. I wanted to protect my eyes, my mouth, my groin. I thought I might need them in the future. But the deeper reason had nothing to do with self-protection but with love. I could not understand what the winner of a fight would gain. Would Diana accept the verdict of our brawl? Like a Kewpie doll at the fairgrounds, would she let herself be claimed by whichever contestant came out on top? If her love could be won by violence, I was not sure I wanted it. I wanted her to love me for who I was, not for how I fought.

My problem, my friends told me then, was that I was too sensitive.   14

Strange how things change. The image of manhood against which I am   15
measured has changed so much that now, almost twenty years later, I am told I am not sensitive *enough*. When tensions build in our relationship, Shelley will admonish me for being out of touch with my feelings. "You are always so defensive, always trying to protect yourself," she will say. "Why can't you be more open to your feelings?"

How can I explain it to her? How can any man explain it to any woman?   16
Women are not raised to abort all tears. They are not measured by their toughness. They are not expected to bang against each other on hockey rinks and football fields and basketball courts. They do not go out into the woods to play soldiers. They do not settle disagreements by punching each other. For them, tears are a badge of femininity. For us, they are a masculine demerit.

Nothing has made me see this more clearly than talking with Richard   17
Ryan, a former alcoholic. Sitting in the sun one afternoon by a lake near his home, Richard reminded me of a masculine rite of passage I had almost forgotten.

"After I gave this rap about alcoholism at the high school, this kid came   18
up to me and said, 'Can I talk with you privately, Mr. Ryan?' Usually that means that either the kid's parents are alcoholic or he is. But not this kid. He said to me, 'Mr. Ryan, I've never been drunk, never smoked a joint. What's wrong with me?'

"So I said to him, 'Nothing's wrong with you, man. You're doin' fine.'   19

"'But why do I feel I have to lie to my friends about it?' he asked. 'If they   20
knew I didn't drink or smoke they'd make fun of me.'"

21   Richard Ryan rolled over onto his stomach as he finished the story. Either the sun or his emotions made him hide his face.

22   "I always felt like I had to lie as a kid," Ryan told me. "I liked to bake cookies. I liked to watch my kid brothers and sisters. I liked to write poetry. But my dad made me feel that was wrong somehow. So I started to pretend I *didn't* want to do it."

23   I had heard the lament so often now that I pushed him for specifics. "But what did your dad do? Did he walk in and say, 'Get out of the kitchen' or 'That's women's work'?"

24   "No, no. Nothing like that. It was more subtle." He thought for a moment. "For example, when my mother's mother died, I wanted to be her pall-bearer. Grandma had been very special to me. I felt like she'd carried me all my life. When she died, I wanted to carry her once. So I asked my dad if I could be a pallbearer. He said, 'Only if you promise not to cry. Pallbearers can't cry!' I knew if I lied and said I wouldn't, he'd let me. But I felt like that'd be betraying her. How could I go to her funeral and not cry? Since I wouldn't promise, my dad refused to let me do it."

25   Now in his mid-thirties, Ryan runs a project called Creative Drug Education. He visits high schools and talks about alcohol and drug abuse. But he doesn't preach. He tells his own story:

26   "When I used to go out and get bombed, guys would say, 'He drinks like a man' or 'He holds it like a man.' Being drunk, I really felt like I was something great. The other guys and I, we were like a pack, and drinking was our bond. We'd get together and, because we drank, we'd say stuff and hug each other and do all sorts of things we'd never let ourselves do if we were sober."

27   Only after reaching the age of thirty did Richard realize he was an alcoholic. "I've only recently felt I can be who I am," he continues. "All those years I felt I had to blot out a whole side of myself. I used alcohol to make myself feel good about myself. After I quit drinking, I thought I was free. But then I realized I was addicted to smoking. And I mean *addicted*. My withdrawal from nicotine was almost as bad as from booze—the shakes, sweating, couldn't sleep. I found it hard to be around people without a cigarette in my hand. It was the whole Marlboro man thing—it made me look cool, made me feel like a man. When a friend told me I should stop, I told him, 'Anybody can quit smoking. It takes a real man to face cancer.' I said it as a joke, but I meant it. That's how sick I was."

28   Richard no longer looks sick. He is big and muscular. We swam out to the middle of the lake and back and, when we dried off, he wasn't even out of breath. He is respected by the people with whom he works. Teachers tell me he is more effective with young people who use drugs than anyone they've ever met.

29   As we walked back to the car, I saw a sadness in him, a wound that had not yet healed.

"What you thinking about?" I asked, not knowing a better way to probe. He laughed. "Oh, I was just thinking about Grandma's funeral. You know what? Every one of those pallbearers cried."

In Western societies, there are clearly no longer any rites of passage. The very existence of terms such as teenager (the German word is *Halbwüchsiger*, half-grown) shows that the absence of this social institution results in an in-between stage. All too often adult society avoids this whole question by regarding those in their teens in terms of the high school health book definition. Adolescence, it says, is the period when the person is no longer a child, but not yet an adult. This is defining the concept of adolescence by avoiding it altogether. This is why we have a youth culture. It is where adolescents go (and sometimes stay) before they become grownups.

Despite the absence of any established initiation rite, young men need one. By default, other institutions take the place of these missing rites. Some commentators on growing up in America point to sports or fraternities for example, to demonstrate that our culture does have various kinds of initiation rites. But they are wrong.

Sports, for instance, can hardly serve as the means for gaining manhood. Sports are games. Except for the professionals who make their living from them, these games have little connection with real life. Moreover, only a small minority of males in American high schools and colleges can participate in athletics. As dozens of articles document, sports play a key role in enabling boys and young men to test their physical prowess, but they do not alone make a boy a man.

Fraternities, too, are a painfully inadequate means for gaining manhood. Except for token community service projects once a year, most fraternities are disconnected from society. How can they provide a socially recognized initiation rite when they involve only members of the younger generation? Frat members do not go off into seclusion with the adults of the "tribe." They go off into seclusion with themselves. They are initiated into youth culture, perhaps, but not into the world of adults.

The young man facing adulthood cannot reach across this great divide. He has only rites of impasse. There is no ritual—not sexual, economic, military, or generational—that can confirm his masculinity. Maturity eludes him. Our culture is famous for its male adolescent pain. From James Dean in *Rebel Without a Cause* and Dustin Hoffman in *The Graduate* to the more recent box office hits *Breaking Away, My Bodyguard,* and *Ordinary People,* young men try to prove they are grown men. But to no avail. None of the surrogate initiation rites—car duels, college diplomas, after-work drinking rituals, first paychecks, sports trophies—answers their deepest needs. None has proven to be what William James called the "moral equivalent of war."

37   The only rituals that confirm manhood now are imitations of war. The military academies, for example, like boot camp itself, involve many of the ingredients of primitive rites of passage. Young men are secluded with older men. They must endure tests of psychological or physical endurance.

38   Pat Conroy's novel *The Lords of Discipline*, which depicts life in a southern military academy, and Lucian K. Truscott IV's *Dress Gray*, which portrays West Point, showed how boys are turned into men—the kind of men the military needs. But, as we have recognized, the Soldier is no longer the hero. The Vietnam war was "billed on the marquee as a John Wayne shoot-'em-up test of manhood," wrote Mark Baker in *Nam*, but it ended up "a warped version of *Peter Pan* . . . a brutal Never Never Land where little boys didn't have to grow up. They just grew old before their time." Similarly, the heroes of Conroy's and Truscott's tales are not the brave soldier but the dissenter. Nevertheless, because military service is the only rite of passage available, men are drawn to it like moths to light. We need to prove our manhood and will take whatever paths our culture offers.

39   With the option of going to war foreclosed, young men seek to prove themselves by performing other manly deeds. The most obvious surrogates for war often involve violence too. It is not directed at the enemy, but at each other, and ourselves.

40   Each week, the news media overflow with accounts of young men between the ages of fifteen and twenty-five who have committed acts of violence. Too old to be boys, too young to have proven themselves men, they are finding their own rites of passage. Here are three, culled from the newspapers:

41   A Boy Scout leader smashes his new car on a country road at 100 miles per hour: he is "showing off" to the four scouts who were riding with him. Now they are all dead.

42   A sixteen-year-old who lives in a comfortable suburb throws a large rock from a freeway overpass through the windshield of a car. The victim, a thirty-one-year-old housewife, suffers a concussion but survives. "You do it for the thrill," the boy says. "It's a boring town," says one of his classmates.

43   A teenage boy is so upset that his girlfriend has jilted him that he threatens to kill himself. Talking to her on the phone, he says he will drive over to her house and smash his car into the tree in her front yard if she will not go out with him. She refuses. So he does it, killing himself.

44   Many movies are made as surrogate rites of passage for young men. They are designed for the guy who, in actor Clint Eastwood's words, "sits alone in the theater. He's young and he's scared. He doesn't know what he's going to do with his life. He wishes he could be self-sufficient, like the man he sees up there on the screen, somebody who can look out for himself, solve his own problems." The heroes of these films are men who are tough and hard, quick to use violence, wary of women. Whether cowboys, cops, or superheroes, they domi-

nate everything—women, nature, and other men. Young men cannot outmaneuver the Nazis as Indiana Jones did in *Raiders of the Lost Ark*, or battle Darth Vader, or outsmart Dr. No with James Bond's derring-do. To feel like heroes they turn to the other sex. They ask young women for more than companionship, or sex, or marriage. They ask women to give them what their culture could not—their manhood.

Half the nation's teenagers have had sex before they graduate from high   45
school. The easiest way to prove oneself a man today is to make it with a girl. First we make out or put the make on her. Then we make it. We are not, like our "primitive" forebearers, joining together with a woman as adults. We are coming together in order to become adults, if not in society's eyes, then in our own.

"You in her pants yet?" one of the high school jocks asks his classmate in   46
Ordinary People, the Academy Award-winning movie directed by Robert Redford. We prove our manhood on the football field or the basketball court by scoring points against other men. We prove our manhood in sex by scoring with women.

The young man, armed with lines like "Don't you love me?" is always ready   47
for action. He wants to forge ahead, explore new territory. After all, he has nothing to lose. He has no hymen, no uterus. He is free to play the role of bold adventurer, coaxing the reluctant girl to let him sow his wild oats in her still virgin land. "I love you, but I don't feel ready," she may say. She may be afraid that her refusal may jeopardize her relationship with her young explorer, but she is even more afraid to get pregnant. She may feel less mature than her sex-hungry companion. But the emotional reality may be precisely the opposite. Certain of her femininity and of her pregnability, she dares to wait until the time is right. Insecure about his masculinity and obsessed with proving it—to himself and his buddies, if not to her—he needs to score in order to feel that he has made the team.

Sonny Burns, the sexually insecure hero of Dan Wakefield's *Going All the*   48
Way, finds himself engaged in an amorous overture on a double date. But he admits to himself, and to a generation of readers, that he is doing so not because he finds his date exciting. On the contrary, she bores him. He does so because he wants to impress his buddy in the front seat. He must prove he is a man, and a man takes whatever "pussy" he can get. Pretending to be passionate, he thinks about the high school rating system, according to which boys reported their sexual scores: "The next day, when the guys asked you what you got the night before, you could say you got finger action inside the pants. That wasn't as good as really fucking but it rated right along with dry-humping and was much better than just the necking stuff like frenching and getting covered-tit or bare-tit. It was really pretty much of a failure if you parked with a girl and got only covered-tit."

49   Even if he wins, the victory is private. There are no fans in the bleachers as he crosses home plate and scores. He has not proved himself a man to adult males, as did young men in traditional rites of passage. His sexual conquest is a rite of passage only in his own mind. If adult society were to pass judgment on these back-seat gymnastics, it would probably be negative. The responsible adult would ask him if he was ready for marriage. Could he support her if he had to? And of course the answers are no. He has become an adult sexually, not socially. He has proved his virility in the dark of night. By the light of day, the proof has vanished.

50   As Margaret Mead pointed out in *Male and Female*, our culture leaves adolescents in a quandary. We give them extraordinary freedom but tell them not to use it. "We permit and encourage situations in which young people can indulge in any sort of sex behavior that they elect," wrote Mead a generation ago. "We actually place our young people in a virtually intolerable situation, giving them the entire setting for behaviour for which we then punish them when it occurs." It is a cultural arrangement for which some young women pay an awful price.

51   Whether veiled in fiction or revealed in autobiography, women recall the ritual of modern courtship with caustic humor at best, more often with bitterness. So objectified do they feel that they develop a detached attitude toward their bodies. Reports the cheerleader heroine in Lisa Alther's *Kinflicks*: "Joe Bob would dutifully knead my breasts through my uniform jacket and padded bra, as though he were a housewife poking plums to determine their ripeness." Later, she would observe him sucking "at my nipples while I tried to decide what to do with my hands to indicate my continuing involvement in the project."

52   But Alther's good-natured response is not typical. Other sagas of car-seat courtships and apartment affairs leave their heroines harboring a deep distaste for men. Some declare themselves feminists or lesbians. Some become depressed. Others, as in Judith Rossner's *Looking for Mr. Goodbar*, are killed by their lovers. And a few, after great turmoil, find a man who will treat them gently, with genuine care.

53   The movie theater, that public living room for a nation of young lovers, reflects this yearning too. For those who have grown weary of the macho hero whose physical prowess is enough, Hollywood has provided a countertype. For those who are not infatuated with the Soldier, there are now movies about the anti-soldier. "In what may be an emerging genre in the movies," wrote Paul Starr in his review of *Coming Home*, *An Unmarried Woman*, and *Alice Doesn't Live Here Anymore*, "there appears a character who expresses in his personality and in his relations with the heroine a new idea of masculinity. He might be described as the emotionally competent hero. . . . He is the man to whom women turn as they try to change their own lives: someone who is strong and

affectionate, capable of intimacy . . . masculine without being dominating." The new hero, though perhaps not rugged and tough in the familiar mold, can be intimate. He can feel. "The new softer image of masculinity seems to represent what is distinctive and significant in recent films, and I expect we will see more of the post-feminist hero because the old, strong, silent type no longer seems adequate as lover—or as person."

Who, then, is to be the young man's hero? The gentle, post-feminist figure   54 extolled by the new genre of films and by the roughly five thousand men's con- sciousness-raising groups across America? Or the self-sufficient, hard-hitting tough that Eastwood tries to embody and that the military breeds? Faced with such polarized and politicized choices, how does a boy become a man? By being hard or by being soft?

From the sensible to the absurd, we have answers. We have so many shift-   55 ing, contradictory criteria for manhood that they confuse rather than inspire.

American boys coming of age encounter sexual chaos. A chorus of libera-   56 tion advocates, now with bass as well as soprano voices, encourages them to free themselves from the oppressive male role, to become softer, and to con- sider themselves women's equals. But another vociferous group beckons them in another direction. For every pro-feminist man, there is his counterpart, who denounces those "fuzzy-headed housemales, purporting to represent 'men's liberation,' but sponsored by NOW." One Minnesota men's rights leader argued, for example, that men who support women's liberation are "eu- nuchs," motivated by an "urge to slip into a pair of panties." According to him and his followers: "Men's liberation means establishing the right of males to be men, not to liberate them from being men."

The hard-liners and soft-liners both have their respective magazines, orga-   57 nizations, and conferences. Repulsed by the cacophony, most young men try to ignore it. But the questions gnaw at them anyway. Although the pro- and anti-feminist activists irritate them, young men cannot deny their own uncer- tainty. They are caught between the competing ideals of chauvinism and lib- eration. The old archetypes do not work; the new ones remain vague and in- complete. If we are not to be John Wayne, then who?

Into the vacuum created by the demise of the old archetypes rush myriad   58 images. Each hopes to inspire a following. Masculinity becomes the target for everyone from toothpaste advertisers to Hollywood superstars. These sales- men of self-help all have their diagnoses for the young man struggling to find his own identity. Some take the pose of proud aging lions, defending the tra- ditional masculine role as Western civilization enters a precipitous, psycho- sexual decline. In *Sexual Suicide*, George Gilder warned of the imminent fem- inization of man and masculinization of woman and called on men to reassert their superiority.

Others do not oppose liberation but rather seem to exploit it. Cynically   59 catering to masculine insecurity, they describe the world of white-collar commuters as a stark and brutal asphalt jungle in which men must constantly flex their aggressive personalities in order to survive. According to Michael Korda, author of *Power!* and *Success!*, life is nothing more than a series of encounters in which one dominates or is dominated, intimidates or is intimidated, achieves power over or is oneself overpowered. "Your gain is inevitably someone else's loss," philosophizes this latter-day Nietzsche, "your failure someone else's victory."

60   There are also the advocates of liberation who seek to free us from the manacles of machismo. Although they are constructive in intent, they too increase the confusion. In their attempt to free us from one-sidedness, they double our load. They now want us to be "assertive *and* yielding, independent *and* dependent, job *and* people oriented, strong *and* gentle, in short, both masculine *and* feminine." The prescriptions are not wrong, just overwhelming. Their lists of do's and don'ts, like Gail Sheehy's *Passages*, seem too neat, too tidy. They write of "masculinity in crisis" with such certainty. They encourage us to cry with such stoicism. They advise us to "be personal, be intimate with men" with such authority. It is all too much.

61   Whichever model young men choose, they know the traditional expectation of their culture. At least until the seventies, Americans of all ages and of all educational and income levels were in wide agreement about what traits are masculine. According to one study, based on more than a thousand interviews, men are expected to be very aggressive, not at all emotional, very dominant, not excitable, very competitive, rough, and unaware of others' feelings. And women are expected to be more or less the opposite.

62   If this is what maleness is, then a young man must find ways to demonstrate those traits. Without a rite of passage he can only prove what he is not. Not a faggot, a pussy, a queer. Not a pushover, a loser, or a lightweight. Not a dimwit or a dunce or a jerk or a nobody. Not a prick or a pansy. Not, above all, anything that is feminine. Indeed, without clear rites of passage, the only way to be a man is essentially negative: to not be a woman.

63   If we are to be masculine, then they must be feminine. We convince ourselves that women are yielding, that they are more interested in our careers than in their own, that they are interested in sex whenever we are, that they are fulfilled by raising children. That, we assume, is who they are. Should one of them act differently, then something is wrong, not with our assumptions, but with her.

64   Having entered physical manhood, we are nevertheless emotionally unsure of ourselves. The more unsure we are, the more we stress that we are not "feminine" and the more we are threatened when women act "masculine." We try to rid ourselves of any soft, effeminate qualities. We gravitate toward all-male cliques in the form of sports teams, social clubs, or professional groups.

When we are with a woman, it is virtually always in a sexually charged atmosphere. To be merely friends is nearly impossible because it suggests that we have something in common. We are trying, after all, to prove precisely the opposite, which is why so many marriages fail.

Paul Theroux

Being a Man

Novelist, teacher, and master of the travel narrative, Paul Theroux (b. 1941) received an early education in writing from the novelist V. S. Naipaul, who was a faculty colleague of Theroux when he was teaching English at Makerere University in Uganda. Theroux has traveled all over the world, usually taking copious notes of both the people and places he visits. Both Theroux's novels and his travel narratives make extensive use of those notes. In "Being a Man," Theroux applies the skills honed from years of travel and observation to a subject much closer to home: the American male.

THERE IS A PATHETIC SENTENCE IN THE CHAPTER "Fetishism" in Dr. Norman   1
Cameron's book *Personality Development and Psychopathology*. It goes, "Fetishists are nearly always men; and their commonest fetish is a woman's shoe." I cannot read that sentence without thinking that it is just one more awful thing about being a man—and perhaps it is an important thing to know about us.

I have always disliked being a man. The whole idea of manhood in Amer-   2
ica is pitiful, in my opinion. This version of masculinity is a little like having to wear an ill-fitting coat for one's entire life (by contrast, I imagine femininity to be an oppressive sense of nakedness). Even the expression "Be a man!" strikes me as insulting and abusive. It means: Be stupid, be unfeeling, obedient, soldierly and stop thinking. Man means "manly"—how can one think about men without considering the terrible ambition of manliness? And yet it is part of every man's life. It is a hideous and crippling lie; it not only insists on difference and connives at superiority, it is also by its very nature destructive, emotionally damaging, and socially harmful. The youth who is subverted, as most are, into believing in the masculine ideal is effectively separated from women and he spends the rest of his life finding women a riddle and a nuisance. Of course, there is a female version of this male affliction. It begins with mothers encouraging little girls to say (to other adults) "Do you like my new dress?" In a sense, little girls are traditionally urged to please adults with a kind of coquettishness while boys are enjoined to behave like monkeys to-

wards each other. The nine-year-old coquette proceeds to become womanish in a subtle power game in which she learns to be sexually indispensable, socially decorative and always alert to a man's sense of inadequacy.

3   Femininity—being lady-like—implies needing a man as witness and seducer; but masculinity celebrates the exclusive company of men. That is why it is so grotesque; and that is also why there is no manliness without inadequacy—because it denies men the natural friendship of women.

4   It is very hard to imagine any concept of manliness that does not belittle women, and it begins very early. At an age when I wanted to meet girls—let's say the treacherous years of thirteen to sixteen—I was told to take up a sport, get more fresh air, join the Boy Scouts, and I was urged not to read so much. It was the 1950s and if you asked too many questions about sex you were sent to camp—boy's camp, of course: the nightmare. Nothing is more unnatural or prison-like than a boy's camp, but if it were not for them we would have no Elks' Lodges, no pool rooms, no boxing matches, no Marines.

5   And perhaps no sports as we know them. Everyone is aware of how few in number are the athletes who behave like gentlemen. Just as high school basketball teaches you how to be a poor loser, the manly attitude towards sports seems to be little more than a recipe for creating bad marriages, social misfits, moral degenerates, sadists, latent rapists and just plain louts. I regard high school sports as a drug far worse than marijuana, and it is the reason that the average tennis champion, say, is a pathetic oaf.

6   Any objective study would find the quest for manliness essentially right-wing, puritanical, cowardly, neurotic and fueled largely by a fear of women. It is also certainly philistine. There is no book-hater like a Little League coach. But indeed all the creative arts are obnoxious to the manly ideal, because at their best the arts are pursued by uncompetitive and essentially solitary people. It makes it very hard for a creative youngster, for any boy who expresses the desire to be alone seems to be saying that there is something wrong with him.

7   It ought to be clear by now that I have something of an objection to the way we turn boys into men. It does not surprise me that when the President of the United States has his customary weekend off he dresses like a cowboy—it is both a measure of his insecurity and his willingness to please. In many ways, American culture does little more for a man than prepare him for modeling clothes in the L. L. Bean catalogue. I take this as a personal insult because for many years I found it impossible to admit to myself that I wanted to be a writer. It was my guilty secret, because being a writer was incompatible with being a man. There are people who might deny this, but that is because the American writer, typically, has been so at pains to prove his manliness that we have come to see literariness and manliness as mingled qualities. But first there was a fear that writing was not a manly profession—indeed, not a pro-

fession at all. (The paradox in American letters is that it has always been easier for a woman to write and for a man to be published.) Growing up, I had
thought of sports as wasteful and humiliating, and the idea of manliness was
a bore. My wanting to become a writer was not a flight from that oppressive
role-playing, but I quickly saw that it was at odds with it. Everything in stereotyped manliness goes against the life of the mind. The Hemingway personality
is too tedious to go into here, and in any case his exertions are well-known,
but certainly it was not until this aberrant behavior was examined by feminists
in the 1960s that any male writer dared question the pugnacity in Hemingway's fiction. All the bullfighting and arm wrestling and elephant shooting diminished Hemingway as a writer, but it is consistent with a prevailing attitude
in American writing: one cannot be a male writer without first proving that
one is a man.

It is normal in America for a man to be dismissive or even somewhat   8
apologetic about being a writer. Various factors make it easier. There is a
heartiness about journalism that makes it acceptable—journalism is the man-
liest form of American writing and, therefore, the profession the most inde-
pendent-minded women seek (yes, it is an illusion, but that is my point). Fic-
tion-writing is equated with a kind of dispirited failure and is only manly
when it produces wealth—money is masculinity. So is drinking. Being a drunk-
ard is another assertion, if misplaced, of manliness. The American male writer
is traditionally proud of his heavy drinking. But we are also a very literal-
minded people. A man proves his manhood in America in old-fashioned
ways. He kills lions, like Hemingway; or he hunts ducks, like Nathanael West;
or he makes pronouncements like, "A man should carry enough knife to defend himself with," as James Jones once said to a *Life* interviewer. Or he says
he can drink you under the table. But even tiny drunken William Faulkner
loved to mount a horse and go fox hunting, and Jack Kerouac roistered up
and down Manhattan in a lumberjack shirt (and spent every night of *The Sub-
terraneans* with his mother in Queens). And we are familiar with the lengths
to which Norman Mailer is prepared, in his endearing way, to prove that he
is just as much a monster as the next man.

When the novelist John Irving was revealed as a wrestler, people took him   9
to be a very serious writer, and even a bubble reputation like Eric (*Love Story*)
Segal's was enhanced by the news that he ran the marathon in a respectable
time. How surprised we would be if Joyce Carol Oates were revealed as a sumo
wrestler or Joan Didion active in pumping iron. "Lives in New York City with
her three children" is the typical woman writer's biographical note, for just as
the male writer must prove he has achieved a sort of muscular manhood, the
woman writer—or rather her publicists—must prove her motherhood.

There would be no point in saying any of this if it were not generally ac-   10
cepted that to be a man is somehow—even now in feminist-influenced Amer-

ica—a privilege. It is on the contrary an unmerciful and punishing burden. Being a man is bad enough; being manly is appalling (in this sense, women's lib has done much more for men than for women). It is the sinister silliness of men's fashions, and a clubby attitude in the arts. It is the subversion of good students. It is the so-called "Dress Code" of the Ritz-Carlton Hotel in Boston, and it is the institutionalized cheating in college sports. It is the most primitive insecurity.

11   And this is also why men often object to feminism but are afraid to explain why: of course women have a justified grievance, but most men believe—and with reason—that their lives are just as bad.

Marie Winn

TV Addiction

Cookies or Heroin?

Born in Czechoslovakia, Marie Winn emigrated to the United States as a child. She has been a writer all her life, writing children's books, translating plays from her native Czech, and even writing a column on bird watching for the *Wall Street Journal*. In 1977, *The Plug-in Drug*, her first book for adults, gained her a national reputation as a careful observer of human nature.

1   THE WORD "ADDICTION" IS OFTEN USED LOOSELY and wryly in conversation. People will refer to themselves as "mystery book addicts" or "cookie addicts." E. B. White writes of his annual surge of interest in gardening: "We are hooked and are making an attempt to kick the habit." Yet nobody really believes that reading mysteries or ordering seeds by catalogue is serious enough to be compared with addictions to heroin or alcohol. The word "addiction" is here used jokingly to denote a tendency to overindulge in some pleasurable activity.

2   People often refer to being "hooked on TV." Does this, too, fall into the lighthearted category of cookie eating and other pleasures that people pursue with unusual intensity, or is there a kind of television viewing that falls into the more serious category of destructive addiction?

3   When we think about addiction to drugs or alcohol, we frequently focus on negative aspects, ignoring the pleasures that accompany drinking or drug-taking. And yet the essence of any serious addiction is a pursuit of pleasure, a search for a "high" that normal life does not supply. It is only the inability to

function without the addictive substance that is dismaying, the dependence of the organism upon a certain experience and an increasing inability to function normally without it. Thus a person will take two or three drinks at the end of the day not merely for the pleasure drinking provides, but also because he "doesn't feel normal" without them.

An addict does not merely pursue a pleasurable experience and need to experience it in order to function normally. He needs to *repeat* it again and again. Something about that particular experience makes life without it less than complete. Other potentially pleasurable experiences are no longer possible, for under the spell of the addictive experience, his life is peculiarly distorted. The addict craves an experience and yet he is never really satisfied. The organism may be temporarily sated, but soon it begins to crave again. 4

Finally, a serious addiction is distinguished from a harmless pursuit of pleasure by its distinctly destructive elements. A heroin addict, for instance, leads a damaged life: His increasing need for heroin in increasing doses prevents him from working, from maintaining relationships, from developing in human ways. Similarly an alcoholic's life is narrowed and dehumanized by his dependence on alcohol. 5

Let us consider television viewing in the light of the conditions that define serious addictions. 6

Not unlike drugs or alcohol, the television experience allows the participant to blot out the real world and enter into a pleasurable and passive mental state. The worries and anxieties of reality are as effectively deferred by becoming absorbed in a television program as by going on a "trip" induced by drugs or alcohol. And just as alcoholics are only inchoately aware of their addiction, feeling that they control their drinking more than they really do ("I can cut it out any time I want—I just like to have three or four drinks before dinner"), people similarly overestimate their control over television watching. Even as they put off other activities to spend hour after hour watching television, they feel they could easily resume living in a different, less passive style. But somehow or other while the television set is present in their homes, the click doesn't sound. With television pleasures available, those other experiences seem less attractive, more difficult somehow. 7

A heavy viewer (a college English instructor) observes: "I find television almost irresistible. When the set is on, I cannot ignore it. I can't turn it off. I feel sapped, will-less, enervated. As I reach out to turn off the set, the strength goes out of my arms. So I sit there for hours and hours." 8

The self-confessed television addict often feels he "ought" to do other things—but the fact that he doesn't read and doesn't plant his garden or sew or crochet or play games or have conversations means that those activities are no longer as desirable as television viewing. In a way a heavy viewer's life is as 9 imbalanced by his television "habit" as a drug addict's or an alcoholic's. He is living in a holding pattern, as it were, passing up the activities that lead to growth or development or a sense of accomplishment. This is one reason people talk about their television viewing so ruefully, so apologetically. They are aware that it is an unproductive experience, that almost any other endeavor is more worthwhile by any human measure.

10   Finally, it is the adverse effect of television viewing on the lives of so many people that defines it as a serious addiction. The television habit distorts the sense of time. It renders other experiences vague and curiously unreal while taking on a greater reality for itself. It weakens relationships by reducing and sometimes eliminating normal opportunities for talking, for communicating.

11   And yet television does not satisfy, else why would the viewer continue to watch hour after hour, day after day? "The measure of health," writes Lawrence Kubie, "is flexibility . . . and especially the freedom to cease when sated." But the television viewer can never be sated with his television experiences—they do not provide the true nourishment that satiation requires—and thus he finds that he cannot stop watching.

William Raspberry

The Handicap of Definition

William Raspberry (b. 1935) is a Pulitzer Prize-winning writer and a professor of journalism and communications at Duke University. His *Washington Post* column on minority affairs now appears in over 180 newspapers. While his columns often cover the difficult issues of race relations and social development, he remains cautiously optimistic. "I am a hopeful person," commented Raspberry in a 1995 interview, "and I think that there is a reasonable chance that people here and there, not all at once, will wake up to what we need to do and not sit around waiting for the politicians to come riding in to save us. It's the only way we're going to get anywhere." In this essay, he comments on the problems created by society's narrow definition of "black."

1   I KNOW ALL ABOUT BAD SCHOOLS, mean politicians, economic deprivation and racism. Still, it occurs to me that one of the heaviest burdens black Americans—and black children in particular—have to bear is the handicap of definition: the question of what it means to be black.

2   Let me explain quickly what I mean. If a basketball fan says that the Boston Celtics' Larry Bird plays "black," the fan intends it—and Bird probably

accepts it—as a compliment. Tell pop singer Tom Jones he moves "black" and he might grin in appreciation. Say to Teena Marie or The Average White Band that they sound "black" and they'll thank you.

But name one pursuit, aside from athletics, entertainment or sexual perfor- 3
mance in which a white practitioner will feel complimented to be told he does it "black." Tell a white broadcaster he talks "black" and he'll sign up for diction lessons. Tell a white reporter he writes "black" and he'll take a writing course. Tell a white lawyer he reasons "black" and he might sue you for slander.

What we have here is a tragically limited definition of blackness, and it 4
isn't only white people who buy it.

Think of all the ways black children can put one another down with 5
charges of "whiteness." For many of these children, hard study and hard work are "white." Trying to please a teacher might be criticized as acting "white." Speaking correct English is "white." Scrimping today in the interest of to-morrow's goals is "white." Educational toys and games are "white."

An incredible array of habits and attitudes that are conducive to success 6
in business, in academia, in the non-entertainment professions are likely to be thought of as somehow "white." Even economic success, unless it involves such "black" undertakings as numbers banking, is defined as "white."

And the results are devastating. I wouldn't deny that blacks often are bet- 7
ter entertainers and athletes. My point is the harm that comes from too nar-row a definition of what is black.

One reason black youngsters tend to do better at basketball, for instance, 8
is that they assume they can learn to do it well, and so they practice constantly to prove themselves right.

Wouldn't it be wonderful if we could infect black children with the notion 9
that excellence in math is "black" rather than white, or possibly Chinese? Wouldn't it be of enormous value if we could create the myth that morality, strong families, determination, courage and love of learning are traits brought by slaves from Mother Africa and therefore quintessentially black?

There is no doubt in my mind that most black youngsters could develop 10
their mathematical reasoning, their elocution and their attitudes the way they develop their jump shots and their dance steps: by the combination of sus-tained, enthusiastic practice and the unquestioned belief that they can do it.

In one sense, what I am talking about is the importance of developing posi- 11
tive ethnic traditions. Maybe Jews have an innate talent for communication; maybe the Chinese are born with a gift for mathematical reasoning; maybe blacks are naturally blessed with athletic grace. I doubt it. What is at work, I suspect, is assumption, inculcated early in their lives, that this is a thing our people do well.

Unfortunately, many of the things about which blacks make this assump- 12
tion are things that do not contribute to their career success—except for that handful of the truly gifted who can make it as entertainers and athletes. And

many of the things we concede to whites are the things that are essential to economic security. So it is with a number of assumptions black youngsters make about what it is to be a "man": physical aggressiveness, sexual prowess, the refusal to submit to authority. The prisons are full of people who, by this perverted definition, are unmistakably men.

13   But the real problem is not so much that the things defined as "black" are negative. The problem is that the definition is much too narrow.

14   Somehow, we have to make our children understand that they are intelligent, competent people, capable of doing whatever they put their minds to and making it in the American mainstream, not just in a black subculture.

15   What we seem to be doing, instead, is raising up yet another generation of young blacks who will be failures—by definition.

Gloria Naylor

"Mommy, What Does 'Nigger' Mean?"

Gloria Naylor (b. 1950) grew up "thinking that black people didn't write books." However, reading Toni Morrison's *The Bluest Eye* in 1977 inspired her to write her first novel, *The Women of Brewster Place*, which won the National Book Award for best first novel in 1983. She has continued to write stories that portray the African-American experience, often mixing realism and fantasy. Her belief that "myth is more powerful and lasting than reality" not only forms a foundation for her mystical characters, but also underlies her perception of society's racial tension. "It took only one generation to remove all the cultural traits of the Africans, except the color of their skin—thus promoting the myth" that some people are more human than others. Here she explores the myth buried in just one word.

1   LANGUAGE IS THE SUBJECT. It is the written form with which I've managed to keep the wolf away from the door and, in diaries, to keep my sanity. In spite of this, I consider the written word inferior to the spoken, and much of the frustration experienced by novelists is the awareness that whatever we manage to capture in even the most transcendent passages falls far short of the richness of life. Dialogue achieves its power in the dynamics of a fleeting moment of sight, sound, smell and touch.

2   I'm not going to enter the debate here about whether it is language that shapes reality or vice versa. That battle is doomed to be waged whenever we seek intermittent reprieve from the chicken and egg dispute. I will simply

take the position that the spoken word, like the written word, amounts to a nonsensical arrangement of sounds or letters without a consensus that assigns "meaning." And building from the meanings of what we hear, we order reality. Words themselves are innocuous; it is the consensus that gives them true power.

I remember the first time I heard the word nigger. In my third-grade class,   3
our math tests were being passed down the rows, and as I handed the papers to a little boy in back of me, I remarked that once again he had received a much lower mark than I did. He snatched his test from me and spit out that word. Had he called me a nymphomaniac or a necrophiliac, I couldn't have been more puzzled. I didn't know what a nigger was, but I knew that whatever it meant, it was something he shouldn't have called me. This was verified when I raised my hand, and in a loud voice repeated what he had said and watched the teacher scold him for using a "bad" word. I was later to go home and ask the inevitable question that every black parent must face—"Mommy, what does 'nigger' mean?"

And what exactly did it mean? Thinking back, I realize that this could not   4
have been the first time the word was used in my presence. I was part of a large extended family that had migrated from the rural South after World War II and formed a close-knit network that gravitated around my maternal grandparents. Their ground-floor apartment in one of the buildings they owned in Harlem was a weekend mecca for my immediate family, along with countless aunts, uncles and cousins who brought along assorted friends. It was a bustling and open house with assorted neighbors and tenants popping in and out to exchange bits of gossip, pick up an old quarrel or referee the ongoing checkers game in which my grandmother cheated shamelessly. They were all there to let down their hair and put up their feet after a week of labor in the factories, laundries and shipyards of New York.

Amid the clamor, which could reach deafening proportions—two or three   5
conversations going on simultaneously, punctuated by the sound of a baby's crying somewhere in the back rooms or out on the street—there was still a rigid set of rules about what was said and how. Older children were sent out of the living room when it was time to get into the juicy details about "you-know-who" up on the third floor who had gone and gotten herself "p-r-e-g-n-a-n-t!" But my parents, knowing that I could spell well beyond my years, always demanded that I follow the others out to play. Beyond sexual misconduct and death, everything else was considered harmless for our young ears. And so among the anecdotes of the triumphs and disappointments in the various workings of their lives, the word nigger was used in my presence, but it was set within contexts and inflections that caused it to register in my mind as something else.

6   In the singular, the word was always applied to a man who had distinguished himself in some situation that brought their approval for his strength, intelligence or drive:

7   "Did Johnny really do that?"

8   "I'm telling you, that nigger pulled in $6,000 of overtime last year. Said he got enough for a down payment on a house."

9   When used with a possessive adjective by a woman—"my nigger"—it became a term of endearment for husband or boyfriend. But it could be more than just a term applied to a man. In their mouths it became the pure essence of manhood—a disembodied force that channeled their past history of struggle and present survival against the odds into a victorious statement of being: "Yeah, that old foreman found out quick enough—you don't mess with a nigger."

10   In the plural, it became a description of some group within the community that had overstepped the bounds of decency as my family defined it: Parents who neglected their children, a drunken couple who fought in public, people who simply refused to look for work, those with excessively dirty mouths or unkempt households were all "trifling niggers." This particular circle could forgive hard times, unemployment, the occasional bout of depression—they had gone through all of that themselves—but the unforgivable sin was lack of self-respect.

11   A woman could never be a "nigger" in the singular, with its connotation of confirming worth. The noun girl was its closest equivalent in that sense, but only when used in direct address and regardless of the gender doing the addressing. "Girl" was a token of respect for a woman. The one-syllable word was drawn out to sound like three in recognition of the extra ounce of wit, nerve or daring that the woman had shown in the situation under discussion.

12   "G-i-r-l, stop. You mean you said that to his face?"

13   But if the word was used in a third-person reference or shortened so that it almost snapped out of the mouth, it always involved some element of communal disapproval. And age became an important factor in these exchanges. It was only between individuals of the same generation, or from an older person to a younger (but never the other way around), that "girl" would be considered a compliment.

14   I don't agree with the argument that use of the word nigger at this social stratum of the black community was an internalization of racism. The dynamics were the exact opposite: the people in my grandmother's living room took a word that whites used to signify worthlessness or degradation and rendered it impotent. Gathering there together, they transformed "nigger" to signify the varied and complex human beings they knew themselves to be. If the word was to disappear totally from the mouths of even the most racist of white society, no one in that room was naïve enough to believe it would disappear

from white minds. Meeting the word head-on, they proved it had absolutely nothing to do with the way they were determined to live their lives.

So there must have been dozens of times that the word "nigger" was spo- 15
ken in front of me before I reached the third grade. But I didn't "hear" it until it was said by a small pair of lips that had already learned it could be a way to humiliate me. That was the word I went home and asked my mother about. And since she knew that I had to grow up in America, she took me in her lap and explained.

Student Essay

Jason Gray

Questioning the Nature of Intelligence

Jason wrote this research paper for an advanced psychology course, but it is also relevant for general readers. Nearly everyone has been exposed to an IQ test at some point during their lives, but few of us understand what the concept of IQ really means. Jason clears up some of these issues by taking a historical approach to his definition, beginning with some of the pioneers of intellegence testing and finishing with contemporary research on the topic.

FROM A VERY YOUNG AGE, INDIVIDUALS BEGIN TO RECOGNIZE differences among 1
their peers. Some friends are faster, some stronger, some taller, and others shorter. Some friends have a different skin color. Some friends seem very bright and others seem never to understand. This incredible range of differences, which makes each human being unique, is the product of a number of different factors. Physical attributes, such as appearance, build, hair color, and eye color are primarily determined by inherited genetic make-up, even though environment can have many dramatic effects on early development (fetal alcohol syndrome, exposure to toxins in infancy, etc.). Mental attributes are much tougher to pin down and harder to accept as strictly the product of DNA. Is an enjoyment of Pearl Jam and chocolate ice cream over Mozart and vanilla really a matter of biochemistry or brain structure?

What about intelligence, where does it fit in? A much less arbitrary at- 2
tribute than one's favorite ice cream flavor; however, individuals still have difficulty accepting brain power as 100% a matter of genes. Formal instruction and other environmental factors seem to affect how intelligent a person appears. Yet, the size of our brains is just as inherited as the size of our nose. Psy-

chologists have been trying to make sense of this issue since the very beginning of the discipline.

3   The most recent and controversial addition to the debate has come from Herrnstein and Murray's publication, *The Bell Curve: Intelligence and Class Structure in American Life*. The book argues strongly in favor of the belief that intelligence is primarily inherited. They use the heritability argument as a explanation of class stratification in America. The poor are poor because they lack the inherited ability to be anything better. Conversely, the successful individuals have become wealthy because of their natural ability to take on more highly skilled professions such as medicine and the law, which pay better. Their theory is reminiscent of Social Darwinism, which was popular in the late 1800s but eventually fell out of favor. Herrnstein and Murray did not go as far as suggesting programs of eugenics, but the tone of their writing has much the same superior feel. However, this does not discount their argument that economic separation of the races is based on genetic differences in intelligence. Science seems to have come full circle. Might Social Darwinism have been correct all those years ago, just lacking significant evidence to back it up? Herrnstein and Murray present a convincing case for the modern equivalent and suggest that unless society is dramatically restructured the situation of the underclass is only going to get worse.

4   Many scholars from a variety of fields launched an all out assault on their work. Some writers, particularly Stephen Jay Gould, opened up a number of interesting holes in their theory which resulted in more unanswered questions. First, Gould points out that their entire argument is based on four principles of intelligence and should any one of them be proven false their entire argument falls apart. He says Herrnstein and Murray's four principles assert that intelligence can be described as "a single number, capable of ranking people in linear order, genetically based, and effectively immutable" (Gould, 1994).

5   Once the accuracy of the four elements underpinning Herrnstein and Murray's notion of intelligence are analyzed, a better assessment of their overall argument can be made. In the end, more unanswered questions will be raised by this process than were started with and consideration will be given to these issues, as well as the direction of future work in the field of intelligence.

6   The earliest scientific investigations of the nature of intelligence are traced to Sir Francis Galton and his book *Hereditary Genius* (1869). Galton establishes the concept of the standard deviation curve (bell curve) and uses it to make clear to the reader what he means by superior intelligence. To Galton, truly superior intellects constituted only the very smallest part of the tail, those who scored more than three standard deviations above the mean on the

Cambridge mathematical exams. Closely examining this very small population, he found that all of these people were somehow distantly related. From this he concluded that intelligence must run in families and therefore be an inherited trait.

Galton became a controversial figure for his suggestion of eugenics programs, where the best and brightest got together to have children and the less intelligent, lower classes are discouraged from having children (Weiten, 1995). Out of *Heriditary Genius* and Darwin's *Origin of Species*, Social Darwinism developed. Important to our modern debate about *The Bell Curve*, Galton argued that intelligence was immutable. He used the analogy of an athlete to describe mental abilities, saying that a man can work out for many years and gain strength and speed, but he inevitably reaches a maximum potential beyond which his strength cannot increase to match other men of greater size. He says that the same is true for mental ability (Galton, 1869).   7

The first test devised solely to be a measure of intelligence was put together by Alfred Binet and Theodore Simon in 1905 to help single out children in need of special assistance. The test turned out to be very good for predicting student success in school. Binet and Simon also developed the concept of mental age in relation to chronological age as a means of measuring whether a student was ahead or behind in their schooling. In 1916 Lewis Terman published his revision to the original Binet scale, called the Stanford-Binet Intelligence Scale. The test was revolutionary because of its incorporation of the new scoring system, developed by William Stern, which we still use today. The system introduced the "intelligence quotient" or IQ. This was defined as the child's mental age divided by their chronological age, multiplied by 100. The Stanford-Binet test became the standard of intelligence by which all future tests were correlated to ascertain their validity (Weiten, 1995).   8

Binet views intelligence as being more malleable than Galton and his athletic analogy. Binet is quoted as saying: 9

The intelligence of anyone is susceptible to development. With practice, enthusiasm and especially with method one can succeed in increasing one's attention, memory, judgement, and in becoming literally more intelligent than one was before (Weiten, 1995).   10

However, this statement does not directly refute what Galton said. Galton agreed that with work one could improve their intelligence, just that there was an upper limit to the amount of improvement and that this upper limit was set by our inheritance.   11

The next major development in the field of testing came from David Wechsler and his construction of the Wechsler Adult Intelligence Scale (WAIS). This was important for two reasons. First, he included problems that   12 required non-verbal reasoning. Second, scoring was based on a normal distribution, akin to the modern day bell curve. Most IQ tests today use a normal distribution, but the term IQ remains. About his test, Wechsler said, "The subtests are different measures of intelligence, not measures of different kinds of intelligence" (Weiten, 1995). The importance of this concept will be brought to light when the modern approaches, suggesting multiple types of intelligences, are discussed.

13   Charles Spearman presented the final development in the historical view of intelligence. Using the method of factor analysis (which he developed), he looked at correlations among different tests that assessed specific cognitive abilities. Among all these correlations, he concluded that all the diverse tests shared a single core component, which he labeled g. g is often considered to be a general mental ability that is expressed through a variety of different mental tasks. Since the emergence of Spearman's theory, intelligence tests have attempted to correlate as highly as possible with g (Weiten, 1995).

14   Some modern theorists have separated from attempts to find a single overarching test and attempted to quantify the different components of intelligence separately. This will be discussed thoroughly in the next section. One other major modern development has been the use of completely non-verbal intelligence tests, the most widely used of these tests being the Raven's Progressive Matrices Test, which has been correlated with traditional intelligence tests in order to yield the same type of numerical value.

15   Already, the issues that Stephen Jay Gould raised in response to *The Bell Curve* are beginning to come to light. Is intelligence necessarily a single, immutable number? Binet and Galton seemed to be of different minds about the issue of immutability. Wechsler expressed the belief that intelligence is a single number that can be quantified in a number of different ways. Most importantly, differences in testing are now being brought forward. The difference between the Stanford-Binet and Raven's test is dramatic. Yet, they each claim to be testing the same thing. Is it possible to make sense of which is better? In order to get a handle on this problem, a better definition of intelligence is necessary. If intelligence is just ability to abstract, then Raven's is likely to be a very good measure. If a broader view of intelligence is taken and acquired general knowledge is included in one's definition, then the Stanford-Binet might be considered to be more accurate. In addition to the knowledge vs. abstraction distinction, the tests also differ in their manner of presentation. The questions in the Stanford-Binet are all verbally based, whereas the Raven's requires no verbal ability to solve its matrices. Clearly, many questions still remained to be answered.

16   Robert Sternberg has pioneered one of the newest fields of assessment, called dynamic testing. The goal of dynamic testing is to quantify specifically the ability to learn, regardless of one's level of acquired knowledge. In most

experiments, equal emphasis is put on testing and intervention, following the test-intervention-retest model. Much of this work has focused on assisting learning-disabled children or children who perform poorly in static testing situations.

Budoff conducted a study in which subjects were given a battery of differ- 17 ent verbal and non-verbal IQ tests. They were then trained in problem solving techniques essential to achieving a good score and retested. Scores were found to improve (Grigorenko & Sternberg, 1998).

Another important distinction is the difference between academic intel- 18 ligence (book smarts) and practical intelligence (street smarts). Individuals who exhibit complicated problem solving and abstraction skills on the job and in other settings but only have minimal education are considered pri-mary examples in favor of practical intelligence as something distinct from academic intelligence. Racetrack handicappers and individuals who work on assembly lines are two specific cases where the average subject has no more than a high school education, but they are able to use complicated strategies to minimize the number of moves they have to make or maximize their profits, which more educated subjects can't figure out initially (Stern-berg, et al., 1995).

However, challengers to the theory of practical intelligence suggest that it 19 is no different from academic intelligence. They argue that individuals who failed to achieve in an academic setting but succeeded on the job may have lacked motivation or been facing other environmental issues when going through adolescence, etc. That does not change their ability to perform com-plex tasks. There is some experimental evidence against this. In a study of smart shoppers in California (individuals who could perform mathematical calculations quickly in their head to decide which size product is the best buy) conducted by Lave, et al., (1995) no relation was found between shopping ac-curacy and performance on the MIT mental arithmetic test.

Although dynamic assessment and practical intelligence are both very new 20 fields, early studies have shown that there exist aspects of mental capacity that traditional psychometric tests fail to quantify. The dynamic tests are clearly better for distinguishing among lower achievers who still have potential and those that may still be beyond help. Psychometric testing, and in fact, pen and paper testing in general may be missing a whole field of cognitive problem solving that is now being defined as practical intelligence. This exposes a num-ber of holes in Herrnstein and Murray's argument. Most importantly these tests seem to speak to the question of immutability of intelligence. For in-stance, why does academic intelligence increase with age until early adulthood when it begins to decline? Also, the traditional psychometric tests do not seem to be accurate predictors of some individuals' ability to learn, weakening their dismissal of the underclass as being unable to achieve.

21   Knowledge about the inner workings of inheritance has greatly improved since the time of Galton. The discovery of DNA and the implications that came along with understanding the mechanism of evolution revolutionized thinking in the fields of psychology and biology. Genetic theory along with other new technologies has sparked a feverish search for the physiological mechanisms connected with brain behavior. This trend can be seen in every field, from sensation and perception to the study of intelligence. The last ten years have been particularly fruitful in the search for what it is about the brain that makes someone smart.

22   These correlative and physiological findings suggest that Herrnstein and Murray are just wrong about the immutability of intelligence, even though a large portion of intelligence may be genetically determined. The data from Reed and Jensen, clearly showing that environmental effects not only manifest themselves as increased test scores but also as structural differences in the brain, can be explained away simply as a person maximizing their genetically given range. This is fine, but also inherent in the argument in *The Bell Curve* is that all people in the lower class are there because that's as smart as they can be. This certainly seems not to be the case. Scarr and Weinberg demonstrated otherwise by their study in which kids were taken into enriched environments and their scores improved. Given all the evidence that has come forward, even prior to the publication of *The Bell Curve*, it is difficult to believe Herrnstein and Murray would put forth the argument they did.

23   In light of the evidence, the four pillars of Herrnstein and Murray's argument do not seem as solid as the authors suggest in *The Bell Curve*. Their principle of immutability of intelligence has been brought into question. Modern methods of dynamic assessment have exposed weaknesses in the traditional tests used as the intelligence measure in *The Bell Curve*. Additionally, new theories of practical intelligence have identified a different type of cognitive reasoning involving both problem solving and abstraction skills that is not quantified by traditional tests. Finally, physiological and correlational studies have shown that despite the large amount of heritability in intelligence, environment can produce dramatic cognitive and structural changes in the subject.

24   This is not to suggest that psychometric testing is dead, only that *The Bell Curve* presents a distasteful social argument based on a number of questionable assumptions about intelligence taken to be fact by the authors. This paper sought to illustrate the inaccuracy of these assumptions as a means of looking at the current work in the intelligence field. Psychometric testing remains, in fact, the best predictor of success that can be economically administered to large populations and give a rough estimate of an individual's ability. Modern methods of testing are more accurate, but cannot be administered efficiently to large populations. These traditional tests will most likely be used as the primary means of roughly assessing a subject's ability for many years to

come. The danger of these IQ tests is when individuals such as Herrnstein and Murray attempt to read too much into what a single number tells.

The fact of the matter is that even psychologists are split over what the 25 number represents. From Spearman's g to Sternberg's theory of practical intelligence, what exactly constitutes intelligence is still uncertain. Also, the new theories of dynamic assessment and practical intelligence have yet to be fully developed. A great deal of investigation into these fields is still necessary. The physiological field is another area which is quite new and has the potential for incredible expansion in the future. The intelligence field is undergoing a time of great change, likely to redefine the way mental capacity is discussed.

References

Carpenter, P., et al. (1990). What One Intelligence Test Measures: A Theoretical Account of the Processing in the Raven Progressive Matrices Test. *Psychological Review, 97(3)*, 404–431.

Daniel, M.H. (1997). Intelligence Testing: Status and Trends. *American Psychologist, 52(10)*, 1038–1045.

Galton, F. (1869). *Hereditary Genius: Its Laws and Consequences*. New York: D. Appleton & Co. pp. 45–88.

Gardner, H. (1994). Cracking Open the IQ Box. *The American Prospect*, Winter 1994.

Gould, S.J. (1994). Curveball. *The New Yorker*, Nov. 28, 1994.

Grigorenko, E. & Sternberg, R. (1998). Dynamic Testing. *Psychological Bulletin, 124(1)*, 75–111.

Herrnstein R.J., & Murray, C. (1994). *The Bell Curve: Intelligence and Class Structure in American Life*. New York: Free Press. p. introduction-summaries-conclusions.

Myerson, J., Rank, M.R., Raines, F.Q., & Schnitzler, M.A. (1998). Race and General Cognitive Ability: The Myth of Diminishing Returns to Education. *Psychological Science, 9(2)*, 139–142.

Neisser, U., et al. (1996). Intelligence: Knowns and Unknowns. *American Psychologist, 51(2)*, 77–101.

Prabhakaran, V., et al. (1997). Neural Substrates of Fluid Reasoning: An fMRI Study of Neocortical Activation during Performance of the Raven's Progressive Matrices Test. *Cognitive Psychology, 33*, 43–63.

Reed, T.E. (1993). Effects of Enriched (Complex) Environment on Nerve

Conduction Velocity: New Data and Review of Implications for the Speed of Information Processing. *Intelligence, 17,* 533–540.

Reed, T.E., & Jensen, A.R. (1991). Arm Nerve Conduction Velocity (NCV), Brain NCV, Reaction Time, and Intelligence. *Intelligence, 15,* 33–47.

Reed, T.E., & Jensen, A.R. (1992). Conduction Velocity in a Brain Nerve Pathway of Normal Adults Correlates with Intelligence Level. *Intelligence, 16,* 259–272.

Reed, T.E., & Jensen, A.R. (1993). A Somatosensory Latency Between the Thalamus and Cortex also Correlates with Level of Intelligence. *Intelligence, 17,* 443–450.

Saccuzzo, D. & Johnson, N. (1995). Traditional Psychometric Tests and Proportionate Representation: An Intervention and Program Evaluation Study. *Psychological Assessment, 7(2),* 183–194.

Sternberg, R.J., Wagner, R.K., Williams, W.M., & Horvath, J.A. (1995). Testing Common Sense. *American Psychologist, 50(11),* 912–927.

Weiten, W. (1995). *Psychology: Themes and Variations* 3rd Ed. Pacific Grove: Brooks/Cole Publishing Co. pp. 333–374.

10

Argument

Argument

1. **Formulate a clear thesis.** Argument is simply writing to convince someone either to agree with your point of view, or to change their behavior in the manner you desire. The best arguments, therefore, must clearly present the action or opinion the author would like the reader to adopt—a thesis statement. Virginia Woolf's thesis is (at least in part) "it would have been impossible, completely and entirely, for any woman to have written the plays of Shakespeare in the age of Shakespeare." Needless to say, you'll never convince your readers to do or think anything unless you know in advance what you want them to do or think.

2. **Anticipate your audience's response.** Will your readers be hostile to your argument? Generally agreeable? Depending on how you expect your audience to respond, you may want to state your thesis right away, or hold it back until the right moment.

3. **Appeal to your audience's emotions.** The theoretical discussion of argument began thousands of years ago with the ancient Greeks. Even then, philosophers realized that one of the most powerful methods of persuasion was to appeal to the audience's emotions. The same holds true today—for most of us, emotions are what make an argument *matter*. The most logical argument in the world won't convince anyone if it can easily be dismissed with "so what?"

4. **Support your argument with sound reasoning.** Logic is the basis for any sound argument. Volumes have been written about logic, but one of the most useful ways to use logic to support an argument is the data-claim-warrant model. This model, devised by the British philosopher Stephen Toulmin, suggests that any argument has three parts:

McGwire holds the single-season home run record
data

Mark McGwire is the best baseball player in history
claim

The best baseball player is the player who can hit the most home runs in a single season
warrant

Any claim an author makes is based on a warrant, which is usually unstated. Only when the warrant is made explicit can the strength or weakness of a given argument be seen. It's a good idea to identify all three parts to each argument you make to ensure that your reasoning is sound.

The American Center for Law and Justice

School Prayer (pro position)

Freedom of religion is one of the fundamental rights on which our nation is based. Many of the first settlers of America came here to escape a government that made it difficult to practice their chosen religion. Isn't it ironic, then, that children are restricted from practicing religion in schools supported by that same government? The Supreme Court has ruled that the Constitution allows student prayer on school grounds during noninstructional time if a school allows other student activities the same privilege (in the *Mergens* case mentioned below). The American Center for Law and Justice, an organization devoted to preserving the freedom of religious speech, argues that that right is not enough. If students can't pray at graduation ceremonies, or are told they can't do book reports on religious figures, all in the name of separation of church and state, then the Constitution itself must be changed.

FOR THE PAST SIX YEARS, WE HAVE DEDICATED a substantial amount of our resources to defend students who desire to pray and have Bible and prayer clubs at the public schools. In 1990, when we argued the Bible club case, *Westside Community Schools v. Mergens* before the U.S. Supreme Court, we committed substantial resources in order for our organization to stand up for students whenever their rights are being denied because of their faith.   1

The amount of requests for assistance for cases involving the public schools are increasing at an unprecedented rate. Despite the passage of the Equal Access Act in 1984 and the Supreme Court's decision in *Mergens*, students across our land are being denied fundamental rights of freedom of speech, including the right to pray.   2

This fact hit home most recently when the U.S. Court of Appeals for the Ninth Circuit, on November 18, 1994, ruled that student prayer at a graduation ceremony was unconstitutional. The Ninth Circuit held that there was "no meaningful distinction between school authorities actually organizing the religious activities and officials merely permitting students to direct the exercises" (*Harris v. Joint School District No. 241*).   3

This decision of the Ninth Circuit runs contrary to the language written by the Supreme Court in the *Mergens* case, which noted that "there is a crucial difference between government speech endorsing religion which the Establishment Clause forbids, and private speech endorsing religion which the Free Speech and Free Exercise Clauses protect."   4

We have consistently taken the position that students have the right to share their faith at graduation ceremonies through testimony, or through prayer. This apparently is not the view of the U.S. Court of Appeals for the   5

Ninth Circuit. This decision, left unchecked, could create a further zone of hostility for religious students on public school campuses. This is why we need some affirmative protection for religious liberty for students.

6   When the debate began on the constitutional amendment for prayer these past few weeks, we initially were hesitant to take a public position. After reviewing the proposed amendment to the Constitution, however, and then recommending to Congressman Istook and others significant changes to the language, we are convinced that if we work through the amendment process we can obtain justice for students in our Nation's public schools.

7   The language we have proposed is this:

8   Nothing in this Constitution shall be construed to prohibit individual or group prayer by students in the public schools, or individual or group prayer in other public institutions. No person shall be required by the United States or by any State to participate in prayer. Neither the United States nor any State shall compose the words of any prayer to be said in public schools.

9   Our proposed language focuses on students not being denied the right to have prayer at their pubic schools. We have seen the abuses that students have been confronted with when they have been threatened with arrest, have been arrested for praying around their school flagpole, suspected for possession of Christian material on campus, or told that establishing a Bible club would violate the separation of church and state. By using the word "students," and possibly including the word student-initiated or student-led, we will be in a position to affirmatively protect students who desire to pray on public school campuses.

10   We need to see affirmative protection for students on the public school campus who want to exercise their faith. We have reached a point in our country where we have more of a freedom from religion than a freedom of religion.

11   When students are told that they cannot pray at graduation ceremonies, when the president of a Christian Bible club is told to remove the word "God" or "Jesus" from a sign advertising the club meetings, and when students are told that they cannot do book reports on historical figures if those figures are referenced in the Bible, we have a serious misunderstanding of freedom and liberty.

12   Based on the surveys we have seen, and the phone calls and letters that pour into our offices, it's time for affirmative protection for students who want to engage in prayer in our Nation's public schools. Do we want to have a constitutional amendment? No. We certainly would have been more satisfied if the courts simply upheld the true understanding of freedom and liberty, but in many circumstances they have not.

13   For those students involved in the Ninth Circuit decision, their freedom was lost on November 18, 1994, when the Court held that students could not pray at graduation. Through this constitutional amendment process not only

is the issue of school prayer placed before the Nation, but we have an opportunity to see a change in the right direction for freedom.

Americans United for the
Separation of Church and State

School Prayer (con position)

Discussing politics or religion has always been a sure way to get into a fight. It's no surprise that the issue of school prayer has caused its own share of conflicts. As this selection points out, Americans have been fighting about prayer in public schools for almost as long as public schools have existed. Why all the strident debate over perhaps one minute of our children's time in schools? Isn't the Constitution clear on this point? Perhaps the problem is the Constitution, for nowhere does the Constitution say "separation of church and state" or "freedom of religion." The actual text of the First Amendment reads as follows: "Congress shall make no law respecting an establishment of religion, or prohibiting the free exercise thereof. . . ." If you place the emphasis on the first part of the passage, you could argue that school prayer respects "an establishment of religion," and so should not be allowed. On the other hand, if you focus on the second part, which says that Congress can't "prohibit the free exercise" of religion, you can come to the opposite conclusion. Here's a reading that takes the first position. It's a statement by Americans United for the Separation of Church and State, whose belief is that the best way to preserve religion is to keep the government out of it.

IN 1843, AN UGLY RIOT ROCKED THE PHILADELPHIA SUBURB of Kensington. For   1
three days, mobs roamed the streets of the City of Brotherly Love as the police struggled to regain control. When it was all over, several buildings had been reduced to rubble, and 13 people were dead.

The Philadelphia riot was notable for its particularly violent character, but   2
what's even more unusual is what sparked it. The country was restless with pre-Civil War tensions at the time, but it wasn't race relations, slavery, or "preserving the union" that tore the community asunder. The people of Philadelphia rioted over prayer in public schools.

Tensions between Roman Catholics and Protestants were near the break-   3
ing point in mid-19th century America, and public schools had become the flash point. When local education officials in southeastern Pennsylvania assented to Catholic demands and ruled that Catholic children could be excused from mandatory daily—and generally Protestant—Bible reading and prayer, the Protestant majority generated a violent backlash.

The incident is worth remembering as the nationwide debate over religion   4 in public schools resumes again, thanks to soon-to-be Speaker of the House Newt Gingrich's promise to hold a congressional vote on a school prayer amendment by July 4.

5   Prayer in schools is one of the most misunderstood social concerns Americans face today. Many people wonder why the issue is so emotional. What is the harm, they ask, in a little prayer.

6   What these people fail to understand is that religious passions run deep. Many Americans are offended by the idea that their children may be forced to participate in religious exercises in public school that clash with what the children are taught at home or at the family's house of worship. These parents rightly see school prayer as a usurpation of parental authority.

7   Other parents have no desire to have their children participate in the type of bland, watered-down prayers that are commonly offered for public consumption. They cite the words of Jesus from the sixth book of Matthew who, in cautioning against gaudy public displays of religion, said, "When you pray, enter your closet and shut the door. Pray to your Father, who is in secret, and your Father, who sees in secret, will reward you openly."

8   As the religious pluralism of the United States continues to expand, it is impossible that a "To-Whom-It-May-Concern" prayer could be fashioned that would please fundamentalist Protestants and Roman Catholics as well as Jews, Buddhists, Muslims, and the thousands of other religious groups. Even if this type of prayer could be written, who would care to recite such theological pablum?

9   Some school prayer advocates suggest letting each community decide what prayer is recited. If Southern Baptists predominate, for example, the Lord's Prayer would be recited. If Catholics hold sway, it will be the Our Father.

10   Such a "majority rules" set-up would violate the right of conscience of millions of American schoolchildren. Their choice would be to either participate in religious ceremonies alien to them or risk ostracism by getting up and leaving the room.

11   In a country that was founded on religious freedom, this is an unfair situation to put any child in, especially very young children, who may not even understand what is going on.

12   The great tragedy of the school prayer debate is that it is unnecessary. Nothing in the Constitution now prohibits children from engaging in truly voluntary prayer. They may pray at the beginning of the day, over lunch, before tests, at any time they have a free moment.

13   Under the Federal Equal Access Act, high school students may even form prayer clubs and meet outside class hours for Bible study and worship. No court in the land has ever struck down personal religious devotions.

14   Despite the rhetoric, what Gingrich and some of his colleagues are offering is not voluntary prayer. The wording of the proposed amendment says that "group prayer" will be permitted in public schools.

In other words, the entire class, at the direction of a teacher or school of- 15
ficial, can be ordered to recite a prayer. The only option for those who choose
not to take part is to grin and bear it or get up and leave. There is nothing
"voluntary" about this type of coercion.

Religion is best left as a private matter, as the Nation's founders intended. 16
It should never be forced onto anyone, especially a child. Public schools are for
educating children about the basics—reading, 'riting, and 'rithmetic. Let's leave
the "fourth R," religion, where it rightly belongs—in the homes and houses of
worship of our country.

Virginia Woolf

If Shakespeare Had Had a Sister

Virginia Woolf (1882–1941) was a poet, essayist, editor, and most notably, a novelist. She was the focus of
the "Bloomsbury Group," a gathering of important thinkers, including T. S. Eliot, John Maynard Keynes, and
E. M. Forster, who had wide influence in the early part of this century. In this passage from *A Room of One's
Own* (1929), she builds a convincing case that a woman in Elizabethan England would never have been allowed the opportunity to create works like Shakespeare's plays.

IT IS A PERENNIAL PUZZLE WHY NO WOMAN WROTE A WORD of that extraordinary 1
[Elizabethan] literature when every other man, it seemed, was capable of song
or sonnet. What were the conditions in which women lived, I asked myself; for
fiction, imaginative work that is, is not dropped like a pebble upon the ground,
as science may be; fiction is like a spider's web, attached ever so lightly perhaps,
but still attached to life at all four corners. Often the attachment is scarcely perceptible; Shakespeare's plays, for instance, seem to hang there complete by
themselves. But when the web is pulled askew, hooked up at the edge, torn in
the middle, one remembers that these webs are not spun in midair by incor-
poreal creatures, but are the work of suffering human beings, and are attached
to grossly material things, like health and money and the houses we live in. . . .

But what I find . . . is that nothing is known about women before the eigh- 2
teenth century. I have no model in my mind to turn about this way and that.
Here am I asking why women did not write poetry in the Elizabethan age, and
I am not sure how they were educated; whether they were taught to write;
whether they had sitting-rooms to themselves; how many women had children
before they were twenty-one; what, in short, they did from eight in the morn-

ing till eight at night. They had no money evidently; according to Professor Trevelyan they were married whether they liked it or not before they were out of the nursery, at fifteen or sixteen very likely. It would have been extremely odd, even upon this showing, had one of them suddenly written the plays of Shakespeare, I concluded, and I thought of that old gentleman, who is dead now, but was a bishop, I think, who declared that it was impossible for any woman, past, present, or to come, to have the genius of Shakespeare. He wrote to the papers about it. He also told a lady who applied to him for information that cats do not as a matter of fact go to heaven, though they have, he added, souls of a sort. How much thinking those old gentlemen used to save one! How the borders of ignorance shrank back at their approach! Cats do not go to heaven. Women cannot write the plays of Shakespeare.

3   Be that as it may, I could not help thinking, as I looked at the works of Shakespeare on the shelf, that the bishop was right at least in this; it would have been impossible, completely and entirely, for any woman to have written the plays of Shakespeare in the age of Shakespeare. Let me imagine, since facts are so hard to come by, what would have happened had Shakespeare had a won-derfully gifted sister, called Judith, let us say. Shakespeare himself went, very probably—his mother was an heiress—to the grammar school, where he may have learnt Latin—Ovid, Virgil and Horace—and the elements of grammar and logic. He was, it is well known, a wild boy who poached rabbits, perhaps shot a deer, and had, rather sooner than he should have done, to marry a woman in the neighbourhood, who bore him a child rather quicker than was right. That es-capade sent him to seek his fortune in London. He had, it seemed, a taste for the theatre; he began by holding horses at the stage door. Very soon he got work in the theatre, became a successful actor, and lived at the hub of the universe, meeting everybody, knowing everybody, practising his art on the boards, exer-cising his wits in the streets, and even getting access to the palace of the queen. Meanwhile his extraordinarily gifted sister, let us suppose, remained at home. She was as adventurous, as imaginative, as agog to see the world as he was. But she was not sent to school. She had no chance of learning grammar and logic, let alone of reading Horace and Virgil. She picked up a book now and then, one of her brother's perhaps, and read a few pages. But then her parents came in and told her to mend the stockings or mind the stew and not moon about with books and papers. They would have spoken sharply but kindly, for they were substantial people who knew the conditions of life for a woman and loved their daughter—indeed, more likely than not she was the apple of her father's eye. Per-haps she scribbled some pages up in an apple loft on the sly, but was careful to hide them or set fire to them. Soon, however, before she was out of her teens, she was to be betrothed to the son of a neighbouring wool-stapler. She cried out that marriage was hateful to her, and for that she was severely beaten by her fa-ther. Then he ceased to scold her. He begged her instead not to hurt him, not

to shame him in this matter of her marriage. He would give her a chain of beads or a fine petticoat, he said; and there were tears in his eyes. How could she disobey him? How could she break his heart? The force of her own gift alone drove her to it. She made up a small parcel of her belongings, let herself down by a rope one summer's night and took the road to London. She was not seventeen. The birds that sang in the hedge were not more musical than she was. She had the quickest fancy, a gift like her brother's, for the tune of words. Like him, she had a taste for the theatre. She stood at the stage door; she wanted to act, she said. Men laughed in her face. The manager—a fat, loose-lipped man—guffawed. He bellowed something about poodles dancing and women acting—no woman, he said, could possibly be an actress. He hinted—you can imagine what. She could get no training in her craft. Could she even seek her dinner in a tavern or roam the streets at midnight? Yet her genius was for fiction and lusted to feed abundantly upon the lives of men and women and the study of their ways. At last—for she was very young, oddly like Shakespeare the poet in her face, with the same grey eyes and rounded brows—at last Nick Greene the actor-manager took pity on her; she found herself with child by that gentleman and so—who shall measure the heat and violence of the poet's heart when caught and tangled in a woman's body?—killed herself one winter's night and lies buried at some cross-roads where the omnibuses now stop outside the Elephant and Castle.

That, more or less, is how the story would run, I think, if a woman in 4 Shakespeare's day had had Shakespeare's genius. But for my part, I agree with the deceased bishop, if such he was—it is unthinkable that any woman in Shakespeare's day should have had Shakespeare's genius. For genius like Shakespeare's is not born among labouring, uneducated, servile people. It was not born in England among the Saxons and the Britons. It is not born today among the working classes. How, then, could it have been born among women whose work began, according to Professor Trevelyan, almost before they were out of the nursery, who were forced to it by their parents and held to it by all the power of law and custom?

Anita K. Blair

Shattering the Myth of the Glass Ceiling

Anita K. Blair is the executive vice president of the Independent Women's Forum, a conservative women's lobbying group based in Arlington, Virginia. She has been outspoken as a defender of the status quo in the women's rights movement. As a trustee of the all-male Virginia Military Institute, she defended the college's decision not to admit women into its ranks. Here, she suggests that women have moved to a position of near-equality with men, and so no special efforts are necessary to "raise" the status of women any further.

1   WE OFTEN HEAR THAT WOMEN HAVE BEEN the biggest beneficiaries of affirmative action. In fact, whether the credit belongs to affirmative action policies, the birth control pill, economic growth or a combination of factors, women have made remarkable progress in the last 30 years. Why have women succeeded so well while other minorities have not?

2   First, of course, women aren't a minority; they constitute more than 51% of the U.S. population. But like racial and ethnic minorities, until the 1960s, women generally lacked access to educational and employment opportunities. What did they do when previously closed doors began to open for them? Government-gathered statistics tell the story.

3   Women went to college. In 1960, only 19% of bachelor's degrees were awarded to women. By 1992, women received 55% of bachelor's degrees and 54% of master's degrees. Note that these figures exceed the percentage of women in the population.

4   In 1960, women received only 5.5% of medical doctor degrees and 2.5% of juris doctor degrees. By 1992, women represented more than 35% of new physicians and 42% of new lawyers. Today, women constitute more than 22% of doctors and almost 25% of lawyers and judges.

5   Women also left home and went to work. Today, women constitute 46% of the civilian work force overall. Among women 25 to 54, 74% work outside the home. This includes 60% of married women, up from 32% in 1960.

6   We often hear about a "wage gap" between women and men. In 1992, the ratio of female to male, year-round, fulltime earnings was 71 cents to the dollar. This includes workers of all ages and all types of jobs. Among workers 25 to 34, the 1992 ratio was 82 cents on the dollar. And in a real "apples to apples" comparison, the gap narrows more. June E. O'Neill, director of the Congressional Budget Office, did a study based on the National Longitudinal Survey of Youth by Ohio State University's Center for Human Resources Research. O'Neill found that among people 27 to 33 who have never had a child, women's earnings were about 98% of men's. Similar results occur if you compare the earnings of women and men of the same education and experience in the same professions.

7   Women outnumber men in several significant job areas. For example, women far outnumber men in health and medicine management (79% female) and personnel and labor relations management (61% female). Women constitute 64% of workers in technical, sales and administrative support and about 60% of workers in service jobs. These are among the fastest growing occupations in America.

Consider, on the other hand, the jobs where men predominate. Women constitute only 24% of machine operators and laborers, 19% of farming, forestry and fishing workers and 9% of production, craft, and repair workers. The Bureau of Labor Statistics says these are among America's fastest declining occupations. Thus women are concentrated in occupations with good prospects for growth.   8

Women also have created jobs, for themselves and others. In 1980, there were about 2 million women-owned businesses with about $25 billion in sales. Today, according to the National Foundation for Women Business Owners, nearly 8 million companies with more than $2.25 trillion in sales are owned by women. One in four American workers is employed by a woman-owned business.   9

Should affirmative action policies receive the credit for women's success? Assume it's true. What lessons can we learn about the future of affirmative action? First, merely opening doors—the classic meaning of "affirmative action"—can accomplish a lot if the people who walk through the doors have done their homework by staying in school and getting the training necessary to qualify for jobs they want.   10

Second, dictating results—as "affirmative action" has come to do through quotas, goals, preferences and set-asides—not only doesn't help but probably hurts. Suppose women had dedicated all their efforts to penetrating the male-dominated trades mentioned above? They'd have a bleak future, as technology would have marched on anyway, and women would have missed the new opportunities made possible by the technological revolution. Instead, women today are well positioned to participate in the information age.   11

Finally, the era of affirmative action should teach us that any program purportedly designed to achieve goals must achieve or die. If affirmative action has served its purpose, it should be ended. If, after 30 years, it has not served its purpose, it definitely should be ended.   12

Susan Bianchi-Sand

The Glass Ceiling Hurts Business Too

Susan Bianchi-Sand began her career path as an advocate of equal pay for equal work in 1969, when she took a job as a stewardess for United Airlines. Appalled by the inequities she saw there, she ran for and won a seat as president of the flight attendants union. Now Chair and Executive Director of the National Committee on Pay Equity, she continues to work for equal pay and affirmative action.

1   IN RECENT MONTHS A CONSERVATIVE GROUP OF THINKERS has been passing off
the report *Women's Figures* as evidence that the glass ceiling is a myth, that the
wage gap doesn't exist and that feminists are on a mission to sucker the American woman into a victim mentality.

Debunking the backlash

2   This theory is circulating widely among the press—perhaps because it is controversial and contradicts what has become rather boring to the media—but
what remains the real life experiences of women and people of color — no real
change in the wage gap and no improvement in the glass ceiling.

3   Let's take a closer look at the glass ceiling "myth."

4   At the urging of former Secretary of Labor Elizabeth Dole, Republican President George Bush appointed a bipartisan Glass Ceiling Commission of leaders
from a balanced constituency of the business community, civil rights groups and
women's organizations to investigate the phenomenon of the "glass ceiling."

5   After two years of intensive study, focus groups, literature reviews and surveys of corporate America, the bipartisan Commission issued a fact-finding report, *Good for Business: Making Full Use of the Nation's Human Capital*. The report concluded that a serious problem exists within business that prevents
highly educated and qualified women and people of color from reaching their
potential in leadership positions within corporations. It said that the glass
ceiling is experienced in various ways for women and people of color depending on their gender, race, ethnicity and national origin, and that it effectively results in the under-utilization of talent, skill and education of some
of this nation's finest workers.

It's homogeneous at the top

6   The Commission found that less than five percent of all senior managers and
executive positions were occupied by women. In addition, it found that 97%
of the top male positions were held by white men.

7   The Commission went to great lengths to capture the subtle as well as
overt experiences of discrimination in the workforce and its relationship to
promotions and pay.

8   It looked at the "pipeline" to executive-level positions and found that
highly-skilled, educated and otherwise qualified women and people of color
were routinely denied admission to this training ground and "weeded out"
while white male workers gained mentoring, assignments and career opportunities that put them on the right track to the top jobs.

9   Moreover, apart from the Commission's work, a mere perusal of the headlines of today's major newspapers indicates that workplace discrimination is
hardly an issue of the past. Consider the problems within Mitsubishi, Texaco,
the Citadel, the Navy and the Army, to name a few.

Gauging the wage gap

Actually, the glass ceiling begins very early, and can be measured through a ⟨10⟩ number of different indicators. One measure is the earnings ratio between women and men—or the wage gap.

According to the U.S. Department of Commerce, Census Bureau, women ⟨11⟩ earned only 71% of men's annual earnings in 1995. Even when one compares earnings data for recent college graduates—as the U.S. Department of Education did in its recent report *Baccalaureate and Beyond*, women earn 15.7% less than men.

Another Education Department study, *Women at Thirtysomething*, found ⟨12⟩ that women who graduated from the class of 1972 failed to earn job opportunities and pay equal to men in all but seven occupations—even when they clearly had surpassed the men in the classroom.

That lower wage haunts women into their careers and becomes part of the ⟨13⟩ "objective" criteria that influences promotion decisions. Consider the case of two sales workers—according to the U.S. Bureau of Labor Statistics, the man who sells insurance earns on average $777 per week compared to the woman who sells insurance at an average weekly wage of $453. When a supervisory position comes open, the man looks better qualified, more "valuable" on paper, simply because he earns higher wages. The woman's lower earnings contribute to the glass ceiling effect.

A foot in the door

Overcoming the glass ceiling means more than just getting the right credentials ⟨14⟩ for the job. Because the reality of the labor market is not just *what* you know, and what you can do, but *who* you know and who will give you a chance.

Affirmative action has never been about substituting opportunity and fair- ⟨15⟩ ness for credentials and qualifications. It simply is ludicrous to maintain that all businesses should hire women and people of color just for representational purposes. Such a policy does no one any good.

Rather, affirmative action is the policy of giving opportunity to all who are ⟨16⟩ qualified. Not only has it been to the advantage of families and individuals, but it has been good for business. Just ask Xerox, Johnson and Johnson, Hewlett Packard and others.

The bottom line

Bottom line—the increased growth of women and people of color into the ⟨17⟩ marketplace has been a bonus and helped to create the strong economy we enjoy currently. The only choice we have is to open the door wider to encourage talent of all shapes, sizes and colors to walk through.

In fact, propagating the glass ceiling as a myth steers a good business prac- ⟨18⟩ tice down a narrow one-way alley of limited talent and potential. Businesses that fail to reach beyond the glass ceiling barrier to effectively utilize all of our nation's talent and skills will cheat only themselves.

<u>Martin Luther King, Jr.</u>

Letter from Birmingham Jail

In 1955, after a resolute Rosa Parks was arrested for refusing to give up her seat to a white man on a Montgomery bus, a young, articulate black minister was thrust into the national spotlight—as the unlikely leader of the ensuing bus boycott which ignited the modern civil rights movement. Over the next twelve years, Martin Luther King, Jr. became one of the most influential figures in American history. A powerful presence on both the podium and the pulpit, his command of written English made him a figure of admiration around the globe. In 1964 he was awarded the Nobel Peace Prize. In 1986, eighteen years after his tragic assassination, he became one of only three Americans honored with a national holiday.

Perhaps the most eloquent statement of King's philosophy of passive resistance, the "Letter from Birmingham Jail" was written in 1963 after King was arrested for demonstrating in defiance of a court order. Soon thereafter, it was widely circulated. It has become a classic of the civil rights movement.

APRIL 16, 1963

1   MY DEAR FELLOW CLERGYMEN:

2   While confined here in the Birmingham city jail, I came across your recent statement calling my present activities "unwise and untimely." Seldom do I pause to answer criticism of my work and ideas. If I sought to answer all the criticisms that cross my desk, my secretaries would have little time for anything other than such correspondence in the course of the day, and I would have no time for constructive work. But since I feel that you are men of genuine good will and that your criticisms are sincerely set forth, I want to try to answer your statement in what I hope will be patient and reasonable terms.

3   I think I should indicate why I am here in Birmingham, since you have been influenced by the view which argues against "outsiders coming in." I have the honor of serving as president of the Southern Christian Leadership Conference, an organization operating in every southern state, with headquarters in Atlanta, Georgia. We have some eighty-five affiliated organizations across the South, and one of them is the Alabama Christian Movement for Human Rights. Frequently we share staff, educational and financial resources with our affiliates. Several months ago the affiliate here in Birmingham asked

us to be on call to engage in a nonviolent direct-action program if such were deemed necessary. We readily consented, and when the hour came we lived up to our promise. So I, along with several members of my staff, am here because I was invited here. I am here because I have organizational ties here.

But more basically, I am in Birmingham because injustice is here. Just as   4
the prophets of the eighth century B.C. left their villages and carried their "thus saith the Lord" far beyond the boundaries of their home towns, and just as the Apostle Paul left his village of Tarsus and carried the gospel of Jesus Christ to the far corners of the Greco-Roman world, so am I compelled to carry the gospel of freedom beyond my own home town. Like Paul, I must constantly respond to the Macedonian call for aid.

Moreover, I am cognizant of the interrelatedness of all communities and   5
states. I cannot sit idly by in Atlanta and not be concerned about what happens in Birmingham. Injustice anywhere is a threat to justice everywhere. We are caught in an inescapable network of mutuality, tied in a single garment of destiny. Whatever affects one directly, affects all indirectly. Never again can we afford to live with the narrow, provincial "outside agitator" idea. Anyone who lives inside the United States can never be considered an outsider anywhere within its bounds.

You deplore the demonstrations taking place in Birmingham. But your   6
statement, I am sorry to say, fails to express a similar concern for the conditions that brought about the demonstrations. I am sure that none of you would want to rest content with the superficial kind of social analysis that deals merely with effects and does not grapple with underlying causes. It is unfortunate that demonstrations are taking place in Birmingham, but it is even more unfortunate that the city's white power structure left the Negro community with no alternative.

In any nonviolent campaign there are four basic steps: collection of the   7
facts to determine whether injustices exist; negotiation; self-purification; and direct action. We have gone through all these steps in Birmingham. There can be no gainsaying the fact that racial injustice engulfs this community. Birmingham is probably the most thoroughly segregated city in the United States. Its ugly record of brutality is widely known. Negroes have experienced grossly unjust treatment in the courts. There have been more unsolved bombings of Negro homes and churches in Birmingham than in any other city in the nation. These are the hard, brutal facts of the case. On the basis of these conditions, Negro leaders sought to negotiate with the city fathers. But the latter consistently refused to engage in good-faith negotiation.

Then, last September, came the opportunity to talk with leaders of Bir-   8
mingham's economic community. In the course of the negotiations, certain promises were made by the merchants—for example, to remove the stores' humiliating racial signs. On the basis of these promises, the Reverend Fred Shut-

tlesworth and the leaders of the Alabama Christian Movement for Human Rights agreed to a moratorium on all demonstrations. As the weeks and months went by, we realized that we were the victims of a broken promise. A few signs, briefly removed, returned; the others remained.

9   As in so many past experiences, our hopes had been blasted, and the shadow of deep disappointment settled upon us. We had no alternative except to prepare for direct action, whereby we would present our very bodies as a means of laying our case before the conscience of the local and the national community. Mindful of the difficulties involved, we decided to undertake a process of self-purification. We began a series of workshops on nonviolence, and we repeatedly asked ourselves: "Are you able to accept blows without retaliating?" "Are you able to endure the ordeal of jail?" We decided to schedule our direct-action program for the Easter season, realizing that except for Christmas, this is the main shopping period of the year. Knowing that a strong economic-withdrawal program would be the by-product of direct action, we felt that this would be the best time to bring pressure to bear on the merchants for the needed change.

10   Then it occurred to us that Birmingham's mayoral election was coming up in March, and we speedily decided to postpone action until after election day. When we discovered that the Commissioner of Public Safety, Eugene "Bull" Connor, had piled up enough votes to be in the runoff, we decided again to postpone action until the day after the runoff so that the demonstrations could not be used to cloud the issues. Like many others, we wanted to see Mr. Connor defeated, and to this end we endured postponement after postponement. Having aided in this community need, we felt that our direct-action program could be delayed no longer.

11   You may well ask, "Why direct action? Why sit-ins, marches and so forth? Isn't negotiation a better path?" You are quite right in calling for negotiation. Indeed, this is the very purpose of direct action. Nonviolent direct action seeks to create such a crisis and foster such a tension that a community which has constantly refused to negotiate is forced to confront the issue. It seeks so to dramatize the issue that it can no longer be ignored. My citing the creation of tension as part of the work of the nonviolent-resister may sound rather shocking. But I must confess that I am not afraid of the word "tension." I have earnestly opposed violent tension, but there is a type of constructive, nonviolent tension which is necessary for growth. Just as Socrates felt that it was necessary to create a tension in the mind so that individuals could rise from the bondage of myths and half-truths to the unfettered realm of creative analysis and objective appraisal, so must we see the need for nonviolent gadflies to create the kind of tension in society that will help men rise from the dark depths of prejudice and racism to the majestic heights of understanding and brotherhood.

The purpose of our direct-action program is to create a situation so crisis- 12
packed that it will inevitably open the door to negotiation. I therefore concur
with you in your call for negotiation. Too long has our beloved Southland been
bogged down in a tragic effort to live in monologue rather than dialogue.

One of the basic points in your statement is that the action that I and my 13
associates have taken in Birmingham is untimely. Some have asked: "Why didn't
you give the new city administration time to act?" The only answer that I can
give to this query is that the new Birmingham administration must be prodded about as much as the outgoing one, before it will act. We are sadly mistaken if we feel that the election of Albert Boutwell as mayor will bring the
millennium to Birmingham. While Mr. Boutwell is a much more gentle person than Mr. Connor, they are both segregationists, dedicated to maintenance
of the status quo. I have hoped that Mr. Boutwell will be reasonable enough
to see the futility of massive resistance to desegregation. But he will not see
this without pressure from devotees of civil rights. My friends, I must say to
you that we have not made a single gain in civil rights without determined
legal and nonviolent pressure. Lamentably, it is an historical fact that privileged groups seldom give up their privileges voluntarily. Individuals may see
the moral light and voluntarily give up their unjust posture; but, as Reinhold
Niebuhr has reminded us, groups tend to be more immoral than individuals.

We know through painful experience that freedom is never voluntarily 14
given by the oppressor; it must be demanded by the oppressed. Frankly, I have
yet to engage in a direct-action campaign that was "well timed" in the view of
those who have not suffered unduly from the disease of segregation. For years
now I have heard the word "Wait!" It rings in the ear of every Negro with
piercing familiarity. This "Wait" has almost always meant "Never." We must
come to see, with one of our distinguished jurists, that "justice too long delayed is justice denied."

We have waited for more than 340 years for our constitutional and God- 15
given rights. The nations of Asia and Africa are moving with jetlike speed toward gaining political independence, but we still creep at horse-and-buggy
pace toward gaining a cup of coffee at a lunch counter. Perhaps it is easy for
those who have never felt the stinging darts of segregation to say "Wait." But
when you have seen vicious mobs lynch your mothers and fathers at will and
drown your sisters and brothers at whim; when you have seen hate-filled policemen curse, kick and even kill your black brothers and sisters; when you see
the vast majority of your twenty million Negro brothers smothering in an air-
tight cage of poverty in the midst of an affluent society; when you suddenly
find your tongue twisted and your speech stammering as you seek to explain
to your six-year-old daughter why she can't go to the public amusement park
that has just been advertised on television, and see tears welling up in her eyes
when she is told that Funtown is closed to colored children, and see ominous

clouds of inferiority beginning to form in her little mental sky, and see her beginning to destroy her personality by developing an unconscious bitterness toward white people; when you have to concoct an answer for a five-year-old son
who is asking: "Daddy, why do white people treat colored people so mean?";
when you take a cross-country drive and find it necessary to sleep night after
night in the uncomfortable corners of your automobile because no motel will
accept you; when you are humiliated day in and day out by nagging signs
"white" and "colored"; when your first name becomes "nigger," your middle
name becomes "boy" (however old you are) and your last name becomes
"John," and your wife and mother are never given the respected title "Mrs.";
when you are harried by day and haunted by night by the fact that you are a
Negro, living constantly at tiptoe stance, never quite knowing what to expect
next, and are plagued with inner fears and outer resentments; when you are
forever fighting a degenerating sense of "nobodiness"—then you will understand why we find it difficult to wait. There comes a time when the cup of endurance runs over, and men are no longer willing to be plunged into the abyss
of despair. I hope, sirs, you can understand our legitimate and unavoidable
impatience.

16   You express a great deal of anxiety over our willingness to break laws. This
is certainly a legitimate concern. Since we so diligently urge people to obey the
Supreme Court's decision of 1954 outlawing segregation in the public
schools, at first glance it may seem rather paradoxical for us consciously to
break laws. One may well ask: "How can you advocate breaking some laws and
obeying others?" The answer lies in the fact that there are two types of laws:
just and unjust. I would be the first to advocate obeying just laws. One has not
only a legal but a moral responsibility to obey just laws. Conversely, one has a
moral responsibility to disobey unjust laws. I would agree with St. Augustine
that "an unjust law is no law at all."

17   Now, what is the difference between the two? How does one determine
whether a law is just or unjust? A just law is a man-made code that squares
with the moral law or the law of God. An unjust law is a code that is out of
harmony with the moral law. To put it in the terms of St. Thomas Aquinas:
An unjust law is a human law that is not rooted in eternal law and natural law.
Any law that uplifts human personality is just. Any law that degrades human
personality is unjust. All segregation statutes are unjust because segregation
distorts the soul and damages the personality. It gives the segregator a false
sense of superiority and the segregated a false sense of inferiority. Segregation,
to use the terminology of the Jewish philosopher Martin Buber, substitutes an
"I-it" relationship for an "I-thou" relationship and ends up relegating persons
to the status of things. Hence segregation is not only politically, economically
and sociologically unsound, it is morally wrong and sinful. Paul Tillich has
said that sin is separation. Is not segregation an existential expression of man's

tragic separation, his awful estrangement, his terrible sinfulness? Thus it is that I can urge men to obey the 1954 decision of the Supreme Court, for it is morally right; and I can urge them to disobey segregation ordinances, for they are morally wrong.

Let us consider a more concrete example of just and unjust laws. An unjust law is a code that a numerical or power majority group compels a minority group to obey but does not make binding on itself. This is *difference* made legal. By the same token, a just law is a code that a majority compels a minority to follow and that it is willing to follow itself. This is *sameness* made legal. **18**

Let me give another explanation. A law is unjust if it is inflicted on a minority that, as a result of being denied the right to vote, had no part in enacting or devising the law. Who can say that the legislature of Alabama which set up that state's segregation laws was democratically elected? Throughout Alabama all sorts of devious methods are used to prevent Negroes from becoming registered voters, and there are some counties in which, even though Negroes constitute a majority of the population, not a single Negro is registered. Can any law enacted under such circumstances be considered democratically structured? **19**

Sometimes a law is just on its face and unjust in its application. For instance, I have been arrested on a charge of parading without a permit. Now, there is nothing wrong in having an ordinance which requires a permit for a parade. But such an ordinance becomes unjust when it is used to maintain segregation and to deny citizens the First-Amendment privilege of peaceful assembly and protest. **20**

I hope you are able to see the distinction I am trying to point out. In no sense do I advocate evading or defying the law, as would the rabid segregationist. That would lead to anarchy. One who breaks an unjust law must do so openly, lovingly, and with a willingness to accept the penalty. I submit that an individual who breaks a law that conscience tells him is unjust, and who willingly accepts the penalty of imprisonment in order to arouse the conscience of the community over its injustice, is in reality expressing the highest respect for law. **21**

Of course, there is nothing new about this kind of civil disobedience. It was evidenced sublimely in the refusal of Shadrach, Meshach, and Abednego to obey the laws of Nebuchadnezzar, on the ground that a higher moral law was at stake. It was practiced superbly by the early Christians, who were willing to face hungry lions and the excruciating pain of chopping blocks rather than submit to certain unjust laws of the Roman Empire. To a degree, academic freedom is a reality today because Socrates practiced civil disobedience. In our own nation, the Boston Tea Party represented a massive act of civil disobedience. **22**

23   We should never forget that everything Adolf Hitler did in Germany was "legal" and everything the Hungarian freedom fighters did in Hungary was "illegal." It was "illegal" to aid and comfort a Jew in Hitler's Germany. Even so, I am sure that, had I lived in Germany at the time, I would have aided and comforted my Jewish brothers. If today I lived in a Communist country where certain principles dear to the Christian faith are suppressed, I would openly advocate disobeying that country's antireligious laws.

24   I must make two honest confessions to you, my Christian and Jewish brothers. First, I must confess that over the past few years I have been gravely disappointed with the white moderate. I have almost reached the regrettable conclusion that the Negro's great stumbling block in his stride toward freedom is not the White Citizen's Counciler or the Ku Klux Klanner, but the white moderate, who is more devoted to "order" than to justice; who prefers a negative peace which is the absence of tension to a positive peace which is the presence of justice; who constantly says: "I agree with you in the goal you seek, but I cannot agree with your methods of direct action"; who paternalistically believes he can set the time table for another man's freedom; who lives by a mythical concept of time and who constantly advises the Negro to wait for a "more convenient season." Shallow understanding from people of good will is more frustrating than absolute misunderstanding from people of ill will. Lukewarm acceptance is much more bewildering than outright rejection.

25   I had hoped that the white moderate would understand that law and order exist for the purpose of establishing justice and that when they fail in this purpose they become the dangerously structured dams that block the flow of social progress. I had hoped that the white moderate would understand that the present tension in the South is a necessary phase of the transition from an obnoxious negative peace, in which the Negro passively accepted his unjust plight, to a substantive and positive peace, in which all men will respect the dignity and worth of human personality. Actually, we who engage in nonviolent direct action are not the creators of tension. We merely bring to the surface the hidden tension that is already alive. We bring it out in the open, where it can be seen and dealt with. Like a boil that can never be cured so long as it is covered up but must be opened with all its ugliness to the natural medicines of air and light, injustice must be exposed, with all the tension its exposure creates, to the light of human conscience and the air of national opinion before it can be cured.

26   In your statement you assert that our actions, even though peaceful, must be condemned because they precipitate violence. But is this a logical assertion? Isn't this like condemning a robbed man because his possession of money precipitated the evil act of robbery? Isn't this like condemning Socrates because his unswerving commitment to truth and his philosophical inquiries precipitated the act by the misguided populace in which they made him drink

hemlock? Isn't this like condemning Jesus because his unique God-consciousness and never-ceasing devotion to God's will precipitated the evil act of crucifixion? We must come to see that, as the federal courts have consistently affirmed, it is wrong to urge an individual to cease his efforts to gain his constitutional rights because the quest may precipitate violence. Society must protect the robbed and punish the robber.

I had also hoped that the white moderate would reject the myth concerning time in relation to the struggle for freedom. I have just received a letter from a white brother in Texas. He writes: "All Christians know that the colored people will receive equal rights eventually, but it is possible that you are in too great a religious hurry. It has taken Christianity almost two thousand years to accomplish what it has. The teachings of Christ take time to come to earth." Such an attitude stems from a tragic misconception of time, from the strangely irrational notion that there is something in the very flow of time that will inevitably cure all ills. Actually, time itself is neutral; it can be used either destructively or constructively. More and more I feel that the people of ill will have used time much more effectively than have the people of good will. We will have to repent in this generation not merely for the hateful words and actions of the bad people but for the appalling silence of the good people. Human progress never rolls in on wheels of inevitability; it comes through the tireless efforts of men willing to be co-workers with God, and without this hard work, time itself becomes an ally of the forces of social stagnation. We must use time creatively, in the knowledge that the time is always ripe to do right. Now is the time to make real the promise of democracy and transform our pending national elegy into a creative psalm of brotherhood. Now is the time to lift our national policy from the quicksand of racial injustice to the solid rock of human dignity.

You speak of our activity in Birmingham as extreme. At first I was rather disappointed that fellow clergymen would see my nonviolent efforts as those of an extremist. I began thinking about the fact that I stand in the middle of two opposing forces in the Negro community. One is a force of complacency, made up in part of Negroes who, as a result of long years of oppression, are so drained of self-respect and a sense of "somebodiness" that they have adjusted to segregation; and in part of a few middle-class Negroes who, because of a degree of academic and economic security and because in some ways they profit by segregation, have become insensitive to the problems of the masses. The other force is one of bitterness and hatred, and it comes perilously close to advocating violence. It is expressed in the various black nationalist groups that are springing up across the nation, the largest and best-known being Elijah Muhammad's Muslim movement. Nourished by the Negro's frustration over the continued existence of racial discrimination, this movement is made up of people who have lost faith in America, who have absolutely repudiated Christianity, and who have concluded that the white man is an incorrigible "devil."

29   I have tried to stand between these two forces, saying that we need emulate neither the "do-nothingism" of the complacent nor the hatred and despair of the black nationalist. For there is the more excellent way of love and nonviolent protest. I am grateful to God that, through the influence of the Negro church, the way of nonviolence became an integral part of our struggle.

30   If this philosophy had not emerged, by now many streets of the South would, I am convinced, be flowing with blood. And I am further convinced that if our white brothers dismiss as "rabble-rousers" and "outside agitators" those of us who employ nonviolent direct action, and if they refuse to support our nonviolent efforts, millions of Negroes will, out of frustration and despair, seek solace and security in black-nationalist ideologies—a development that would inevitably lead to a frightening racial nightmare.

31   Oppressed people cannot remain oppressed forever. The yearning for freedom eventually manifests itself, and that is what has happened to the American Negro. Something within has reminded him of his birthright of freedom, and something without has reminded him that it can be gained. Consciously or unconsciously, he has been caught up by the *Zeitgeist*, and with his black brothers of Africa and his brown and yellow brothers of Asia, South America, and the Caribbean, the United States Negro is moving with a sense of great urgency toward the promised land of racial justice. If one recognizes this vital urge that has engulfed the Negro community, one should readily understand why public demonstrations are taking place. The Negro has many pent-up resentments and latent frustrations, and he must release them. So let him march; let him make prayer pilgrimages to the city hall; let him go on freedom rides—and try to understand why he must do so. If his repressed emotions are not released in nonviolent ways, they will seek expression through violence; this is not a threat but a fact of history. So I have not said to my people, "Get rid of your discontent." Rather, I have tried to say that this normal and healthy discontent can be channeled into the creative outlet of nonviolent direct action. And now this approach is being termed extremist.

32   But though I was initially disappointed at being categorized as an extremist, as I continued to think about the matter I gradually gained a measure of satisfaction from the label. Was not Jesus an extremist for love: "Love your enemies, bless them that curse you, do good to them that hate you, and pray for them which despitefully use you, and persecute you." Was not Amos an extremist for justice: "Let justice roll down like waters and righteousness like an ever-flowing stream." Was not Paul an extremist for the Christian gospel: "I bear in my body the marks of the Lord Jesus." Was not Martin Luther an extremist: "Here I stand; I cannot do otherwise, so help me God." And John Bunyan: "I will stay in jail to the end of my days before I make a butchery of

my conscience." And Abraham Lincoln: "This nation cannot survive half slave and half free." And Thomas Jefferson: "We hold these truths to be self-evident, that all men are created equal. . . ." So the question is not whether we will be extremists, but what kind of extremists we will be. Will we be extremists for hate or for love? Will we be extremists for the preservation of injustice or for the extension of justice? In that dramatic scene on Calvary's hill three men were crucified. We must never forget that all three were crucified for the same crime—the crime of extremism. Two were extremists for immorality, and thus fell below their environment. The other, Jesus Christ, was an extremist for love, truth, and goodness, and thereby rose above his environment. Perhaps the South, the nation and the world are in dire need of creative extremists.

I had hoped that the white moderate would see this need. Perhaps I was 33 too optimistic; perhaps I expected too much. I suppose I should have realized that few members of the oppressor race can understand the deep groans and passionate yearnings of the oppressed race, and still fewer have the vision to see that injustice must be rooted out by strong, persistent, and determined action. I am thankful, however, that some of our white brothers in the South have grasped the meaning of this social revolution and committed themselves to it. They are still all too few in quantity, but they are big in quality. Some—such as Ralph McGill, Lillian Smith, Harry Golden, James McBride Dabbs, Ann Braden and Sarah Patton Boyle—have written about our struggle in eloquent and prophetic terms. Others have marched with us down nameless streets of the South. They have languished in filthy, roach-infested jails, suffering the abuse and brutality of policemen who view them as "dirty nigger-lovers." Unlike so many of their moderate brothers and sisters, they have recognized the urgency of the moment and sensed the need for powerful "action" antidotes to combat the disease of segregation.

Let me take note of my other major disappointment. I have been so greatly 34 disappointed with the white church and its leadership. Of course, there are some notable exceptions. I am not unmindful of the fact that each of you has taken some significant stands on this issue. I commend you, Reverend Stallings, for your Christian stand on this past Sunday, in welcoming Negroes to your worship service on a nonsegregated basis. I commend the Catholic leaders of this state for integrating Spring Hill College several years ago.

But despite these notable exceptions, I must honestly reiterate that I have 35 been disappointed with the church. I do not say this as one of those negative critics who can always find something wrong with the church. I say this as a minister of the gospel, who loves the church; who was nurtured in its bosom; who has been sustained by its spiritual blessings and who will remain true to it as long as the cord of life shall lengthen.

When I was suddenly catapulted into the leadership of the bus protest in 36

Montgomery, Alabama, a few years ago, I felt we would be supported by the white church. I felt that the white ministers, priests and rabbis of the South would be among our strongest allies. Instead, some have been outright opponents, refusing to understand the freedom movement and misrepresenting its leaders; all too many others have been more cautious than courageous and have remained silent behind the anesthetizing security of stained-glass windows.

37   In spite of my shattered dreams, I came to Birmingham with the hope that the white religious leadership of this community would see the justice of our cause and, with deep moral concern, would serve as the channel through which our just grievances could reach the power structure. I had hoped that each of you would understand. But again I have been disappointed.

38   I have heard numerous southern religious leaders admonish their worshippers to comply with a desegregation decision because it is the law, but I have longed to hear white ministers declare: "Follow this decree because integration is morally right and because the Negro is your brother." In the midst of blatant injustices inflicted upon the Negro, I have watched white churchmen stand on the sideline and mouth pious irrelevancies and sanctimonious trivialities. In the midst of a mighty struggle to rid our nation of racial and economic injustice, I have heard many ministers say: "Those are social issues, with which the gospel has no real concern." And I have watched many churches commit themselves to a completely otherworldly religion which makes a strange, un-Biblical distinction between body and soul, between the sacred and the secular.

39   I have traveled the length and breadth of Alabama, Mississippi and all the other southern states. On sweltering summer days and crisp autumn mornings I have looked at the South's most beautiful churches with their lofty spires pointing heavenward. I have beheld the impressive outlines of her massive religious-education buildings. Over and over I have found myself asking: "What kind of people worship here? Who is their God? Where were their voices when the lips of Governor Barnett dripped with words of interposition and nullification? Where were they when Governor Wallace gave a clarion call for defiance and hatred? Where were their voices of support when bruised and weary Negro men and women decided to rise from the dark dungeons of complacency to the bright hills of creative protest?"

40   Yes, these questions are still in my mind. In deep disappointment I have wept over the laxity of the church. But be assured that my tears have been tears of love. There can be no deep disappointment where there is not deep love. Yes, I love the church. How could I do otherwise? I am in the rather unique position of being the son, the grandson and the great-grandson of preachers. Yes, I see the church as the body of Christ. But, oh! How we have blemished and scarred that body through social neglect and through fear of being nonconformists.

41   There was a time when the church was very powerful—in the time when

the early Christians rejoiced at being deemed worthy to suffer for what they believed. In those days the church was not merely a thermometer that recorded the ideas and principles of popular opinion; it was a thermostat that transformed the mores of society. Whenever the early Christians entered a town, the people in power became disturbed and immediately sought to convict the Christians for being "disturbers of the peace" and "outside agitators." But the Christians pressed on, in the conviction that they were "a colony of heaven," called to obey God rather than man. Small in number, they were big in commitment. They were too God-intoxicated to be "astronomically intimidated." By their effort and example they brought an end to such ancient evils as infanticide and gladiatorial contests.

Things are different now. So often the contemporary church is a weak, in-   42
effectual voice with an uncertain sound. So often it is an archdefender of the status quo. Far from being disturbed by the presence of the church, the power structure of the average community is consoled by the church's silent—and often even vocal—sanction of things as they are.

But the judgment of God is upon the church as never before. If today's   43
church does not recapture the sacrificial spirit of the early church, it will lose its authenticity, forfeit the loyalty of millions, and be dismissed as an irrelevant social club with no meaning for the twentieth century. Every day I meet young people whose disappointment with the church has turned into outright disgust.

Perhaps I have once again been too optimistic. Is organized religion too in-   44
extricably bound to the status quo to save our nation and the world? Perhaps I must turn my faith to the inner spiritual church, the church within the church, as the true *ekklesia* and the hope of the world. But again I am thankful to God that some noble souls from the ranks of organized religion have broken loose from the paralyzing chains of conformity and joined us as active partners in the struggle for freedom. They have left their secure congregations and walked the streets of Albany, Georgia, with us. They have gone down the highways of the South on tortuous rides for freedom. Yes, they have gone to jail with us. Some have been dismissed from their churches, have lost the support of their bishops and fellow ministers. But they have acted in the faith that right defeated is stronger than evil triumphant. Their witness has been the spiritual salt that has preserved the true meaning of the gospel in these troubled times. They have carved a tunnel of hope through the dark mountain of disappointment.

I hope the church as a whole will meet the challenge of this decisive hour.   45
But even if the church does not come to the aid of justice, I have no despair about the future. I have no fear about the outcome of our struggle in Birmingham, even if our motives are at present misunderstood. We will reach the goal of freedom in Birmingham and all over the nation, because the goal of America is freedom. Abused and scorned though we may be, our destiny is tied up with America's destiny. Before the pilgrims landed at Plymouth, we

were here. Before the pen of Jefferson etched the majestic words of the Declaration of Independence across the pages of history, we were here. For more than two centuries our forebears labored in this country without wages; they made cotton king; they built the homes of their masters while suffering gross injustice and shameful humiliation—and yet out of a bottomless vitality they continued to thrive and develop. If the inexpressible cruelties of slavery could not stop us, the opposition we now face will surely fail. We will win our freedom because the sacred heritage of our nation and the eternal will of God are embodied in our echoing demands.

46   Before closing I feel impelled to mention one other point in your statement that has troubled me profoundly. You warmly commended the Birmingham police force for keeping "order" and "preventing violence." I doubt that you would have so warmly commended the police force if you had seen its dogs sinking their teeth into unarmed, nonviolent Negroes. I doubt that you would so quickly commend the policemen if you were to observe their ugly and inhumane treatment of Negroes here in the city jail; if you were to watch them push and curse old Negro women and young Negro girls; if you were to see them slap and kick old Negro men and young boys; if you were to observe them, as they did on two occasions, refuse to give us food because we wanted to sing our grace together. I cannot join you in your praise of the Birmingham police department.

47   It is true that the police have exercised a degree of discipline in handling the demonstrators. In this sense they have conducted themselves rather "nonviolently" in public. But for what purpose? To preserve the evil system of segregation. Over the past few years I have consistently preached that nonviolence demands that the means we use must be as pure as the ends we seek. I have tried to make clear that it is wrong to use immoral means to attain moral ends. But now I must affirm that it is just as wrong, or perhaps even more so, to use moral means to preserve immoral ends. Perhaps Mr. Connor and his policemen have been rather nonviolent in public, as was Chief Pritchett in Albany, Georgia, but they have used the moral means of nonviolence to maintain the immoral end of racial injustice. As T. S. Eliot has said: "The last temptation is the greatest treason: To do the right deed for the wrong reason."

48   I wish you had commended the Negro sit-inners and demonstrators of Birmingham for their sublime courage, their willingness to suffer and their amazing discipline in the midst of great provocation. One day the South will recognize its real heroes. They will be the James Merediths, with the noble sense of purpose that enables them to face jeering and hostile mobs, and with the agonizing loneliness that characterizes the life of the pioneer. They will be old, oppressed, battered Negro women, symbolized in a seventy-two-year-old woman in Montgomery, Alabama, who rose up with a sense of dignity and with her people decided not to ride segregated buses, and who responded with ungrammatical profundity to one who inquired about her weariness: "My feets

is tired, but my soul is at rest." They will be the young high school and college students, the young ministers of the gospel and a host of their elders, courageously and nonviolently sitting in at lunch counters and willingly going to jail for conscience' sake. One day the South will know that when these disinherited children of God sat down at lunch counters, they were in reality standing up for what is best in the American dream and for the most sacred values in our Judaeo-Christian heritage, thereby bringing our nation back to those great wells of democracy which were dug deep by the founding fathers in their formulation of the Constitution and the Declaration of Independence.

Never before have I written so long a letter. I'm afraid it is much too long 49 to take your precious time. I can assure you that it would have been much shorter if I had been writing from a comfortable desk, but what else can one do when he is alone in a narrow jail cell, other than write long letters, think long thoughts and pray long prayers?

If I have said anything in this letter that overstates the truth and indicates 50 an unreasonable impatience, I beg you to forgive me. If I have said anything that understates the truth and indicates my having a patience that allows me to settle for anything less than brotherhood, I beg God to forgive me.

I hope this letter finds you strong in the faith. I also hope that circum- 51 stances will soon make it possible for me to meet each of you, not as an integrationist or a civil-rights leader but as a fellow clergyman and a Christian brother. Let us all hope that the dark clouds of racial prejudice will soon pass away and the deep fog of misunderstanding will be lifted from our fear-drenched communities, and in some not too distant tomorrow the radiant stars of love and brotherhood will shine over our great nation with all their scintillating beauty.

Yours for the cause of Peace and Brotherhood, 52
MARTIN LUTHER KING, JR.

Patricia Curtis

The Argument Against Animal Experimentation

In 1978, Patricia Curtis shocked many readers of the *New York Times* with her graphic depiction of the world of animal experimentation. Today the animal rights movement is well known, and many of the practices Curtis describes have been banned. Now an author of children's books on animals, Curtis's most recent book is *Animals You Never Even Heard Of*.

1   THE PROFESSOR WAS LATE LEAVING THE MEDICAL SCHOOL because he'd had to review papers by his third-year students in experimental surgery. It was well after 11 when he wearily drove his car into the garage. The house was dark except for a hall light left on for him. His wife and youngsters were already asleep, he realized, and the professor suddenly felt lonely as he fit his key in the lock. But even as he pushed open the door, Sabrina was there to welcome him. She was always waiting for him, lying on the rug just inside the door.

2   The little dog leaped up ecstatically, wagging her tail and licking the professor's hand. The professor stroked her affectionately. She flopped on her back and grinned at him as he tickled her chest and belly; then she jumped to her feet and danced around his legs as he walked into the kitchen to get something to eat. Sabrina's exuberant joy at his return never failed to cheer him.

3   Early next morning, the professor drove back to the medical school and entered the laboratory. He noticed that a dog on which one of his students had operated the previous afternoon still had an endotracheal tube in its throat and obviously had not received pain medication. He must be more strict in his orders, he thought to himself. Another dog had bled through its bandages and lay silently in a pool of blood. Sloppy work, the professor thought—must speak to that student. None of the dogs made any sounds, because new arrivals at the laboratory were always subjected to an operation called a ventriculocordectomy that destroyed their vocal cords so that no barks or howls disturbed people in the medical school and surrounding buildings.

4   The professor looked over the animals that would be used that day by his surgery students. He came across a new female dog that had just been delivered by the dealer. Badly frightened, she whined and wagged her tail ingratiatingly as he paused in front of her cage. The professor felt a stab. The small dog bore an amazing resemblance to Sabrina. Quickly he walked away. Nevertheless, he made a note to remind himself to give orders for her vocal cords to be destroyed and for her to be conditioned for experimental surgery.

5   American researchers sacrifice approximately 64 million animals annually. Some 400,000 dogs, 200,000 cats, 33,000 apes and monkeys, thousands of horses, ponies, calves, sheep, goats and pigs, and millions of rabbits, hamsters, guinea pigs, birds, rats and mice are used every year in experiments that often involve intense suffering. The research establishment has generally insisted that live animals provide the only reliable tests for drugs, chemicals and cosmetics that will be used by people. Researchers also believe that animal experiments are necessary in the search for cures for human illnesses and defects.

There is no question that many important medical discoveries, from polio vaccine to the physiology of the stress response, have indeed been made through the use of animals. Thus universities, medical and scientific institutions, pharmaceutical companies, cosmetics manufacturers and the military have always taken for granted their right to use animals in almost any way they see fit.

But increasing numbers of scientists are beginning to ask themselves some 6 hard ethical questions and to re-evaluate their routine use of painful testing tools such as electric shock, stomach tubes, hot plates, restraining boxes and radiation devices. A new debate has arisen over whether all such experiments are worth the suffering they entail.

Strongly opposing curtailment of animal experimentation are groups such 7 as the National Society for Medical Research, which insists that any such reduction would jeopardize public safety and scientific progress. The N.S.M.R. was formed to resist what it considers the threat of Government regulation of animal research and to refute the charges of humane societies. Many scientists, however, although they firmly believe that some animal research is necessary, no longer endorse such an absolutist approach to the issue.

"Some knowledge can be obtained at too high a price," writes British phys- 8 iologist Dr. D. H. Smyth in his recent book *Alternatives to Animal Experiments*.

"The lives and suffering of animals must surely count for something," says 9 Jeremy J. Stone, director of the Washington-based Federation of American Scientists, which has devoted an entire newsletter to a discussion of the rights of animals.

According to physiologist Dr. F. Barbara Orlans of the National Institutes 10 of Health, "Within the scientific community there's a growing concern for animals that has not yet had a forum." Dr. Orlans is president of the newly formed Scientists' Center for Animal Welfare, which hopes to raise the level of awareness on the part of fellow scientists and the public about avoidable suffering inflicted on lab animals, wildlife, and animals raised for meat. "We will try to be a voice of reason. We can perhaps be a link between scientists and the humane organizations," Dr. Orlans explains. "We hope also to provide solid factual data on which animal-protection decisions can be based."

Another link between researchers and humane organizations is a new 11 committee comprising more than 400 doctors and scientists that has been formed by Friends of Animals, a national animal-welfare group. Headed by eight M.D.s, the committee is making a survey of Federally funded animal-research projects. Friends of Animals hopes that the study will expose not only needless atrocities performed on animals, but also boondoggles involving taxpayers' money.

One reason scientists are no longer so indifferent to the suffering they in- 12 flict on animals is the discoveries that science itself has made. We now know that many animals feel, think, reason, communicate, have sophisticated social systems, and even, on occasion, behave altruistically toward each other. Communication by sign language with higher primates, demonstrations of the intelligence of dolphins and whales, observations of the complex societies of wolves and other animals, and many other investigations have narrowed the gap between ourselves and the rest of the animal kingdom, making it more difficult to rationalize inhumane experiments. Dr. Dallas Pratt, author of *Painful Experiments on Animals*, points out that "among the rats and mice, the computers and oscilloscopes, there is Koko"—referring to the young gorilla whom a California primatologist has taught a working vocabulary of 375 words and concepts in sign language and who has even learned to take snapshots with a Polaroid camera. It's hard not to feel squeamish about subjecting animals to inhumane experiments when they possess almost-human intelligence.

13   The thinking of researchers is also beginning to be affected by the growing movement for animal rights. The rising concern for the welfare of animals is seen by some people as a natural extension of contemporary movements promoting civil rights, women's rights, homosexual rights, human rights, and children's rights. Public interest in preserving endangered species is based first on an increasing awareness of the complexity and fragility of ecosystems, and second on the notion, still much debated, that any species of plant or animal, from the lowly snail darter to the blue whale, has the right to continue to exist. From here it is only a short logical step to the belief that animals have the right to exist without suffering unnecessarily.

14   Near the top of the list of animal-welfare activists' causes is putting an end to inhumane experiments on laboratory animals. In Great Britain, where a vigorous antivivisection movement has existed for more than a century, a clandestine group called the Animal Liberation Front conducts commando-style raids on laboratories, liberating animals and sabotaging research equipment. A.L.F. members have also been known to slash tires and pour sugar in the gas tanks of trucks used by animal dealers who supply labs. To be sure, this group of zealots hasn't made much of a dent in England's vast research community, but it does appeal to a gut reaction on the part of many Britons against animal research.

15   Animal-rights activists are not merely sentimental do-gooders and pet-lovers. They have mounted a philosophical attack on the traditional Western attitude toward animals, branding it as "speciesist" (like racist or sexist), a term derived from the word "speciesism," coined by psychologist and author Dr. Richard Ryder. The Australian philosopher Peter Singer, in his influential 1975 book *Animal Liberation*, argued that the "speciesist" rationalization, "Human beings come first," is usually used by people who do nothing for either human or nonhuman animals. And he pointed out the parallels between the oppression of blacks, women, and animals: Such oppression is usually rationalized on the grounds that the oppressed group is inferior.

In 1977, when outraged antivivisectionists heard about some highly un- 16
pleasant electric-shock and burn experiments conducted on young pigs in Den-
mark, they wasted no time in pointing out the irony that the tests were being
conducted by Amnesty International, the human-rights organization. Amnesty
International was attempting to prove that human prisoners could be tortured
without leaving any marks, and pigs were used because of the similarity of their
skin to ours. (The tests were subsequently discontinued.)

Paradoxically, the public tends to be "speciesist" in its reaction to animal 17
experimentation: For many people, a test is permissible when it inflicts pain
on a "lower" animal like a hamster, but not when the victim is a dog. When
it was discovered in the summer of 1976 that the American Museum of Natural History was damaging the brains of cats and running painful sex experiments on them, hundreds of people picketed in protest. The museum's Animal Behavior Department defended itself on the grounds that the research
was intended to gain a better understanding of human sexual responses. Animal-rights groups, scientists among them, were not convinced of the necessity
of the tests, which came to an end only when the chief researcher retired. But
the protesters made no stir about the pigeons, doves, and rats that suffered in
the same laboratory.

If United States Army researchers had used guinea pigs instead of beagles 18
when they tried out a poison gas, they probably would not have provoked the
public outcry that resulted in the curtailment of their funding in 1974. When
a few Avon saleswomen quit their jobs last spring after reading about painful
eye-makeup tests the company conducts on rabbits, they did not complain
about the thousands of guinea pigs and rats Avon routinely puts to death in
acute-toxicity tests.

It is not known whether any single vertebrate species is more or less im- 19
mune to pain than another. A neat line cannot be drawn across the evolutionary scale dividing the sensitive from the insensitive. Yet the suffering of
laboratory rats and mice is regarded as trivial by scientists and the public alike.
These rodents have the dubious honor of being our No. 1 experimental animals, composing possibly 75 percent of America's total lab-animal population.
As Russell Baker once wrote, "This is no time to be a mouse."

Rats and mice are specifically excluded from a Federal law designed to give 20
some protection to laboratory animals. The Animal Welfare Act, passed in
1966 and amended in 1970, is administered by the Department of Agriculture and covers only about 4 percent of laboratory animals. Animal advocates
worked hard for the bill, which sets some standards for the housing of animals
in laboratories and at the dealers' facilities from which many of them are obtained. But the law places no restrictions on the kinds of experiments to
which animals may be subjected. It does indicate that pain-relieving drugs
should be used on the few types of animals it covers—but it includes a loop-

hole so as not to inhibit researchers unduly. If a scientist claims that pain is a necessary part of an experiment, anesthetics or analgesics may be withheld.

21   One standard test conducted on rats by drug companies is called the "writhing test" because of the agonized way the animals react to irritants injected into their abdomens. Paradoxically, this test assesses the efficacy of pain-killers, which are administered only after the rats show signs of acute suffering.

22   Equally common are psychological experiments in "learned helplessness" that have been conducted on rats, dogs, and other kinds of animals. In some of these tests, caged animals are given painful electric shocks until they learn certain maneuvers to obtain their food. As they become adept at avoiding the shocks, the researchers keep changing the rules so that the animals have to keep learning more and more ways to avoid shocks. Ultimately no way remains to escape, and the animals simply give up and lie on the floors of their cages, passively receiving shock after shock. Researchers have attempted to draw parallels between "learned helplessness" and depression in human beings, but some critics have difficulty perceiving their necessity. "What more are we going to learn about human depression by continuing to produce immobility in animals?" asks former animal experimenter Dr. Roger Ulrich, now a research professor of psychology at Western Michigan University.

23   Electric shock is widely used on many different kinds of animals in various types of research. In one experiment typical of a series that has been under way since 1966 at the Armed Forces Radiobiology Research Institute in Bethesda, Md., 10 rhesus monkeys were starved for 18 hours and then "encouraged" with electric prods to run rapidly on treadmills. This went on for several weeks before the monkeys were subjected to 4,600 rads of gamma-neutron radiation. Then they were retested on the treadmills for six hours, and subsequently for two hours each day until they died. Mean survival time for the vomiting, incapacitated monkeys was recorded in A.F.R.R.I.'s report as 37 hours. Dogs have been used in similar experiments, whose purpose is to get an idea of the effects of radiation on human endurance.

24   Now A.F.R.R.I. and other American research facilities are having to look for new sources of monkeys. In March 1978, the Government of India banned further export of rhesus monkeys to the United States. The native population was dwindling and Prime Minister Morarji R. Desai cited violations of a previous agreement that restricted the use of rhesus monkeys to medical research under humane conditions. "There is no difference between cruelty to animals and cruelty to human beings," the ascetic Prime Minister stated. The International Primate Protection League, a four-year-old watchdog group whose members include many scientists and especially primatologists (Jane Goodall, for one), had spread word in the Indian press that American scientists were using rhesus monkeys in grisly trauma experiments. According to the Primate

Protection League, these tests included dipping monkeys in boiling water at the University of Kansas, shooting them in the face with high-powered rifles at the University of Chicago, and slamming them in the stomach with a cannon-impactor traveling at a speed of 70 miles per hour at the University of Michigan.

"I feel justified in stating that fully 80 percent of the experiments involv- 25 ing rhesus monkeys are either unnecessary, represent useless duplication of previous work, or could utilize nonanimal alternatives," wrote Illinois Wesleyan University biologist Dr. John E. McArdle, a specialist in primate functional anatomy, in a letter to Prime Minister Desai, who so far has held firm despite pressure from the American scientific community to rescind the ban. In the meantime, researchers are making do with non-Indian rhesus monkeys and a close relative, the crab-eating macaque.

One of the arguments in favor of animal tests is that under the controlled 26 circumstances of the experimental laboratory they are likely to be objective and consistent. But the results of the same tests conducted on the same kinds of animals often differ from one laboratory to the next. When 25 cooperating companies, including Avon, Revlon, and American Cyanamid, conducted a comprehensive study of eye- and skin-irritation tests using rabbits, the results varied widely. The study concluded that these tests "should not be recommended as standard procedures in any new regulations" because they yielded "unreliable results."

One of these tests, the Draize Ophthalmic Irritancy Test, is used to evalu- 27 ate the effect upon the eyes of household and aerosol products, shampoos, and eye makeup. Rabbits are used because their eyes do not have effective tear glands and thus cannot easily flush away or dissolve irritants. The animals are pinioned in stocks and their eyes are exposed to a substance until inflammation, ulceration, or gross damage occurs.

Many investigators concede that the data provided by such experiments 28 are often inconsistent and that the stresses caused by crowded cages, callous treatment, pain, and fear can affect animals' metabolisms and thus confuse test results. "Since there is hardly a single organ or biochemical system in the body that is not affected by stress," says Dr. Harold Hillman, a British physiologist, "it is almost certainly the main reason for the wide variation reported among animals on whom painful experiments have been done."

Very often, different species respond differently to substances or situa- 29 tions. The rationale for many animal tests is that they predict human reactions, but thalidomide, for example, did not produce deformities in the fetuses of dogs, cats, monkeys, and hamsters. On the other hand, insulin has been proved harmful to rabbits and mice although it saves human lives.

Researchers are becoming increasingly dubious about the efficacy of the 30 LD/50, a test for acute toxicity that consists of force-feeding a group of animals a specific substance until half of them die, ostensibly providing a quantitative measure of how poisonous the substance is. In *Painful Experiments on Animals,* Dr. Pratt asks what we learn from forcing hair dye or face powder into a dog or rat through a stomach tube until its internal organs rupture.

31   One small victory for animal-welfare activists that was hailed by many American scientists was the 1975 Canadian ban on the use of vertebrate animals by students participating in science fairs. Children had been awarded prizes for attempting heart-transplant surgery on unanesthetized rabbits, amputating the feet of lizards, performing Caesarean operations on pregnant mice, bleeding dogs into a state of shock and blinding pigeons. Remarking that such "experiments" were a distortion of the spirit of research, science fair officials ruled out all such projects except observations of the normal living patterns of wild or domestic animals.

32   In this country, the search for adequate substitutes for laboratory animals was officially launched last summer when the year-old American Fund for Alternatives to Animal Research made its first grant—$12,500 to a biology professor at Whitman College in Walla Walla, Wash. The award to Dr. Earl William Fleck will help finance his development of a test substituting one-celled organisms called tetrahymena for animals in screening substances for teratogens, agents that can cause birth defects. It is expected that the test, if and when perfected, will be cheaper, quicker, more accurate, and certainly more humane than putting thousands of pregnant animals to death.

33   According to veterinarian Thurman Grafton, executive director of the National Society for Medical Research, people who talk about alternatives to animals are creating false hopes. "These new technologies can only be adjuncts to the use of animals," he claims. "While they serve a purpose in furnishing clues as to what direction a type of research might take, you will always ultimately need an intact animal with all its living complications and interchanging biochemical functions to properly assay a drug."

34   "Not so," says Ethel Thurston, administrator of the American Fund for Alternatives. "Enough progress has already been made to indicate that certain techniques can completely replace animals."

35   Several of these techniques have been developed over the last five years in Great Britain, where the Lord Dowding Fund for Humane Research has given grants totaling more than $400,000 to dozens of scientists engaged in research aimed at finding experimental substitutes for animals. Dowding is currently financing several developmental studies of the Ames Test, a promising technique invented by a Berkeley biochemistry professor, Dr. Bruce Ames, that uses salmonella bacteria rather than animals to determine the carcinogenic properties of chemicals. (It was the Ames Test that recently revealed the possible carcinogenic dangers of certain hair dyes.) Another Dowding Fund re-

cipient, research physician Dr. John C. Petricciani, now with the Food and Drug Administration, has devised a method of assessing how tumors grow by inoculating the tumor cells into skin from 9-day-old chicken embryos instead of into living animals.

Animal tests are frequently replaced by other methods discovered and de- 36 veloped by scientists like Dr. Ames who are not trying to avoid the use of animals per se but are simply searching for simpler and more cost-efficient ways to achieve their goals. Dr. Hans Stich, a Canadian cancer researcher, for example, has devised a new test for detecting carcinogenicity in chemicals; it uses human cells, takes one week and costs only about $260. The traditional method, using rats and mice, takes three years and costs approximately $150,000.

In addition to egg embryos, bacteria, and simple organisms, possible sub- 37 stitutes for animals include tissue cultures, human and other mammal cells grown in test tubes, and organ banks. Preserved human corneas, for instance, might be used to spare rabbits the agony of the Draize test. Computers could also play a role if researchers used them fully to analyze experimental data, predict the properties of new drugs, and test theoretical data. Computers can even be programmed to simulate living processes. Mechanical models and audio-visual aids can and do substitute for animals as teaching instruments. Simulated human models could provide valid information in car-crash tests.

Last winter, Representative Robert F. Drinan, Democrat of Massachusetts, 38 introduced a bill authorizing the Department of Health, Education and Welfare to fund projects aimed at discovering research methods that would reduce both the numbers of animals used in laboratories and the suffering to which they are subjected.

Meanwhile, medical and military research and an unending stream of new 39 pharmaceutical, cosmetic, and household products are resulting in an ever-increasing use of animals in the laboratory.

The most recent and thorough exploration of alternatives is Dr. D. H. 40 Smyth's book *Alternatives to Animal Experiments*, which examines every option and weighs its pros and cons. He concludes that there is certainly reason to hope that the numbers of laboratory animals can be drastically reduced, but also warns that it is unlikely a complete phasing out of animal experimentation will happen soon. "By the time we can produce complete alternatives to living tissue," Dr. Smyth writes, "we will not need those alternatives because we will already understand how living tissues work."

Still, Dr. Smyth asks, "Does this mean we can perpetrate any cruelty on 41 animals to satisfy scientific curiosity in the hope that it will one day be useful? To me it certainly does not. . . . Everyone has a right to decide that certain procedures are unacceptable."

Richard Ryder calls animal experimenters to task for trying to have it both 42 ways: Researchers defend their work scientifically on the basis of the *similarities* between human beings and animals, but defend it morally on the basis of the *differences*.

43   And there's the rub: The differences aren't as reassuringly clearcut as they once were. We now know that some animals have a more highly developed intelligence than some human beings—infants, for example, or the retarded and the senile. Dr. Ryder asks, "If we were to be discovered by some more intelligent creatures in the universe, would they be justified in experimenting on us?"

Stephen Rose

Proud to be Speciesist

The animal rights movement has had a powerful impact on scientific research in the academic community. While philosophers like Tom Regan were carefully crafting bulletproof arguments for animal rights, biologists, biochemists, neuroscientists, and psychologists were busily carrying on their research in the same manner they had for decades, largely ignoring the efforts of what they thought to be a few eccentric radicals. Then college administrators started listening to these "radicals," and animal research laboratories began closing. Now scientists are beginning to respond to the animal rights movement, and they are doing it with the same bulletproof logic so adeptly used against them by the philosophers. Stephen Rose, a professor of biology at Open University in England, is one of the scientists who is beginning to fight back. "Proud to Be Speciesist" takes a term near to the heart of many animal rights activists—"speciesism"—and turns it around, using it to make his own case for using animals in research.

1   I RESEARCH ON ANIMALS. I STUDY THE INTIMATE CHEMICAL and electrical processes that are the brain's mechanisms for storing information, for learning and memory. To discover those mechanisms, I analyze the cellular changes that occur when young chicks learn and remember simple tasks. An antivivisectionist once asked me whether my research didn't make me feel rather like Dr. Mengele. No, it doesn't, though I can't resist pointing out that the only country ever to have moved to ban animal experimentation was Germany in the Nazi 1930s, showing a sensitivity that certainly didn't extend to those categories of humans regarded as "lives not worth living."

2   I won't cheapen the justification for my work by claiming that it will have *immediate* health benefits in helping children with learning problems or in treating the devastating consequences of Alzheimer's disease, though the fundamental biological mechanisms I am uncovering are certainly of relevance to

both. I will insist that what I do is part of that great endeavor to understand human biological nature, and to interpret some of the deepest of philosophical questions about the nature of mind and brain. Of course, science is a social activity, and in a democratic society should be democratically controlled.

But the absolutists within the animal rights movement care little for that   3
sort of democratic control. They want to have their argument both ways. On the one hand they claim the *discontinuities* between animals and humans are so great that animal experiments can tell us nothing relevant to the human condition. On the other, they say that because animals are sentient, the *continuities* between animals and humans mean that to privilege the latter over the former is an abuse, for which the perjorative term "speciesism" has been coined. The first statement is plain wrong; the second, the claim that animals have "rights," is sheer cant.

The biological world is a continuum. The base biochemical mechanisms   4
by which we tick are very similar to those in most other organisms. If they weren't, even the food we eat would poison us. Many human diseases and disorders are found in other mammals—which is why we can learn how to treat them by research on animals. Sure, there are differences, as the thalidomide case so tragically demonstrated. But given the choice between testing the toxicity of a new product on animals and not testing, there is no doubt which would be safer.

Of course, we may ask whether so many new drugs, cosmetics or other   5
products are necessary at all, or whether such proliferation is merely the consequence of the restless innovatory needs of capitalist production. But that is not how the animal activists argue. Instead, they claim that there are alternatives to the use of animals. In some cases this is possible, and research to extend the range of such tests should have a high priority. But for many human diseases, understanding and treatment has demanded the use of animals and will continue to do so for the foreseeable future. There is no way, for instance that the biochemical causes of the lethal disease diabetes, or its treatment with insulin, could have been discovered, without experiments on mammals. And we can't use tissue cultures, or bacteria, or plants, to develop and test the treatments needed to alleviate epilepsy, Parkinsonism or manic depression. Anyone who claims otherwise is either dishonest or ignorant.

Equally, however, no biologist can or should deny the sentience of other   6
large-brained animals. The Cartesian myth—that non-human animals are mere mechanisms, pieces of clockwork whose expressions of pain or suffering are no more than the squeak of a rusty cog—is just that, a myth. It was necessary to the generations of Christian philosophers who, following Descartes, wished to preserve the spiritual uniqueness of "Man" whilst accepting the hegemony of physics and biology over the rest of nature. And it was convenient to some 19th-century physiologists in absolving them from responsibil-

ity for the consequences of their experiments. But if I believed for one moment that my chicks were mere clockwork, I might as well stop working with them at all, and go play with computers instead.

7   Unless, of course, I experimented on humans. And this, the privileging of humans, is the nub of the question. Just because we are humans, any discussion of rights must begin with human rights. How far are those rights to be extended—does it even make sense to talk of extending them—to the "animal kingdom"? The animal kingdom isn't composed only of cats and dogs, mice and monkeys. It includes slugs and lice, wasps and mosquitoes. How far can the concept of right be extended—to not swatting a mosquito that is sucking your blood? To prevent your cat from hunting and killing a rat? Does an ant have as many rights as a gorilla?

8   Most people would say no—though I have met one activist who argued that even viruses had souls! I think most animal righters are really arguing that the closer animals are to humans, biologically speaking—that is, evolutionarily speaking—the more rights they should have. So where does the cut-off come? Primates? Mammals? Vertebrates? The moment one concedes that question, it is clear that the decision is arbitrary—that it is *we*, as humans, who are conferring rights on animals—not the animals themselves.

9   Put like this, the spurious nature of the term *speciesism* becomes apparent. It was coined to make the claim that the issue of animal rights is on a par with the struggles for women's rights, or black people's rights, or civil rights. But these human struggles are those in which the oppressed themselves rise up to demand justice and equality, to insist that they are not the objects but the subjects of history.

10   Non-human animals cannot conceive or make such a claim, and to insist the terms are parallel is profoundly offensive, the lazy thinking of a privileged group.

11   Indeed, it is sometimes hard to avoid the impression that, for some among the animal rights movement, non-human animals take precedence over humans. The movement's absolutism and its seeming openness to members of extreme right-wing groups, reinforce the view that, for many of its activists, there is no automatic relationship between a concern for animal rights and one for human rights. Among others, there is an air of sanctimonious hypocrisy. They may, if they wish, refuse insulin if they are diabetic, L-dopa if they have Parkinsonism, antibiotics or surgical procedures that have been validated on animals before being used with humans—but I deny them any right to impose their personal morality on the rest of suffering humanity.

12   Nonetheless, it is essential to listen to the message that the movement carries. Its strength, despite its inchoate ideology, is, I believe, in part a response to the arrogant claim to the domination of nature that western scientific culture drew from its scriptural roots. The animal rights movement is part of a widespread romantic reaction to the seemingly cold rationality of science. Sci-

entists who ignore the strength of this reaction do so at their peril—which is why this week sees the launch, by the British Association for the Advancement of Science of a "Declaration on Animals in Medical Research" signed by more than 800 doctors and scientists, defending the controlled use of animals.

The argument about how non-human animals should be treated is at root 13 about how we as humans should behave. It is here that the biological discontinuities between humans and other animals become important. Our concern about how we treat other species springs out of our very humanness, as biologically and socially constructed creatures. We do not expect cats to debate the rights of mice. The issue is not really about animal rights at all, but about the *duties* that we have just because we are human.

And I am sure that we do have such duties, to behave kindly to other animals, with the minimum of violence and cruelty, not to damage or take their lives insofar as it can be avoided, just as we have duties to the planet's ecology in general. But those duties are limited by an overriding duty to other humans. I have a much-loved and exceedingly beautiful cat. But if I had to choose between saving her life and that of any human child, I would unhesitatingly choose the child. But I would save my cat at the expense of a fish. And so would the vast majority of people. That is species loyalty—speciesism if you like—and I am proud to be a speciesist.

Linda Hasselstrom

The Cow versus the Animal Rights Activist

People often ask Linda Hasselstrom (b. 1943) why she doesn't devote herself full-time to either writing or ranching, although she's been quite successful doing both. Her response is characteristically down-to-earth: "I'm often tired, but never bored. When I'm confronted with a job I detest, six other jobs I prefer can delay it another day." Her writings often focus on her own connection to the land and the lessons she has learned from that association. While the result, in less apt hands, would soon devolve into dogmatic drivel, Hasselstrom somehow strikes the right balance—she rarely sounds like she's preaching. In this excerpt from *Land Circle*, Hasselstrom again uses her own experience as a rancher to dispute animal rights activists' claims that raising and killing animals for food is immoral.

I'M A RANCHER; BEEF CATTLE PROVIDE MOST OF MY MONEY and food. I *like* cows; 1 I've had a warm partnership with them for thirty-five years. I admire a cow's instincts, and suspect her of having a sense of humor, as well as of knowing more than we think. I envy her adaptation to the arid plains, and her apparent serenity in emergencies.

2   I also love to cut into a tender sirloin steak with a hint of pink in the center, and dip each bite into the luscious brown juice surrounding the potatoes on my plate. I relish each mouthful, thinking dreamily of the cow whose flesh I'm eating; I remember when she was born, how she became crippled so that her destiny became the dark freezer in my basement rather than the meat department of a brightly lighted supermarket. I have always considered that the relationship between me and my cattle was a little like a good marriage, with good days and bad days, but considerable satisfaction on both sides.

3   Suddenly my personal paradox has frightening possibilities, because animal rights activists are declaring in sizeable headlines that it is not possible to love animals and also kill them. Anyone who says so, they declare, is vicious, sadistic, and untrustworthy. Some extremists declare that doing anything at all with an animal but letting it follow its normal patterns is immoral, and others declare that we have no right to experiment with animals even to save human lives. Ranchers are targets because we confine cattle in pastures, brand them with hot irons, and cut sections out of their ears to show ownership. Those, say the activists, are the actions of exploiters, unfit to be environmentalists or associate with your daughter. Activists have destroyed research labs to free the animals, sometimes loosing dangerous bacteria. Some deer and bison lovers follow hunters into the woods, shouting to frighten the game. One screaming activist repeatedly whacked and poked a bison hunter with the point of a ski pole; the hunter, a model of nonviolence, neither screamed back nor made threatening gestures with his Rolling Block .45-70, capable of decimating an activist with one shot. In a middle-sized town near our ranch, activists scream obscenities and spit on women in fur coats. At a National Cattlemen's Association meeting, a speaker warned ranchers that new employees may work undercover for animal rights groups. An auction yard in Dixon, California, and a meatpacking plant in San Jose were torched by arsonists, and an unlit Molotov cocktail lobbed into the offices of the California Cattlemen's Association. A popular country singer, k.d. lang, was part of a "Meat Stinks" campaign supported by People for the Ethical Treatment of Animals, a group that opposes using animals "other than for companionship." Radio and television stations in beef-producing areas, including South Dakota, promptly stopped playing all of lang's records. I was disappointed; watching lang croon sweet nothings into the ear of a dairy cow—in no danger of being eaten because she is too valuable as a milk factory, and tough as guitar strings—was the highlight of my television watching.

4   Her problem, and the difficulty of the ski pole-wielding activist confronting the bison hunter, is lack of information. The beef cattle industry has three major phases. First, farmers and ranchers own basic herds and

produce breeding cattle, or yearlings sold as feeders. They keep the breeding cattle, and sell the yearlings at a sale market where the price is determined by supply and demand, and by bidders. When the ranchers sell, they have no opportunity to add costs of materials to the product, passing expenses on to the consumer as most businesses do. Ranchers take the price offered on sale day, or take the cattle home—where they will require more care, more expense.

The second phase of the beef cattle industry consists of stocker operators whose pastures put additional weight on feeder cattle before they enter feedlots, the third phase. Confined in muddy, stinking feedlots, cattle consume huge quantities of pesticide-laced grain designed to make the meat fat enough for consumer preference, and produce immense amounts of polluted runoff. The dangers posed to humans by the chemicals in both the meat and runoff have drawn environmentalists' attention to the cattle industry—but they are attacking the wrong end of production. Feedlots are generally operated by corporations that control feeding, butchering, and in some cases supermarket sales of meat, grain, and associated products. In 1988, three companies—Iowa Beef Packing (IBP, owned by Occidental Petroleum), ConAgra, and Excel (Cargill)—accounted for 70 percent of all fed cattle slaughtered in the United States. These monopolies, which also control a considerable amount of the nation's grain, flour, pork, egg, and poultry production, do pass costs to the consumers, hiking prices far above what ranchers get for their labor. But enormous corporations are tough to find and difficult to move; it's easier to attack individual hunters and ranchers.

I'm afraid that one day I'll be sweating and swearing in the corral, struggling to brand calves twice my weight, and suddenly find I'm surrounded by people with no sense of humor who have come to "liberate" my cows.

I'd like to discourage that kind of behavior, partly because some ranchers are impatient and armed, and partly because it's based on lack of information. Unchecked ignorance and paranoia can escalate misunderstandings to bloodshed. And some of my cows, unaccustomed to noise and rudeness, might kick the strangers, who would sue me, not the cows.

I recognize the difficulty many people face in reconciling their love of animals with their love of meat, but I believe the problem is increasing because we are getting further from the realities of human existence. As we developed our large brain, we also built a complicated set of desires that seems to imply that enough wealth will allow us to sit still. We want our food to be easily obtainable; now that we no longer have to run it down and beat it to death, many of us buy it precooked. When someone markets predigested dinners, there will be buyers. But many of us will continue to wear leather shoes, lust after leather skirts and jackets and leather upholstery on our car seats, and relish a good steak or hamburger. As long as humans have such desires but remain unwilling or unable to slaughter and skin the animals that can satisfy them, ranchers will be needed.

9   In defense, beef industry representatives say a pregnant woman produces four hundred thousand times as much estrogen every day as she would get from the average serving of beef injected with growth-inducing hormones. I've spent my life doing hard physical labor while eating organically raised cattle, so I understand the healthy properties of red meat, and I despair at the perception among many Americans that this tasty stuff isn't good for them. I am part of an industry that requires me to donate one dollar from each animal sold to the Beef Check-Off plan, which promotes the facts about eating beef and health—a group defense instituted, reluctantly, by cattle ranchers in response to misinformation spread by antibeef activists. In part, this idea comes from paranoia about cholesterol and growth hormones; in part, it's a result of government-subsidized campaigns by producers of other foods. In many countries, the beef I eat in a year would make a family wealthy, but I am frustrated by being unable to sell directly to consumers beef raised on grass that is the natural product of my land.

10   Like most ranchers, I work more closely with cows than any animal rights activist I've ever met. I kneel in steaming cow manure and hot urine while talking kindly to a cow and urging a calf from her birth canal. I must brand calves so they won't stray or be stolen; castrate bulls to make them edible steers and protect bloodlines. I've cut cows' throats, helped gut and skin them, and canned every edible part of them for my family's use; in the process I've gained a deep appreciation for what killing our own meat can mean to humans. Because of this close involvement with the lives of cows, I feel I have worked hard for the right to eat their flesh. My relationship with cows is intimate, balanced—the cow is capable of killing or injuring me—and demands the most complete responsibility from the human half of the equation. The relationship is reviewed by both parties almost daily, and its implications carefully considered at least by the human half. Who knows what the cows are thinking?

11   Animal rights activists seem to me guilty of simplistic thinking and tunnel vision, although I envy people who forswear *all* killing and eating of flesh; I believe they have an easier road than those of us who try to strike a balance between exploitation and love. Similarly, I don't consider strolling along behind a fur-wearing woman screaming epithets, or shooting a cow, or burning a packing plant, to be meaningful activism; such actions are too simplistic, and too close to terrorism. During the easy environmentalism of the 1960s, one could lie on the lawn smoking grass on "Gentle Thursdays," sing "We Shall Overcome" and shout "No More War," and go back to class, one's pacifist duty done for the week. During that period, a few hard-working environmentalists passed strict laws which gave us a sense of power, but were some-

times as narrow and poorly thought out as the actions behind the corporate greed that made them necessary.

All of us—ranchers, environmentalists, and animal rights activists—if we expect to be taken seriously, should put as much work into defining and achieving realistic, fair goals as ranchers spend trying to keep cows alive. Few of us are born with that kind of dedication; we have to develop an interest in detail, a respect for our fellow animals—even Democrats, feminists, and snail darters—and an understanding of our responsibilities to the whole spectrum of life on the planet. What E. B. White wrote nearly sixty years ago is still true: 12

> Before you can be an internationalist you have first to be a naturalist and feel the ground under you making a whole circle. It is easier for a man to be loyal to his club than to his planet; the by-laws are shorter, and he is personally acquainted with the other members. 13

> The effect of any organization of a social and brotherly nature is to strengthen rather than to diminish the lines which divide people into classes; the effect of states and nations is the same, and eventually these lines will have to be softened, these powers will have to be generalized. It is written on the wall that this is so. I'm not inventing it, I'm just copying it off the wall. 14

Statistics from a few years ago declared that the average American ate fourteen cows in a lifetime, but consumption will drop to a twenty-five-year low in 1990 as hysterical and ill-informed folks screech about the dangers of beef. I've eaten more than my share in an effort to make up for vegetarian relatives and friends. When I calculated this my own family consisted of my parents, and my husband and me; we would butcher two animals, usually heifers, per year. Assuming each of us ate about one-fourth of each animal, I was eating an entire cow every four years, which means I've gobbled upwards of ten so far. If I live to be eighty, as I hope to do, I'll have eaten at least twenty of my own herd, not to mention the beef I eat in restaurants when I'm upholding the honor and economy of ranchers while surrounded by midwesterners lying about how good the frozen fish tastes. I am willing to take responsibility for the deaths of those twenty bovines, because I've saved the lives of many more than that. 15

Vegetarians may whittle the number of beefeaters down, but I'm confident beef will remain part of the American diet. Ranchers are learning to produce lean meat; I believe we will soon begin to move away from the dangerous chemicals and growth hormones we've been talked into using in order to raise productivity above sensible limits. At the same time, we are becoming aware of growing criticism of the damage cattle do to public lands by poorly controlled grazing. Little has been done, however, to control the meat and grain 16 monopolies which will eventually control our food supplies and determine grocery prices.

17   It's a popular pastime now to debunk the myth of the independent cowboy and the cattle baron, and rightly so in many ways. Although there's truth to the legends, they were popularized and distorted by dime novels and bad movies; and some cow folk even bought their own advertising campaign or fantasy, and played their roles more eagerly than pulp heroes. They deserve to be reminded of reality.

18   But simply pronouncing the death of the age of the cattle baron and cowboy is too simple. Sure, those men—and their womenfolk—treated the West as if it was their kingdom. They battled its hardships, "civilized" it as they thought best—because they were given a challenge to do so by the wisest spirits of their age. Where I live was "the Great American Desert," shunned by all but the hardiest explorers. Later, the thinkers in their comfy New England offices decided that "rain follows the plow," and all that was needed to make the desert bloom were a few hardy souls to build claim shanties and plow to the horizon. The New England philosophers had no idea what difficult conditions westerners faced, but the westerners went right on working until they controlled everything but the weather.

19   We now see their errors, but we might have been guilty of the same actions, now seen as abuse, had we been cattle barons in those days. And some changes have been made not out of lack of concern, but through economic necessity. Cowboys, paid "forty a month and found," used to ride the range constantly, moving cattle around so that grazing was spread evenly over a wide area. Today workers who might once have become cowboys and cowgirls are instead making big wages in a city, and many ranchers operate alone, or assisted only by their smaller number of children or seasonal help. They have tried to adapt the advice given to farmers by agricultural experts within the government to invest more money, get big, and become efficient, but it didn't work as well on mobile cattle as on rows of corn; it didn't work on corn either, but that's another story, and Wes Jackson is telling it in his sustainable agriculture research at The Land Institute.

20   This generation's heroes are people who work to save our environment: the dead Saint Ed Abbey, Wendell Berry, Wes Jackson, Annie Dillard, Ann Zwinger, Gary Snyder, Barry Lopez, Gretel Ehrlich, Bil Gilbert, Kim Stafford, and other writers who contemplate humanity and nature. Some have attained almost mythical stature themselves, and we all try to learn from and imitate them. We believe, fervently, that they are right; those old ranchers believed in Manifest Destiny and the American Way just as passionately. What if we're wrong again?

21   Instead of blaming ranchers and farmers for doing what they were told to do, environmentalists need to show us what's wrong with the way we graze cat-

tle, if they know. Most of the complainers have never been personally introduced to a cow, have no clear idea what's wrong with her grazing habits, and
wouldn't know a good stand of native grass if they were lying in it reciting poetry or reading Abbey. They're willing to take someone else's word—just as the
ranchers took the government's word for how to use the land. Too many environmentalists condemn without knowledge. None of the rhetoric changes
the fact that the grasslands are in trouble, and only the people who own the
land are likely to resolve the problems.

When I left the ranch, bound for a life of comfortable academic superi-   22
ority in some ivory tower, I cared considerably less about cows than I do now,
though I already knew more than the average American about the brutal facts
of bovine life. Living beside a packing plant for a few months made a tempo-
rary vegetarian out of me. I saw cows unloaded daily, heard the thud as the
knacker's maul struck their foreheads, the bawl of pain as they were swung,
only stunned, off their hooves by a hook thrust into an ankle. Sometimes, I
could hear the bubbling, choking screech cut short as a worker finally opened
a steer's throat. My cat grew sleek dragging home fleshy bones larger than he
was, and I watched smugly when a steer escaped and ran through the streets,
ineffectually pursued by a police force with little experience in cattle management. But as soon as I moved back to South Dakota, where I look out on my
walking larder through every window, I went back to eating meat without hes-
itation. I earn every mouthful. The outmoded butchering practices used in
packing plants have been changed; animals are killed with a gun, rather than
stunned, before butchering begins. Other changes in the beef industry show
increased awareness of public scrutiny.

When I returned to the ranch, I had shed some of the narrow attitudes   23
with which I grew up, and I became involved in the complicated process of
keeping a cow alive. I've learned, but I've remained a part of a wider world.
Critics think ranch men read only *Farm Journal* and their wives do nothing
but cook and raise children, but many are college graduates, and even those
who aren't read more widely than their ancestors did. They also watch television; the rest of the world is no longer distant and inaccessible to them. They
are informed about conditions in the "outer" world, and aware that most consumers know little about ranching or the food processing industry. For example, while farmers and ranchers know a good deal about what happens to
their products—meat, grains, hay—when these leave the land, many folks who
buy those products or by-products neatly wrapped in polyethylene haven't a
clue about their production, and don't want to. Knowing the origins of our
food and frivolities helps us make sensible choices about what we really want;
in some cases, the sacrifice is not worth the benefit. When I shop for groceries, I carry a booklet that categorizes products by how socially responsible
the producer is. I avoid products if the Council on Economic Priorities re-

ports no reductions in animal testing by those companies, and no company contributions toward alternative research. On the other hand, I wouldn't hesitate to use any compatible animal heart to save the life of a child. But if the child was cocaine-addicted in the womb, and the operation was at taxpayers' expense, I could not support it.

24   Cattle have been domesticated for centuries, and belong in a separate category from animals bred for laboratory tests, and from wildlife; we are not likely to stop eating and managing cattle herds, nor should we. Wild cattle herds would be hardly more aesthetically satisfying than tame ones, as Indians have discovered while dodging sacred cows. A poorly managed herd of cattle can be as repugnant as Edward Abbey insisted, but that's the fault of the human manager, not the cows. With adequate feed and water and space to move while grazing selectively, a herd of cattle can be at least as acceptable in polite society as the average dog or child. Cattle do attract flies; before poisonous sprays and other costly forms of fly control existed, we built "oilers," slinging old feed sacks on a wire between two posts. We poured used crankcase oil on the cloth (recycling!) and cows rubbed oil on their bodies to discourage flies and lice. When the chemical companies noticed us using a product we didn't buy, they developed spray, injections, and fly-killing ear tags.

25   But most folks don't know this, because they spend more time with domesticated cats and dogs, and half-savage children, than with cows; and it is the activities that result from ignorance that bother me. Since I have become moderately well known as an articulate ranch woman, I've been questioned several times about animal rights.

26   What do I think of proposed laws to make branding illegal, for example? My reply: the folks who pass that law can find and return or replace the stolen cattle, catch and prosecute the thieves, and pay the costs of the confusion and crime. Branding does hurt, but it places a permanent mark on a cow, so even if she's illegally butchered, an owner has some chance of proving it. No other method is as useful, and I'll consider another method of marking my cattle when we stop licensing cars to identify them and prevent their theft. Every few years, someone suggests that acid brands are more merciful; I'd like that idea tested on the folks who suggest it: which hurts most, a burn with a hot iron, or an acid burn? Even if they are less painful, acid brands might not be enough; local old-timers talk about the days when government agencies used them. Enterprising cowboys sometimes roped the cows, smeared axle grease on the brands to neutralize the acid, turned the cows out until the hair grew back, and a few months later branded cows that appeared ownerless. Speaking of pain, what about breeds of dogs—Boxers, Doberman Pinschers, Schnauzers—not considered attractive unless their ears and tails are chopped off? Poodles, among the most widely popular dog breeds, just have their tails trimmed,

though dogs with extremities intact are now allowed in some shows. What about the thousands of pets killed each year because owners couldn't be bothered with them any longer? Is it more merciful to keep a wild predator like a cat confined to an apartment for its entire life than to brand a cow once? So-called "pet" cats slaughter wild songbirds by the millions in most cities, but few animal rights activists picket pet owners. Why do suburbanites let their dogs run loose to chase and kill wildlife and calves?

Today's cattle live very well compared to their ancestors, perhaps too well 27 for the health of the species; some old breeds are dying out. We may need their genetic diversity in coming years, if we continue to breed cattle for beef and milk production instead of their ability to survive, coddling them with medications until they can no longer resist disease. The average calf is observed and protected from predators at birth, and quickly vaccinated against many diseases. When necessary operations like branding, earmarking, castration, and dehorning occur, they are done with sterile equipment, supplemented with healing sprays to keep flies and maggots from the wounds. In the wild, only the fittest animals would survive a tough winter; modern cattle operators carefully control herd feed throughout the year for maximum gain, and maximum protection of pasture. Sick, weak, crippled, or otherwise unfit animals are culled from the herd, instead of being allowed to suffer and pass on their genes and illnesses. Ranchers who habitually abuse their cattle damage their own income and endanger themselves, both indirectly—by hurting their own profits—and directly; an abused or frightened cow can be a dangerous proposition.

As the rancher's awareness of chemical dangers increases, and as costs 28 climb, some of us are realizing that we could raise organic, lean beef with less effort and expense, with the help of a real demand in the market from an informed public. Some ranchers already nervous about growth hormone implants would give them up if the steers didn't gain; heavier steers mean more income. As I write this, several tuna-packing companies have finally instituted policies that will make the killing of dolphins unprofitable. If the public demands chemical-free beef, it will be produced; ideally, South Dakota could encourage the sale of cattle straight from the organic grass of our pastures to the hungry customer—rather than selling the land for garbage dumps. I have heard of no state-sponsored efforts to keep native grass unplowed and grazed by cows for organic beef. If state officials put half the energy and cash spent on tourism into promoting the state's ranchers—whose product can keep the land relatively undamaged—we might discover a strong demand for grass-fed beef. And why not give tourists the chance to visit real, working ranches?

So if you like beef but don't like chemicals, cholesterol, or high food 29 prices, get acquainted with a rancher who raises cattle on grass. Get a few

friends together, buy a fat young "beef," and butcher it yourself—or ask a
hunter to help. If one person does it, you'll just be a well-fed oddity. If two
people do it, or five, it might become a movement. Think of it! Ranchers and
beef eaters, joining together to beat chemical companies and monopolies;
why, it's the stuff democracy is made of.

30   I'll say it again: I love cows, and consider my care and understanding of
them superior to the treatment they'd get at the hands of the average animal
rights activist.

Jonathan Swift

A Modest Proposal

Jonathan Swift (1667–1745), Irish writer, poet, and clergyman, used his works as an opportunity to comment
on the society he lived in. He is best known for his novel, *Gulliver's Travels*, but "A Modest Proposal" is perhaps his most effective social commentary. At the time "A Modest Proposal" appeared, Ireland was afflicted by
a great famine, made worse by the oppressive rule of England. Harsh taxation by the invading English made it
difficult for all but a few to sustain themselves at a reasonable level. Master of satire, Swift offered his "Modest Proposal" as a means of solving the tremendous problems Ireland faced. If "A Modest Proposal" didn't accomplish that, it has, for over two centuries, enlightened us all on the art of satire.

1   IT IS A MELANCHOLY OBJECT TO THOSE WHO WALK through this great town or
travel in the country, when they see the streets, the roads, and cabin doors
crowded with beggars of the female sex, followed by three, four, or six children, all in rags and importuning every passenger for an alms. These mothers,
instead of being able to work for their honest livelihood, are forced to employ
all their time in strolling to beg sustenance for their helpless infants, who, as
they grow up, either turn thieves for want of work, or leave their dear native
country to fight for the Pretender in Spain, or sell themselves to the Barba-
does.

2   I think it is agreed by all parties that this prodigious number of children
in the arms, or on the backs, or at the heels of their mothers, and frequently
of their fathers, is in the present deplorable state of the kingdom a very great
additional grievance; and, therefore, whoever could find out a fair, cheap, and
easy method of making these children sound, useful members of the com-
monwealth, would deserve so well of the public as to have his statue set up for
a preserver of the nation.

But my intention is very far from being confined to provide only for the [3] children of professed beggars; it is of a much greater extent, and shall take in the whole number of infants at a certain age who are born of parents in effect as little able to support them as those who demand our charity in the streets.

As to my own part, having turned my thoughts for many years upon this [4] important subject, and maturely weighed the several schemes of other projectors, I have always found them grossly mistaken in their computation. It is true, a child just dropped from its dam may be supported by her milk for a solar year, with little other nourishment; at most not above the value of two shillings, which the mother may certainly get, or the value in scraps, by her lawful occupation of begging; and it is exactly at one year old that I propose to provide for them in such a manner as instead of being a charge upon their parents or the parish, or wanting food and raiment for the rest of their lives, they shall on the contrary contribute to the feeding, and partly to the clothing, of many thousands.

There is likewise another great advantage in my scheme, that it will pre- [5] vent those voluntary abortions, and that horrid practice of women murdering their bastard children, alas! too frequent among us! sacrificing the poor innocent babes I doubt more to avoid the expense than the shame, which would move tears and pity in the most savage and inhuman breast.

The number of souls in Ireland being usually reckoned one million and a [6] half, of these I calculate there may be about two hundred thousand couples whose wives are breeders; from which number I subtract thirty thousand couples who are able to maintain their own children, although I apprehend there cannot be so many, under the present distresses of the kingdom; but this being granted, there will remain an hundred and seventy thousand breeders. I again subtract fifty thousand for those women who miscarry, or whose children die by accident or disease within the year. There only remain a hundred and twenty thousand children of poor parents annually born. The question therefore is, how this number shall be reared and provided for? which, as I have already said, under the present situation of affairs, is utterly impossible by all the methods hitherto proposed. For we can neither employ them in handicraft or agriculture; we neither build houses (I mean in the country) nor cultivate land. They can very seldom pick up a livelihood by stealing, till they arrive at six years old, except where they are of towardly parts; although I confess they learn the rudiments much earlier, during which time they can, however, be properly looked upon only as probationers; as I have been informed by a principal gentleman in the county of Cavan, who protested to me that he never knew above one or two instances under the age of six, even in a part of the kingdom so renowned for the quickest proficiency in that art.

I am assured by our merchants, that a boy or a girl before twelve years old [7] is no saleable commodity; and even when they come to this age they will not yield above three pounds or three pounds and half a crown at most on the Exchange; which cannot turn to account either to the parents or the kingdom, the charge of nutriment and rags having been at least four times that value.

8   I shall now therefore humbly propose my own thoughts, which I hope will not be liable to the least objection.

9   I have been assured by a very knowing American of my acquaintance in London, that a young healthy child well nursed is, at year old, a most delicious, nourishing, and wholesome food, whether stewed, roasted, baked, or boiled; and I make no doubt that it will equally serve in a fricassee or a ragout.

10   I do therefore humbly offer it to public consideration that of the hundred and twenty thousand children already computed, twenty thousand may be reserved for breed, whereof only one-fourth part to be males; which is more than we allow to sheep, black cattle, or swine; and my reason is, that these children are seldom the fruits of marriage, a circumstance not much regarded by our savages; therefore one male will be sufficient to serve four females. That the remaining hundred thousand may, at a year old, be offered in sale to the persons of quality and fortune through the kingdom, always advising the mother to let them suck plentifully in the last month, so as to render them plump and fat for a good table. A child will make two dishes at an entertainment for friends; and when the family dines alone, the fore or hind quarter will make a reasonable dish, and seasoned with a little pepper or salt will be very good boiled on the fourth day, especially in winter.

11   I have reckoned upon a medium that a child just born will weigh twelve pounds, and in a solar year, if tolerably nursed, will increase to twenty-eight pounds.

12   I grant this food will be somewhat dear, and therefore very proper for landlords, who, as they have already devoured most of the parents, seem to have the best title to the children.

13   Infant's flesh will be in season throughout the year, but more plentiful in March, and a little before and after: for we are told by a grave author, an eminent French physician, that fish being a prolific diet, there are more children born in Roman Catholic countries about nine months after Lent than at any other season; therefore, reckoning a year after Lent, the markets will be more glutted than usual, because the number of popish infants is at least three to one in this kingdom; and therefore it will have one other collateral advantage, by lessening the number of papists among us.

14   I have already computed the charge of nursing a beggar's child (in which list I reckon all cottagers, laborers, and four-fifths of the farmers) to be about two shillings per annum, rags included; and I believe no gentleman would repine to give ten shillings for the carcass of a good fat child, which, as I have said, will make four dishes of excellent nutritive meat, when he has only some particular friend or his own family to dine with him. Thus the squire will

learn to be a good landlord, and grow popular among his tenants; the mother will have eight shillings net profit, and be fit for work till she produces another child.

Those who are more thrifty (as I must confess the times require) may flay 15 the carcass; the skin of which artificially dressed will make admirable gloves for ladies, and summer boots for fine gentlemen.

As to our city of Dublin, shambles may be appointed for this purpose in 16 the most convenient parts of it, and butchers we may be assured will not be wanting: although I rather recommend buying the children alive, and dressing them hot from the knife as we do roasting pigs.

A very worthy person, a true lover of his country, and whose virtues I 17 highly esteem, was lately pleased in discoursing on this matter to offer a refinement upon my scheme. He said that many gentlemen of this kingdom, having of late destroyed their deer, he conceived that the want of venison might be well supplied by the bodies of young lads and maidens, not exceeding fourteen years of age nor under twelve; so great a number of both sexes in every county being now ready to starve for want of work and service; and these to be disposed of by their parents, if alive, or otherwise by their nearest relations. But with due deference to so excellent a friend and so deserving a patriot, I cannot be altogether in his sentiments. For as to the males, my American acquaintance assured me from frequent experience that their flesh was generally tough and lean, like that of our schoolboys by continual exercise, and their taste disagreeable; and to fatten them would not answer the charge. Then as to the females, it would, I think, with humble submission be a loss to the public, because they soon would become breeders themselves; and besides, it is not improbable that some scrupulous people might be apt to censure such a practice (although indeed very unjustly) as a little bordering upon cruelty; which, I confess, has always been with me the strongest objection against any project, how well soever intended.

But in order to justify my friend, he confessed that this expedient was put 18 into his head by the famous Psalmanazar, a native of the island Formosa, who came from thence to London above twenty years ago, and in conversation told my friend that in his country when any young person happened to be put to death, the executioner sold the carcass to persons of quality as a prime dainty; and that in his time the body of a plump girl of fifteen, who was crucified for an attempt to poison the emperor, was sold to his imperial majesty's prime minister of state, and other great mandarins of the court, in joints from the gibbet, at four hundred crowns. Neither indeed can I deny that if the same use were made of several plump young girls in this town, who without one single groat to their fortunes cannot stir abroad without a chair, and appear at the playhouse and assemblies in foreign fineries which they never will pay for, the kingdom would not be the worse.

19   Some persons of a desponding spirit are in great concern about that vast number of poor people who are aged, diseased, or maimed, and I have been desired to employ my thoughts what course may be taken to ease the nation of so grievous an encumbrance. But I am not in the least pain upon that matter, because it is very well known that they are every day dying and rotting by cold and famine, and filth and vermin, as fast as can be reasonably expected. And as to the younger labourers, they are now in almost as hopeful a condition. They cannot get work, and consequently pine away for want of nourishment, to a degree that if at any time they are accidentally hired to common labour, they have not strength to perform it; and thus the country and themselves are in a fair way of being soon delivered from the evils to come.

20   I have too long digressed, and therefore shall return to my subject. I think the advantages by the proposal which I have made are obvious and many, as well as of the highest importance.

21   For first, as I have already observed, it would greatly lessen the number of papists, with whom we are yearly overrun, being the principal breeders of the nation as well as our most dangerous enemies; and who stay at home on purpose with a design to deliver the kingdom to the Pretender, hoping to take their advantage by the absence of so many good Protestants, who have chosen rather to leave their country than stay at home and pay tithes against their conscience to an idolatrous Episcopal curate.

22   Secondly, the poor tenants will have something valuable of their own, which by law may be made liable to distress, and help to pay their landlord's rent, their corn and cattle being already seized and money a thing unknown.

23   Thirdly, whereas the maintenance of an hundred thousand children from two years old and upward, cannot be computed at less than ten shillings apiece per annum, the nation's stock will be thereby increased fifty thousand pounds per annum, besides the profit of a new dish introduced to the tables of all gentlemen of fortune in the kingdom who have any refinement in taste. And the money will circulate among ourselves, the goods being entirely of our own growth and manufacture.

24   Fourthly, the constant breeders, besides the gain of eight shillings sterling per annum by the sale of their children, will be rid of the charge of maintaining them after the first year.

25   Fifthly, this food would likewise bring great custom to taverns, where the vintners will certainly be so prudent as to procure the best receipts for dressing it to perfection, and consequently have their houses frequented by all the fine gentlemen, who justly value themselves upon their knowledge in good eating; and a skillful cook, who understands how to oblige his guests, will contrive to make it as expensive as they please.

26   Sixthly, this would be a great inducement to marriage, which all wise nations have either encouraged by rewards or enforced by laws and penal-

ties. It would increase the care and tenderness of mothers towards their children, when they were sure of a settlement for life to the poor babes, provided in some sort by the public, to their annual profit instead of expense. We should see an honest emulation among the married women, which of them could bring the fattest child to the market. Men would become as fond of their wives during the time of their pregnancy as they are now of their mares in foal, their cows in calf, their sows when they are ready to farrow; nor offer to beat or kick them (as is too frequent a practice) for fear of a miscarriage.

Many other advantages might be enumerated. For instance, the addition 27 of some thousand carcasses in our exportation of barreled beef, the propagation of swine's flesh, and improvement in the art of making good bacon, so much wanted among us by the great destruction of pigs, too frequent at our tables, and which are no way comparable in taste or magnificence to a well-grown, fat, yearling child, which roasted whole will make a considerable figure at a lord mayor's feast or any other public entertainment. But this and many others I omit, being studious of brevity.

Supposing that one thousand families in this city would be constant cus- 28 tomers for infants' flesh, besides others who might have it at merry meetings, particularly weddings and christenings, I compute that Dublin would take off annually about twenty thousand carcasses, and the rest of the kingdom (where probably they will be sold somewhat cheaper) the remaining eighty thousand.

I can think of no one objection that will possibly be raised against this 29 proposal, unless it should be urged that the number of people will be thereby much lessened in the kingdom. This I freely own, and it was indeed one principal design in offering it to the world. I desire the reader will observe, that I calculate my remedy for this one individual kingdom of Ireland and for no other that ever was, is, or I think ever can be upon earth. Therefore let no man talk to me of other expedients: of taxing our absentees at five shillings a pound: of using neither clothes nor household furniture except what is of our own growth and manufacture: of utterly rejecting the materials and instruments that promote foreign luxury: of curing the expensiveness of pride, vanity, idleness, and gaming in our women: of introducing a vein of parsimony, prudence, and temperance: of learning to love our country, wherein we differ even from Laplanders and the inhabitants of Topinamboo: of quitting our animosities and factions, nor act any longer like the Jews, who were murdering one another at the very moment their city was taken: of being a little cautious not to sell our country and conscience for nothing: of teaching landlords to have at least one degree of mercy toward their tenants: lastly, of putting a spirit of honesty, industry, and skill into our shopkeepers; who, if a resolution could now be taken to buy only our native goods, would immediately unite to cheat and exact upon us in the price, the measure, and the goodness, nor could ever yet be brought to make one fair proposal of just dealing, though often and earnestly invited to it.

30   Therefore, I repeat, let no man talk to me of these and the like expedients, till he has at least a glimpse of hope that there will ever be some hearty and sincere attempt to put them in practice.

31   But as to myself, having been wearied out for many years with offering vain, idle, visionary thoughts, and at length utterly despairing of success, I fortunately fell upon this proposal, which, as it is wholly new, so it has something solid and real, of no expense and little trouble, full in our own power, and whereby we can incur no danger in disobliging England. For this kind of commodity will not bear exportation, the flesh being of too tender a consistence to admit a long continuance in salt, although perhaps I could name a country which would be glad to eat up our whole nation without it.

32   After all, I am not so violently bent upon my own opinion as to reject any offer proposed by wise men, which shall be found equally innocent, cheap, easy, and effectual. But before something of that kind shall be advanced in contradiction to my scheme, and offering a better, I desire the author or authors will be pleased maturely to consider two points. First, as things now stand, how they will be able to find food and raiment for a hundred thousand useless mouths and backs. And secondly, there being a round million of creatures in human figure throughout this kingdom, whose whole subsistence put into a common stock would leave them in debt two millions of pounds sterling, adding those who are beggars by profession to the bulk of farmers, cottagers, and labourers, with their wives and children who are beggars in effect; I desire those politicians who dislike my overture, and may perhaps be so bold to attempt an answer, that they will first ask the parents of these mortals, whether they would not at this day think it a great happiness to have been sold for food at a year old in the manner I prescribe, and thereby have avoided such a perpetual scene of misfortunes as they have since gone through by the oppression of landlords, the impossibility of paying rent without money or trade, the want of common sustenance, with neither house nor clothes to cover them from the inclemencies of weather, and the most inevitable prospect of entailing the like or greater miseries upon their breed for ever.

33   I profess, in the sincerity of my heart, that I have not the least personal interest in endeavouring to promote this necessary work, having no other motive than the public good of my country, by advancing our trade, providing for infants, relieving the poor, and giving some pleasure to the rich. I have no children by which I can propose to get a single penny; the youngest being nine years old, and my wife past child-bearing.

Student MLA Essay

Eileen Williams

Mandatory AIDS Testing for Job Applicants

There is no need to shy away from controversial topics in research papers. Here, Eileen puts forth a very convincing case for banning AIDS testing of job applicants. Note that her case is consistently supported by research—she doesn't just make undocumented assertions.

AIDS IS A RAPIDLY SPREADING DISEASE that is reaching epidemic proportions. 1
According to a brochure entitled *Facts About AIDS* put out by the Public
Health Service, AIDS was first reported in the United States in 1981. By early
1987, an estimated 1.5 million Americans had been infected with the AIDS
virus, more than 30,000 had developed AIDS, and 17,000 had died from it.
Researchers are predicting that by 1991, these latter two figures will be ten
times as high. An issue evolving from the AIDS problem is that of whether or
not employers can require job applicants to take a blood test for AIDS before
the employers will consider hiring them. Although many workers feel they
have the right to refuse to work with an AIDS victim because they do not want
to risk contracting the illness, and although an employer might not want to
invest in a person whose condition ends in death, these tests should not be
made mandatory. They will only lead to discrimination in both the workplace
and with insurance, and they are an invasion of privacy.

Once an AIDS test for a job applicant has come back positive, discrimi- 2
nation is likely to start. Many employees feel they do not have to work with a
person infected with AIDS because they risk contracting the disease. This
shows ignorance because over and over the U.S. Public Health Service has assured the public that AIDS cannot be transmitted through casual contact.
The only ways known to transmit the virus are through sexual contact, the
sharing of needles for intravenous drugs, blood transfusions, and rarely, a
mother's breast milk (*Facts*). One cannot contract the AIDS virus from a toilet seat or from sharing someone's eating utensils. These concerned employees
have no logical or medical evidence to support them, only emotional input.

An employer might also want to require AIDS testing so he'll know if he 3
wants to invest in a person whom he expects always to be sick and to have a
short life expectancy. But in the *Facts About AIDS* brochure, it is stated that it
might be up to five years after a person is infected with the virus before he starts
experiencing symptoms. So even though he may have several good years to live

and work, the employer will probably label him an AIDS victim and not hire him. This is discrimination because a person's life should not end the moment he or she is diagnosed as having AIDS. As long as he can, he should be allowed to lead a normal life, including working for as long as he is able. Fortunately, according to the article, "Workplace AIDS," most authorities feel that people with AIDS are included in the laws that protect the handicapped from discrimination. So if they don't have any symptoms that interfere with their work ability, they cannot be fired. In all fairness, this should apply to hiring as well.

4   Discrimination doesn't remain only in the workplace, though. If job applicants' test results are passed on to insurance companies, they sometimes discriminate also. Fortunately, as stated in a *U.S. News and World Report* article, "contract law forbids insurers from barring newly diagnosed AIDS patients from group health plans". Yet, according to another *U.S. News* article, a man in Colorado sent a copy of his negative AIDS test to his insurance company, and they still refused him "on the basis that the fact he got tested at all made him too great a risk". These companies are presently fighting bills that would keep them from refusing AIDS victims.

5   Along with causing discrimination, the AIDS tests are invading persons' privacy. Employers, by testing job applicants for AIDS, are prying into their personal lives. Employers don't test prospective employees for other diseases that aren't contagious through casual contact such as cancer, syphillis, and cerebral palsy, and for that matter, for diseases that are more easily contagious, such as hepatitis and pneumonia, so why should AIDS be an exception? Besides, once employers explore all aspects of applicants' health and discover positive AIDS tests, what's to stop employers from looking into causes and discriminating against the applicants, not necessarily because of AIDS, but perhaps because they are homosexual? That is quite a generalization, and perhaps most employers are more unbiased than this, but it is certainly possible that discrimination could become this out-of-hand.

6   Yes, the population of AIDS victims is rapidly growing, and it is frightening because everyone is afraid of contracting this dreadful illness. But if we refrain from the activities known to transmit AIDS, we have no need to worry, even in the workplace. AIDS victims—like everyone else—have the right to live normal lives, and as long as they are able to perform their job duties, they should not be discriminated against. So, until the medical community finds any evidence that AIDS can be transmitted through casual contact, I don't see any risk with an AIDS victim in the workplace. Therefore, mandatory blood tests to check for AIDS in job applicants are unnecessary.

Works Cited
"AIDS: No Need for Worry in the Workplace." *Newsweek* 25 Nov. 1985: 51.
"AIDS: What We Know Now." *McCall's* Apr. 1987: 143–44.

Facts About AIDS. U.S. Dept. of Health and Human Services, Spring 1986.

"Mandatory Tests for AIDS?" *U.S. News & World Report* 9 March 1987: 62.

"Workplace AIDS." *Nation's Business* Nov. 1986: 30.

Alan Hirsch

Don't Blame the Jury

A graduate of Yale Law School, Alan Hirsch is now a freelance writer and an adjunct professor of English at Hartwick College. His articles have appeared in the *Washington Times* and *Troika Magazine,* and he has written several books, including *For the People: What the Constitution Really Says about Your Rights.* The following essay originally appeared in *Troika.*

SEVERAL RECENT HIGH-TRIALS, ESPECIALLY THOSE of O.J. Simpson, the Menendez brothers, and the police officers who pummeled Rodney King, have spawned recognition that the criminal justice system doesn't work. Unfortunately, the precise problem has been misdiagnosed.   1

A growing chorus of commentators argues that the problem lies with ordinary people (jurors), who cannot be trusted to decide difficult cases. This gets things backwards. The professionals (judges, lawyers, and legislators) have created an irrational system that makes it impossible for ordinary citizens to play their proper role.   2

The problem begins with jury selection. The pool of prospective jurors is whittled down to a jury of twelve through two means: attorneys dismiss prospective jurors without giving any reason (the "peremptory challenge"), or the judge, with or without prompting from either side, dismisses prospective jurors "for cause." For better or worse, the peremptory challenge has deep roots in our criminal law and is here to stay. We must, however, give serious thought to sharply narrowing the basis of for-cause dismissals.   3

Clearly, some for-cause dismissals are necessary. At a minimum, the selection process should establish that no jurors are acquainted with any of the parties, attorneys, or key witnesses. Beyond that, prospective jurors should be asked whether they have a predisposition in the matter and if they are capable of following the judge's instructions. Assuming satisfactory answers to these questions, it would seem that they should be eligible to serve on the case. Under current law, however, for-cause dismissals involve much more than rooting out conflicts of interest or bias. Whole categories of people are   4 dismissed based on speculation that some circumstance could unconsciously compromise their impartiality. If the case deals with business fraud, the judge is apt to dismiss all business persons.

5   If the case involves a school, bid farewell to teachers, students, and administrators. In child molestation cases, prospective jurors with young children are often dismissed. People with lawyers or police in their family are bounced from all kinds of cases. Anyone with stock investments may be tossed from an insider trading case.

6   Such people could swear under oath that they have no axes to grind, but they will be dismissed on the ground that they may have axes to grind of which they are unaware. Increasingly, there is a sense that to be an impartial juror one must be a blank slate with respect to the facts and issues in the case.

7   This idea reflects a double standard. Judges often have knowledge and opinions (and children and stocks), but only palpable conflicts of interest tend to be considered a basis for disqualification. Why do we trust judges so much more than jurors? Indeed, juror bias may be less problematic than judge bias, because a juror is only one of twelve decision makers, whereas a biased judge can singlehandedly manipulate proceedings.

8   The dismissal of prospective jurors whose background suggests any conceivable bias is bad enough. Even more disturbing, people who have heard anything about the charged crime or the defendant are likely to be excused. Even if these people have formed no opinions and have no discernible bias, they are viewed as contaminated by any awareness of the underlying facts or parties.

9   In high-profile cases, this leads to the search for jurors unattuned to the world around them. In the McMartin child abuse case in California, a survey found that 97% of adults in the community had heard about the case. Seeking jurors from the remaining 3% invited an unqualified jury.

10   To capture the absurdity of this state of affairs, we cannot improve on Mark Twain's characterization. In a highly-publicized murder case of his time, the court kept off the jury anyone familiar with the facts. Twain described the result with characteristic panache:

11   "A minister, intelligent, esteemed, and greatly respected; a merchant of high character and known probity; a mining superintendent of intelligence and unblemished reputation; a quartz-mill owner of excellent standing, were all questioned in the same way, and all set aside. Each said the public talk and the newspaper reports had not so biased his mind but that sworn testimony . . . would enable him to render a verdict without prejudice and in accordance with the facts. But of course such men could not be trusted with the case. Ignoramuses alone could mete out unsullied justice."

12   That Twain penned these words in 1871 suggests that the foibles of jury selection are nothing new. However, it ought not be inferred that the Found-

ing Fathers endorsed the equation of impartiality with ignorance. They valued "local" juries (the Sixth Amendment requires trial by a jury of "the State and district wherein the crime shall have been committed") in part so that jurors would be acquainted with the context of the case and grounded in the shared values and understanding of the community.

However, our criminal law increasingly moves in the opposite direction, 13 with the situation reaching comic proportions in some cases. Take the case of Oliver North. North testified before Congress in hearings televised nation-wide and widely discussed. At his subsequent criminal trial, the judge decided to dismiss all jurors familiar with North's testimony before Congress. From a pool of 235 jurors, 212 were removed on this basis. Not surprisingly, the ac-tual jury left something to be desired. The juror who became forewoman told the court, "I don't like the news. I don't like to watch it. It's depressing." Other jurors confessed to not reading newspapers or not understanding what-ever they had heard about the case.

In the O.J. Simpson case, the task of finding a sufficiently ignorant jury 14 was captured by a joke that made the rounds. "Knock knock. . . . Who's there? . . . O.J. . . . O.J. who? . . . Congratulations, you're on the jury!"

While these high-profile cases are particularly prone to producing an ig- 15 norant jury, the notion that jurors should lack even slight knowledge or ten-tative opinions relative to a case applies across the board. All too often, intel-ligent and well-informed jurors are dismissed precisely because they are intel-ligent and well-informed.

Obviously, jurors should base their decisions on the evidence in the case, 16 not on preconceived notions or outside information, and should be emphat-ically instructed to this effect. But we do prospective jurors an injustice to assume that any familiarity with a case renders it impossible to render a fair verdict. And we do a larger injustice when we skew the jury toward the least informed members of the community.

Then too, the problem with the jury system transcends the selection 17 process. The wisest, best-informed members of the community could sit in the jury box and we'd still have no right to expect an accurate verdict, given the rules governing juror conduct. In some jurisdictions, jurors are not permitted to take notes. In most jurisdictions, they may not discuss the case among themselves prior to deliberations. And if, during deliberations, they request to see transcripts of testimony or the judge's instructions, in many jurisdictions the request is denied. Each of these practices is justified by assorted rationales, but they all come down to the fact that jurors are not trusted to behave like other decision makers.

These restrictions on juror conduct have come under attack in recent 18 years, and reform is underway. However, another practice that poses a more profound threat to jury decision making has gone largely unchallenged: a rule of evidence in all jurisdictions that deprives jurors of relevant evidence when judges fear they would misuse it.

19   The precise wording differs from jurisdiction to jurisdiction, but typically provides that evidence, though relevant, must be excluded if its value is "outweighed by the danger of unfair prejudice." While taken for granted by most participants in the criminal justice system, this rule (the "prejudicial evidence" rule) interferes with a jury's ability to reach a sound verdict.

20   The parties in a trial obviously cannot be allowed to introduce into evidence everything they believe will influence the jury. One reasonable limitation is that evidence must be relevant. For example, defense lawyers would love to introduce testimony that the defendant's family will suffer if he is convicted, or that the victim is a despicable character. But in a trial to determine whether the defendant committed a particular offense, such matters are clearly irrelevant.

21   So far, so good. The prejudicial evidence rule, however, permits the exclusion of relevant evidence if the judge deems that its legitimate value or "weight" is outbalanced by its potential for unfair prejudice—that is, if the jury would likely attach too much or the wrong significance to it. Insofar as assigning the proper weight to evidence is central to the jury's role, it seems bizarre to deprive jurors of relevant material on the ground that they cannot weigh it properly.

22   That is not to say all relevant evidence must be admitted. A party may wish to call a dozen witnesses to give identical testimony about a minor matter. The judge's authority to limit such repetitious, time-consuming material is necessary to ensure an orderly trial. Other rules excluding relevant material, such as that privy to lawyer/client or physician/patient privileges, derive from public policy. Legislatures have determined that, absent these privileges, people would be less willing to confide in lawyers and physicians, to the detriment of the public interest.

23   These rules reflect the fact that the jury's access to relevant evidence must sometimes be tempered by other considerations. But the prejudicial evidence rule is different: it permits judges to exclude relevant material even absent a public policy reason, and even if the material does not violate any specific evidentiary taboo (such as "hearsay"). This is a rule of evidence designed to protect the jury from itself.

24   Traditionally, the prejudicial evidence rule was used sparingly, primarily in cases of stark exhibits such as bloody photographs. Today, judges invoke this rule frequently, and exclude all kinds of material they believe would overwhelm jurors.

25   George Fletcher's recent book about high-profile criminal cases, *With Justice for Some*, suggests the significance of this rule. In case after case, the rule played a role. In the 1st trial of Lyle and Erik Menendez, accused of murdering their parents for money, evidence was excluded that Erik wrote a play

about a man who kills his parents for money. In the William Kennedy Smith rape case, evidence that Smith assaulted three other women was excluded. In the trial of police for beating Rodney King, the court excluded evidence that a defendant characterized a fight between blacks as "gorillas in the mist." And in the case of the subway vigilante Bernard Goetz, Goetz' statement that the way to clean up the street is to "get rid of spics and niggers" was excluded.

In each of these cases, the judge's doubts about the jury's ability deprived 26 the jury of relevant evidence. As it happens, in these cases the exclusions helped the defense. But the prejudicial evidence rule is an equal opportunity truth-defeater—it can harm as well as help a defendant. Thus, in the O.J. Simpson case, the rule led to the exclusion of potentially critical evidence showing Detective Mark Furhman's propensity to plant evidence.

In one sense, the defense got what it deserved. Throughout the trial, de- 27 fense counsel invoked the prejudicial evidence rule as a basis for excluding prosecution evidence, including: photographs of the victims' bodies; Simpson's history of spousal abuse; and a videotape in which he joked about wife-beating. They were particularly outraged that Judge Ito allowed evidence of Simpson's abusive past. This, they claimed, would sway the jury improperly.

Exploring the basis of their claim clarifies the problem with the prejudi- 28 cial evidence rule. The defense's concern was twofold. First, the jury could improperly conclude that anyone who committed past acts of violence must be guilty of the violent act with which he is charged. Alternatively, the jury might decide to convict Simpson because, whether or not he committed the murders, he'd shown himself to be a bad man who deserves punishment. (Although the latter might seem farfetched, it is often advanced as a basis for excluding evidence of a defendant's prior bad acts.)

Both rationales rest on a painfully dim view of juries. It assumes that the 29 jury will either disregard its duty to decide the case before it, or prove incapable of putting evidence in its proper perspective.

Are such notions justified? Actually, they are unproven. Following the ver- 30 dict, the Simpson jurors said they were not overly impressed with the evidence of abuse: just because Simpson battered his ex-wife didn't mean he killed her. Arguably, these jurors gave too little weight to the evidence of spousal abuse. Certainly, their elementary inference—not all abusers commit murder—is one most jurors can draw.

Or, take the exercise video in which Simpson jokes about wife-beating. His 31 attorney, Robert Shapiro, argued that the prejudicial evidence rule required exclusion of this portion of the video, insisting that it had hardly any evidentiary value since Simpson was clearly joking. Shapiro protested too much; if Simpson's remarks were patently meaningless jests, why did he care whether the jury heard them? At the end of his lengthy statement about the irrelevance of the jokes, Shapiro added that the video was "highly prejudicial."

32　How can you have it both ways? How can material be meaningless yet highly prejudicial? The only way these statements can be reconciled is if we assume the jurors are dimwits. Simpson's jokes were of limited significance, a miniscule piece in the prosecution puzzle, but there was reason to fear that jurors would think them a huge piece. While it is true that the flawed selection process produces too many uninformed jurors, even the least educated know the difference between joking about violence and committing it.

33　Rather than arguing that the admission of evidence will create unfair prejudice, lawyers should show the jury the weakness of the evidence and defuse the potential prejudice. In the marketplace of ideas, the proper response to weak arguments is not censorship but strong arguments. So too with weak evidence.

34　The various rules and practices discussed above inhibit the ability of jurors to reach an accurate verdict. Their task is then compounded by the fact that, unless they reach unanimity, they may not render a verdict at all—a hung jury results. While the Supreme Court has said the Constitution does not require a unanimous verdict, the federal courts and all but two states prohibit nonunanimous verdicts. As a result, juries are sometimes defined by their worst members: one or two obstinate or biased dissenters can hang the jury even in the face of clear evidence.

35　There are two primary rationales behind the unanimity requirement. First, it is said that if a nonunanimous verdict were permitted, juries would not bother to deliberate: they would essentially vote and disband. However, if this argument is accepted, it should lead not just to a unanimous jury requirement but a unanimity requirement in every multimember decision-making body (at least those that are expected to deliberate).

36　Deliberative bodies deliberate not because they must reach consensus, but because that is their job and they are committed to a decision that takes into account the concerns of all the members. Does the Supreme Court, for example, eschew argument in favor of mere nose-counting?

37　The risk of insufficient deliberations should be dealt with directly, rather than by requiring unanimity. Jurors should be emphatically instructed to take the views of dissenting colleagues seriously and make every effort to persuade one another, ceasing deliberations only when they have exhausted such efforts. Moreover, when a jury announces that it has reached a verdict, the judge can poll the jurors to assure that deliberations were not cut off prematurely.

38　The second argument for requiring unanimity is that, as long as any jurors vote to acquit, it cannot be said that the government proved guilt beyond a reasonable doubt. However, this argument fails to explain why unanimity is required not only for convictions but also for acquittals. More importantly, this argument defies common sense. Will the proposition that the earth is round not be proven beyond a reasonable doubt until the Flat Earth Society disbands? Does the existence of persons denying the Holocaust cast reasonable doubt that it took place? It is clearly a mistake to suggest that something cannot be proven beyond a reasonable doubt absent unanimity.

The various rules and practices discussed combine to create an artificial 39 environment obstructing the capacity of jurors to deliberate intelligently and reach an accurate verdict. A vicious cycle results. Whenever a jury renders a dubious verdict, critics call into question entrusting critical decisions to ordinary citizens. This distrust leads to more constraints that further impede the jury's ability to function well.

It's time to ask whether the fault is that of ordinary citizens (jurors), or the 40 elites who make and apply these rules. When jurors are selected in a way that eliminates informed members, are denied the most universal and time-tested means of obtaining and processing information, deprived of key evidence, and required to reach unanimity or else no verdict at all, why should we expect just decisions?

James Zigarelli

Hand It Over

James Zigarelli teaches G.E.D. and Adult Basic Education classes in Philadelphia. He graduated with a B.A. in English from Rutgers University in 1998. He has worked as a reporter and a freelance writer while studying abroad in South Africa. He has also been an editorial assistant at *The Village Voice*. Currently, he is working on a collection of short fiction. "Hand It Over" originally appeared in the online magazine *citypaper.net*.

IT'S NOT SOMETHING THAT HAPPENS AT YOUR FAVORITE Fairmount pub every 1 night: two young men, appearing at the open front door, guns pointed, demanding that the cash register be open.

It happens quickly. A short, dark figure is swiftly behind the bar, removing the contents of the cash drawer. The other man is three feet behind me, 2 over my right shoulder. In a heavy, demanding voice, he says, "All the money, everybody's money on the table!" Everyone empties the cash from their wallets onto the table. I drop my money, and in an act of spirited self-preservation, let my eyes gaze, out of focus, at the counter.

They flee. My friend alertly pulls the door shut and locks it. Out of a window on the side of the bar one patron sees them get into a red getaway car. 3

The bartender calls the police. There are 10 of us in the bar, not counting 4 the bartender.

5   After the initial crash that follows any rush or release, we all agree that the job took under a minute.

6   "Those guys are making about $60,000 an hour."

7   "Not a bad wage!"

8   The volume of conversation continues to rise. Repeatedly, the bartender is imploring us to keep it down.

9   But containing people's vigor is not easy. A liveliness and grand camaraderie begins to inhabit the bar. People are at once intimates, caused by one unchangeable swoop of chance.

10   When the bartender hangs up, he announces that drinks are on the house. We all have to wait for the detectives to arrive and question us.

11   "I feel like I've experienced something," someone says. "I feel like we've all bonded," someone else says across the bar.

12   "I just finished peddling all night delivering pizzas," one guy says. He plopped his hard-earned $80 down on the table when the robbers requested, but didn't seem to mind very much. "I can earn it again tomorrow," he says with a shrug and a smile.

13   This cool nonchalance to victimization expressed by the pizza deliverer is the prevailing sentiment. None of the money just stolen from us is irreplaceable. Much of it would have been dropped at the bar anyway. The only irreplaceable thing in all of our lives at this moment seems to be a warped sense that being robbed is some sort of extreme-sport gut-check. We are all taking inventory, asking ourselves how we fared. If that were lights, camera, action, was I ready to go?

14   An hour passes as we wait for the detectives. The cops have already arrived, but this sort of thing is mundane for them, and I gain a new sense of awe for the life of a cop. One of them finds a television screen perched in a high corner of the bar far more absorbing than the details of the armed robbery we are all discussing.

15   While we sit, drinking mugs of ale and porter, I begin to consider the other people involved, the two gunmen. It seems they had given us so much, an intense experience that will last a lifetime; and we have given them so little, enough money perhaps to live for a week. My more Marxist leanings beg me to understand the robbery as a very natural occurrence, just a simple redistribution of wealth in a capitalist society. Yet beyond textbooks and theories, I had seen the horror in the turbulent face of the young man, not a day over 18, who was robbing the cash register. The delight I had taken from the incident was perverse, I knew, but to what degree was I complicit in this robbery? Was I a witness or a participant? How badly did he wish he didn't have to walk into that bar with a gun to get what America says we can all have?

16   I found my answer moments later, when the bartender, in the voice of a victor, revealed that in his haste, the young gunman had not even grabbed the twenties out of the register.

17   Apparently, his gaze was as out of focus as mine.

Credits